Social Science Methodology

This book offers a one-volume introduction to social science methodology relevant to the disciplines of anthropology, economics, history, political science, psychology, and sociology. It is written for students and practitioners, as well as methodologists, and applies to work conducted in qualitative and quantitative styles. While offering a handy overview of this vast and diverse subject, the book is also an argument about how we should conceptualize methodological problems. Tasks and criteria, the author argues – not fixed rules of procedure – best describe the search for methodological adequacy. Thinking about methodology through this lens provides a new framework for understanding and conducting work in the social sciences.

John Gerring is Associate Professor of Political Science at Boston University. He is author of *Party Ideologies in America, 1828–1996* (Cambridge 1998) and articles appearing in *Social Science History, Political Research Quarterly, Polity, Journal of Policy History, Party Politics,* and *Studies in American Political Development.*

D0721245

Social Science Methodology
A Criterial Framework

John Gerring

Boston University

CAMBRIDGE
UNIVERSITY PRESS

PUBLISHED BY THE PRESS SYNDICATE OF THE UNIVERSITY OF CAMBRIDGE
The Pitt Building, Trumpington Street, Cambridge, United Kingdom

CAMBRIDGE UNIVERSITY PRESS
The Edinburgh Building, Cambridge CB2 2RU, UK
40 West 20th Street, New York, NY 10011-4211, USA
10 Stamford Road, Oakleigh, VIC 3166, Australia
Ruiz de Alarcón 13, 28014 Madrid, Spain
Dock House, The Waterfront, Cape Town 8001, South Africa

http://www.cambridge.org

© John Gerring 2001

This book is in copyright. Subject to statutory exception
and to the provisions of relevant collective licensing agreements,
no reproduction of any part may take place without
the written permission of Cambridge University Press.

First published 2001

Printed in the United States of America

Typeface Sabon 10/12 pt.   *System* QuarkXPress™   [HT]

A catalog record for this book is available from the British Library.

Library of Congress Cataloging in Publication Data

Gerring, John, 1962–
Social science methodology : a criterial framework / John E. Gerring.
p. cm.
Includes bibliographical references and index.
ISBN 0-521-80113-3 – ISBN 0-521-80513-9 (pb.)
1. Social sciences – Methodology.   I. Title.
H61.G47 2001
300 – dc21   00-054662

ISBN 0 521 80113 3   hardback
ISBN 0 521 80513 9   paperback

To have mastered "method" and "theory" is to have become a self-conscious thinker, a man at work and aware of the assumptions and the implications of whatever he is about. To be mastered by "method" or "theory" is simply to be kept from working, from trying, that is, to find out about something that is going on in the world. Without insight into the way the craft is carried on, the results of study are infirm; without a determination that study shall come to significant results, all method is meaningless pretense.

— C. Wright Mills (1959: 120–1)

Contents

vii

List of Tables and Figures

Tables

Figures

ix

Preface

Those sciences, created almost in our own days, the object of which is man himself, the direct goal of which is the happiness of man, will enjoy a progress no less sure than that of the physical sciences, and this idea so sweet, that our descendants will surpass us in wisdom as in enlightenment, is no longer an illusion. In meditating on the nature of the moral sciences, one cannot help seeing that, as they are based like physical sciences on the observation of fact, they must follow the same method, acquire a language equally exact and precise, attaining the same degree of certainty.

– Condorcet (1782)[1]

In reading the work of older generations of social scientists one thing stands out as fundamentally different from today's writings. Through the mid-twentieth century, most writers who considered the subject were enthusiastic and self-confident about the promise of these fields.[2] Two centuries ago, Condorcet prophesied that his descendants would surpass him in "wisdom as in enlightenment," acquiring a language "exact and precise," just as in the natural sciences. A century ago, Comte, Durkheim, Freud, Malinowski, Marshall, and Mark were equally confident – though with somewhat different notions of science in mind. During the postwar era, major intellectual movements like behavioralism, structural-functionalism, and modernization theory seemed once again to inaugurate new epochs of progress in the sciences of man.

It would be difficult to muster an equivalent level of enthusiasm today. To write about social science at the turn of the twenty-first cen-

---

1. Quoted in Scott (1998: 91).
2. See, for example, Barnes (1925), Myrdal (1944), Small (1910), Smith and White (1929), White (1930), White (1956), and Wirth (1940).

tury is to invite criticism from many quarters. Skeptical perspectives on truth and knowledge – poststructuralism, postmodernism, deconstruction, critical theory, among others – suggest that there is no such thing as social science, or that a science of society is pernicious.[3] Popular commentators on the right and left find much to criticize, and little to extol. Opinions among the general public vary from indifference to incomprehension.

Even among self-identified social scientists there is a striking diffidence. We introduce our subjects with humility. We apologize for the thinness of our data, the crudeness of our methods, the inexactitude of our findings. We are despondent about the state of research, and the lack of resolution of long-standing problems. We remark upon how much we do not know. In sum, we are no longer certain of the capacity of humankind to understand humankind. To be sure, members of the human sciences take great pride in their own work, and perhaps, their particular subfield. Notably absent, however, is an abiding faith in *social science*.[4]

Why is it that social science has come to evoke skepticism, and more than occasional ridicule? Why must it be placed in quotation marks ("social science") and accompanied by a lengthy apologia-cum-explanation? What is social science's problem?

Let us begin by noticing that complaints registered against social science stem from two very different perspectives. Those who, following Condorcet, look to natural science as a model for the social sciences fault these disciplines for their lack of precision, their inconstancy and indeterminacy (five writers on a given subject, it is said, will produce five different explanations), their lack of progress and cumulation, their lack of unifying theory, and their lack of objectivity and neutrality. There is too much impressionistic narrative in the work of the social sciences, too much rhetoric, and not enough scientific ballast. From the

---

3. On poststructuralism and its cousins (deconstruction, critical theory, and so forth), see Norris (1997) and Rosenau (1992). See also work in history of science that focuses on science's "constructed" or "paradigmatic" qualities (e.g., Feyerabend 1975; Latour and Woolgar 1979), radical work in the interpretivist genre (e.g., Winch 1958), and feminist methodology (Shulamit 1992).

4. On this general point, see Converse (1986), as well as Adams et al. (1982), Fiske and Shweder (1986), Kruskal (1982), Simon (1982: 19), and Smelser and Gernstein (1986). To be sure, the natural sciences have also been subject to criticism. Yet, they have also been stoutly defended. Their prestige, I should think, is as high at the close of the twentieth century as it was at the outset, and perhaps higher. Nor do physicists, chemists, and biologists shrink from "science," as sociologists and their brethren often do when confronted with the label "social science." Any way one looks at it, the fate of social science seems fundamentally more troubled.

perspective of critics in the naturalist tradition social science is bad science, or immature science.[5]

Ironically, critics in the humanist tradition are even more inclined to highlight social science's failings as a purported science. Social science, humanists point out, is forever awaiting its Newton, its Darwin, its Einstein; forever constructing grand theoretical foundations that are then, after a decade or two (or less!), abandoned; forever setting out on voyages with no real hope of arrival. It is a condition of permanent paradigmatic revolution. Yet, humanists attribute this failure not to poor execution and insufficient rigor, but rather to the *impossibility* of the naturalist ideal. Problems encountered in a science focused on human actions and institutions, humanists argue, are quite different from those encountered in a science focused on inanimate objects, mathematical regularities, and genetically programmed behavior. It is not simply that the social sciences have a harder task cut out for them (this leaves open the possibility that we could still apply the natural science model, even if only imperfectly). More important, the methods useful for investigating human action and the sorts of questions we are inclined to ask are quite different from those applied to the study of nature. Thus, the scientific impulse is said to have a desiccating effect on the study of humankind. Contemporary social science is overly quantitative, obsessed with abstract models that have few real-life applications, too limited in scope – leaving out normative questions, questions that cannot be quantified, questions that hinge on human agency and cultural meaning – and steeped in an arcane ("scientistic") rhetoric. It reads poorly, and does not satisfy.

The fields of social science have occupied a shifting, liminal position within the academy. Condemned by one set of observers for being insufficiently scientific, they are condemned from the other side for being too scientific. Not quite *Naturwissenschaft,* nor quite *Geisteswissenschaft,* these disciplines have stood between a rock and an uncomfortably soft

---

5. See, in particular, Wilson (1998: ch 9). Versions of naturalism can be found in Hempel (1965), Kincaid (1990/1994), King et al. (1994), Kornblith (1985), McIntyre (1996), Popper (1936/1957), and earlier work in the "logical positivist" vein (not all were official members of the Vienna Circle) – for example, Ayer (1936/1950; 1959), Carnap (1967), and Wittgenstein (1921/1988). Critiques of naturalism from the humanities perspective can be found in Dray (1952; 1956), Gadamer (1975), Hoy (1982), Natanson (1963), Taylor (1962; 1967; 1970; 1985), Winch (1958), and articles by Gadamer, Geertz, Ricoeur, and Taylor in Rabinow and Sullivan (1979). For arguments pro and con, see Dray (1966), Martin and McIntyre (1994), Mazlish (1998), Polkinghorne (1983), and Thomas (1979). The early history of these debates is covered in Brown (1984) and Smith (1997).

place. They are, collectively, bad science *and* bad narrative. So conceived, they cannot help but fail.[6]

Yet, we do not need to conceptualize the subject in this dichotomous fashion. Rather than approaching the social sciences as quasi-science or quasi-humanities, let us entertain the hypothesis that these disciplines strive for somewhat different objectives, and utilize rather different methodological tools, than their cousins on the hard and soft ends of the academic spectrum. Perhaps, that is, we have held a false set of expectations about what social science is.[7]

Can there be science without laws of nature, mathematical language, and laboratory experiments? We may take heart from a brief look at the word's meaning in other linguistic contexts. "The English usage," notes Donald McCloskey, "would puzzle an Italian mother boasting of her studious son, *mio scienziato,* my learned one. Italian and other languages use the science word to mean simply 'systematic inquiry' (as do for example French, German, Dutch, Spanish, Swedish, Polish, Hungarian, Turkish, Korean, Hindi, and Tamil)." Only English – and, indeed, only the English of the past century – has promoted physical and biological science into the dominant paradigm for science at-large. It would be a good idea, concludes McCloskey, "to claim the word back for reasonable and rigorous argument."[8] I heartily agree.

This is not an argument *against* science. It is an argument for a broader view of science than is generally understood by the natural science referent. Quine writes of natural science as "a continuation of common sense."[9] Whether this correctly describes quantum mechanics may be debated; however, it seems an excellent characterization for most of what is valuable in the fields of the social sciences.

Social science, I argue, finds its rightful place *between* the natural sciences and the humanities; it is not simply an imperfect version of physics

---

6. See Converse (1982: 83; 1986) and Lindblom (1997: 251).

7. Zald (1990) makes similar points, but is content to rest with the conclusion that sociology (and the social sciences more generally) are quasi-sciences *and* quasi-humanities. This does not leave us much ground to stand on.

8. McCloskey (1990: 7). One of the first statements of the autonomy of social science from natural science came from J. S. Mill, who, in 1831, wrote: "If we contemplate the whole field of human knowledge, attained or attainable, we find that it separates itself obviously, and as it were spontaneously, into two divisions, which stand so strikingly in opposition and contradistinction to one another, that in all classifications of our knowledge they have been kept apart. These are *physical* science, and *moral* or psychological science" (quoted in Mazlish 1998:83). Yet, in his *System of Logic* (1843/1872) he argues, somewhat to the contrary, that methods developed in the physical sciences ought to be applied to the moral sciences.

9. Quine (1953: 45). See also Myrdal (1970: 450).

or a tortured version of hermeneutics. So conceived, we can arrive at a more realistic set of methodological goals for the various fields of the social sciences. So conceived, the ongoing methodological crisis of social science is somewhat mitigated.

What, then, *is* this niche between natural science and the humanities? If social science is to claim a status that is more than residual, we will have to struggle with the problem of definition. This is not an easy task, since social science may be defined in many ways. But it is an important one, because whatever we say about social science must be premised on our delineation of this key concept.

Social science, I propose – following the work of many writers – is any scientific study of human action focusing on elements of thought and behavior that are in some sense social (nonbiological). "The object of the social sciences," writes Hans Morgenthau, "is man, not as a product of nature but as both the creature and the creator of history in and through which his individuality and freedom of choice manifest themselves."[10] Wherever nurture matters more than nature, or where some significant decisional element is involved, we are on the turf of social science. (In previous eras one would have referred to these disciplines as "moral" or "human" sciences.) At the same time, and in marked contrast to the humanities, writers in the social sciences take their moniker seriously. They aspire to *science* – which is to say, they intend to study human action in a systematic, rigorous, evidence-based, generalizing, nonsubjective, and cumulative fashion.

Our definition takes its cues from the twin terms *social* and *science*. The two terms are in tension with one another, as the *Geisteswissenschaft/Naturwissenschaft* dispute suggests. But not irreconcilably so. Indeed, the framework presented in this book may be viewed as an attempt to meld these often estranged elements into a single, unified methodology. So defined, social science may be said to comprise the present-day fields of economics, political science, and sociology, along with various offshoots such as communications, education, public policy, and social work. That portion of psychology focused on decisional elements of human behavior might also be included.

The most troublesome question of classification concerns cultural anthropology, history, and the "theory" subfields of political science and sociology. They are clearly social, but are they science? About all one can say without risk of offense is that many writers in these fields see their own approaches as systematic, rigorous, evidence-based, generalizing,

---

10. Morgenthau (1955: 441). See also Almond and Genco (1977/1990).

nonsubjective, and cumulative – as scientific, in the loose sense in which we have employed the term here. To this extent, then, these fields may also be included in the subject matter of the book.

To clarify: this is *not* an argument for a rigid separation among the three major paradigms of the modern academy – natural science, social science, and the humanities. These divisions will always be blurred around the edges, as the foregoing discussion of fields and subfields suggests. Moreover, we have much to learn from one another. The proposed definition for social science is therefore an ideal-type, applying differentially to disciplines, writers, and works across the fields of anthropology, economics, history, political science, psychology, and sociology.[11]

It should also be clear that in adopting social science as our unit of analysis we are not attempting to conflate the very real distinctions that exist *within* these fields. The argument, rather, is that we will gain better purchase on methodological agreement and disagreement by considering these fields as part of a common quest.

Let me put the matter this way. Both Kenneth Arrow and Clifford Geertz claim to be engaged in an effort to understand society in a scientific manner.[12] Let us take these claims seriously. There is no reason why these paragons of social science should not speak to one another, engaging each others' ideas and empirical findings. The framework developed in this book is designed to do just that.

There *is* a valued place for social science in contemporary academic life. It is not the grand place claimed by early enthusiasts, but it is an important place nonetheless. And we can also do better. Doing better

---

11. For discussion of ideal-type concepts, see Chapter 4.
12. It is worth quoting Geertz – the paragon of interpretivism – at length on this point. He writes (1973: 24): "The besetting sin of interpretive approaches to anything – literature, dreams, symptoms, culture – is that they tend to resist, or to be permitted to resist, conceptual articulation and thus to escape systematic modes of assessment. You either grasp an interpretation or you do not, see the point of it or you do not, accept it or you do not. Imprisoned in the immediacy of its own detail, it is presented as self-validating, or, worse, as validated by the supposedly developed sensitivities of the person who presents it; any attempt to cast what it says in terms other than its own is regarded as travesty – as, the anthropologists' severest term of moral abuse, ethnocentric. For a field of study which, however timidly (though I, myself, am not timid about the matter at all), asserts itself to be a science, this just will not do. There is no reason why the conceptual structure of a cultural interpretation should be any less formulable, and thus less susceptible to explicit canons of appraisal, than that of, say, a biological observation or a physical experiment – no reason except that the terms in which such formulations can be cast are, if not wholly nonexistent, very nearly so. We are reduced to insinuating theories because we lack the power to state them." For Geertz, at least at this point in his career, interpretivism is clearly part of the overall project of social science, not a separate and incommensurable activity. Contrast Geertz (1983).

will involve thinking more clearly about our use of concepts, propositions, and research designs, and reaching agreement on some basic points. The framework proposed in this book is designed to lay out the full range of choices available to us, clarifying the tradeoffs involved in these choices. Ultimately, it is hoped, we can preserve a pluralism of methods and models without sacrificing the cumulation of knowledge necessary to the progress of any scientific discipline.

Methodology

The field of methodology has been an active one over the past few decades. Methods, models, and paradigms have multiplied and transformed themselves with dizzying speed, fostering a burst of interest in a heretofore moribund topic. One sign of the growing status of this field is the scholarly vituperation it inspires. Terms such as *interpretivism, rational choice, poststructuralism, constructivism,* and *feminist theory* are not just labels for what we do; they are also fighting words.

Meanwhile, venerable debates over power, class, and status seem to have subsided. It is not that we no longer talk about these subjects. Yet, our talking occurs without the rancor that accompanied these subjects in previous eras. This may not be entirely a bad thing, but it is surely noteworthy. Over the past few decades methodological disagreements have largely displaced disagreements over substantive issues at conferences, at faculty meetings, and on editorial boards. Methodology, not ideology, defines the most important cleavages within the social sciences today.

Readers disturbed by this development may feel that there is altogether too much methodology running around the social sciences today – too much discussion about how to get there, and not enough about what's there. They may be partial to C. Wright Mills's admonition: "Methodologists, get to work!" However, the question naturally arises, *how* is one to go to work, and what is one to work on? It is unlikely that these questions are best answered in a seat-of-the-pants manner.

Moreover, the stakes in our current *Methodenstreit* are high. At issue is not merely who will make it into the first-tier journals and who will make tenure, but also the shape and focus of the social sciences as we head into the twenty-first century. The winners of these methodological wars will determine the sort of training that is offered to students, the sort of advice that is offered to policymakers, and the sort of guidance that is offered to the lay public. Social science matters – perhaps not as much as we might like, but a good deal nonetheless. And because of its prominent place in shaping the course of social science, *methodology* matters.

This book is a synthesis of existing work in the rich and heterogeneous field of social science methodology. Yet, my approach to the

subject deviates from most of this work in ways that should be emphasized from the outset.

First, I take *social science* as my primary unit of analysis. Social science, I have already argued, is not simply an offshoot of the natural sciences, or of the humanities. It is, rather, a distinctive realm of inquiry
with a distinctive set of norms and practices. Thus, rather than focusing on a particular field, or on science at-large, this book addresses all
fields whose primary focus is on human action and human institutions
– anthropology, economics, history, political science, psychology, and
sociology. Insofar as the book succeeds, it should help to restore a
sense of common purpose to the myriad vocabularies, topics, and
methods that currently populate these fields.

Second, this book aims to address the subject of social science
methodology in ways that will be useful to practitioners. We should
remind ourselves that there is little point in studying methodology if the
discoveries of this field are shared only among methodologists. Rather
than highlighting my arguments with the literature, therefore, I have
sought to place these arguments in footnotes or chapter appendices, or
have omitted them altogether. The tables and chapter sections of the
book are organized to facilitate easy access and reference. Specialized
vocabulary is avoided, with two important exceptions: where specialized
references are needed to tie together arguments from different language
regions, and where no everyday term exists for the subject at hand. In
general, the text sticks close to everyday language and requires no prior
knowledge of methodological subjects.

Third, this book places the subject of social science methodology in a
broad historical and intellectual context. It is helpful to remember that
most of the questions we find ourselves grappling with today are itera-
tions of classic methodological debates and are encountered in virtually
all fields of the social sciences. Many were addressed as far back as 1843,
when J. S. Mill published his pathbreaking *System of Logic*. Some go
back even farther. Arguably, the introduction of new methods (for example, statistical tools of analysis) has had relatively little effect on the
underlying logic of social science analysis. The same difficulties crop up
in different circumstances. This may serve as cause for dismay or con-
tentment, depending on one's orientation. From my perspective, it is
another indication that there is something central to the social sciences
that distinguishes this enterprise from others. We are defined, one might
say, by our methodological predicaments.

Finally, this book intends to impart a deeper understanding of methodological questions than is usual in most methods texts. "God," write
Charles Lave and James March, "has chosen to give the easy problems to

the physicists."[13] What the authors mean by this provocative comment is not, of course, that it is easy to practice physics, but rather that it is fairly easy to know when one has obtained a *result* in this field. The implications of this fact are momentous. The natural scientist can afford to cultivate a method, confident that her results, if significant, will be recognized. The social scientist, by contrast, must justify not only how she obtained her findings – questions of method, narrowly construed – but also why those findings are important and why they are true – questions of *methodology*, broadly construed. This book is concerned, therefore, with what social scientists do, what they say they do, and what they ought to be doing. These three issues, together, constitute social science methodology.

Our blessing and our curse is to be implicated in the subjects that we study and to study subjects who are subjects, in the full Kantian sense. As a consequence, those working in the social sciences have harder problems, methodologically speaking. We disagree on more points, and on more basic points, and spend much more time debating these points than our cousins in the natural sciences. Indeed, methodology is central to the disciplines of the social sciences in a way that it is not to the natural sciences. Clark Glymour observes, "Exactly in those fields where impressive and dominant results are difficult to obtain, methodological considerations are likely to be most explicit, and innovations in method are likely to occur most often."[14] To do good work in the social sciences, therefore, requires more than mastering a set of techniques. It requires understanding why these techniques work, why one approach might be more appropriate for a given task than another, and how a given approach might be adapted to diverse research situations. Good work in the social sciences is necessarily *creative work*, and creative work requires a broad grounding in methodology.[15]

The great philosopher of science, Henry Poincare, put it this way: "The natural sciences talk about their results. The social sciences talk about their methods."[16] This was true at the turn of the last century, and it is true today. Arguments among behavioralists, critical theorists, formal theorists, interpretivists, positivists, post-positivists, and partisans of other methodological camps are symptoms of an ongoing controversy over what it means to be doing social science. In order to understand social science, one must understand these arguments. The goal of this book, therefore, is to explore the logic of inquiry that guides work in the

---

13. Lave and March (1975: 2).
14. Glymour (1980: 291).
15. "More than other scientists," notes Milton Friedman (1953/1984: 236), "social scientists need to be self-conscious about their methodology."
16. Attributed to Poincare by Berelson and Steiner (1964: 14). See also Samuelson (1959: 189).

social sciences, as well as the pragmatic rationale that, I claim, underpins these norms. Methods are inseparable from methodology; we can hardly claim to understand one without delving into the other.

No one could plausibly claim expertise in all the areas of the social sciences, and I am certainly no exception. My own experience is primarily in political science, a fact that probably colors the following narrative (perhaps in ways that I am scarcely aware of). I have done my best to familiarize myself with the literature outside my own field, to cite this literature where appropriate, and to employ examples that cross disciplinary boundaries. For helping me overcome my own disciplinary parochialisms I owe a debt of gratitude to numerous scholars in other fields – many of them listed below. For the inevitable shortcomings, I must beg the reader's forbearance.

Generous comments and suggestions were provided by Tom Burke, Dave Campbell, Pearson Cross, Marshall Ganz, Kristin Goss, David Hart, Alan Jacobs, Dan Kryder, Rob Mickey, Paul Pierson, Theda Skocpol, and other members of the American Politics workshop at Harvard University, where an early version of this manuscript was presented. (Members of the workshop will be relieved to discover that this version was substantially revised.)

Portions of later editions were read by Neil Beck, Dave Campbell, David Collier, Michael Coppedge, David Hart, Orit Kedar, Marcus Kurtz, David Lyons, Michael Martin, Dawn Skorczewski, Laurel Smith-Dorr, and John Williamson. More informal – but no less useful – were conversations and e-mail exchanges with Nik Blevins, Ben Campbell, Russ Faeges, Garrett Glasgow, Lincoln Greenhill, Cathy Harris, Patrick Johnston, Samantha Luks, Jeff Miron, Jim Schmidt, Laura Stoker, Strom Thacker, and Ned Wingreen. Their input was well received and, I hope, graciously integrated. A draft of the entire manuscript was read and critiqued by students in a graduate research seminar at UMass Amherst, whose comments greatly aided in the process of revision. I was also fortunate to have the input of scholars at the University of Connecticut, Boston University, and University of California, Berkeley, where portions of the book were presented.

I owe a special round of thanks to Bob Bullock, Steve Hanson, Jim Mahoney, Howard Reiter, Rudy Sil, Craig Thomas, David Waldner, and two reviewers for Cambridge University Press, who gave detailed comments on lengthy portions of the manuscript. David Collier's support throughout the long process of formulation and revision was invaluable, and greatly appreciated.

A final acknowledgment belongs to all the published work on methodology that I borrow from. Although it would be tedious to list authors by name, the lengthy bibliography and crowded footnotes provide ample testimony of my indebtedness.

1

The Problem of Unity Amid Diversity

One of the chief practical obstacles to the development of social inquiry is the existing division of social phenomena into a number of compartmentalized and supposedly independent non-interacting fields.

– John Dewey[1]

The social sciences today are divided. They are divided, first of all, among the separate disciplines – anthropology, economics, history, political science, psychology, and sociology. Although scholars occasionally cross these borders, such crossings are arduous and often problematic. It is no surprise that for the most part, anthropologists associate with other anthropologists, and economists with other economists. Whether sustained by methodological differences, organizational incentives, or simple inertia, members of the different scholarly tribes tend to stick to their own kind.

The social sciences are divided, second, among subdisciplinary fields. The American Political Science Association recognizes thirty-four sections, the American Historical Association over one hundred, and the American Economics Association several hundred (depending on how one counts the affiliation categories). Similar divisions may be found in other disciplines. These cubbyholes define courses, jobs, conferences, journals, and scholarly activity generally. They are the de facto boundaries of most academic lives.

The social sciences are divided, third, among those who are comfortable with statistical analysis and mathematical models, and those who prefer the time-honored expedient of natural language. This division, in evidence for well over a century, continues to provoke and offend. As the

---

1. Dewey (1938: 509).

I

reader is no doubt aware, quantoids and qualtoids have developed different languages and different approaches to their topics. They are accustomed to arguing with each other or ignoring each other. It is a case of mutual un-belief or dis-belief (it hardly matters which).[2]

The social sciences are divided, finally, among theoretical frameworks, each with its own more or less explicit methodology – for example, behavioralism, conflict theory, ethnomethodology, exchange theory, institutionalism, interpretivism, ordinary language, rational choice, structural-functionalism, symbolic interactionism, systems theory (cybernetics), and the research schools associated with Freud, Marx, and Weber. Each offers its own research *Weltanschauung.*

Methodological divisions within the contemporary social sciences are therefore deep and complex, involving disciplinary, subdisciplinary, theoretical, method-ological, philosophical, as well as old-fashioned ideological cleavages. What are we to make of this diversity? Surely, some specialization is necessary in order for social science, or any field of endeavor, to thrive. Perhaps, the current fragmentation of social science is the happy outcome of different scholars doing what they, individually, do best. Perhaps, that is, we ought to regard diversity as a mark of disciplinary maturity, rather than as a mark of confusion and disarray.

This is a critical issue. To argue, as I shall, that the social sciences ought to be more unified goes against the grain of some methodological work, and many predilections. Are we better off with a unified, or pluralistic, methodology? In the process of discussing this vital question we will have occasion to specify in a more adequate way just what kind, and what degree, of unity is envisioned in the criterial framework.

---

2. An impression exists among some quantitativists that their colleagues writing prose (particularly those writing *good* prose) are compensating for a lack of rigor. "If you can't measure it," goes the unstated premise, "that ain't it." A corresponding impression exists among some qualitativists that to measure something – to "reduce it to a variable" – is to demean the topic and deprive historical actors of the possibility of speaking for themselves. "If you *can* measure it," goes their credo, "that ain't it." Kaplan (1964: 206) attributes this dictum to members of the University of Michigan faculty (satirizing the anti-quantoids). The same opposing sentiments can also be found in statements by Lord Kelvin ("When you cannot measure it, when you cannot express it in numbers, your knowledge is of a meagre and unsatisfactory kind") and Jacob Viner ("When you can measure it, when you can express it in numbers, your knowledge is still of a meagre and unsatisfactory kind"), quoted in Berelson and Steiner (1964: 14). See also the words of Robert Fogel (on the quant side) and Carl Bridenbaugh and Arthur Schlesinger, Jr. (on the qual side), recorded in Landes and Tilly (1971: 12). Anti-quantificationist manifestos may be found in Winch (1958) and Wolin (1969). For other examples, including statements by Daniel Boorstin, Carl Bridenbaugh, Barrington Moore, Arthur Schlesinger, and E. P. Thompson, see Fischer (1970: 94–6).

The Argument for Unity

From the obvious fragmentation of the social sciences today, it is a small step for writers to posit a pluralistic methodology for the social sciences. Thus, Richard Miller argues,

> there is no framework of empirical principles determining what counts as an explanation in all social sciences. Rather, there are particular frameworks for particular fields. Each specific framework is, in turn, highly complex, with components serving many functions. Whether a true hypothesis explains, or whether a hypothesis should be accepted as explaining, in light of given data, is determined by facts specific, say, to the study of power structures or investment decisions.[3]

Methodological pluralism has an appealing air to it, suggesting tolerance for approaches employed by other scholars and pragmatism in selecting one's own approach to a topic. Be a good craftsman, C. Wright Mills advises us in a famous passage.

> Avoid any rigid set of procedures. Above all seek to develop and to use the sociological imagination. Avoid the fetishism of method and technique. Urge the rehabilitation of the unpretentious intellectual craftsman and try to become such a craftsman yourself. Let every man be his own methodologist; let every man be his own theorist: let theory and method again become part of the practice of the craft.[4]

Mills's advice is attractive. Yet, before embracing a thoroughgoing methodological pluralism it is vital to distinguish between pluralism in *methods* (specific rules and procedures), *theoretical frameworks* (e.g., interpretivism, rational choice, behavioralism), and *methodology*. With respect to methods and theoretical frameworks, pluralism is easy to justify. There are many ways to do good social science. Methods may be statistical or nonstatistical, large-*N* or small-*N*, historical or nonhistorical, and so forth. Theories may be useful for one project, and useless for another. Much depends on the nature of the evidence available and the

---

3. Miller (1983/1991). See also Little (1991), Miller (1987), and Roth (1987). An extreme version of methodological pluralism – associated with poststructuralism, deconstruction, and post-Kuhnian history of science/philosophy of science – supposes that there are no viable standards of science at all, or at least none worthy of upholding. Because this vision of the social science enterprise has not been embraced by most social scientists, I will not attend to these arguments in any detail. On poststructuralism/deconstruction and its implications for social science, see Norris (1997) and Rosenau (1992). For skeptical work in history of science and sociology of science, see Barnes and Bloor (1982), Feyerabend (1975), Latour and Woolgar (1979), and Woolgar (1988).
4. Mills (1959: 224), quoted in Eldridge (1983: 37).

nature of the question under investigation. It would be folly, therefore, to propose a uniform method or theoretical framework for social science, or even for a single discipline.

But what makes one method or theory better for a given task? How should we choose our methods and theoretical frameworks, and how, at the same time, might we judge the product of our choices? Although some standards rightfully apply to particular fields or topics, there must also be standards applying to social science at-large; otherwise, we cannot possibly make decisions among available methods and theoretical frameworks. On what basis does the method-pluralist choose her method? It does not make sense to argue that norms of truth should be field-specific, or steeped in a particular tradition. For if standards of truth are understandable only within the context of specific fields or theoretical traditions, then there is no way to adjudicate among contending views. Whatever scholars in a subfield decide becomes, ipso facto, true (as long as these scholars do not violate their own, self-constructed norms). This sort of epistemological relativism is probably not what Miller, Mills, and others intend, but it does seem a necessary conclusion *if* one is to accept the assertion that methodological norms are field-specific.

A discovery in sociology must be understandable, and appraisable, by those who are *not* sociologists; otherwise, it cannot claim the status of truth, as that term is generally understood.[5] Nor will it suffice to conclude that methodologies must be appropriate to "context."[6] Which contexts, and how many, will be privileged? And how might one justify one's choice of tools and arguments within a given context? It is all very well to say, as hard-nosed practitioners are wont to say, that the proof is in the pudding (i.e., that we can judge social science work only by its product, not its method). Indeed, the approach advocated in this book supposes that we need to broaden methodology's traditional preoccupation with methods so as to include discussion of *results*. But if the proof is in the pudding, by what standards shall we judge the pudding?

No escape is possible from broader interdisciplinary standards if the enterprise of social science is to prove useful to humanity. Indeed, the rationale for a professional caste of scholars, financed at public expense, breaks down if we deny transdisciplinary standards. Naturally, scholarly consensus is not always possible. But surely there are certain things –

---

5. "The theoretical aim of a genuine discipline, scientific or humanistic, is the attainment of truth," writes E. D. Hirsch (1967: viii–ix), "and its practical aim is agreement that truth has probably been achieved. Thus the practical goal of every genuine discipline is consensus – the winning of firmly grounded agreement that one set of conclusions is more probable than others – and this is precisely the goal of valid interpretation."

6. See van Fraassen (1980).

phrenology, for example – that may safely be excluded from consideration. And if phrenology is to be rejected, then we must appeal to transdisciplinary standards in doing so. Otherwise, we must leave the question of phrenology to the phrenologists.

The telling point is that while one can ignore methodology, one cannot choose not to have a methodology. In teaching, in research, and in analyzing the work of colleagues, scholars must separate the good from the bad, the beautiful from the ugly. In so doing, broader criteria of the good, the true, and the beautiful necessarily come into play. Social science, in this sense, is a normative endeavor. Like members of any community, social scientists create and enforce norms, rewarding good behavior and punishing – or, at the very least, ignoring – bad behavior. The gatekeeping functions of the academy cannot be abolished by a wistful appeal to diversity.[7]

Finally, as a matter of good scholarship, writers in the social sciences ought to be able to converse with those in other fields. Hayek once remarked, "The physicist who is only a physicist can still be a first-class physicist and a most valuable member of society. But nobody can be a great economist who is only an economist – and I am even tempted to add that the economist who is only an economist is likely to become a nuisance if not a positive danger."[8] Political scientists interested in political economy should be cognizant – and should seek to incorporate, wherever possible – work in economics. And vice versa. Indeed, cross-disciplinary research is perhaps the most fertile area of research in the social sciences today. Alas, it is not as common as it should be.

The problem posed by academic parochialism stems from the fact that the world of human endeavor, which it is the business of social scientists to study, is remarkably interconnected.[9] It is difficult, for example, to understand features of a political system without understanding something about the economic system. Yet, if political scientists and economists conduct their work with different vocabularies and are guided by a narrow conception of method, they will not have the intellectual equipment to share insights. They may not read each others' work or understand it when they do, even when working on similar topics.

---

7. Moreover, if interdisciplinary standards are to be maintained it will have to be by the widespread and voluntary compliance of the academic community. No arm of government is willing or able to take up the demarcation problem (what is science and what is pseudoscience), and it is not a problem that ordinary citizens are well-prepared to address.
8. Hayek (1956: 462–3; quoted in Redman 1991: epigraph). We should note that the problem of academic parochialism is by no means new. For further discussion – by a self-proclaimed champion of methodological unity – see Wilson (1998).
9. "The domain of truth," Kaplan (1964: 4) writes, "has no fixed boundaries within it."

Because the various methods and theories that populate the social sciences are not effectively unified by a single methodology, less cumulation of knowledge and insight occurs than we might wish. The numbers and narrative camps, for example, are solidly entrenched. Rarely do they raise their heads above the barricades other than to mount a charge against their opponents. It is obvious that knowledge cannot progress unless there is some shared ground on which such knowledge can rest.[10] Even arguments demand a common frame of reference; without such shared ground, they are merely statements of position. In the latter circumstance, science degenerates into a chorus of yeas and nays reminiscent of Monty Python's "Argument Clinic" sketch.

We need to get proponents of different methods and theories back on talking terms. In order to do so we need to provide a common vocabulary – a common framework according to which arguments and evidence can be evaluated, and alternative methods understood. If each has something to contribute (as the phrase goes), then we ought to be able to explain what these contributions are. Whether, in point of fact, norms exist that might provide grounds for judgments of adequacy across the social sciences is the question taken up in the following chapters. For the moment it is sufficient to note that the normative argument for norms is strong. There is no profit in "incommensurability."[11] To the extent that academics employ idiosyncratic or field-specific theoretical frameworks, we become islands in a boatless archipelago. Knowledge will not cumulate; progress – define it how you will – will not occur.

To be sure, the need for agreement varies by topic. Those subjects firmly embedded in the past – those, that is, with few contemporary ramifications – can afford a wider diversity of views. We are less concerned with reaching consensus on the causes of the Spanish Inquisition than

10. For discussion of what "progress" might mean in this context, see Laudan (1977).
11. Incommensurability is a term that entered the lexicon of philosophy of science with the work of Thomas Kuhn. It refers (broadly and ambiguously) to a condition where persons are unable to understand one another because of their different ideological, theoretical, or methodological commitments. It is a very old problem, of course. Bacon noticed that error was the likely result whenever "argument or inference passes from one world of experience to another" (quoted in Wilson 1998: 10), a condition we would now label incommensurability. It should be noted that pluralism and uniformity are matters of degree. All but the most rabid deconstructionists will admit that there are *some* general perspectives on truth and knowledge that tie the social sciences together. See Laudan (1983: 1996), Wallerstein et al. (1996: 92–3), and Wilson (1998) for further defenses of a unified ("objective") methodology. See Hollis and Lukes (1982) and Laudan (1983: 1996) for general discussions of relativism. For arguments in favor of unifying the "qualitative" and "quantitative" dimensions of social science methodology, see Lazarsfeld and Rosenberg (1955: 387–91) and King et al. (1994). For doubts on this score, see McKeown (1999).

the causes of underdevelopment in the third world. (Unfortunately, there is also greater likelihood of consensus on questions in the distant past than on questions that bedevil us in the present.)

The larger point is easier, and more significant: social science should always *strive* for agreement, and the greater agreement it achieves (ceteris paribus) the more useful it is likely to be. Whether the issue is a declaration of war or a capital-gains tax, wherever a policy question lies before us we will seek scholarly consensus on the appropriate course to take. Profound scholarly disagreement over these matters hampers effective public action. How can we justify the expenditure of millions of dollars of public funds if the effectiveness of a program is openly and repeatedly challenged by experts? Indeed, support for social welfare programs has been undermined by suggestions from prominent policy experts that these programs are not achieving their intended purposes.[12] Similarly, support for antimissile defense systems has been weakened by expert testimony questioning the technological viability of these visionary weapons.[13] Citizens are rightfully loath to surrender their earnings in order to pay for programs that cannot demonstrate workability, a judgment we rely on experts to provide.

It is not very useful, let us say, if the social science community generates fourteen different and conflicting perspectives on the causes of crime, on the causes of low educational attainment among African Americans, or on the causes of war in the former Yugoslavia. If this is the end result of academic endeavor, then we have not advanced very far over sheer intuition. Perhaps we have increased our "understanding" of these matters by looking at them from such varied perspectives. However, if we have no way of adjudicating between conflicting visions – if dissensus reigns supreme among academics who study these matters – then we have little to offer policymakers or the general public. Of course, insofar as scholarly dissensus is warranted by the uncertain nature of the evidence we will want that uncertainty to be reflected in public debate. The point is, there is no advantage per se in cultivating diversity. One may applaud *différance* (a Derridean neologism) in the humanities, but not in the social sciences.[14]

---

12. See, for example, Murray (1984).
13. See, for example, Lakoff and York (1989).
14. "Uncertainty" refers here to both fundamental uncertainty (about phenomenal world) and estimation uncertainty (about our sample or methods of analysis). The quest for consensus might also be referred to as a quest for *objectivity*. The trouble with this much-abused term is that it fosters the illusion that such agreement will arise unproblematically from an empirical reality insofar as we view that reality neutrally (without prejudice). My argument for agreement is grounded in the pragmatic need for agreement, rather than in a particular theory of knowledge – empiricist, inductivist, verificationist, falsificationist or what-have-you (see Postscript).

The Search for Unity

If there are good reasons to seek consensus in the social sciences, how might we craft such a consensus? What methodological principles might provide grounds for agreement in the fields of anthropology, economics, history, political science, psychology, and sociology? More to the point, how can we construct a unified framework that is useful for practitioners – that is, reasonably concise, precise, comprehensive, and comprehensible?

Four general approaches may be distinguished among the vast and heterogeneous body of work on social science methodology: *theoretical frameworks, rules, mathematics,* and *philosophy of science.* Although each of these methodological traditions has much to offer, none provides an adequate overall framework for work in the social sciences.

In issuing this critique it should be understood that I am criticizing writers for failing to achieve a goal that they have not, by and large, pursued (at least not in a systematic fashion). Methodologists, historians, and philosophers have other purposes in mind, largely centered on their respective fields and subfields. (Ironically, the field of social science methodology is itself tightly constrained by disciplinary boundaries.) The polemic of this literature review is therefore largely a polemic about what *hasn't* been done. In order to bring this omission into view, and at the same time to set the stage for my own arguments (presented in Chapter 2), we must briefly survey the literature.[15]

Theoretical Frameworks

Social science is inconceivable without the guidance provided by theoretical frameworks such as rational choice, behavioralism, and interpretivism. Each specifies a set of interconnected questions, hypotheses, terms, and methods of analysis that are then used by scholars in the field to define a research project. One must start somewhere. Yet, the scope of these frameworks is small relative to the totality of social science. Interpretivism, for example, sounds eminently reasonable as a description of what many historians, sociologists, and cultural anthropologists do. But what would an interpretivist study of public opinion or public policy look like? Would it tell us things that we want to know? Would it provide the appropriate tools of analysis? To be sure, these "science-y" could probably benefit from an interpretivist's perspective. However, no

---

15. It should be emphasized that this is a highly abbreviated survey, intended only to convey the uses and limitations of different styles of methodological work for the present project. More extended reviews of the literature can be found in footnote references in each section.

one would propose a *purely* interpretivist approach to public opinion (excluding, say, all survey research). Interpretivism, whatever its merits (and they are many), is simply not persuasive as a general framework for the social sciences.[16]

Without engaging in a long and tendentious discussion of other theoretical frameworks we may grant that they, too, are limited in scope. Rational choice, for example, accurately describes the work of most economists, many political scientists, and a few sociologists. But it is simply not plausible as a unifying framework for the social sciences.[17]

More important, these theoretical frameworks are not generally *intended* to answer broader questions of methodological goodness. If we wish to judge the relative success of a study we must go beyond labeling exercises ("interpretivist!" "rational choicer!" "behavioralist!").[18] I suppose one could say that "*A* is a good study in the rational choice genre." However, if genre analysis was the only sort of judgment we could render about a work of social science then we would have to admit something that most social scientists would be loath to admit: that methodological niches are essentially incommensurable and our knowledge of the world highly relativistic. Insofar as we wish to make such cross-theory comparisons – between, say, a rational-choice study of *Y* and an interpretivist study of *Y* – we can do so only with a set of standards that are viable *across* these theoretical divides.[19]

Rules

A second approach to methodological unity reaches for uniform rules, usually garnered from the natural sciences, that might guide scholarly endeavor in the various fields of the social sciences. This tradition has its roots in Aristotle, and traces its lineage through centuries of Aristotelian

---

16. On interpretivism (near-synonyms include *Verstehen* and hermeneutics), see Dray (1952: 1956), Gadamer (1975), Hoy (1982), Natanson (1963), Taylor (1962: 1967/1994; 1970: 1985), Winch (1958), and articles by Gadamer, Geertz, Ricoeur, and Taylor in Rabinow and Sullivan (1979). See also discussion in Mazlish (1998), and Polkinghorne (1983).

17. On rational choice and its variants (analytic narrative, decision theory, formal modeling, formal theory, game theory, marginal theory, new institutionalism, political economy, positive theory, public choice, utility theory), see Barry (1988), Becker (1976), Blaug (1978: 1980), Bohman (1991: 67–76), Coleman (1990), Elster (1986; 1989a), Friedman (1996), Green and Shapiro (1994), Hahn and Hollis (1979), Mueller (1997), Ordeshook (1986), Rosenberg (1992), and Skyrms (1966).

18. On behavioralism (which I employ in its broad, interdisciplinary sense), see Berkhofer (1969), Burgess and Bushell (1969), Charlesworth (1962), Dahl (1961/1969), Eulau (1969), Homans (1951), and Rachlin (1970).

19. On the deleterious effects of a too-great attachment to theory, see Eckstein (1992: 7).

and post-Aristotelian logic.[20] The rulebook approach finds its twentieth-century apogee in the deductive-nomological (or "covering law") model pioneered by Carl Hempel. An explanation for an event, according to this model, should consist of "an adequate description of the event's initial conditions and a general law which 'covers' the case in question, both of which are necessary and sufficient conditions for the occurrence of an explanandum event."[21] Thus, all explanations in the natural and social sciences should take the form of universal laws that are causal, predictive, and testable (and preferably expressed in a mathematical form).

The notion that general laws be substituted for all "particular" explanations (explanations focused on single events) seems somewhat awkward, at least as pertains to the social sciences. In the case of the French Revolution, for example, Hempel proposes something like the following: "A revolution will tend to occur if there is a growing discontent, on the part of a large part of the population, with certain prevailing conditions."[22] As we will discuss later on, an explanation with great breadth is preferable to one with less breadth. Yet, as we will also remark, when an explanation is stretched to include more cases, as in the preceding example, there is generally some sacrifice in accuracy, precision, depth, or some other virtue. Thus, it is not clear that Hempel's call for covering-law explanations will always produce the most useful explanation for a phenomenon of interest to the social sciences.

We may wonder, second, about the designation of explanations as "law-like." One would have to reject a stringent reading of this dictum, since this would toss out most of the explanations that social scientists produce, or could produce. A soft reading of the dictum leaves us just about where we are – striving for perfection, but rarely achieving it. There are a few *so-called* laws in social science (e.g., Duverger's law). But, following the metaphor, one must conclude that they aren't well-

---

20. J. S. Mill's masterpiece (1843/1872), though much richer than traditional logic, probably also belongs in this category. For mainstream work in logic, see Cohen and Nagel (1934). Tarski's "semantic" theory of truth may be understood as a variant of this long tradition (Tarski 1944; Field 1972). The early Wittgenstein and so-called logical positivists (G. Bergmann Carnap, Feigl, Neurath, Schlick, and Waisman), along with their admirers and associates (e.g., A. J. Ayer and Bertrand Russell) in England were also on a mission to use logic to reduce the ambiguities of ordinary language. See Ayer (1959), Carnap (1957), Wittgenstein (1921/1988), and commentary in Friedman (1992) and Gillies (1993).

21. Bohman (1991: 18). See Hempel (1965; 1966). Among philosophers of science, Braithwaite (1955), Nagel (1961), and Popper (1934/1968) are often associated with the deductive-nomological model. Social scientists influenced by this body of work include Przeworski and Teune (1970).

22. Quoted in Bohman (1991: 19).

enforced. We may wonder, finally, about the dictum that all explanations are, at the same time, predictions. It is difficult to see much productive historical work occurring under these conditions. One would like to achieve such a state of grace, but it does not seem to be a realistic goal for most questions that social scientists are concerned to answer.[23]

Hempel, many would say, offers an absurd vision of science (it may not even be applicable to physics). In any case, few in the social sciences invoke Hempel today, so we ought not tar the rulebook vision with a deductive-nomological brush. Softer versions abound, but they pose a different sort of problem, one of ambiguity.

For heuristic purposes, Larry Laudan offers a list of ten rules found commonly in methods texts and philosophical treatises: "propound only falsifiable theories; avoid ad hoc modifications; prefer theories which make successful surprising predictions over theories which explain only what is already known; when experimenting on human subjects, use blinded experimental techniques; reject theories which fail to exhibit an analogy with successful theories in other domains; avoid theories which postulate unobservable entities; use controlled experiments for testing causal hypotheses; reject inconsistent theories; prefer simple theories to complex ones; accept a new theory only if it can explain all the successes of its predecessors."[24] King, Keohane, and Verba, in one of the best recent texts in social science methodology, advise us to "construct falsifiable theories; build theories that are internally consistent; select dependent variables carefully; maximize concreteness; and state theories in as encompassing a way as possible."[25]

Many additional rules might be added to this compendium. And, as can be observed from these two lists, there is some degree of consensus over the proper *do's* and *don'ts* of science. Indeed, rules provide a good point of departure for the beginning student. However, they also create a fundamentally misleading image of what good social science is, instilling a false sense of certainty and simplicity into the undertaking. The point is perhaps best illustrated by a caveat that King, Keohane, and Verba attach to the introduction of their book.

23. For work critical of Hempel, and of the nomothetic ideal of natural science generally, see Almond and Genco (1977/1990), Bohman (1991), Dray (1952), Kaplan (1964), Miller (1987), Murphey (1994), Natanson (1963). For work generally sympathetic to Hempel (as applied to social science), see Brodbeck (1968), and McIntyre (1996). Essays for and against can be found in Boyd et al. (1991), Dray (1966), and Martin and McIntyre (1994).

24. Laudan (1996: 132).

25. Brady (1995: 12), summarizing King et al. (1994: ch 3). Elsewhere, King et al. (1994: 6) claim to delineate "the rules of scientific inference."

We do not provide recipes for scientific empirical research. We offer a number of precepts and rules, but these are meant to discipline thought, not stifle it. In both quantitative and qualitative research, we engage in the imperfect application of theoretical standards of inference to inherently imperfect research designs and empirical data. Any meaningful rules admit of exceptions, but we can ask that exceptions be justified explicitly, that their implications for the reliability of research be assessed, and that the uncertainty of conclusions be reported. We seek not dogma, but disciplined thought.[26]

No one could argue with these modest and sensible caveats. But they betray an uncertainty at the heart of rule-based approaches to social science methodology. No sooner are rules issued than the reader is assured that there are viable exceptions to those rules, or that the rules are subject to a (ubiquitous) ceteris paribus clause. As one wag has noted, when is ceteris ever really paribus? Indeed, rules often contradict one another, leaving the reader to judge which among them should be granted priority. When all these qualifications and caveats are taken into account rules begin to function like soft desiderata, not firm requirements.

Finally, as Timothy McKeown observes, methods texts like *Designing Social Inquiry* do not have much to say about *why* we should follow their rules, and not someone else's.[27] They cannot, therefore, make sense of disputes about which of several methods to employ, or how to evaluate rival hypotheses. The ground is thin, and travelling is precarious.[28]

---

26. King et al. (1994: 7). To this, they add later (22), "social science does not operate strictly according to rules: the need for creativity sometimes mandates that the textbook be discarded!"
27. McKeown (1999).
28. The limits of this sort of work were noted several decades ago by Giovanni Sartori (1970: 1033). Methods texts, he wrote, have "little if anything to share with the crucial concern of 'methodology,' which is a concern with the logical structure and procedures of scientific enquiry. In a very crucial sense there is no methodology without *logos*, without thinking about thinking. And if a firm distinction is drawn – as it should be – between methodology and technique, the latter is no substitute for the former. One may be a wonderful researcher and manipulator of data, and yet remain an unconscious thinker." The profession as a whole, concluded Sartori, "is grievously impaired by methodological unawareness. The more we advance technically, the more we leave a vast, uncharted territory behind our backs." Sartori's words, penned in 1970, are perhaps even truer today. As data become available on a wider range of topics, and as quantitative techniques become more and more sophisticated, and more accessible to the lay researcher via user-friendly data packages, the gap between what we do and what we mean to do has grown wider and wider. For further discussion of the traditional methods text – with particular attention to King et al. (1994) – see Bartels (1995), Brady (1995), Caporaso (1995), Collier (1995b), Laitin (1995), McKeown (1999), Munck (1998), Rogowski (1995), Tarrow (1995), and the response of the authors (King et al. 1995).

Mathematics

Closely related to the rulebook approach to social science methodology is the mathematical approach.[29] Indeed, to say methodology is to imply, by common usage, *quantitative* methodology. This is understandable, given the importance of mathematics to contemporary social science. Yet, it is a mistake to suppose that methodology is equivalent to, or reducible to, mathematical methods and/or logical symbols. If this were true, one would be obliged to argue that those employing qualitative methods in the social sciences do not really have a method, or have worse methods, than those practicing quantitative methods. Perhaps some people (and a few methodologists) agree with this appraisal. Nonetheless, it is probably as easy to lie with statistics as without them. The more important point is that there are many cases of both, and what determines the truth or falsity of a proposition is *not* whether the argument is couched in equations or in narrative prose.

If we must assign priority to math or prose – a dubious assignation, but one that occupies many minds – we must assign it to the latter. Mathematical expressions are meaningless if they cannot be translated into prose. Prose, however, is eminently meaningful without a companion formula. Indeed, many useful expressions in social science *cannot* be expressed mathematically (or are transformed beyond recognition in so doing). Qualitative research, notes Larry Bartels, "has produced most of the science in most of the social sciences over most of their history."[30] Math, and more specifically that branch of math known as statistics, is best understood as a tool of social science, like surveys or computer software. It is not social science itself. In some cases the reduction of a long narrative explanation to a parsimonious equation is wonderfully useful. In other cases, it creates an incomprehensible mess. Moreover, if social science is to be of any use to the world, it must culminate in work that

29. This might be called the Cartesian approach to social science methodology, since Descartes was the first to propose a mathematical paradigm for the sciences (Wilson 1998: 31). A variety of approaches to probability theory (e.g., Bayesian, frequentist, and likelihood) have provided mathematical models of causation and of scientific knowledge in general. See Glymour (1997), Horwich (1982), Jeffrey (1983), King (1989), King et al. (1994: 6), Rosenkrantz (1977), Salmon (1967), Suppes (1970), and discussion in Miller (1987). Of these efforts, Pearl (2000: xiii) writes: "In the last decade, owing partly to advances in graphical models, causality has undergone a major transformation: from a concept shrouded in mystery into a mathematical object with well-defined semantics and well-founded logic. Paradoxes and controversies have been resolved, slippery concepts have been explicated, and practical problems relying on causal information that long were regarded as either metaphysical or unmanageable can now be solved using elementary mathematics. Put simply, causality has been mathematized."
30. Bartels (1995: 8).

ordinary people can understand. What occurs within the restricted realm of scholarly discourse must therefore retain a footing in everyday language and ordinary modes of comprehension. When it loses touch with that ordinary-ness it is likely to become sterile and meaningless.[31]

In all these respects mathematical logic is secondary to the basic logic of social science inquiry, which the present volume is intended to uncover. This book should be viewed as a complement, therefore – not a replacement for, or an opponent to – texts that cover quantitative methods.

Philosophy of Science

A final approach to methodological unity in the social sciences may be found in philosophy of science and history of science (the fields are closely intertwined and will be referred to henceforth as philosophy of science). The vastness and heterogeneity of this field precludes any attempt at synthesis. Yet, we may briefly discuss some of its more prominent representatives and thereby indicate the uses and limits of philosophy of science for the present venture.[32]

Most practicing social scientists would agree that good work must be *falsifiable*. This ideal, elaborated in Karl Popper's 1934 classic, *The Logic of Scientific Discovery,* has become a shibboleth of social science.[33] If a statement cannot be proven false, Popper demonstrated, there is very little sense in which it may be considered true. Thus, although we may never be able to tell, at least not with great certitude, whether a theory is true, we can at least eliminate those theories that are demonstrably false *if we adhere to standards of falsifiability.* The sign of a nonfalsifiable proposition, Popper points out, is that virtually "any conclusion we please can be derived from it."[34] It may be true *by definition,* but it is not true by any standards that we might test – which is to say, by empirical standards.

The trouble with falsifiability as a standard of social science is that it is at once vague *and* limited in purview. This abstract principle may refer to operationalization, specification, precision, simplicity, boundedness, variation in the dependent variable, logical consistency, confirmationist

---

31. This is one of the messages contained in Wassily Leontief's (1982/1983: x–xi) indictment of the economics profession.
32. Recent introductions to the literature can be found in Bohman (1991), Boyd et al. (1991), Brodbeck (1968), Brody (1970), Fiske and Shweder (1986), Kaplan (1964), Krimerman (1969), Martin and McIntyre (1994), McIntyre (1996), Miller (1987), Murphey (1994), Natanson (1963), Rosenberg (1988), and Trigg (1985).
33. See Popper (1934/1968), as well as Popper (1945: 1969: 1976). See de Marchi (1988) and Levinson (1988) on Popper's influence on the social and natural sciences. Most contemporary philosophy of science, and all methods texts that I am aware of, pay obeisance to the goal of falsifiability (e.g., King et al. 1994: 19–20, 100, 109–12).
34. Popper (1934/1968: 92).

strategies of research, as well as broader philosophy-of-science questions such as the so-called demarcation problem. (Popper invokes most, if not all, of these meanings.) Thus, like the *verification* standard it was intended to replace, falsifiability is an unwieldy vehicle for parsing the adequacy of specific tasks and specific work. It is true but not always useful. More important, it does not encompass all that we rightly identify with the scientific ideal (see Table 2.1 on page 21). In some situations, it may even conflict with other desiderata that we hold dear. (For example, we may prefer an exploratory rather than a confirmatory approach to investigation, even though the former is less falsifiable, as discussed in Chapter 10.)

Quite different in tone is the work of Popper's successor, and longtime adversary, Thomas Kuhn.[35] Kuhn's work, unlike Popper's, focused exclusively on the natural sciences. Yet, he is perhaps even better known among social scientists, who draw from Kuhn enlightenment about their own fate. In Kuhnian terms, the social sciences are preparadigmatic or multi-paradigmatic, which is to say that work stems from the diverse impulses of myriad methods, frameworks, and subfields, each with its own more or less specialized vocabulary and parochial sensibility.[36] The natural sciences, by contrast, conduct "normal" science, work that is relatively unified in scope and method around a single paradigm or mutually compatible theoretical frameworks, like those provided by Darwin and Einstein.

This description may be challenged, but let us assume that it is correct in its essentials. Where, then, does it leave us? Are we to embrace this nonparadigmatic status? (Should we strive for *more* paradigms?) Or should we work instead toward an eventual unification of paradigms, as the "preparadigmatic" designation implies? If the latter, on what basis might we expect to achieve reconciliation? Kuhnians, and Kuhn himself, are not clear on these questions. Because of this normative ambiguity, there is not much one can conclude on the basis of Kuhn's work. At best, the Kuhnian framework offers a provocative description of the social sciences today. At worst, it offers an excuse for those who would avoid or deny the importance of methodology.

The work of Kuhn's generally recognized successor, Imre Lakatos, is more useful, since Lakatos is interested in explaining theoretical *progress* – a term with obvious normative connotations. Scientific progress occurs, according to Lakatos, when successive theories offer "some excess empirical content over its predecessor" – including both the empirical content of the predecessor plus some additional empirical content.[37] This is the core insight of the Lakatosian oeuvre as it pertains to normative issues in methodology.

35. See Kuhn (1962/1970) and Lakatos and Musgrave (1970).
36. See, for example, Gutting (1980).
37. Lakatos (1978: 33).

Yet, there are qualifications. Laudan notes that progress cannot always be judged in a straightforward "quantitative" manner, for two empirical facts are not always of equal theoretical importance. Thus, he writes, "the overall problem-solving effectiveness of a theory is determined by assessing the number and importance of the empirical problems which the theory solves and deducting therefrom the number and importance of the anomalies and conceptual problems which the theory generates."[38] Geoffrey Levey proposes a third, and still broader, version of progress.[39] Indeed, if one considers the Lakatosian question in any detail (i.e., in terms more specific than generalized "progress") it will be granted that there are *many* versions, and many essential elements, of theoretical progress.[40] In this light, the work of Lakatos and his followers must be regarded as useful additions to an ongoing debate, but not a final resolution of the question. (Indeed, at this point the Lakatosian framework merges with the rulebook approach.)

The question of progress is inseparable from the larger methodological framework that Lakatos, along with most contemporary philosophers of science, situate themselves within. *Realism,* born out of dissatisfaction with Kuhnian and other post-positivist perspectives, may be understood as an attempt to look closely at what constitutes progress within the natural sciences for clues about the overall methodological project of natural science. "That science succeeds in making many true predictions, devising better ways of controlling nature, and so forth, is an undoubted empirical fact," begins Hilary Putnam, one of realism's leading exponents. "If realism is an *explanation* of this fact, realism [as a methodology of science] must itself be an overarching scientific *hypothesis.*"[41]

---

38. Laudan (1977: 68). See also Simowitz and Price (1990).
39. "Second-order empiricism stipulates … that a theory may explain the apparent success of its rival by situating its content in regard to its own, by inverting its causal logic, or by comprehensively, as against totally, covering what the rival covers" (Levey 1996: 54).
40. See, for example, Eckstein (1975: 88), Hempel (1991: 81), Laudan (1996: 18, 131–2), Przeworski and Teune (1970: 20–3), Stinchcombe (1968: 31), Van Evera (1997: 17–21), and Wilson (1998: 216). This topic is taken up in Chapter 5.
41. Putnam (1984: 141). Richard Boyd's (1984: 41–2) four-point synthesis of realism is longer, but hardly more concrete. "1. Theoretical terms in scientific theories (i.e., nonobservational terms) should be thought of as putatively referring expressions; that is, scientific theories should be interpreted 'realistically.' 2. Scientific theories, interpreted realistically, are confirmable and in fact are often confirmed as approximately true by ordinary scientific evidence interpreted in accordance with ordinary methodological standards. 3. The historical progress of mature sciences is largely a matter of successively more accurate approximations to the truth about both observable and unobservable phenomena. Later theories typically build upon the (observational and theoretical) knowledge embodied in previous theories. 4. The reality which scientific theories describe is largely independent of our thoughts or theoretical commitments." For additional work, see Aronson (1984), Little (1998), Sayer (1992), and various essays in Boyd et al. (1991) and Leplin (1984). Bhaskar (1975/1978) attempts to apply realism to the social sciences.

Realism may be applied to the social sciences, just as it has been applied to the natural sciences. Indeed, this book might be conceived (if the reader was generous) as an effort in the realist mode. But it is not clear what, if anything, this broad hypothesis settles, except insofar as it rules out the rather extreme proposals of poststructuralists and other antiscience critics. Moreover, it is difficult to apply the hypothesis of progress to the social sciences in the way that realists have applied it to the natural sciences. Few would dare proclaim social science's success "an undoubted empirical fact," for example. Appeals to success in a social science field – to productivity, fecundity, or sheer staying power – run into the problem that practitioners in the social sciences are of so many minds, and change their minds with such remarkable frequency. The appeal to consensus, to praxis, and to a theory's track record will get us somewhere – it may, for example, allow us to eliminate methods and methodologies that are highly unorthodox – but it will not adjudicate between two theoretical frameworks or methods, each solidly entrenched within a field or subfield. For this, we must look further.

One could spend much more time discussing philosophy of science. And different versions of these various philosophies could be distinguished from one another, rather than lumped crudely together, as I have done here. Yet, one conclusion would likely remain intact. With a few exceptions (e.g., work by Popper and Lakatos and their followers), philosophy of science does not tell us much about how to improve work in the social sciences, or how to distinguish good work from bad; for most of it is written at a rather lofty ("philosophical") level.[42]

For this reason, philosophy of science has had rather limited effect on the practice of social science. However, it has had great effect on the question of social science's *methodology,* and it is here that we have some cause for concern. Rather than clarifying the methodological debates within the social sciences and fostering greater interdisciplinary harmony, work in the philosophy-of-science genre has had a centrifugal effect. This is not entirely the fault of philosophers. It stems also from the ways in which philosophical work is used and interpreted by the laity (i.e., by social scientists). At a popular level (which is, of course, the level of most social scientists), terms such as constructivism, covering law, determinism, empiricism, falsification, hermeneutics, holism, idealism, inductivism, methodological individualism, naturalism, objectivity, paradigm,

---

42. Some writers are especially forthright on this point. Secord (1986: 197) alerts his readers to the fact that, "as in any philosophical analysis, no specific methodological prescriptions are given for how to do research." The field of epistemology – closely related to philosophy of science – suffers the same limitation. For further discussion, see Kirkham (1992), and the Postscript to this book.

positivism, realism, relativism, subjectivity, value-neutrality, and verification are dogmas. They carve up the universe of social science into mutually incompatible schools and sects.

I do not mean to imply that these terms, and others like them, are useless; indeed, the reader will find most of them employed in the following text. Yet, their utility is limited by their enormous heft. If we ask specific questions about the past, present, and future (e.g., *What was the cause, or causes, of the Civil War?*), it is unlikely that "falsificationists" will come up with vastly different answers than their colleagues in the "relativist" camp. Perhaps those whose work falls under different epistemological labels will choose to investigate different topics. This is significant; but it should not lead us to conclude that social scientists are fundamentally, epistemologically, at odds with one another. We need to pay attention not only to the work of philosophy of science, but also to its uses; and its uses, I would argue, are unfortunate. Kuhn and his progeny are evidence of that. Too often, philosophy of science has served as a sanctuary for those who would prefer *not* to struggle with questions of method.

Conclusions

From my perspective, work in the various genres of social science methodology is either too narrow in scope, or too ambiguous, to guide work and set standards across the social sciences.[43] Theoretical frameworks, rules, mathematics, and philosophy of science are eminently useful, but not for the project undertaken here. In order to provide a model of social science methodology that is useful for practitioners we will have to reconceptualize this complex subject in a framework that is concise, precise, comprehensive, and comprehensible. This, in brief, is the task of the following chapters. The criterial framework is thus correctly understood as a systematization, not a rejection, of extant work on social science methodology. To this framework we now turn.

---

43. Much the same complaint was made several decades ago by Przeworski and Teune (1970: x).

2

A Criterial Framework

There is no royal road to science, and only those who do not dread the fatiguing climb of its steep paths have a chance of gaining its luminous summits.
– Karl Marx[1]

I have argued that there are good reasons to seek greater methodological unity in the social sciences, but that existing approaches do not fully achieve this objective. I shall take a nuts-and-bolts approach to this problem. What makes a work of social science true, useful, or convincing ("scientific")? Why do we prefer one treatment of a subject over another? What reasons do we give when we accept or reject a manuscript for publication? These are the sorts of ground-level judgments that define the social sciences and their various subfields. These are the points of agreement and disagreement that we encounter in the normal course of a day, in interaction with students, colleagues, and in our own work. This is our local knowledge.

How, then, can we systematize this ubiquitous, and often unstated, set of intuitions? Are there unifying threads that tie our intuitions together into a broader framework of norms and practices across the social sciences? Can local knowledge be transformed or reorganized into general knowledge – without losing contact with the workaday tasks of academic inquiry? These are the questions that guide this project of methodological reconstruction.

It is a bottom-up approach, by and large, though it builds on the prodigious literature of social science methodology. Naturally, it is highly synthetic endeavor. Its purpose is to rearrange what we already know, or think we know, into a more useful framework. For the most part, then, the book may be read as a compendium of common sense.

---

1. Marx, "Preface to the French Edition," *Capital* (299), quoted in Levi (1999: 171).

Yet, I also stake some claims. In these cases I beg the reader to follow the logic of the argument carefully in order to perceive the utility that may (if I am correct) justify these departures from standard wisdom. Work on methodology is useful to the extent that it can point the way to more productive norms and practices. This book is thus both a description of, and an argument about, social science methodology.[2]

A Brief Summary

I argue that the work of social science is usefully divided into three interdependent tasks: *concept formation, proposition formation,* and *research design.* Each calls forth a somewhat different set of criterial demands (or goals). The vast and complex subject of social science methodology may be conceptualized, therefore, as a set of tasks and their attendant criteria, as set forth in Table 2.1.

Concepts answer the *what?* question. In order to talk about anything at all one must call it by a name. Since some names are better than others, and some definitions better than others, we cannot escape the problem of concept formation. Adequacy in concept formation requires us to consider eight criteria simultaneously: coherence, operationalization, validity, field utility, resonance, contextual range, parsimony, and analytic/empirical utility. Juggling these criteria successfully is the art of forming good concepts.

Propositions involve the formulation of general statements about the empirical world. Arguments, hypotheses, predictions, explanations, and inferences are all "propositions" in the sense that I employ this term. All such propositions respond to ten criteria of adequacy: specification, accuracy, precision, breadth, depth, parsimony, analytic utility, innovation, intelligibility, and relevance. Additional criteria are attached to propositions of a classificatory, predictive, or causal nature, as indicated in Table 2.1.

---

2. It is appropriate to point out that *any* work on methodology – except perhaps for the most assiduously historical – treads on normative ground. Why else would one write, or read, a treatise on this subject, if not to discover a *should* or a *should not?* Another way of stating this point is to say that the relevance of methodological study stems from its capacity to orient and direct research in the field. A purely descriptive study, assuming such a book could be written, is less interesting because it takes no positions on the methodological battles of the day. Moreover, as a practical matter, a book that traversed this territory while granting equal coverage to every method, practice, and premise would become too large and too heterogeneous to be of assistance to practitioners. Thus, I have self-consciously excluded or downplayed certain tendencies that seemed, to my way of thinking, idiosyncratic or unproductive.

Table 2.1 *The Criterial Framework Summarized*

	Chap.	Table
I. Concepts		
General criteria . . . . . . Coherence, Operationalization, Validity, Field utility, Resonance, Contextual range Parsimony, Analytic/empirical utility	3	3.1
Strategies . . . . Minimal, Ideal-type	4	4.1
II. Propositions		
General criteria . . . . . . Specification, Accuracy, Precision, Breadth, Depth, Parsimony, Analytic utility, Innovation, Intelligibility, Relevance, *plus* ...	5	5.1
Description		
Generalization . . . [no additional criteria]	6	6.1
Classification . . . . Mutual-exclusivity, Exhaustiveness, Comparability	6	6.2
Prediction . . . . Covariation, Priority	6	6.3
Causation . . . . Differentiation, Priority, Independence, Contingency	7	7.2
III. Research Design (in causal analysis)		
General criteria . . . . . . Plenitude, Boundedness, Comparability, Independence, Representativeness, Variation, Analytic utility, Replicability, Mechanism, Causal comparison	8	8.2
Methods . . . . Experimental, Statistical, QCA, Most-similar, Most-different, Extreme-case, Typical-case, Crucial-case, Counterfactual	9	9.1
Strategies . . . . Confirmatory, Exploratory	10	

Research design, finally, involves the evidence, selection of cases, treatment of cases (if any), and methods of analysis that are mustered to demonstrate a given proposition.[3] Since causal inference is by far the most complicated form of argument (at least from a logical point of view), I focus on research design in causal explanation. This task responds to ten criteria: plenitude, boundedness, comparability, independence, representativeness, variation, analytic utility, replicability, mechanism, and causal comparison.

3. Research design has a broader meaning as well, encompassing concepts and propositions. I choose the narrower meaning here.

The book is organized around these three general subjects. Part I sets forth the eight criteria of concept formation (Chapter 3) and discusses various strategies of definition (Chapter 4). Part II sets forth the ten criteria pertaining to all social science propositions (Chapter 5) and then discusses specific kinds of propositions – descriptive, predictive, and causal – and their additional criteria (Chapters 6 and 7). Part III tackles the complex subject of research design in three sections: general criteria (Chapter 8), specific methods (Chapter 9), and basic strategies (Chapter 10).

Further elaboration on these difficult points will have to await later chapters. For the moment, let us consider the implications of the criterial framework. How helpful is it in making sense of the complex enterprise of social science and in sorting out traditional methodological problems?

Circularities and Tradeoffs

We have already noted the insufficiencies of a rulebook methodology (Chapter 1). The problem, in brief, is that of arriving at a comprehensive set of rules applicable to all disciplines. We invariably discover that rules developed for use in one methodological context are burdensome in another. Even within the *same* methodological context different rules may impose conflicting demands on an investigation. This leads methodologists to introduce every rule with a "ceteris paribus" caveat, which in turn forces rules to function in a non-rulelike manner. The rulebook approach usual to methods texts breaks down.

By contrast, a criterial approach to social science emphasizes the *circularity* of this enterprise. There is no obvious point of entry for a work of social science, no easy way to navigate between what we know (or think we know) and what we would like to know "out there" in the empirical world. One might begin with a hunch, a question, a clearly formed theory, or an area of interest. With questions of method, we may paraphrase Peirce: "There is only one place from which we ever can start, ... and that is from where we are."[4]

Once begun, our procedure of concept formation, proposition formation, and research design is difficult to diagram in a series of temporally discrete "steps" – unless one imagines hopping to-and-fro and back-and-forth in a rather frenetic fashion. Empirical investigation is necessarily contingent on preformed concepts and theories, as well as our general notions of the world; yet, our investigation is likely to alter these notions in unpredictable ways. In so doing, we shall revise our conception of what

---

4. Paraphrased in Kaplan (1964: 86).

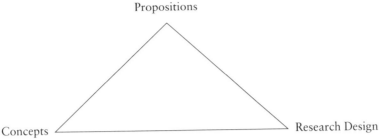

Figure 2.1. Social Science Tasks: A Triangular Relationship.

we (think) we are studying. The definition of one's dependent variable often changes once one has analyzed the data. Indeed, social science is an exceptionally good example of the so-called hermeneutic circle.

The high level of interdependence among the three tasks of social science can hardly be overemphasized. It is difficult to imagine a useful concept independent of a useful proposition, and vice versa. Research design makes no sense at all unless it is attached to a particular proposition and set of concepts. Thus, any alteration of one of these elements necessarily upsets the other two. *Tradeoffs,* rather than fixed formula, best describe this dynamic process of mutual adjustment.[5]

The criterial approach thus places the ceteris paribus caveat at the center of social science methodology. Adequacy involves attempting to satisfy criteria that, even *within* a given context, are often in conflict with one another. The hard work of social science thus begins when a scholar begins to prioritize tasks and criteria. It is this prioritization that defines one's approach to a given subject. Consequently, the process of putting together concepts, propositions, and a research design involves circularities and tradeoffs (among tasks *and* criteria); it is not a linear follow-the-rules procedure. Figure 2.1 portrays the triangular relationship obtaining among concepts, propositions, and research design.

More than a century ago, the great dramatist and orator, Richard Sheridan, offered the following commentary on a Ministerial speech: "It contained a great deal both of what was new and what was true, but unfortunately what was new was not true and what was true was not new."[6] If new, not true; if true, not new – it is a standard social science

5. The importance of tradeoffs of various sorts is emphasized in the work of David Collier, Larry Laudan, Adam Przeworski, Giovanni Sartori, Rudra Sil, Henry Teune, and others.

6. Sykes and Sproat (1967: 100).

rejoinder, an all-purpose critique. Of course, one hopes that this is not *entirely* the case. But clearly there is a nagging tradeoff between innovation and accuracy in social science.

Another common propositional tradeoff is the tug of war between breadth and depth. A prefers to say a little about a great many things, whereas B prefers to say a lot about a few things. (In stats vernacular, A explains 10% of the variance across 100 cases, whereas B explains 90% of the variance across several cases.) The general topic of interest may be identical, but the results of these two studies may diverge dramatically.

A third example, combining a large number of criteria, is provided by J. H. Hexter's contrast between "lumpers" and "splitters" in the historical discipline:

> *Splitters* like to point out divergences, to perceive differences, to draw distinctions. They shrink away from systems of history and from general rules, and carry around in their heads lists of exceptions to almost any rule they are likely to encounter. They do not mind untidiness and accident in the past; they rather like them.
>
> *Lumpers* do not like accidents; they would prefer to have them vanish. They tend to ascribe apparent accidents not to the untidiness of the past itself but to the untidiness of the record of the past or to the untidiness of mind of splitting historians who are willing to leave the temple of Clio a shambles. Instead of noting differences, lumpers note likenesses; instead of separateness, connection. The lumping historian wants to put the past into boxes, all of it, and not too many boxes at that, and then to tie all the boxes together into one nice shapely bundle. The latter operation turns out to be quite easy, since any practiced lumper will have so selected his boxes in the first place that they will fit together in a seemly way.[7]

The same clash of preferences can be found in many disciplines and, more important, *between* disciplines. Economists, political scientists, and sociologists are likely to be found lumping their facts together; cultural anthropologists and historians generally prefer to pry them apart. Thus, political scientists generally look for similarities among cultures – so as to "hold culture constant." Anthropologists, by contrast, are more often "seeking out diversity."[8] Historians, by the same token, are keen to emphasize the "differentness" of a historical period vis-à-vis their own era. In general, idiographs contrast, while nomothets compare. Each is unsatisfied with what the other has to offer. Each has a different view of what social science is, or should be.

Yet, these are not dichotomous worldviews. There are no "pure" splitters or lumpers; lumping and splitting are always matters of degree. (Any

---

7. Hexter (1979: 242); attributed to Donald Kagan.
8. Barth (1999: 82).

description of an event will involve some lumping and some splitting.) And both lumping and splitting rely on the same logical process of *comparison* (see Chapter 8). Indeed, few writers, I imagine, would wish to classify themselves entirely in one camp. Thus, the bifurcated categories themselves are extremely lumpy. A more precise way of understanding this debate, I think, is to say that splitters give preference to propositional criteria like accuracy, precision, and depth, while lumpers give preference to breadth, parsimony, analytic utility, and relevance. Rather than looking on these two camps as hostile and irreconcilable, therefore, it may be more useful to observe this long-standing argument, as a matter of criterial prioritization.

Many of the other dichotomies that we employ to categorize work in the social sciences – theoretical/empirical, small-N/large-N, experimental/nonexperimental, qualitative/quantitative, and so forth – might be understood as choice-sets along various dimensions of tasks and criteria. The same might be said for various theoretical frameworks that divide up the landscape of social science research such as behavioralism, rational choice, and interpretivism. Each of these research traditions is an effort to maximize some particular set of virtues, while ignoring a corresponding set of vices.

Arguments among schools, theories, and methods usually appeal to a *shared* set of norms. Lumpers accuse splitters of ignoring the big picture, but they can hardly deny the importance of depth and precision. Splitters, by the same token, cannot deny that there is some benefit to generalization. Similarly, debates over rational choice involve the question of whether rational choice is falsifiable (among other things); they do *not* question falsifiability as a general goal of social science. In short, there is less disagreement than meets the eye in the constant to-and-fro among partisans of different methodological camps. Each has chosen to maximize different goods, but the goods themselves are generally recognized.

Indeed, the construction of theoretical frameworks is of limited utility in illuminating the adequacies and inadequacies of work in the social sciences. Schools and traditions are difficult to specify (what is "rational choice"?), and all such arguments hinge on this problem of definition. Moreover, however specified, these schools are quite diverse. Thus, we are likely to find falsifiable rational choice as well as nonfalsifiable rational choice, theoretically-informed interpretivist work and nontheoretical interpretivist work. It makes little sense to speak of these schools as if they were unitary entities. What we *can* confidently conclude relates to particular work and the concepts, propositions, and research designs that compose that work. Here, the relevant dimensions are not the school or tradition that a study happens to fall into but rather the degree to which it satisfies the criterial framework of adequacy. Criteria, not theoretical traditions, provide the underlying normative framework of social science.[9]

Beyond Tradeoffs

I have presented work in the various fields of social science as a series of theoretical and disciplinary frameworks, each emphasizing certain goods and downplaying others. This "tradeoffs" perspective is troubling in one respect. If scholars are free to prioritize criteria as they see fit, can we ever say that a writer has made a wrong choice? Are all criterial compromises equally satisfactory? Because no school or tradition can make a priori truth-claims, the usual answer to this question is that it all comes down to a matter of taste. Different writers, and different research traditions, exemplify different aesthetic preferences. It would seem that we have landed ourselves in a relativistic swamp, after all.

There are several responses to this apparent dilemma. First, as the criterial framework indicates, the dimensions of what might qualify as good taste are not limitless. Although scholars working within different traditions choose which criteria to prioritize in a given study, they do not create their own unique criteria. Criterial demands are fixed and determinate across the disciplines of the social sciences. Thus, when an author relinquishes her hold on one criterion for the more full possession of another, the value of the resulting work gains and loses accordingly. An author may be forthright about such tradeoffs; she may restrict her gaze to a single case, ignoring other examples of a phenomenon. Such forthrightness is exemplary, but does *not* obviate the need for breadth. Readers are still entitled to wonder whether her arguments hold across a broader set of cases.

Second, although we shall never be able to judge concepts, propositions, and research designs according to a single metric, we can aim for a *comparative* approach that judges one concept, proposition, or research design against others that might be substituted in its place (i.e., others that would explain the same general phenomenon). There are no absolute standards, only relative ones. Thus, readers might ask what level of propositional goodness could be achieved by a study that

---

9. The concept *criterion* is central to this investigation. Here, I rely on everyday usage rather than specialized usage in philosophical realms. Cavell (1979: 9), following a review of several examples of usage-patterns and a seven-part definitional typology, offers the following gloss: "criteria are specifications a given person or group sets up on the basis of which (by means of, in terms of which) to judge (assess, settle) whether something has a particular status or value." This seems clear enough. (For further commentary, see additional passages in Cavell [Ibid.].)

reversed the original author's choices – sacrificing depth, perhaps, for greater breadth, or specification for greater analytic utility. Would the resulting argument be stronger along other dimensions (more accurate, more precise, more relevant)? In some situations, one would likely conclude that each approach has its merits. In other situations, one might conclude that there *is* a best way of approaching a topic, others being faulty on one ground or another. Some adjustments are zero-sum (pure tradeoffs); others are positive-sum (payeto optimal).

The phrase "inference to the best explanation" is apt.[10] However, the criterial framework endows this pat phrase with a more specific content. (*Of course* one wishes to find the proposition that best explains a given state of affairs; the critical question is, how do we know this proposition when we see it?) We ought to be able to identify the best explanation for a given phenomenon by its superior performance along the three tasks (concepts, propositions, and research design), and their attendant criteria.

The methodological framework set forth in this book is quite different, therefore, from a methodological pluralism that considers all approaches equally valid or fruitful, and worlds away from "relativism" and "incommensurability."[11] I should like to think of it as pluralism within limits, a happy medium between the straitjacket of logical positivism and the anything-goes style of poststructuralism.[12]

---

10. There is considerable dispute over what inference to the best explanation (IBE) means. According to Day and Kincaid (1994: 282), "IBE names an abstract pattern whose force and success depends on the specific background assumptions involved. Without substantive assumptions both about explanation in general and about specific empirical details, IBE is empty. In short, appeals to the best explanation are really implicit appeals to substantive empirical assumptions, not to some privileged form of inference. It is the substantive assumptions that do the real work." See also Harman (1965). For work emphasizing the importance of comparison in evaluating theories and other products of social science, see Gruenbaum (1976), Hanson (1961), Hausman (1992: 306), Lakatos (1978), Laudan (1977: 71; 1996: 86), Levey (1996), and Miller (1987: ch 4).

11. See Laudan (1996: 19) for a brief summary of relativist positions.

12. Of course, *most* methodologies seek to avoid the Scylla of logical positivism and the Charybdis of poststructuralism. Neither is very popular among social scientists today. Yet, we must reach some accommodation between constraint and freedom (objectivity and subjectivity, consensus and dissensus...) in academic work. The scholar must be free to innovate, but within limits; otherwise, her innovations will not be understood. In hermeneutical terms, one might say that innovation occurs, but only within the context of tradition. If it breaks too radically with that tradition, then it no longer constitutes innovation at all. It is merely nonsense. Where, precisely, to strike a balance between uniformity and pluralism in social science inquiry is a question that probably cannot be answered in generalities. We can only hope to prove the argument by laying out a specific resolution to this eternal dilemma, and counterposing its virtues to other possible frameworks (such as those explored, fleetingly, in Chapter 1).

The search for greater unity is inextricably intertwined with the search for *progress,* another sticking point for the social sciences. Consider the following anecdote, related by Charles Lindblom. The writer of a review essay concludes that significant progress has been made in his subfield. Yet, Lindblom notes, "these claims were not posited by detailing findings but rather by alleging that political scientists had 'illuminated,' 'were concerned with,' 'gave special emphasis to,' 'developed insights, hypotheses, and analytical categories,' 'codified,' 'stressed the importance of,' 'examined the significance of,' 'placed in the context of,' 'treated variables theoretically,' 'produced good work,' 'were fruitful,' 'applied concepts and models to,' 'vastly improved our understanding,' 'dealt with,' and 'increased the level of rigor.'"[13] The reviewer's methodological difficulties are characteristic of the social sciences at large. We have no clear way of charting progress, or noting deviation.

The criterial framework will not alleviate argument. Indeed, it should be remembered that argument is a prerequisite for progress; a perfectly consensual social science is perfectly dystopic. What the criterial framework may provide is a substructure of consensus among contending methods, fields, and theoretical frameworks: a way of organizing our disagreements, and hence a common ground on which these arguments might be debated.

One of the reasons why arguments in the social sciences tend to fly past one another (the proverbial ships in the night) is that we apply norms indiscriminately, failing to distinguish between those that are proper to particular tasks. We have also developed a panoply of overlapping, and ultimately rather confusing, terms to describe the things we like and dislike. The criterial approach does not depend on establishing a uniform vocabulary, but it does depend on seeing the interconnections among different lexicons. Thus, a good deal of attention in the following chapters is devoted to elucidating alternative terms for more or less similar ideas. Concepts, not terms, should be the focus of debate; in order for this to happen we must pay heed to terminology.

Although we are continually struck by social science's fissiparous quality, there is also a sense in which the whole project hangs together. It is downright clingy. This is the twin difficulty that besets any methodological work in the social sciences: the seamless and holistic quality of methodological "goodness." One is at pains to evaluate one vice or virtue without addressing a host of neighboring issues. Concepts, propositions, and research designs intermingle, as do the various criteria

---

13. Lindblom (1997: 257).

applying to each task. This confusion is embedded in the terms we use, which invariably refer to a variety of overlapping methodological features. Only by putting these pieces together into a single, comprehensive framework can we hope to grasp the interconnections and redundancies of social science methodology.

Whatever agreement is possible in social science will be provided by a foundation that we can all (more or less) agree on. Such a framework is present already in our everyday judgments about good work, strong arguments, and solid evidence. By contrast, consensus is *not* likely to arise through our conversion to a single paradigm (inaugurating that heavenly state known as "normal science"). We are not likely to wake up one Monday morning to find ourselves all doing game theory, or hermeneutics. Fortunately, agreement on theories, models, and methods is not necessary. Indeed, it would be foolhardy and unproductive for social scientists to pursue the same questions in the same ways. Triangulation is useful.

Such knowledge will cumulate only if we are able to put diverse evidence and argumentation together into a common framework. Progress *is* a realistic goal, so long as we understand that lasting progress is more likely to occur in small steps than in revolutionary ("paradigmatic") leaps. If the criterial framework will not resolve all our strife, it will at least point the way to a more productive style of debate: where arguments meet each other on common ground, where the advantages and disadvantages of different approaches to a problem can be specified and evaluated, and where cumulation can reasonably be assessed.

Clarifications

Before moving on to a discussion of concepts, propositions, and research designs – the topics of Parts I, II, and III of the book – we must clear up several possible points of confusion.

First, it should be clarified that the criterial framework does not involve considerations of *expediency*. We might choose a concept, a proposition, or a research design because it is more convenient for us to do so – for example, because we lack the language skills to study something else, because political or cultural barriers prevent us from gathering that information, because data or nonstatistical information is limited for other cases, because we have received funding to study that subject (and not others), because the researcher has a personal interest in that area, and so forth. All of these considerations are perfectly defensible. Indeed, nothing is so common as the scholar's explanation that she has collected data for all cases for which data were available.[14] Yet, these practical considerations are not, themselves, criteria of good concepts, propositions, or research designs. One could hardly argue, for example, that a given research design is superior to another because it was more practical. This might have been the reason *behind* a study's success or failure, but it cannot be the grounds on which we accept or reject it. If another writer comes along with more money, better language skills, or better access to key cases, she will be able to construct a better research design. It is the latter, goodness in research design, that we are concerned with here.

Readers have probably been told the tale of the hapless drunk who searched repeatedly for her lost keys under a lamppost. When a bystander inquired why she looked only in this one small area, the drunk replied that it was the only spot where she could see clearly. That sample of cases which is most convenient may not be the most plentiful, transparent, comparable, independent, representative, variable, or analytically useful. Yet, the latter criteria are the grounds on which the writer must ultimately justify her selection of cases. Similarly, for concept formation and proposition formation. I underline these rather obvious points to differentiate the criterial framework from the more practical sort of advice that students of politics, economics, cultures, and societies might benefit from (often included in methods textbooks). It is advisable to familiarize oneself with a research venue before beginning to collect one's data, to conduct exploratory work before administering a survey, to have sufficient resources available to complete one's work, to avoid antagonizing your informants (and your thesis adviser!), and so forth. Ethical considerations also apply. But one could hardly call this one's methodology.[15]

A second clarification concerns the length and structure of the criterial framework. To some, this framework may seem like an unduly long and complicated laundry list. To others, it undoubtedly appears short and reductivist. Indeed, books have been written about some of the subjects that I cover (rather cavalierly, it must seem) in a page or two. I do not claim to have ended discussion on these points. My claim is simply

---

14. We should note that when cases are said to have been selected according to convenience (i.e., data availability), the implication that the writer wishes to convey is not that convenience confers some special methodological status upon her cases but rather that she has not used other (more suspicious) methods of case selection. Convenience, in certain circumstances, may be considered a method of random selection. Again, the relevant question is comparability and representativeness, not "convenience" per se.

15. Van Evera (1997) is perceptive on these practical and ethical considerations.

to have covered this territory as thoroughly as possible *at this level of analysis.* An intermediate level of analysis was chosen so as to afford us the benefits of breadth and parsimony, with some regrettable, but unavoidable, sacrifice of depth. Readers hungry for more discussion on various topics may follow the trail of footnotes or survey the references listed at the end of the book.

I should also acknowledge the obvious: the typology set forth here could be subdivided in different ways. There is nothing sacrosanct about the numbers 8 (for concepts), 10+ (for propositions), and 10 (for research designs), as set forth in Table 2.1. In my mind, these categories seemed to divide up the subject in the most clear and efficient manner possible. Other scholars might slice the pie somewhat differently. But not *that* differently, I should think.

The reader will note that the criterial framework is an effort in classificatory inference (see Chapter 6). As such, it depends on a large number of categorical distinctions, primarily between different tasks and criteria. None of these distinctions is hard and fast, as the saying goes. (This is true, of course, for any classification.) Yet, the utility of a classificatory schema must be judged by the easy cases as well as the problem cases. Successes must be weighed against apparent failures. By this accounting, I think the criterial framework earns high marks.

PART I
Concepts

3

Concepts: General Criteria

As we are ... prisoners of the words we pick, we had better pick them well.
– Giovanni Sartori[1]

Concept formation concerns the most basic question of social science research: *What are we talking about?* Specifically, how do we make connections between the phenomenal world, the presumed subject matter of social science, and the linguistic world within which social science takes form? Concept formation thus lies at the heart of all social science endeavor. It is impossible to conduct work without using concepts. It is impossible even to conceptualize a topic, as the term suggests, without putting a label on it.

More important, concepts are not static. Work on a subject necessarily involves *reconceptualization* of that subject. Work on the nation-state, for example, if at all persuasive, alters our understanding of "nation-state." No use of language is semantically neutral. Authors make lexical and semantic choices as they write and thus participate, wittingly or unwittingly, in an ongoing interpretive battle. This is so because language is the tool kit with which we conduct our work, as well as the substance on which we work. Progress in the cultural sciences occurs, if it occurs at all, through changing terms and definitions. This is how we map the changing terrain.[2]

---

1. Sartori (1984a: 60).
2. Weber (1905/1949: 105–6) writes: "The history of the social sciences is and remains a continuous process passing from the attempt to order reality analytically through the construction of concepts – the dissolution of the analytical constructs so constructed through the expansion and shift of the scientific horizon – and the reformulation anew of concepts on the foundations thus transformed... The greatest advances in the sphere of the social sciences are substantively tied up with the shift in practical cultural problems and take the guise of a critique of concept-construction." The progress of the social sciences is thus ineluctably tied to "reconstruction of concepts through which we seek to comprehend reality" (Ibid.).

But all is not well in the land of concepts. For many years it has been a standard complaint that the terminology of social science lacks the clarity and constancy of the natural science lexicon. "Ideology," for example, a concept explored at length in the following chapter, has been found to contain at least thirty-five possible attributes, forming a conceptual apparatus with some 2^{35} definitional possibilities. Other concepts, such as justice, democracy, the state, and power, are similarly fraught. Truly, it might be said, we do not know what it is we are talking about when we use these terms, for when *A* says ideology she may mean something quite different from *B*. Concepts are variously employed in different fields and subfields, within different intellectual traditions, among different writers, and sometimes – most alarmingly – within a single work. Concepts are routinely stretched to cover instances that lie well outside their normal range of use.[3] Or they are scrunched to cover only a few instances (ignoring others). Older concepts are redefined, leaving etymological trails that confuse the unwitting reader. New words are created to refer to things that were perhaps poorly articulated through existing concepts, leaving a highly complex lexical terrain (for the old concepts continue to circulate). Words with similar meanings crowd around each other, vying for attention and stealing each others' attributes. Thus we play musical chairs with words, in Sartori's memorable phrase.[4]

This sort of semantic confusion throws a wrench into the work of social science. Arguments have a tendency to fly past each other, and work on these subjects does not progress. Concepts seem to get in the way of a clear understanding of things.

Those with a humanities vision of how to study the social world may look on this state of disrepair as further evidence of the natural and irrevocably chaotic state of language.[5] Ordinary language analysis, for

---

3. On conceptual stretching, see Collier and Mahon (1993) and Sartori (1970: 1984a).
4. Sartori (1975: 9). See also Sartori (1984a: 38, 52–53).
5. Words, writes Virginia Woolf in *The Death of the Moth*, "are the wildest, freest, most irresponsible, most unteachable of all things. Of course, you can catch them and sort them and place them in alphabetical order in dictionaries. But words do not live in dictionaries; they live in the mind ... Thus to lay down any laws for such irreclaimable vagabonds is worse than useless. A few trifling rules of grammar and spelling are all the constraint we can put on them. All we can say about them, as we peer at them over the edge of that deep, dark and only fitfully illuminated cavern in which they live – the mind – all we can say about them is that they seem to like people to think and to feel before they use them, but to think and to feel not about them, but about something different. They are highly sensitive, easily made self-conscious. They do not like to have their purity or their impurity discussed... Nor do they like being lifted out on the point of a pen and examined separately. They hang together, in sentences, in paragraphs, sometimes for whole pages at a time. They hate being useful; they hate making money; they hate being lectured about in public. In short, they hate anything that stamps them with one meaning or confines them to one attitude, for it is their nature to change" (quoted in Robinson 1954: 65). For a more formal discussion, see work in the ordinary language tradition (e.g., Pitkin 1972: 4).

example, implies that no sort of scientific reconstruction beyond that already evident in everyday understandings and dictionary definitions is likely to clear up this semantic mess. Scholars in the humanities are also likely to challenge the existence of an ("objective") physical reality out there. Language, they might claim, lies prior to, or is at least implicated in, our understandings of the world. There are no "things" to appeal to for help in straightening out our conceptual difficulties.[6]

Suffice to say, the external world exerts *some* influence (leaving aside exactly how much) on our construction of concepts; we define words like "democracy" with regard to actually existing practices. Concept formation in the social sciences may be understood as an attempt to mediate between the world of language (as well as our prelinguistic cognitive world) and the world of things (beyond language); it is neither entirely one nor the other. One aim, among many, is to represent that phenomenal world as accurately as possible.

The second claim, that agreement on words and meanings is impossible, may also be understood as a matter of degree. The purpose of this chapter and the next is not to attain complete consensus on words and meanings, but rather to attain a higher level of agreement in the social sciences than we currently possess.

Granted, then, that disambiguation is a worthy goal, and that we might move marginally closer to this goal, let us examine some of the approaches one might take toward greater conceptual clarity and standardization in the social sciences.

One solution to our endless conceptual disputation is to bypass conceptual disputes entirely by focusing on the phenomena themselves (rather than the labels and definitions we attach to them). If, as Galileo observed, all definitions are arbitrary, then we might as well begin with a recognition of this fact.[7] It is commonly said, for example, that one can prove practically anything simply by defining terms in a convenient way. This is, no doubt, what prompts certain commentators to say that we ought to pay less attention to the terms we use, and more to the things out there that we are talking about. "Never let yourself be goaded into taking seriously problems about words and their meanings," Karl Popper argues in his vehement fashion. "What must be taken seriously are questions of fact, and assertions about facts, theories, and hypotheses; the problems they solve; and the problems they raise."[8]

This seems reasonable. On the other hand, as we have already suggested, we are unable to talk about questions of fact without getting

---

6. See, for example, Taylor (1985) or, more radically, Whorf (1956).
7. Paraphrased in Robinson (1954: 63).
8. Popper (1976: 19; quoted in Collier 1998).

caught up in the language that we use to describe such questions. If *A* calls it "fascism" while *B* calls it "authoritarianism," does this not matter? Would it be possible to carry on a productive dialogue when *A* and *B* employ different terms for the same (ostensibly the same) phenomenon? It seems that at some point *A* and *B* would be compelled to reach an understanding about what to call the thing at issue, and how to define that key term. They would be compelled, in other words, to engage in concept formation in a formal and self-conscious manner. Indeed, the frequent and often extreme ambiguities encountered in social science language militates against a blithely empirical approach to social science.

A second approach to alleviating conceptual stress in the social sciences advises us to avoid high-order concepts in preference for less abstract ("concrete") concepts. Because most of the conceptual ambiguities of social science concern abstract concepts like democracy, power, and ideology, perhaps we would be better off paring down our conceptual universe to more manageable units such as deaths, votes, and purchasing power. Again, this seems like reasonable advice. But again, there are important tradeoffs to such a strategy (known to philosophers as *physicalism*). Most obviously, we would be limited in what we could talk about. We could indeed discuss deaths, votes, and purchasing power, but *not* democracy, power, or ideology. And although this concretized lexicon might lead to greater agreement among social scientists, we should have to wonder about the overall utility of a social science reconstructed along such lines. Does the act of voting matter outside a framework of democracy? Is it meaningful at all? Arguably, a social science limited to observable entities would have very little of importance to say. Moreover, it would have no way of putting these small-order ideas together into a coherent whole. Large-order concepts comprise the scaffolding on which we hang observables. Without general concepts, science cannot generalize. A social science without abstract concepts would be a series of disconnected facts and microtheories.

A third approach to conceptual disambiguation lies in the familiar admonition to carefully define our terms and to maintain a reasonable level of consistency in our use of those terms within a given work. This is excellent advice, but also begs an antecedent question: *which* terms, and *which definitions* for those terms, should we choose? Purely stipulative definitions (deriving solely from the authority of the author) can be difficult to comprehend and, equally important, to remember. We are likely to refer to such definitions as arbitrary if they do not fit with our intuitive understandings of the term or the subject matter. Humpty-Dumpty insisted that when he used a word, "It means just what I choose it to mean – neither more nor less." To this Alice responded: "The question is, whether you *can* make words mean so many different things."[9] We must side with Alice in this controversy; social science is not at all like Wonderland. It matters *how* we define our terms, not merely that we define them.

A final approach to resolving conceptual difficulty in the social sciences suggests that concept formation is irreducibly a matter of "context." There is little one can say in general about this vexed subject because different concepts will be appropriate for different research tasks. This hoary bit of wisdom is true as well. Even so, conceptual disputes in the social sciences are rarely resolved by an appeal to context. Indeed, it is rather uncertain what "context" means, or how one would employ it to guide the process of concept formation. The appeal to context is thus highly ambiguous.[10]

In short, commonsense approaches to concept formation are all true, but only to a point. Similarly, the more theoretically ambitious efforts of philosophers and social scientists to delineate the *do's* and *don'ts* of concept formation are enlightening, but not conclusive (see Chapter 4). The approach taken here is to isolate the various desiderata identified by common sense and academic wisdom into a concise and reasonably comprehensive framework. Thus situated, goodness in concepts may be understood as an attempt to mediate between eight criteria: *coherence, operationalization, validity, field utility, resonance, contextual range, parsimony,* and *analytic/empirical utility,* as shown in Table 3.1.[11]

The chapter proceeds in two stages. In the first section I set forth the eight criterial demands, showing why each is important and, at the same time, why concept formation is not reducible to that criterion alone. In the next section, I discuss some broader the implications of this framework for the conduct of social science research. Chapter 4 delineates a strategy for forming good concepts around troubled terms (e.g., "ideology").

Before we begin, we must clarify our topic. Conventionally, a concept refers to an alignment among three intertwined components: the term (a linguistic label comprised of one or a few words), the phenomena to be defined (the *referents, extension,* or *denotation* of a concept), and the properties or attributes that define those phenomena (the *definition, intension,* or *connotation* of a concept). This has come to be known as

9. Carroll (1939: 187).
10. For further discussion, see Chapter 4.
11. This framework revises arguments put forth originally in Gerring (1999).

Table 3.1   *Criteria of Conceptual Goodness*

---

1. Coherence (differentiation, definition, clarity, boundedness) (*antonyms:* fuzziness, arbitrariness, ambiguity). How internally coherent and externally differentiated are the attributes of the concept vis-à-vis neighboring concepts and entities?

2. Operationalization (measurement, indicators, precision) (*antonyms:* fuzziness, ambiguity). Can the concept distinguish its own referents from other, similar referents? How clear are a concept's borders? How do we know it when we see it?

3. Validity (construct, measurement or cue validity, accuracy, truth, reliability). Is the concept valid? Are we measuring what we purport to be measuring?

4. Field Utility (natural kinds, classificatory utility). How useful is the concept within a field of closely related terms?

5. Resonance (familiarity, normal usage) (*antonyms:* neologism, idiosyncracy). How resonant is the concept – in ordinary and/or specialized contexts?

6. Contextual range (breadth, scope, compass, reach, stretch) (*antonyms:* parochialism). Across how many linguistic contexts (language regions) is a concept viable? How far can it travel?

7. Parsimony. How short is (a) the term and (b) its list of defining attributes (the intension)?

8. Analytic/empirical utility. How useful is the concept within a particular analytic (theoretical) context or research design?

---

the Ogden–Richards Triangle and is illustrated in Figure 3.1.[12] Concept *formation,* therefore, refers to the process of adjusting terms, referents, and definitional attributes to maximize a concept's performance along the eight criteria.

12. See Sartori (1984a: 22), adopted from Ogden and Richards (1923/1989: 11). If these terms are unfamiliar to readers it is doubtless because so little attention has been devoted to the subject of concept formation within the social sciences. Stephen Toulmin (1972: 8) notes, "the term *concept* is one that everybody uses and nobody explains." To be sure, concepts are a central concern for philosophers, political theorists, sociological theorists, intellectual historians, linguists, and cognitive psychologists. On the phenomenon of "contested concepts," see Clarke (1979), Connolly (1974/1983), Gallie (1956/1962), and Gray (1977). On conceptual change through history, see Ball (1988), Ball et al. (1989), and Kosselleck (1989). On the differences between researchers' and subjects' definitions of key concepts, see Brown and Taylor (1972). On epistemological and linguistic issues pertaining to concept formation, see Austin (1961), Fodor (1998), Gardner and Schoen (1962), Held (1973), Kalleberg (1969), Lakoff (1987), Lamberts and Shanks (1997), Natanson (1963), Palmer (1988), Pitkin (1972), Rosch et al. (1976), and Taylor (1995). On the definition of "concept," see Adcock (1998). These scholars are primarily interested in concepts as they function in ordinary or philosophical contexts, rather than in the specialized realm of social science.

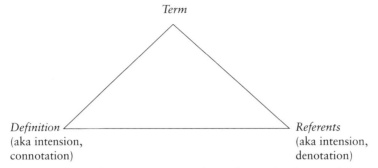

Figure 3.1. What Is A Concept? The Ogden–Richards Triangle.

Coherence

All referential concepts perform a grouping or sorting function. A concept gathers together things that are alike in some respect, distinguishing them from those things that are different. Apples, insofar as they share similar properties, are rightfully grouped under the rubric "apple." Oranges, insofar as they are different from apples and similar to each other, are rightfully grouped under the label "orange." And so forth. Similarly, with social science concepts like "nation-state." *Coherence* and *differentiation* are the key terms here, the one referring to how similar a set of phenomena are to each other and the other referring to how different they are from surrounding phenomena.

The importance of differentiation is embedded in the words "definition," and "term." Definition, says the OED, is "the act or product of marking out, or delimiting, the outlines or characteristics of any conception or thing."[13] "Term" has similar connotations, John Dewey points out. It is "derived from the Latin *terminus* meaning both *boundary* and terminal *limit*."[14] Hanna Pitkin explains, "the meaning of an expression is delimited by what might have been said instead, but wasn't. Green leaves off where yellow and blue begin, so the meaning of 'green' is delimited by the meanings of 'yellow' and 'blue.'"[15]

13. Reprinted in Chapin (1939: 153). The *Dictionary of Philosophy* finds the Latin origins of the term in the verb *definire*, which is translated as "to limit," "to end," "to be concerned with the boundaries of something" (Angeles 1981: 56).
14. Dewey (1938: 349).
15. Pitkin (1972: 11). "We call a substance silver," writes Norman Campbell (1919/1957: 49), "so long as it is distinguished from other substances and we call all substances silver which are indistinguishable from each other. The test whether a property is a defining or a non-defining property rests simply on the distinction between those properties which serve to distinguish the substance from others and those which it possesses in common with others. Any set of properties which serve to distinguish silver from all other substances will serve to define it."

The flip side of external differentiation is internal coherence. (Because it is ponderous to employ twin terms at every juncture, I will designate "coherence" as the central signifier; readers should understand that external differentiation is implied whenever coherence is invoked.)[16] A concept can hardly be distinguished from neighboring concepts if its attributes and entities have nothing in common. Social science concepts, like all concepts, do not make sense unless the attributes that define the concept *belong* to one another in some logical or functional manner. This is what we usually mean when we point to a concept's coherence or incoherence. Within the United States, for example, the concept of "the West" is vulnerable to the charge that western states do not share many features in common. Thus, although one can stipulate a precise set of borders (e.g., the seven western-most states) one cannot help but feel that these borders are a trifle artificial. Although it does not make the concept wrong, certainly it is less useful, less meaningful. The deeper or richer a concept the more convincing is its claim to define a class of entities deserving of being called by a single name. A coherent term carries more of a punch: it is, descriptively speaking, more powerful, allowing us to infer many things (the common characteristics of the concept) with one thing (the concept's label). The concept of "the South," following the opinion of most historians, would have to be considered more coherent than the West, since a much longer list of accompanying attributes could be constructed and differences vis-à-vis other regions are more apparent. At the other extreme, proper nouns (e.g., "Tom") tell us virtually nothing about the object in question beyond matters of sex (usually) and ethnicity (sometimes). Tom's share few similarities relative to Dick's and Harry's.

The most coherent definitions are those that are able to identify a core, or "essential," meaning.[17] Robert Dahl, in his influential work on power, sets out to discover "the central intuitively understood

16. The twin desiderata of coherence and differentiation correspond to "lumping and splitting" operations in social classification (Zerubavel 1996) and to "similarity and difference" judgments in cognitive linguistics (Tversky and Gati 1978). The twin desiderata may also be recognized in Rosch's work on basic-level categories, which "(a) maximize the number of attributes shared by members of the category; and (b) minimize the number of attributes shared with members of other categories" (Rosch, quoted in Taylor 1995: 50–1).

17. An "essential" or "real" definition is defined as: "Giving the essence of a thing. From among the characteristics possessed by a thing, one is unique and hierarchically superior in that it states (a) the most important characteristic of the thing, and/or (b) that characteristic upon which the others depend for their existence" (Angeles 1981: 57). See also Mill (1843/1872: 71).

meaning of the word,"—"the primitive notion [of power] that seems to lie behind all [previous] concepts."[18] This essentializing approach to definition is common (and, indeed, often justified). The essential meaning of democracy, for example, is often thought to be rule by the people. This may be viewed as the single principle behind all other definitional characteristics, associated characteristics, and usages of the term. When one says democracy, what one is *really* talking about is rule by the people. To the extent that this reductionist effort is successful – to the extent, that is, that a single principle is able to subsume various uses and instances of the concept – the highest level of coherence has been achieved in that concept. (Essentializing definitions often take the form of "minimal" definitions, as discussed in the next chapter.)

Implicit in this discussion is the notion that coherence is a matter of degrees. Contrary to the classical vision (discussed later), where defining attributes are those found *always* and *only* in the extension, social science concepts usually take a more pragmatic approach. The borders of most concepts are established in a piecemeal fashion: property X is invoked to distinguish the concept from one neighboring concept, and property Y to distinguish it from another, since neither resides uniquely within the extension.

Operationalization

Since the key concepts of social science are referential, the task of establishing coherence involves not only the logical or semantic ordering of attributes but also the ordering of *referents* – things, objects, phenomena, entities, events "out there" (I use these words more or less interchangeably). Democracy, if defined as rule by the people, seems clear enough. But we are bound to wonder what a writer really means (i.e., what sort of regimes she considers to be ruled by the people) when she uses this term. One might call this a problem of differentiation at the phenomenal level; more commonly, it is referred to as a problem of *operationalization*.

The critical question raised by operationalization is *How do we know it when we see it?* Can power be distinguished from powerlessness, for example? With respect to this key word Dahl writes, "The gap between the concept and operational definition is generally very great, so great, indeed, that it is not always possible to see what relation there is between the

---

18. Dahl (1957/1969: 79–80).

operations and the abstract definition."[19] Indeed, many terms in the social science lexicon suffer from this problem. Alienation, anomie, charisma, civil society, collective conscience, crisis, democracy, dogmatism, equality, false consciousness, hegemony, ideology, legitimacy, mass society, national character, pattern variable, petty bourgeois, rationalization, sovereignty, state, and status anxiety are all "fuzzy" concepts. (Other examples probably leap to the reader's mind.) We may be able to define them in a *general* way, but we have immense difficulty locating their referents in empirical space. Barbara Geddes notes that *state autonomy* is generally

> inferred from its effects rather than directly observed. No one, it seems, is quite sure what "it" actually consists of. State autonomy seems at times to refer to the independence of the state itself, the regime, a particular government, some segments or agencies of the government, or even specific leaders. It seems the phrase can refer to any independent force based in the central government.[20]

The physicalist approach suggests that we eschew such terms in favor of concrete, if not actually observational, concepts. The virtue of small concepts is their tangible nature. Indeed, it is difficult to imagine a larger concept being more operational than the smaller concepts within its purview. "State" is less operational than "executive," "parliament," and "bureaucracy." Even so, Quine observes that the most directly observable concepts are commonly vague in at least two ways: "as to the several boundaries of all its objects and as to the inclusion or exclusion of marginal objects." He offers the example of a mountain, noting "it is vague on the score of how much terrain to reckon into each of the indisputable mountains, and it is vague on the score of what lesser eminences to count as mountains at all."[21] Thus, the avoidance of abstract concepts will not necessarily solve problems of operationalization (not to mention problems of validity and analytic utility).

We may distinguish not only between terms, but also among definitions for a single term that may be more or less operational. Consider the following two definitions of *power*.

> (1) "Power is a word that will be used to describe the acts of men going about the business of moving other men to act in relation to themselves or in relation to organic or inorganic things" (Floyd Hunter).[22]
> (2) "*A* has power over *B* to the extent that he can get *B* to do something that *B* would not otherwise do" (Robert Dahl).[23]

---

19. Dahl (1968: 414), quoted in Debnam (1984: 2).
20. Geddes (1996: 5).
21. Quine (1960: 126).
22. Hunter (1963: 2), quoted in Debnam (1984: 3).
23. Dahl (1957/1969), quoted in Debnam (1984: 3).

Whatever the merits and demerits of these two definitions on other dimensions, Dahl's must be judged more operational. It is not as operational as "chair" or "horse," to be sure, but it is considerably easier to locate in empirical space than Hunter's proposed definition. (It is perhaps not coincidental that definition #1 is almost entirely forgotten.)

According to the classical tradition of concept formation, successful definition involves the identification of attributes that provide necessary and sufficient conditions for locating examples of the term (i.e., the phenomenon itself). "In defining a name," writes Mill, "it is not usual to specify its entire connotation, but so much only as is sufficient to mark out the objects usually denoted by it from all other known objects. And sometimes a merely accidental property, not involved in the meaning of the name, answers this purpose equally well."[24] Following this tack, a later logician writes: "A class must be defined by the invariable presence of certain common properties. If we include an individual in which one of these properties does not appear, we either fall into a logical contradiction, or else we form a new class with a new definition. Even a single exception constitutes a new class by itself."[25] To define human as an animal that is featherless and bipedal, for example, is to offer a definition that successfully differentiates one species from all others. The combination of these two traits occurs always and only among humans.

We may think of the classical approach as privileging one aspect of concept formation (operationalizability) over all others. The problem, evidently, is that operationalization is not the *only* demand that we seek to satisfy when forming concepts. Humans are indeed featherless and bipedal, but these are not the only properties that come to mind. Definitions in social science are referential, but they are not *merely* referential. Moreover, even if we *were* to privilege operationalization over all other conceptual desiderata, achieving the goal of the classical concept (whose attributes always identify its referents, and no others) is simply not possible in many instances. Consider the term "mother." If defined as a person who gives birth to a child we would appear to satisfy the always-and-only criterion. But how are we to refer to foster mothers and adoptive mothers? Are they not also, in some basic sense, mothers?

---

24. Mill (1843/1872: 73).
25. Jevons, quoted in Kaplan (1964: 68). See also Cohen and Nagel (1934), Lazarsfeld (1966), Sartori et al. (1975), and Zannoni (1978). Although Sartori's work is too wide-ranging to fit into any single model, his repeated injunction to "seize the object" (1984a: 26), to "identify the referent and establish its boundaries" (1984a: 33), puts him closer to the classical camp than to any other. "The defining properties are those that bound the concept extensionally... Confine your defining to the necessary properties," writes Sartori (1984a: 55). For further discussion of the classical concept, see Adcock (1998) and Taylor (1995).

Even the "featherless and biped" definition breaks down in the face of accident victims and birth defects. Problems multiply when one begins to consider social science concepts. Which attributes of democracy, for example, should be considered necessary and sufficient to identify instances of democracy? The classical ideal is an ideal rarely satisfied, as many writers have pointed out.[26]

Nevertheless, the classicists are correct in emphasizing the significance of operationalization in concept formation. All social science concepts aspire to capture something – something "real" – in the world around us. The reference may be highly attenuated, but it is nonetheless always present. The more easily these referents can be located and differentiated from other similar referents the more useful, ceteris paribus, that concept will be. A theory about democracy that cannot tell us which phenomena are democratic and which are not is less useful than one that can do so. Theories of justice, capitalism, socialism, ideology, or anything else in the social science universe are subject to the same demand.

Consider justice. If ever there was a social science concept of high-order abstraction, this is surely it. Yet, one is at pains to find a social science discussion of the topic without an external (real-life, actual, physical, observational) referent. Even philosophers and social theorists are concerned with concrete instances and specific policies. John Rawls, whose *Theory of Justice* is the fount of contemporary debate, is an excellent case in point. Rawls, along with his challengers (e.g., Michael Walzer, Robert Nozick, and Ronald Dworkin), wish to know not only what justice is "in the abstract" but also how it might enter into questions of taxing and spending.[27] "Concepts without percepts are empty; percepts without concepts are blind," wrote Kant.[28]

---

26. See Collier and Levitsky (1997), Collier and Mahon (1993), Kaplan (1964: 68), and Lakoff (1987).
27. See Dworkin (1977), Nozick (1974), Rawls (1971), and Walzer (1983). That these projects have not entirely succeeded in making contact with reality (Mapel 1989) is no reason to dismiss the goal. For explicitly empirical work on justice, see Cohen (1986), Frohlich and Oppenheimer (1992), and Soltan (1982; 1987). "It would be a mistake," writes Mill (1843/1872: 98) in the same vein, "to represent these difficult and noble inquiries [into the meaning of rhetoric, justice, truth, and so forth] as having nothing in view beyond ascertaining the conventional meaning of a name. They are inquiries not so much to determine what is, as what should be, the meaning of a name; which, like other practical questions of terminology, requires for its solution that we should enter, and sometimes enter very deeply, into the properties not merely of names but of the things named." Although the borderline between the phenomenal world ("things") and language ("words") is by no means hard and fast, there remains enough boundedness between these two realms to make the distinction useful.
28. Kant, quoted in Hollis (1994: 71).

I have employed operationalization as a general goal of concept formation, a goal that all concepts strive toward. It is important to note that
this goes somewhat against the grain of current usage, where one often
speaks of a concept and its operationalization as separate linguistic facts.
Indeed, there are many research circumstances in which one might wish
to distinguish a core concept and various possible operationalizations; I
refer to the latter as contextual definitions in Chapter 4. Separating these
two elements is not harmful so long as one keeps in mind the fact that
an unoperationalized concept is not a very useful concept. Indeed, it
does not have a specific empirical content, and therefore can do no
empirical work. It is "merely" conceptual. My general argument may be
bluntly stated: operationalization is *integral* to the process of forming
concepts, not just an afterthought. If one term is easier to specify in
physical space, it is better (ceteris paribus) than another near-synonym.
If one definition is easier to operationalize, it is better (ceteris paribus)
than other possible definitions.

Of course, like our other desiderata, operationalization is a matter of
degrees. As originally devised (in a 1927 physics textbook by P. W.
Bridgman), it referred to the actual physical operations a person would
employ to locate a phenomenon. One can imagine an absurd standard
of operationalization in the social sciences in which the definition of
election involved a 100-page manual with such instructions as "First,
hire a fleet of monitors to observe the purported election. Second, make
sure that all the monitors are unbiased. Check for bias by examining past
backgrounds..." The distance between a relatively high-order concept
(democracy) and the operationalization of that concept in the empirical
world is always somewhat problematic.

In constructing a reasonable standard of operationalization we must
fall back on what reasonable people would agree on. Borrowing language from George Schlesinger, we can say "That which is conceptualized need not be completely defined in terms of operations, although it
must make contact with the world of public experience."[29] Quantitative
measures (indicators) may or may not be necessary. Operationalization,
in any case, should not be equated with measurement. If we can judge
by sight whether the sky is purple there is no need to develop a color
meter to gauge the frequency of light waves. The critical test here, as
elsewhere, is what level of specification reasonable people with proper
training would require to locate the referents in question, and what level
of precision is required for the research purpose at hand.

---

29. Quoted in Connolly (1974/1983: 16). For further discussion, see Kaplan (1964: 57–60).

Michael Coppedge describes the procedure of concept formation as a correlational exercise with four essential steps.

> First, the analyst breaks the mother concept up into as many simple and relatively objective components as possible. Second, each of these components is measured separately. Third, the analyst examines the strength of association among the components to discover how many dimensions are represented among them and in the mother concept. Fourth, components that are very strongly associated with one another are treated as unidimensional, that is, as all measuring the same underlying dimension, and may be combined. Any other components or clusters of components are treated as indicators of different dimensions.[30]

Thus, instead of looking for "absolute" (always-and-only) attributes, as the classical concept demands, we look for *groupings* of attributes. These groupings provide the break points between neighboring concepts. Establishing operationalizability is thus much like searching for "natural kinds," or "carving nature at the joints" (see Field Utility, below) – except that here the relevant information is phenomenal, rather than semantic.[31]

Validity

In addition to being coherent and operational, one would like a concept to be true. Concept (construct, cue, or measurement) validity may be considered the truth element of concept formation. It refers to the degree of alignment between a term's definition (its defining attributes, including its operationalization) and its extension (the phenomena "out there" that the term is intended to capture).[32]

Researchers concerned with justice, as we have intimated, struggle with the problem of how to distinguish justice from injustice. What is a just act, or a just situation, these writers ask. Work on democracy cannot avoid the problem of how to measure this concept across countries that differ in culture (and hence in their understanding of democracy), in political practices, and in economic settings. A variety of measures

---

30. Coppedge (1999: 469).
31. The only quarrel I have with Coppedge's procedure, quoted above, is the implication (which I do not believe Coppedge subscribes to) that concept formation is driven purely by phenomenal (empirical) considerations.
32. The accuracy of a given attribute in distinguishing one concept from a field of related concepts has been named "cue validity" by Rosch, et al. (1976; discussed in Lakoff 1987: 52). On validity more generally, see Kaplan (1964: 198–206), Neuman (1997: 138–45), and – most extensively – Adcock and Collier (2000).

have been used, each of which seem to capture different dimensions of democracy, but they are not always highly intercorrelated.[33] Which is most valid? As a final example we might consider research in cognitive psychology on the question of intelligence. Is intelligence accurately measured by IQ tests, or by some other test? Is it measurable at all?[34]

Evidently, all these concepts can be operationalized – we can stipulate definitions that allow us to sort entities in empirical space into conceptual slots ("Yes, it is an example of justice," or "No, it is not"). And, as we have pointed out, the operationalization of a concept plays an important, and legitimate, part in the ongoing definition of that concept. Edwin Boring's famous quip about the concept of intelligence – intelligence is whatever it is that intelligence tests measure – is not entirely facetious.[35] But surely, it is not *only* the measurement of a concept that determines its meanings. Surely, some operationalizations are better than others. What makes a definition or operationalization (the distinction is not important here) adequate to its task is the degree to which it *accurately* portrays some portion of the empirical world.[36] Have we achieved an accurate rendering of things with words? Better, have we achieved a good "fit" between words and things? Concept formation is a representational act. To say that a concept is valid is to say that its referents are, in fact, as they are purported to be. To say that a concept is invalid, or less valid, is to say that we have not identified the right empirical referents.

Problems of conceptual validity may be created when terms are "stretched" (i.e., employed in unfamiliar settings). Thus, if corporatism is defined as an institution of peak bargaining among relatively autonomous units within civil society it might be considered a conceptual stretch to extend this concept to include Latin American cases, where unions and other actors in civil society are often manipulated by the state. Yet, if corporatism is defined more broadly – as, say, including *any* formal bargaining among organized sectors of civil society (with or without state control) – then it is perfectly appropriate to employ this concept in the Latin American context. This may be stretching the established meaning of the

---

33. See Munck and Verkuilen (2000).
34. See Sternberg and Detterman (1986).
35. Boring (1923).
36. If we regard operationalization as a separate and differentiable element of concept formation, then we must make room for two kinds of validity – one connecting the definition and the operationalization and another connecting the operationalization and the actual entities under definition (Adcock and Collier 2000). If not, we may regard validity as connecting the definition (including the operationalization) with the entities under definition, as I have. These are slightly different ways of articulating the same general dilemma.

term (compromising its resonance, as discussed below), and it may compromise its field utility (see the following section), but it is not a problem of validity: the intension and extension correspond.[37]

Field Utility

Concepts are defined in terms of other concepts: boys in terms of girls, nation-states in terms of empires, parties in terms of interest groups. At issue, therefore, is the way in which a given concept relates to most-similar concepts: synonyms, near-synonyms, antonyms, and terms that are superordinate or subordinate to the concept under definition. These neighboring terms form the semantic field within which a term gains meaning. Precisely because of the interconnectedness of language, the definition of a single term necessarily involves some resettling of the semantic field. It is impossible to redefine one term without also, at least by implication, redefining others. Any redefinition of "corporatism" changes our understanding of "pluralism," as a redefinition of "democracy" changes our understanding of "authoritarianism."

What is it then that constitutes virtue at the *field* level? The ancient carving-the-joints metaphor is a useful point of departure. "What makes a concept significant," writes Abraham Kaplan,

> is that the classification it institutes is one into which things fall, as it were, of themselves. It carves at the joints, Plato said. Less metaphorically, a significant concept so groups or divides its subject-matter that it can enter into many and important true propositions about the subject-matter other than those which state the classification itself. Traditionally, such a concept was said to identify a "natural" class rather than an "artificial" one. Its naturalness consists in this, that the attributes it chooses as the basis of classification are significantly related to the attributes conceptualized elsewhere in our thinking. Things are grouped together because they resemble one another. A natural grouping is one which allows the discovery of many more, and more important, resemblances that those originally recognized. Every classification serves some purpose or other...: it is artificial when we cannot do more with it than we first intended.[38]

The better we can "cover" a given phenomenal and terminological terrain the better are the individual concepts that inhabit that terrain. (It is here that the criteria of concept formation, and of classificatory propositions, discussed in Chapter 6, dovetail.)

---

37. The notion of conceptual stretching, as introduced by Sartori (1970; see also Collier and Mahon 1993), thus refers to one, or several, elements of conceptual adequacy.
38. Kaplan (1964: 50–1). See also Hempel (1965: 147) and Jevons (1877/1958: 679).

Ideally, every distinct thing (referent) in a semantic field has a distinct name, and every name a distinct referent: a one-to-one correspondence between words and things. Of course, correspondences are rarely so perfect. However, all social science conceptualizations strive for this ideal, which, as Sartori points out, maximizes the efficiency and clarity of language in describing the world around us.[39] One wishes, in other words, to avoid the problem of the "homeless entity" – a phenomenon that is important and distinctive, but does not possess a name.[40] Dewey refers to this as "an unoccupied no-man's-land."[41] Mill's words on this subject are simple, but definitive: "we should possess a name wherever one is needed; wherever there is anything to be designated by it, which it is of importance to express."[42]

One wishes, at the same time, to avoid the problem of the entityless concept, a term without a corresponding referent. In redefining concepts it is easy to steal referents from neighboring terms, thus creating empty categories.[43] Consider the question of American political culture. Perhaps the easiest way to make a name for oneself in this overcrowded field is to select one word among the field of terms competing to describe American political norms and folkways (e.g., liberalism, republicanism, protestantism, individualism, equal opportunity, pragmatism, libertarianism, democratic capitalism, freedom, Algerism, Americanism, the frontier spirit) showing how this term, rather than all the others, is really the key to understanding a vexed subject. There is nothing wrong with establishing coherence in a definition. However, if all one is doing is rearranging the same parts into essentially the same whole (with a new label) then not much has been accomplished. Alternatively, one may promote a fundamentally new term (e.g., "American jeremiad" or "American mission") to refer to the established field of referents. It all makes perfect sense. In fact, it makes sense much too easily. If one keeps in mind that one is reconceptualizing not simply a single term but rather a *field* of terms, then it becomes apparent why this sort of terminological legerdemain is problematic; other, neighboring terms have been deprived of their referents.

Field utility refers to the extent to which a given concept respects the coherence, operationalization, validity, resonance, contextual range, parsimony, and analytic utility of neighboring concepts. It refers to the adequacy of a single concept within a field of concepts.

39. "Different things should have different names," writes Sartori (1984a: 50).
40. Gardiner (1952/1961: 55), from whom I steal this phrase, has a somewhat different point in mind.
41. Dewey (1938: 349–50).
42. Mill (1843/1872: 436).
43. See Sartori (1984a).

Resonance

The degree to which a definition makes sense, or is intuitively clear, depends critically on the degree to which it conforms or clashes with established usage – both within everyday language and within whatever specialized language region the term may be deployed. A term defined in a highly idiosyncratic way is unlikely to be understood, and if not understood will either cause confusion or be ignored. The achievement of clarity involves *resonance,* among other things.

Resonance in the *definition* of a given term is achieved by incorporating as many of its standard meanings in the new definition as possible, or at least by avoiding any glaring contradiction of those meanings. "The supreme rule of stipulation," writes Richard Robinson, "is surely to *stipulate as little as possible.* Do not change received definitions when you have nothing to complain of in them."[44] To be sure, the criterion of resonance is a matter of degrees. There should be, in any case, a demonstrable fit between new and old meanings of a given term.

Resonance in the *term* is achieved by finding that word within the existing lexicon which, as currently understood, most accurately describes the phenomenon under definition. Where several existing terms capture the phenomenon in question with equal facility – as, for example, the near-synonyms *worldview* and *Weltanschauung* – achieving resonance becomes a matter of finding the term with the greatest common currency. Simple, everyday English terms are (by definition) more familiar than terms drawn from languages that are dead, foreign, or highly specialized. Where *no* term within the existing general or social science lexicon adequately describes the phenomena in question the writer is evidently forced to invent a new term. Neologism is the greatest violation of the resonance criterion, for it involves the creation of an entirely new term with little resonance in normal usage. All other things being equal, a writer should turn to this expedient only when no other semantic options present themselves.[45]

Even so, the invention of "new" terms is never entirely removed from the redefinition of old terms. Neologisms, while rejecting ordinary language, strive to reenter the universe of intelligibility. They are rarely nonsense words; they are, instead, new combinations of existing words (e.g., *bureaucratic-authoritarianism*) or roots (e.g., *polyarchy, heresthetic*), or terms bor-

---

44. Robinson (1954: 80).

45. "Let us not stipulate until we have good reason to believe that there is no name for the thing we wish to name," notes Robinson (1954: 81) emphatically. See also Connolly (1983), Durkheim (1895/1964: 37), Mahon (1998), Mill (1843/1872: 24), Oppenheim (1975), and Pitkin (1972).

rowed from other time periods (e.g., *corporatism*), other language regions (e.g., *equilibrium*), or other languages (e.g., *laissez-faire*).[46] By far the most fertile grounds for neologism have been Classical (e.g., *Id, communitas, polis, hermeneutics*), and eponymous (e.g., *Marxism, Reaganism*). In all these cases words, or word roots, are imported from their normal contexts to a rather different context where their definition takes on new meaning, or additional senses. However severe the semantic stretch, at least some of the original properties of such terms remain intact.[47]

We may think of resonance as the criterial embodiment of ordinary-language philosophy. The meaning of a word, declares Wittgenstein, "is its use in the language."[48] Yet, I have argued, since social science vocabulary is explicitly referential in function we cannot rely *solely* on norms of usage to achieve conceptual adequacy. Even "justice," we have demonstrated, pursues a phenomenal reality. We wish to describe and to explain situations "out there" that are just, or unjust, and these empirical referents rightfully influence the way we think about justice (the concept). Indeed, as philosophers and linguists are quick to point out, norms of usage generally provide a *range* of terminological and definitional options, rather than a single definition. Thus, although ordinary usage may be an appropriate place to begin, it is usually an inappropriate place to end the task of concept formation. Given the diversity of meanings implied by ordinary usage there is rarely a *single* "normal" definition to which one might appeal in settling semantic disputes.

Nor is there any good reason to suppose that social science should restrict itself to ordinary meanings when defining terms for social scientific use. Social science concepts, Durkheim pointed out,

46. On polyarchy, see Dahl (1971); on heresthetic, see Riker (1986); on corporatism, see Collier (1995a) and Schmitter (1974).
47. Robinson (1954: 55) notes: "Men will always be finding themselves with a new thing to express and no word for it, and usually they will meet the problem by applying whichever old word seems nearest, and thus the old word will acquire another meaning or a stretched meaning. Very rarely will they do what A. E. Housman bade them do, invent a new noise to mean the new thing." For a survey of contemporary neologisms, see Algeo (1991).
48. Wittgenstein (1953: 43), quoted in Sartori (1984a: 57). Pitkin (1972: 173) expatiates: "The meaning of a word ... is what one finds in a good dictionary – a word or phrase that can be substituted for it. The meaning of 'justice' has to do with what people intend to convey in saying it, not with the features of the phenomena they say it about." For other work in the ordinary-language tradition, see Austin (1961), Caton (1963), Chappell (1964), Ryle (1949), Ziff (1960), as well as the various writings of G.E.M. Anscombe, Stanley Cavell, Jerry Fodor, Jerrold Katz, Norman Malcolm, and John Wisdom.

do not always, or even generally, tally with that of the layman. It is not our aim simply to discover a method for identifying with sufficient accuracy the facts to which the words of ordinary language refer and the ideas they convey. We need, rather, to formulate entirely new concepts, appropriate to the requirements of science and expressed in an appropriate terminology.[49]

Social science, like all language regions (e.g., medicine, law, street gangs, baseball) requires a specialized vocabulary. This does not mean, that a premium should be placed on "scientific," as opposed to ordinary, usage. Indeed, I have argued that departures from natural language impose costs, and should not be taken lightly. However, it seems indisputable that such departures must be embraced on some occasions.[50] Social science cannot accept words simply as they present themselves in ordinary speech. Some fiddling with words and definitions is incumbent on the researcher, if only because ordinary usage is unsettled.

Contextual Range

We have said that the degree to which a definition makes sense, or is intuitively clear, depends critically upon the degree to which it conforms with established usage. It is merely an extension of the resonance criterion to say that the more contexts within which a given concept makes sense, the better that concept will be (ceteris paribus). A concept that applies broadly is more useful than a concept with only a narrow range of application. A good concept stretches comfortably over many contexts; a poor concept, by contrast, is parochial – limited to a small linguistic turf.

Contextual range should not be equated with the number of referents covered by a concept (the number of phenomena contained in its extension). Consider nuclear war. There is only one case of this, or perhaps none (since the U.S. deployment of nuclear weapons effectively ended World War II). Does this make it a poor concept? Is war a better concept by virtue of having more referents? By this logic, the farther one moves up the ladder of abstraction the more useful concepts should be (e.g., "military conflict," "conflict," etc.). This is clearly nonsense. The number of referents falling into a concept's domain does not appear to be a feature, by itself, that will make a concept more useful.

To be sure, there are numerous instances in which we might, for *analytic* purposes, wish to increase our sample size (see the section titled

---

49. Durkheim (1895/1964: 36–7).
50. See Robinson (1954: 73) and Sartori (1984a).

Analytic/Empirical Utility). In order to do so we might either redefine the original concept *or* choose a different concept with a higher order of magnitude. Whether we choose option (a) or (b) depends on the availability of nearby terms. In the case of nuclear war it is fairly easy to climb the ladder of abstraction (to "war," or "military conflict," or somesuch). In other cases, owing to a paucity of terms, it may be necessary to redefine the original term. Thus, if we wish to combine racial and ethnic conflict in the same general category we might refer to it awkwardly as intergroup conflict (a term with neither resonance nor parsimony), or we might redefine ethnicity to include racial definitions of group identity – an option that also involves some loss of resonance (vis-à-vis normal definitions of ethnicity). Here, as in so many situations of concept formation, there are no hard-and-fast rules of procedure. We must simply consider the pros and cons of different options, as set forth in the criterial framework. For present purposes we need only note that the phenomenal range of a concept is quite different from a concept's contextual or linguistic range; it is the latter, not the former, that qualifies a concept as good.

The utility of contextual range is perhaps most clearly visible in work of a cross-cultural nature, where bridging linguistic boundaries is essential.[51] If one is studying family structures it will not be helpful to define "family" in a way that is specific to a particular cultural group. Indeed, even if a study is restricted to a single cultural community (i.e., if the explicit population of that study is culturally delimited), we are likely to accord that work more importance if its terms link up to work on the same subject in other cultural areas. If, by contrast, those terms are resonant only within a restricted language region we will find the work less useful in the broader enterprise of social science. Here we can observe the distinct advantage of "etic" over "emic" styles of analysis. The former can be fit into cross-cultural categories; the latter, by definition, is culturally bound.

But the utility of contextual range is by no means limited to cross-cultural work. If one is studying political parties it is not proper to adopt a definition of party that is derived from a single case. Ditto for "regime," or "nation-state." All seek, or should seek, cosmopolitan definitions. Otherwise, they cannot contribute to the cumulation of knowledge on that topic.

We should also contemplate the virtues of contextual range among different regions of social science, and between social science and everyday

51. See Collier (1995a), Collier and Mahon (1993), Coppedge (1999), Ember and Otterbien (1991), Hammel (1980), Ross (1988), Van Deth (1998), and Vijver and Leung (1997).

language. It is troubling, for example, that terms like "exchange" and "institutions" are used so differently in the disciplines of sociology and economics. It is equally troubling that so many of the terms employed in statistical work (e.g., admissibility, parameter, regression, sufficiency) bear scant resemblance to their everyday cognates. Such radical conceptual disparities do not enhance the prospects for cross-disciplinary understanding, or lay understanding for that matter. Even neologisms that catch on within the restricted ambit of social science are still neologistic (i.e., offenses against the resonance criterion) within the context of everyday speech. What is ordinary in one context may be extraordinary in another, and to no good purpose (if there are everyday analogs that might have been adopted).

The importance of everyday language as a basic medium of communication in the social sciences will be taken up in the following chapter. For the moment it is sufficient to observe that since there is no cross-disciplinary language (aside from mathematical languages) the only way social science can overcome disciplinary parochialisms is by cultivating its connections to what is often called natural language. This everyday-ness will allow social science to maintain a relatively uniform vocabulary across fields, as well as to promote its intelligibility among the general public.

Before letting go of this topic we must also note the costs that often accompany a broad contextual range. To begin with, a concept that is stretched to multiple languages or language regions is likely to lose some of its coherence. We can more easily preserve a univocal meaning for a concept when its range is limited; sending our concepts off into foreign climes is likely to involve some alteration of meaning. Like the Catholic church, we may find that proselytizing our concepts leads to a formal adoption of codes, but little transference of meaning (or an indigenization of meaning).

This raises a second sort of problem. If a word is understood differently in different language regions then the problem of resonance is vexed: what is resonant in one context will violate the resonance criterion in another. This sort of conflict-of-contexts problem is frequently encountered in the definition of social scientific terms – where ordinary usage *within* the academic community is likely to conflict with ordinary usage within the broader community (or among other academic communities). Which resonance should we respect? There is little one can say *in general* about this problem beyond noting that this difficulty, like most, exemplifies the criterial tradeoffs of concept formation. All things being equal, a definition that promises greater contextual breadth is better.

Parsimony

A definition, writes Cicero, "is a certain brief and circumscribed account of the properties of the thing we wish to define."[52] Good concepts do not have endless definitions. A long intension, even if composed of closely related attributes, will create a cumbersome and unappealing semantic vehicle. "Ideology," as we will observe, is so overloaded with definitional baggage that it barely manages to shuffle across the page. We may suppose that it is their sheer number, not simply their incoherence (criterion #1), that makes them burdensome.

Less often noted, the goal of parsimony also properly applies to the *term* itself. Consider the options for ideology-like phenomena. One might call it a belief-system, a symbol-system, or a value-system, but none of these possible replacements is as short and to-the-point as that old standby, ideology. If qualified by the adjective "political" (e.g., political belief-system), these alternate terms become clumsier still. Arguably, ideology's endurance, in the face of repeated assaults, is due to its admirable compactness.

Concept formation itself is an exercise in semantic reduction. "By the stipulative substitution of a word for a phrase, language is abbreviated," notes Robinson.

> What can now be said could also have been said previously, without using the new rule or the new name; but it can now be said in fewer words, because the thing cannot be indicated by a single name, whereas formerly a descriptive phrase was required. The value of such timesaving does not lie merely or mainly in leaving more time for other activities. Abbreviation not merely shortens discourse; it also increases understanding. We grasp better what we can hold in one span of attention, and how much we can thus hold depends on the length of the symbols we have to use in order to state it. Abbreviations often immensely increase our ability to understand and deal with a subject.[53]

The Chinese language takes this quest for reduction to an extreme, utilizing single characters where English employs a phrase or sentence. Logical and mathematical languages also prize brevity. But languages of *any* sort must drastically abridge our experience of the world.

Reduction, of course, is not the only task of language, just as it is not the only task of concepts in social science. But consider: key concepts are likely to be employed repeatedly and insistently in a given work. To say "political

---

52. Paraphrased in Robinson (1954: 2). Brevity is implied in Aristotle's *Topics* (Robinson 1954: 3). See also Sartori (1984a: 40, 54–55) and Riggs (1975).
53. Robinson (1954: 68).

belief-system" once in a paragraph is enough; to say it thrice in a paragraph is tendentious. Single-word concepts, particularly those that trip easily off the tongue, can be used again and again without calling attention to themselves. All other things being equal "worldview" is preferable to "Weltanschauung," "walking" preferable to "perambulation."[54]

Bentham's words on this matter are amusing and instructive:

> Blessed be he forevermore, in whatever robe arrayed, to whose creative genius we are indebted for the first conception of those too short-lived vehicles which convey to us as in a nutshell the essential character of those awful volumes which at the touch of the sceptre become the rules of our conduct and the arbiters of our destiny: "The Alien Act," "The Turnpike Act," "The Middlesex Waterworks Bill," and so on. How much better they serve than those authoritative masses of words called *titles*, by which so large a proportion of sound and so small a proportion of instruction are at so large an expense of attention granted to us, such as – "An Act to explain and amend an act entitled An Act to explain and amend...." Coinages of commodious titles are thus issued day by day throughout the session from an invisible though not unlicensed mint.[55]

Coining words fit to be used entails finding words, or combinations of words, that are *parsimonious*. "An Act to explain and amend..." cannot be remembered; nor, if it could, would it facilitate communication.

Analytic/Empirical Utility

The goal of a social science concept is to aid in the formulation of theories. Concepts are the building blocks of all theoretical structures and the formation of many concepts is clearly, and legitimately, theory-driven. "Theory formation and concept formation go hand in hand," Hempel stresses; "neither can be carried on successfully in isolation from the other."[56] *Anomie, libido, mode of production,* and *charisma* owe their endurance, at least in part, to the theories of Durkheim, Freud,

---

54. It may be observed that parsimony in a term occasionally conflicts with parsimony in a definition. "Ideology," for example, scores well on the first and poorly on the second. "Belief-system" scores poorly on the first, but well on the second.

55. Bentham (1834/1952: 10–11).

56. Hempel (1965: 113; see also 139). Kaplan (1964: 53) calls this the paradox of conceptualization: "The proper concepts are needed to formulate a good theory, but we need a good theory to arrive at the proper concepts." A slightly different version of the "theoretical" approach is offered by Murphey (1994: 23–4). Rather than seeing concepts performing functions within theories, Murphey proposes that "theories that explain the behavior and properties of instances of the concept *are* the meanings of concepts" (emphasis added). Thus, the best definition of gold is "the element whose atomic number is 79." See also Faeges (1999), Murphy and Medin (1985), and Quine (1977).

Marx, and Weber. Indeed, these terms have little meaning in the social sciences without these broader theoretical frameworks.

Innumerable examples of "theoretical" concepts may be discovered in the fields of the social sciences. Ideology, for example, within the field of political psychology, has been used to refer to the highest (i.e., most sophisticated) level of political understanding.[57] This brings with it an emphasis on certain traits, particularly abstraction, sophistication, and knowledge. Other commonly understood features of the concept must be excluded or else the theoretical schema will be violated. Although this involves some sacrifice of resonance, it may make more sense to appropriate the general term ideology, with all its warts, than to resort to neologism.

One can think of concepts whose existence is almost *wholly* dependent on their utility within a theoretical framework. Wildavsky's *fatalism* and Luebbert's *traditional-authoritarianism,* have few external referents.[58] Indeed, they are virtually empty categories. However, these concepts are redeemed to some degree by their utility within broader causal arguments, which they help to define and delimit. These are extreme cases but they illustrate the more general point that concepts categorize.[59]

We can make the following general points about the ways in which theoretical concerns insert themselves into the business of concept formation. First, the definition of key concepts allows a writer to define the boundaries of her subject. If a study advances a theory of ideology, then this theory ought to be differentiable from a theory of political culture. Alternatively, if the latter is included in the theory, the writer's definition of ideology must be broad enough to encompass it. This is fairly commonsensical. However, it should be recognized that one of the principle influences on concept formation in the social sciences is a writer's need to "define in" those elements of the world that she wishes to talk about, and "define out" those elements that she wishes to ignore.[60]

Second, a causal theory will choose terms, and define those terms, in ways that allow for a clear separation between independent and dependent variables (cause and effect). If I propose to explain the causes of ideology, for example, I ought not define ideology so as to include characteristics that I am using to *explain* ideology. If, similarly, I propose to use ideology to explain a particular event, or pattern of behavior, I must be careful to purge from my definition all of those elements that I

---

57. See, for example, Converse (1964).
58. See Thompson et al. (1990) and Luebbert (1991).
59. Indeed, these two terms – concept and category – are often used synonymously (Collier and Mahon 1993; Taylor 1995).
60. The *boundedness* of a study (see Chapter 8) is established largely by its definition of key concepts.

am seeking to explain. Otherwise, I will be making a circular argument (see Chapter 7).

The broader point is that concepts rest within propositions, and propositions rest within research designs. Consequently, the criteria applying to propositions (discussed in Part II of the book) and those applying to research designs (discussed in Part III) rightly impinge on the process of concept formation. Social science concepts strive for analytic and empirical utility.

Conclusions

This chapter suggests that concept formation is a more wide-ranging and unpredictable process than is indicated by previous approaches to the subject. No fewer than eight criteria impinge on the complex task of choosing terms and definitions. Moreover, as we have seen repeatedly, satisfying one criterion is likely to have ramifications for other criteria. The oft-noted instability of terms such as ideology arises from the plural, and often contradictory, nature of the demands to which they are expected to respond.

Since the elements of a concept – the term, the intension, and the extension – are interdependent, the process of concept formation is necessarily one of mutual adjustment. To achieve a higher degree of adequacy one may choose a different term, adjust the properties of the intension, or adjust the members of the extension (see Figure 3.1). Concept formation thus offers an excellent illustration of the so-called hermeneutic circle: a change in any one aspect of a concept will normally affect the other two.[61] For this reason, concept formation must be viewed holistically. It is difficult to separate out tasks that pertain only to the "phenomenal" realm from those that pertain only to "linguistic" or "theoretical" realms.

Acknowledging the interdependent nature of concept formation leads us away from a static, rule-bound model of concept formation. Forming concepts in the social sciences is a *dynamic* process. The best we can do in guiding conceptualization is to keep track of its multiple parameters. Tradeoffs, rather than fixed rules, best make sense of this vexing enterprise.[62] A concept that shares few characteristics in common, that cannot be easily located in the physical world, that does not appear where it is alleged to appear, that cuts the semantic field in an unnatural fashion, that

61. See Hoy (1982).
62. The notion of concept formation as a set of tradeoffs is not new. See Cohen (1989: 131–45), Cohen and Nagel (1934: 33), Collier (1998), Collier and Mahon (1993), Collier and Levitsky (1997), Jevons (1877/1958: 26), Sartori (1970: 1041), Weber (quoted in Burger 1976: 72), and discussion in Chapter 4. What has not been generally recognized is that the number of demands placed on a single concept – and hence the number of possible tradeoffs – reaches well beyond two or three.

does not build on standard usage, that applies to a restricted language region, that is lengthy in term or definition, or has little theoretical utility is *for any one of these sins* less useful. It will not make sense, or will make less sense. In sum, we are probably better off thinking of social science concepts as pragmatic, and often temporary, expedients, rather than as fixed and determinate entities in semantic space. Recurring confusion in concept formation may not be due to the limited methodological skills of the conceptualizer so much as to the tradeoffs entailed in conceptualization.

Yet, we may still distinguish between good and bad concepts. Such standards are assessable in terms of the goals achieved by a given concept *relative to that which the concept might otherwise attain with a different choice of words, properties, or phenomena*. It would be pointless, in other words, to complain that a certain definition of "justice" was insufficiently operational because it was more difficult to locate in the empirical universe than a certain definition of "chair." The relevant standard of comparison is other definitions of justice, or other neighboring terms that might more adequately describe the instances in question. Just as any new theory must account for the relative success of all rival explanations, any new definition must encounter and surpass all rival definitions and terms. The test of adequacy may be stated as follows: Is there a term, or another set of attributes, that would better fulfill the eight tasks of concept formation in this proposition?

Approaching the task of concept formation from a criterial framework reduces the uncertainty of this complicated process, specifying the various demands that must be taken into consideration and, in so doing, allowing us to make better choices. Where concepts remain flawed – as, in a certain sense, all social science concepts are – we will at least comprehend the nature of those flaws. "When it is impossible to obtain good tools," writes Mill, "the next best thing is to understand thoroughly the defects of those we have."[63]

Appendix: Explications and Implications

I have argued that concepts are liable to eight criteria of adequacy: coherence, operationalization, validity, field utility, resonance, contextual range, parsimony, and analytic/empirical utility. Readers may wonder whether these criteria truly exhaust the norms governing concept formation in the social sciences. Specifically, how are we to account for norms like clarity, power, adequacy, value-neutrality, and other desiderata that do not appear in the eight-part framework?

---

63. Mill (1843/1872: 31–2).

Most of these desiderata are beyond reproach. (Who could argue with the notion that a definition "must not be ambiguous"?[64]) Yet, these familiar admonitions are also, ironically, highly ambiguous, referring to several criterial demands at once. "Clarity" and "precision," like their antonyms "ambiguity," "vagueness," and "indefiniteness," may refer to coherence or operationalization, in our terms. "Power" may refer to coherence, resonance, parsimony, analytic/empirical utility, or field utility. "Adequacy" and "utility" may refer to any or all criteria. In short, it seems useful to disaggregate the project of concept formation into smaller, more specific parts, as our framework proposes.

What about other norms, such as *value-neutrality* (the absence of bias) and *sonority* (how a term sounds)? These options, I will argue, are either unwarranted or considerably less important than the eight criteria already identified. The appendix ends with a brief discussion of various concept types (e.g., "ideal-type") and their implications for the criterial framework. Although concept types correctly identify different sorts of conceptual tasks, none are exempt from the criterial framework.

Value-neutrality. The oft-expressed goal of value-neutrality[65] is plainly impossible to achieve in many contexts. Imagine trying to craft definitions of *slavery, fascism, terrorism,* or *genocide* without recourse to pejorative attributes, or *human rights, democracy,* or *peace* without valorizing attributes. These are stark examples, but the same general problem confronts the choice of definitional attributes of all social science concepts. Ideology, for example, is sometimes defined as dogmatic behavior and thought-patterns,[66] a characteristic few would aspire to. The point is, the desirability of an attribute or term-label is irrelevant to its utility in social science research. The most offensive word may be, in some circumstances, the most appropriate.[67] To be sure, biased terms and definitions may pose a problem to social science. But the problems they pose are not due to the normative connotations of these concepts. They are, rather, owing to errors or misrepresentations of fact, which introduce problems of validity. Thus,

---

64. Angeles (1981: 56).
65. See, for example, Oppenheim (1961, 1975, 1981).
66. See Sartori (1970).
67. The larger point at issue over this criterion is whether it is at all possible to create a truly value-neutral social science language. For comments generally critical of this project, see Connolly (1974/1983), Lakoff (1987), Pitkin (1972), Taylor (1967/1994), and Winch (1958). Finley's (1963: 22–3) discussion of the word "slave" is apropos. At the same time – and despite suggestions in Connolly (1974/1983) – there is no reason to give *preference* to evaluative connotations (over less evaluative ones) when defining a term. Stripping notions of goodness from "democracy" may indeed be preferable for many social science purposes – not because goodness is evaluative, but because it is so difficult to operationalize.

the norm of value-neutrality is incorporated in the criterial framework, insofar as it matters at all to social science concept formation.

Sonority. Why do some terms stick while others, with virtually identical meanings, disappear? Why are some efforts successful at reformulating a field or a problem, and others (with the same general argument) often overlooked? One factor in the knowledge game that relates directly to concept formation is the sound of a given term, its sonority. "Makers, Breakers, and Takers," "Exit, Voice, and Loyalty," and "Civic Culture" are all examples of sonority at-work.[68] Sonority among a group of terms may be achieved through prefixes (alliteration), suffixes (rhyming), or syllables (rhythm). (If not identical, the last term in a typology should have the most syllables; hence, Exit, Voice, and Loyalty, *not* Loyalty, Exit, and Voice.) Each of these auditory devices indicates the coherence of the typology, and hence the belongingness of the individual terms.

Yet, the importance, and *legitimacy,* of sonority does not parallel the importance of our other criteria in the formation of social science concepts. We are unlikely to fault a writer for insufficient attention to sonority, or, if we do, it will be a parenthetical note. Indeed, we are more likely to fault a writer for being drawn to catchy labels: labels that sound good, but violate other criteria of conceptual adequacy. They are terminological tinsel. Phrase making is not central to social science research.

Concept Types. Another objection to the criterial framework set forth in this chapter might be that concepts are not really, as claimed, part of a single enterprise. Rather, what we may have is a set of widely varying conceptual exercises, each responding to different criteria of adequacy. Indeed, considering the number and diversity of concept-types – circular, classical, classificatory, comparative, connotative, contextual, core, deductive, denotative, dispositional, empirical, essential, essentially contested, experiential, family-resemblance, functional, *genus et differentia,* ideal-type, inductive, lexical, metrical, minimal, nominal, object, observable, operational, ostensive, persuasive, polar, precising, property, radial, real, residual, stipulative, technical, theoretical, and so forth[69] – claims for uniformity in this process may seem strained.

---

68. See Krasner (1978), Hirschman (1970a), and Almond and Verba (1963). See also discussion in Collier and Levitsky (1997: 450).
69. See Adjdukiewicz (1969), Angeles (1981: 56–58), Bierstedt (1959), Burger (1976), Chapin (1939), Cohen (1989), Collier and Mahon (1993), DiRenzo (1966a), Dumont and Wilson (1967), Graham (1971), Hempel (1952), Kaplan (1964), Lakoff (1987), Linsky (1969), Miller (1980), Olshewsky (1969), Pap (1969), Putnam (1975), Robinson (1954), Russell (1969), Sartori (1975: 28–30; 1984a: 72–85), Stinchcombe (1968), and Strawson (1969).

Although there are important differences among concept types (see Chapter 4 for a discussion of several), I would argue that these differences are better understood as differences of degree, rather than of kind. Moreover, most of these differences can be readily mapped across the eight dimensions of our framework. Concept types, in other words, are subsumable within the criterial framework. "Classical" concepts privilege operationalization, as we have noted. Ideal-type, radial, and family-resemblance concepts emphasize resonance. Each concept type (or each individual concept) emphasizes a different conceptual task or tasks – *but not to the total exclusion of other tasks.* Ideal-type concepts have not renounced all claims to operationalization; classical concepts do not eschew resonance; and so forth.[70] In sum, although concept types offer a useful shorthand way of talking about certain issues in concept formation, they do not offer a comprehensive explanation of that process. Particular concept types are best understood as a matter of *prioritization,* a sacrifice of certain conceptual virtues for the more firm possession of others.

70. On the connection between ideal-types and empirical reality, Weber (1905/1949: 97) writes: "All expositions for example of the 'essence' of Christianity are ideal types enjoying only a necessarily very relative and problematic validity when they are intended to be regarded as the historical portrayal of empirically existing facts." However tenuous the connection to reality, it seems clear from Weber's exposition that ideal-type concepts must bear *some* relationship to "empirically existing" phenomena in order to be of use to social science. The *relative* nature of conceptual adequacy is also recognized (at least implicitly) in the following comments by Hempel (1991: 81). "Cognitive significance in a system is a matter of degree: significant systems range from those whose entire extralogical vocabulary consists of observation terms, through theories whose formulation relies heavily on theoretical constructs, on to systems with hardly any bearing on potential empirical findings."

4

Strategies of Definition

There is ... progress in the social sciences, but it is much slower [than in the natural sciences], and not at all animated by the same information flow and optimistic spirit. Cooperation is sluggish at best; even genuine discoveries are often obscured by bitter ideological disputes. For the most part, anthropologists, economists, sociologists, and political scientists fail to understand and encourage one another.... Split into independent cadres, they stress precision in words within their specialty but seldom speak the same technical language from one specialty to the next. A great many even enjoy the resulting overall atmosphere of chaos, mistaking it for creative ferment.

– Edward O. Wilson[1]

It matters how we define words, not merely that we define them. Yet, as we have seen in the previous chapter, the task of concept formation is irreducibly complex, involving claims for coherence, operationalization, validity, field utility, resonance, contextual range, parsimony, and analytic/empirical utility (see Table 3.1). Not surprisingly, natural scientists like E. O. Wilson find the lexicon of social science to be confusing and unstable terrain, an apparently orderless field of churning terms, definitions, and referents. Three problems, in particular, plague the social science lexicon: homonymy (multiple meanings for the same term), synonymy (different terms with the same, or overlapping, meanings), and instability (unpredictable changes in the foregoing). As a result, studies of the same subject appear to be talking about different things, and studies of different subjects appear to be talking about the same thing. Knowledge cumulation is impeded, and methodological fragmentation encouraged.

The case for semantic reconstruction seems strong, and many plans have been proposed. Although the goals and methods of these reconstructions differ, all aim for a simplification of terms and meanings in

1. Wilson (1998: 198).

65

the social sciences so that a greater level of agreement (call it "objectivity") and a more logical relationship among terms might be achieved. Many strive toward the classical ideal (discussed in Chapter 3), in which terms are defined by unique properties along a genus-et-differentia ladder of abstraction, and in which a one-to-one relationship obtains between word and meaning (thus overcoming problems of homonyny and synonymy).[2] Some, like the original "logical positivists," go further, proposing a language for science that is reduced to basic symbols and operators.[3] All concur in a general way with Sartori's call for "the formulation of a special and specialized language ... whose distinctive characteristic is precisely to correct the defects of ordinary language."[4]

None of these reconstructive attempts have been very successful (witness, our current conceptual malaise). The first problem is that they invariably depart from norms of ordinary usage, or elevate one particular meaning for a word over others (equally ensconced in ordinary usage). Such reconstructions may be helpful for the writer or for a small band of followers, but for the broader realm of social science these reconstructions turn out to be either objectionable (on empirical or theoretical grounds) or incomprehensible. The net effect is often to *add* to our sense of confusion, for the reconstructed and unreconstructed concepts now sit side-by-side, vying for attention. Thus is another layer of meaning added to an already overflowing semantic field.

A second problem is more basic. Even if social scientists were to accept such a reconstruction, we might wonder about the utility of such a lexi-

2. The classical approach to concept formation may be traced back to Aristotle and the *scholastic* philosophers of the Middle Ages. For later variants, see Chapin (1939), Cohen and Nagel (1934), DiRenzo (1966), Dumont and Wilson (1967), Hempel (1952, 1963, 1965, 1966), Landau (1972), Lasswell and Kaplan (1950), Lazarsfeld (1966), Meehan (1971), Stinchcombe (1968; 1978), Zannoni (1978), and most important, Sartori (1970; 1984a; 1984b), and Sartori et al. (1975). For further discussion see Adcock (1998) and Taylor (1995). For a somewhat different reconstructive approach, based on the analytic philosophic tradition, see Oppenheim (1961, 1975, 1981).

3. For work representative of the so-called Vienna Circle (G. Bergmann, Carnap, Feigl, Neurath, Schlick, and Waisman), see Ayer (1959), Carnap (1962; 1967), and commentary in Friedman (1992), Gillies (1993), and Katz (1966). Wittgenstein's early work (1921/1988), which was a principal inspiration for this group, remains perhaps the most important statement of logical positivism Pitkin (1972: 29). summarizes Wittgenstein's approach in the *Tractatus* as follows: "Language ... is a kind of logical calculus operating according to strict, definite rules, and the job of philosophy is to study these rules and make them explicit. Whatever in language cannot be analyzed into elementary propositions is either lacking in sense or nonsensical." Tarski's "semantic" theory of truth is closely related (Tarski 1944; Field 1972).

4. Sartori (1984a: 57–58).

con. The world of human endeavor that the social sciences seek to describe and explain is characterized by a great deal of messiness and *in*discreteness. Phenomena "out there" – particularly when it concerns phenomena of a decisional sort – do not readily group together in bundles with clear borders and hierarchical interrelationships. They do not, that is, conform to the classificatory neatness of the classical vision. Thus, to employ a simplified language in the work of social science might reduce our semantic confusion, but at the cost of reducing our capacity to understand the world. We could agree on a lot – having the limited terms and uniform meanings that such a gridwork provides – but we could not say very much.[5]

Obviously, "complexity" is a matter of degree. No language can hope to capture the complexity of the world because the world is infinitely complex. This is a truism. My argument is simply that the language available to social science should not be more reductionist than the language of everyday discourse (i.e., "natural" language). Social science should be allowed to use the same tools available to journalists, poets, and the proverbial man in the street. To deprive the social science community of certain words, or of certain uses of commonly understood words, is bound to create confusion, and also to limit the usefulness of social science as a way of apprehending the world. It is to tie our hands behind our backs prior to heavy lifting.

Everyday language should thus be regarded as setting the *minimum* level of linguistic complexity above which social science might reach (by the creation of new terms or the specialized redefinitions of established terms) but below which it should not fall. None of this precludes the use of a more restricted language, including mathematical languages, for specific tasks in social science. The preservation of the complexity inherent in everyday language is not an assault on statistics or formal modeling. It simply says that for some tasks at least we will want to have access to the full range of terms and meanings contained in the English (or some other natural) language.

In direct contrast to the reconstructive approach is the philosophical movement known as "ordinary language."[6] Ordinary language philoso-

5. When we define, Edmund Burke wrote, "we seem in danger of circumscribing nature within the bounds of our own notions" (quoted in Robinson 1954: 6).
6. See Ammerman (1965), Austin (1961, 1962/1975), Caton (1963), Cavell (1969), Chappell (1964), Fodor and Katz (1964), Pitkin (1967; 1972), Ryle (1953/1964), Wittgenstein (1953), Ziff (1960). Pitkin (1972: 5–6) discusses the three branches of ordinary language philosophy, each of which is associated with a distinct location: Oxford, where Wittgenstein taught, Cambridge, where Austin and Ryle taught, and the United States, where Chomsky, Fodor, Katz, and Ziff taught. The differences are significant (see Katz 1966: ch 3). Nonetheless, like Pitkin and Katz, I treat this heterogeneous family of scholars as part of a single intellectual movement, "ordinary language."

phers, as the term suggests, look upon norms embedded in everyday usage as a source of orderliness. Rather than endeavoring to straighten out ordinary language, ordinary language approaches aim to figure it out. After all, ordinary language makes sense to its users (by all appearances); why should it not make sense to philosophers, or social scientists? It is clear, writes Wittgenstein,

> that every sentence in our language is "in order as it is." That is to say, we are not *striving after* an ideal, as if our ordinary vague sentences had not yet got a quite unexceptional sense, and a perfect language awaited construction by us. On the other hand, it seems clear that where there is sense there must be perfect order. So there must be perfect order even in the vaguest sentence.[7]

Wittgenstein's critique of linguistic reconstructionism is strongly stated. (What is "perfect order"?) Yet, it seems a useful corrective to the enthusiasms of the Vienna Circle and Wittgenstein's own early work (the aptly titled *Tractatus logico-philosophicus*).

It is less clear what this critique portends for the practice of social science. Although a great deal has been written about ordinary language since Wittgenstein's startling lectures at Cambridge in the 1930s, its application to social science remains relatively unexplored. Mainly, I suspect, this is because those who are enamored of ordinary-language philosophy tend *not* to be enamored of social science, and vice versa. The twain seldom meet, except in adversity.[8]

What would it mean to practice a social science rooted in ordinary language? Would it mean a social science limited to everyday language? Or would it respect terms and definitions as understood within specialized language regions (e.g., subfields of social science)?[9] Finally, once we have engaged in an ordinary language analysis of key terms, how should we define those terms? This last question is most critical, for the strength of

---

7. Quoted in Oppenheim (1981: 178). There is some debate over the degree to which philosophic analysis in the ordinary language tradition should leave language "as it is" (Fodor 1966: ch 3). Nonetheless, at least with respect to the reconstructive tradition, this is the salient characteristic of ordinary language analysis.
8. But see Fearon and Laitin (2000) and Schaffer (1998).
9. Pitkin (1972: 19) remarks that the ordinary language philosopher is not "opposed to the introduction of new technical terms or new definitions. He is interested only in a certain characteristic kind of deviation from ordinary usage that does not involve any technical terms or redefinitions, and that is paradoxically unable really to leave ordinary usage behind." The implication is that the ordinary language approach is limited to everyday language, other language regions being "deviations" from this set of norms. Ryle (1964: ch 6) interrogates this question, but with inconclusive results (so far as I can see).

ordinary language analysis has been in elucidating the complexity of terms, not in taming that complexity. Ordinary language analysis, as pioneered by John Austin and others, is an exercise in splitting, not lumping. Definitions are collected, usages reviewed, and meanings parsed. But Humpty-Dumpty is left on the ground. If ordinary language analysis is to facilitate empirical analysis – if it is to elucidate *usable* concepts – an effort must be made to put Humpty-Dumpty back together again.[10]

The task of this chapter is to combine the virtues of reconstructive and ordinary language analysis. We wish, following the later Wittgenstein, to leave language more or less as it is. This means, among other things, avoiding the attachment of a word to a particular theory – unless of course that theory is so pervasive, and so generally accepted, that it might provide firm footing for the word in a wide variety of contexts (a rare occurrence in the social sciences). Yet we wish at the same time to avoid the pitfalls of ordinary language analysis – (a) an exclusive focus on natural language and (b) endless definitional possibilities. We wish to redescribe ordinary usage in a way that will provide general definitions for difficult terms and also provide the ground on which more specific definitions can be constructed.

Broadly, there are two sorts of questions one might ask about a term's definition: (1) what does it mean *generally*? and (2) what should it mean *here* (in this particular context)? The first question refers to a general context of usage – a language or language region – the second to a more particular context, perhaps a research problem. The first question is essentially descriptive; it aims simply to describe the meanings and usages attached to a particular word within the specified language region. The second is more normative in aim, insofar as it must reach beyond these general semantic possibilities toward a particular resolution of attributes and referents. The first offers a general definition, applicable to a wide range of particular uses; the ambit of the second sort of definition will be more restricted. We shall refer to the first sort of definition as *general* definition, and the second as *contextual* definition (or a definition-in-use).[11]

It will be seen that the difference between general and contextual definitions is largely a product of their differing contextual range – the num-

---

10. Indeed, some studies in the ordinary language tradition *have* succeeded in constructing reasonably concise frameworks for understanding complex terms – for example, Pitkin (1967) on "representation," and Westen (1990) on "equality." Kroeber and Kluckhohn's (1952/1963) work on "culture," by contrast, is little more than a compendium of definitions.
11. See Robinson (1954).

ber of linguistic contexts that the definition aims to embrace, a matter
discussed in the previous chapter. It is of course a difference of degrees.
As one broadens the contextual range of a contextual definition (the confusion in terms is regrettable but unavoidable) it approaches the status
of general definition, and vice versa.

Because of its broad range, general definitions normally do not consider "empirical" matters, such as operationalization, validity, and ana-
lytic/empirical utility. We are not really concerned, in any case, with
whether a term is useful empirically; we are primarily concerned with
what it *means* (conventionally). Thus, our focus is on "formal" criteria
of concept formation: contextual range, coherence, field utility, and
most important, resonance.

There is a temptation to dismiss general definitions, focused as they
are on formal criteria, as *merely* definitional. The real work of concepts
is performed by contextual definitions, according to this view. However,
it is also the case that we must know what a word is generally understood to mean before we define it contextually. All contextual definitions
are parasitic on general definitions, even though (regrettably) general
definitions are often bypassed. Our goal, therefore, is to make general
definition more accessible and more helpful in the task of contextual definition, not to deprecate the latter.

We might also consider the fact that terms, like theories, are best
approached from a wide-angle perspective. Our approach takes more
time than the quick-and-dirty stipulative definition. Yet, if we do not
engage in a reasonably comprehensive search of the many definitional
options available we risk constraining our understanding of the term,
and the phenomena to which the term refers. We also risk ending up
with a highly idiosyncratic definition: one that will not travel to other
research sites, that will not cumulate with other work on the subject, and
that will not (for both these reasons) advance the field.

It should also be pointed out that the concepts that cause the most
trouble in social science – concepts such as justice, democracy, power,
and ideology – are problematic because we do not know what they *mean*
(generally), not because we lack contextual definitions. To be sure, contextual definitions clarify meaning; but insofar as they clash with each
other they are likely to cause confusion about the general concept. If
empirical work on democracy employs different definitions of democracy, or if it occurs under different labels (eschewing the ambiguity of
"democracy"), it becomes difficult to integrate this work into a single
discussion. This is the sort of semantic confusion and disciplinary
parochialism that we wish to avoid.

Table 4.1 *General Definition*

1. *Sample:* sample representative usages and definitions
2. *Typologize:* arrange nonidiosyncratic attributes in a single typology
3. *Define:*
(a) *Minimally* (identify those few attributes that all nonidiosyncratic uses of the term have in common)
(b) *Ideal-typically* (identify those attributes that define a term in its purest, most "ideal," form)

How, then, shall we go about crafting general definitions? This task is broken down into three steps: sampling usages, typologizing attributes, and the construction of minimal and ideal-type definitions, as specified in Table 4.1. The chapter lays out these procedures (which build upon both reconstructive and ordinary language precedents), and then discusses their implications for contextual definition. I will carry forth the exposition by working through the definition of *ideology,* a key concept in the social science lexicon and one of its most problematic entries. If we can bring order to this troublesome concept, then we have presumably achieved a most-difficult case of concept formation.

The Sample

How broad a swath do we wish to cut with a definition? What is its rightful contextual range? This is always a difficult question, as we have discussed. At the very least, we ought to consider everyday language and the language region(s) within which our work belongs. We might also consider historical uses of the term (etymology), its near-synonyms in other languages, and its usage within other fields (if any).

A second question is easier to solve: how do we know when we have adequately covered a territory in our search for definitions? The answer, I suggest, is when we have reached the point of redundancy – when further searches through the literature seem to garner only repetitions of meanings that we have already encountered.

A final question concerns which cognates of a core term, and which meanings of that core term, to include in our survey. The general rule is *inclusivity:* include as many cognates and alternate meanings as possible (i.e., without sacrificing the coherence of the concept). Thus, we extend our survey to include not only "ideology," but also "ideological," and "ideologue." This does not mean that we ignore differences among cognates; it means that we see greater conceptual gain from treating them together than from treating them separately.

Table 4.2   *A Sampling of Influential Definitions of "Ideology"*

"An organization of opinions, attitudes, and values – a way of thinking about man and society. We may speak of an individual's total ideology or of his ideology with respect to different areas of social life; politics, economics, religion, minority groups, and so forth" (Adorno et al. 1950: 2).

"A consistent and integrated pattern of thoughts and beliefs explaining man's attitude towards life and his existence in society, and advocating a conduct and action pattern responsive to and commensurate with such thoughts and beliefs" (Loewenstein 1953: 52).

"A particularly elaborate, close-woven, and far-ranging structure of attitudes. By origin and usage its connotations are primarily political, although the scope of the structure is such that we expect an ideology to encompass content outside the political order as narrowly defined … A highly differentiated attitude structure, [with] its parts … organized in a coherent fashion.… Must be capped by concepts of a high order of abstraction.… [Must supply] a manageable number of ordering dimensions that permit the person to make sense of a broad range of events" (Campbell et al. 1960: 192–93).

"A body of concepts [which]: (1) deal with the questions: Who will be the rulers? How will the rulers be selected? By what principles will they govern?, (2) constitute an argument; that is, they are intended to persuade and to counter opposing views, (3) integrally affect some of the major values of life, (4) embrace a program for the defense or reform or abolition of important social institutions, (5) are, in part, rationalizations of groups interests – but not necessarily the interests of all groups espousing them, (6) are normative, ethical, moral in tone and content, (7) are … torn from their context in a broader belief system, and share the structural and stylistic properties of that system" (Lane 1962: 14–15).

"Systems of belief that are elaborate, integrated, and coherent, that justify the exercise of power, explain and judge historical events, identity political right and wrong, set forth the interconnections (causal and moral) between politics and other spheres of activity" (McClosky 1964: 362).

A belief-system that includes: (1) a wide range of opinions, (2) high attitude consistency (*aka* "constraint" or "economy"), and (3) abstract conceptualizations (e.g., "liberal," "conservative") (paraphrase of Converse 1964).

"Maps of problematic social reality and matrices for the creation of collective conscience" (Geertz 1964/1973: 220).

"The reflection of process and structure in the consciousness of those involved – the *product* of action" (Nettl 1967: 100).

"A typically dogmatic, i.e., rigid and impermeable, approach to politics" (Sartori 1969: 402).

(continues)

Table 4.2 *Continued*

"A logically coherent system of symbols which, within a more or less sophisticated conception of history, links the cognitive and evaluative perception of one's social condition – especially its prospects for the future – to a program of collective action for the maintenance, alteration, or transformation of society" (Mullins 1974: 235).

"Sets of ideas by which men posit, explain and justify ends and means of organised social action, and specifically political action, irrespective of whether such action aims to preserve, amend, uproot or rebuild a given social order" (Seliger 1976: 11).

"A system of collectively held normative and reputedly factual ideas and beliefs and attitudes advocating a particular pattern of social relationships and arrangements, and/or aimed at justifying a particular pattern of conduct, which its proponents seek to promote, realise, pursue or maintain" (Hamilton 1987: 38).

"An emotion-laden, myth-saturated, action-related system of beliefs and values about people and society, legitimacy and authority, that is acquired to a large extent as a matter of faith and habit. The myths and values of ideology are communicated through symbols in a simplified, economical, and efficient manner. Ideological beliefs are more or less coherent, more or less articulate, more or less open to new evidence and information. Ideologies have a high potential for mass mobilization, manipulation, and control; in that sense, they are mobilized belief systems" (Rejai 1991: 11).

An initial sampling of well known definitions is presented in Table 4.2. Evidently, with a word so varied and so ubiquitous we will need to search much further than these thirteen definitions before we can presume to have collected a representative sample. More than 100 articles and books were ultimately consulted in the course of this survey. In collecting these definitions I paid attention not simply to formal definitions, but also to usages – how "ideology" was employed in social science contexts.

The task of gathering definitions might be coded quantitatively: *X*-number of definitions of type *A*, *X*-number of definitions of type *B*, and so forth. The exercise is doable, but unnecessary, for we are interested in general usage patterns, not precise fluctuations. The purpose is to discover which attributes are universal, which are selectively employed, and which may be discarded as idiosyncratic (those which pose the greatest violation of the resonance criterion).

The Typology

Having taken a look at the extant uses of a word, and having eliminated the most idiosyncratic, we are probably still faced with a large number of definitional options. This is certainly true for ideology. Countless books and articles have been written about this concept, each purporting to clarify its meaning. As a consequence, countless definitions now populate academic discourse (Table 4.2 barely scratches the surface of this heterogeneity). One is struck not only by the cumulative number of different attributes that writers find essential, but also by their contradictions. To some, ideology is dogmatic, while to others it carries connotations of political sophistication. To some it refers to dominant modes of thought, and to others it refers primarily to those most alienated by the status quo. To some it is based in the concrete interests of a social class, while to others it is characterized by an absence of economic self-interests. One could go on.

Given this state of conceptual disarray, how does one go about choosing a single definition for such a term? One common expedient is to consult a classic work on the subject and appropriate the author's definition. Yet, since the definition used by the author was crafted for a specific context (the context of the work itself), it is not at all clear that this will be the best possible choice for the writer's own project. Clifford Geertz, whose work on ideology has been enormously influential, defines ideologies as "maps of problematic social reality and matrices for the creation of collective conscience."[12] Although useful for some types of work (particularly of the interpretive variety), this is probably not the best definition one could choose for a behavioral study of ideology.

A second common approach to definition is to arrive at a causal-explanatory understanding of the term. Such an approach defines a concept by what explains it, or by what it explains. In the case of ideology, for example, writers have asked how ideologies originate, what shapes and sustains them, and what influences their transformation. Accordingly, the origin of the modern phenomenon called ideology has been located in the English Revolution, the French Revolution, and in a long chain of interconnected developments – the displacement of traditional modes of thought, the appearance of nation-states, the invention of mass communications, and the rise of democratic politics. Ideological thinking has been explained by basic cognitive features of the human psyche, patterns of childrearing, social strain, personality structures, irrational features of the cultural landscape, situations of crisis, pre-

12. Geertz (1964/1973: 220).

modern cleavages, the absence of economic development, particular organizational structures, types of electoral systems, levels of political mobilization and communications technologies, group interests, constituencies, the intelligentsia, critical historical events, and ideologies themselves.[13] Interesting as such theories are, they are probably not helpful in the initial task of definition. One would not wish one's study of post-Communist party ideologies in Eastern Europe to hinge on a particular *causal* theory of ideology, for example. Causal explanations are rarely appropriate for crafting general definitions.

The scholar might also turn to an intellectual history of the concept.[14] But this approach is equally vexing. Historians and political theorists have shown how the concept of ideology figures in the work of Machiavelli, Bacon, Locke, Condillac, Comte, Feuerbach, Hegel, Pareto, Sorel, Durkheim, Lukacs, Gramsci, Weber, Mannheim, Kuhn, Freud (and later psychoanalytically oriented theorists like Ricoeur and Lacan), Marx, the Frankfurt School, and a range of neo- and post-Marxists (e.g., Castoriadis, Lefort, Habermas), structuralists (e.g., Lévi-Strauss, Kristeva, Barthes), and poststructuralists (e.g., Bourdieu, and the *Tel Quel* crew). Each of these writers and traditions has been incorporated in the ongoing debate over what ideology means. Indeed, virtually all social theorists, linguists, and political philosophers worth their salt now seem to possess a "concept of ideology," which surely qualifies it as one of the most versatile concepts in political theory.[15] The fecundity of this word – its variety of traditions and the variety of usages even *within* a tradition – augurs poorly for an intellectual-history approach to general definition.[16]

What I propose here is a melding of ordinary language analysis with the conceptual work conducted by Sartori and his colleagues. Having sampled a field of definitions, I propose that we focus on *specific definitional attributes* that each definition or use of the word presents. In so doing, we will

---

13. For citations to the literature and further discussion of the concept of ideology, see Gerring (1997).

14. See, for example, Ball et al. (1989), and Williams (1983), on various concepts. Most of the entries in Sills (1968) take an intellectual-history approach to definition.

15. See Adams (1989), Althusser (1971), Bergmann (1951), Birnbaum (1960), Carlsnaess (1981), Cox (1969), Cunningham (1973), Dittberner (1979), Eagleton (1991), Elster (1982), Goldie (1989), Hall et al. (1977), Halle (1972), Hirst (1979), Huaco (1971), Keohane (1976), Laclau (1977), Larrain (1979, 1983), Lichtheim (1967), Manning (1980), Manning and Robinson (1985), McLellan (1986), Partridge (1961), Plamenatz (1970), Ritsert (1990), Roucek (1944), Seliger (1976; 1977), Therborn (1980), Thompson (1984), and Williams (1988).

16. I am assuming that the writer is intending to address more than a single intellectual tradition herself. If not, a survey of that single tradition may be appropriate.

Table 4.3 *"Ideology": Typology and General Definitions*

Typology of definitional traits

1. Location
a. Thought
b. Behavior
c. Language

2. Subject matter
a. Politics
b. Power
c. The world at-large

3. Subject
a. Social class
b. Any group
c. Any group or individual

4. Position
a. Dominant
b. Subordinate

5. Function
a. Explaining
b. Repressing
c. Integrating
d. Motivating
e. Legitimating

6. Motivation
a. Interest-based
b. Noninterest-based
c. Nonexpedient

7. Cognitive/affective structure
a. Coherence (internal)
b. Differentiation (external)
c. Abstraction

d. Specificity
e. Hierarchy
f. Stability (endurance)
g. Knowledge
h. Sophistication
i. Facticity
j. Simplicity
k. Distortion
l. Conviction
m. Insincerity
n. Dogmatism
o. Consciousness
p. Unconsciousness

Minimal definition

Ideational (values, beliefs, ideas, et al. – with or without institutional or behavioral elements)
About power
Coherent (internally consistent, interdependent)
Stable (enduring)
Differentiated (vis-à-vis other ideologies)
Nonexpedient

Ideal-type definition

Ideational
About politics (implied: about relationships of power)
Coherent
Stable
Differentiated
Nonexpedient
Constraining (causally significant)
Programmatic (action-oriented)
Shared (within a group or community)
Abstract as well as specific
Hierarchical (in its arrangement of parts)
Dogmatic
Conscious, manifest, explicit (but perhaps with unconscious, latent, implicit elements as well)
Not reducible to (nonideological) structures

try to group together attributes that are similar to one another. The result is a typology of definitional options that is not, we hope, unduly long but nonetheless represents the semantic diversity of the term. The product of this effort should resemble the framework illustrated in Table 4.3, which contains all attributes regularly associated with "ideology" and its cognates in contemporary social science discourse (with glances to everyday usage), arranged in logically related parts.

This is a highly condensed form of presentation, so it is worth reviewing the findings, if only briefly. Writers have disagreed, first, over ideology's location. Is it to be found primarily in thought (a view prevalent among political scientists), in behavior (a view common among traditional anthropologists), or in language (a view popular in contemporary cultural studies)? Writers have also disagreed over the subject matter of ideology. Is it politics *tout court,* power, or the world at-large? Third, writers have entertained differing views of the ideologists (the holders of ideologies). Are they primarily to be thought of as social classes (the traditional Marxist view), any group (e.g., trade union, secret society, political party), or any group or individual (the broadest, most permissive view)? Fourth, writers have seen ideology as an attribute of the dominant class or establishment, but also as a tool in the struggle *against* such domination. Fifth, writers have debated the functions of ideology. Ideology has been seen variously as explaining things about the world (the location of power, the rights and privileges of citizens,...), repressing certain interests and values, integrating individuals into a social whole, motivating individuals to participate in political acts, and legitimating certain actions or authority-relations. Sixth, writers have divided over whether ideology is grounded in concrete material interests (e.g., a class interest), or whether the hallmark of ideology is the *submergence* of interest-based political activity. Another possibility is that ideology may be either interest-based or not; but it must not, under any circumstances, be reducible to expedience. Finally, one finds a host of disagreements over the particular cognitive/affective structure evidenced in an ideology, as enumerated in Table 4.3.

It should be clear by now, why ideology is a conceptual morass. Yet when measured against the thousands of extant definitions, and even more numerous usages, the typology summarized in Table 4.3 is a considerable feat of semantic reduction.

Of course, this typology could be constructed in somewhat different ways. One could choose different terms to label the categories. One could lump some of the foregoing categories together, or split them apart to create a larger typology. One could perhaps discover, after diligent search through the literature (or different, more extended, literatures) several connotations of the term that are reasonably common and *not* included in the foregoing analysis. Nonetheless, I venture to say that any effort of this sort would result in a table of similar dimensions.

The important point is that it *is* possible to reduce the field of meanings emanating from "ideology" to manageable proportions. Presumably, similar typologies could be produced for other, equally conflicted, terms such as justice, democracy, or power. Such reduction is essential to the conceptualizer because there is no other way for her to comprehend, and hence knowledgeably choose among, a large field of definitional options. We must have some way of getting a handle on these slippery terms if they are to play a productive role in social science research.

Minimal Definition

At this point, we are still faced with a multitude of possible meanings for this vexed term. Indeed, no concept could possibly carry all these meanings and serve as a useful semantic vehicle in social science research. What does ideology *really* mean? one is obliged to ask.

Two complementary approaches to general definition are presented here: minimal definition and ideal-type definition. A minimal definition refers to a definition that would apply to all usages of a term within a specified language region (when a term is employed in a nonidiosyncratic manner). Ideally, it should be perfectly substitutable. We ought to be able to replace "ideology" in any sentence with our minimal definition without contradicting the intended meaning of these sentences. A useful minimal definition is a capacious one. It spreads its semantic net widely.[17]

Here we go.

All definitions of ideology assume that the location (l) of "ideology" is, at the very least, in *thought* (a) – which is to say, in attitudes, values, and/or beliefs. This is universally understood (though sometimes tacit). Some would add behavior (b) and language (c) as locations of ideology, but because not all writers agree on these additional attributes, their claims to resonance are weaker. We therefore retain (a) and discard the others in our minimal definition.

Many writers propose that ideologies imply a sense of *conviction* on the part of an ideologue (7l). But ideologies are also commonly spoken

17. Minimal definition strategies have been employed by many writers, though not always by this name and not always in the precise manner suggested here. See, e.g., Debnam (1984), Freeden (1994: 146), Hamilton (1987), Murphey (1994: 23–4), and Pitkin (1967: 10–11). Sartori endorses minimal definition in his early work (1975: 34–5; 1976: 61), but drops the matter in his classic formulation (1984a).

of as "mere ideologies," hollow ideational shells in which few truly believe. The ideology of communism in Eastern Europe prior to the fall of the Soviet Union seems to have approximated this sense of ideology as *insincerity* (7m). Both these attributes may be dropped from our minimal definition. Similarly, the attribute *dominant* (4a) conflicts with *subordinate* (4b); and *consciousness* (7o) contradicts *unconsciousness* (7p). These, too, must be jettisoned. To those who would claim that ideology is an example of *abstract* (7c), *hierarchically ordered* (7e), *knowledgeable* (7g), and/or *sophisticated* (7h) cognition, one must also observe that ideological thought has often been defined by its *simplicity* (7j) and *distortion* (7k). Neither side of this debate has a strong claim to definitional priority.

Many troubling definitional conflicts can be found on the *motivation* dimension. Here, *interest-based* (6a) and *noninterest-based* (6b) definitions collide. Indeed, this would seem to be the source of a good deal of ideology's semantic strife; some evidently wish to define ideological activity as instrumental and others as noninstrumental. The authors of *The American Voter* offer a sensible way out of this definitional dilemma. They propose that ideology be understood as *nonexpedient* ideas and behavior. "[I]t matters whether self-interest proceeds in a simple and naked sense, or has indeed become imbedded in some broader ideological structure."[18] What the writers wish to distinguish is "self-interest in a primitive and short-sighted sense, and the operation of self-interest within a structure of attitudes that might reasonably be labeled an 'ideology.'"[19] Here is a resolution that does not directly contradict either (6a) or (6b), and echoes common usage of the term (though it is not common among formal definitions). It makes good sense for purposes of minimal definition.

Another time-worn dispute concerns whether ideology should be restricted to explicitly *political* subject matter (2a), to relationships mediated by *power* (2b), or to the *world at-large* (2c). Of these associations, only "power" seems universal. Ideology always refers to relationships mediated by power.

The importance of *coherence* (7a) – aka "consistency" or "constraint" – is virtually unchallenged in the social science literature. Ideology, at the very least, refers to a set of idea-elements that are bound together, belonging to one another in a nonrandom fashion. On what principles they intercorrelate, and to what degree, remain matters of dispute, but

---

18. Campbell et al. (1960: 203–04).
19. Ibid.

the notion of coherence is difficult to gainsay. I would add, as corollaries, *differentiation* (7b) and *stability* (7f): the one implying coherence vis-à-vis competing ideologies and the other implying coherence through time. An ideology (as the term is commonly employed) must be different from other neighboring idea-systems, and it must not be evanescent.

A minimal definition of ideology, then, may be formulated as follows: *ideational elements (values, attitudes, beliefs, et al.) about power relationships which are relatively coherent, differentiated, stable, and nonexpedient.* All contemporary usages of the term – and certainly, those usages common in social science contexts – include these minimal features. We have not defined-out any implications of the term and thus prejudged our topic. Thus, the minimal definition serves its primary function. It identifies what we mean, in a general sort of way, by "ideology."

Ideal-Type Definition

Having arrived at a minimal definition – a definition minimally applicable to all contexts within a given language region – we may now proceed to the *ideal-type*. Ideal-type definition aims for a collection of attributes that is maximal – that is, including all (nonidiosyncratic) characteristics that help to define the concept in its purest, most "ideal" (and perhaps its most extreme) form. An ideal-type, Weber writes,

> is not a *description* of reality but it aims to give unambiguous means of expression to such a description.... An ideal type is formed by the one-sided *accentuation* of one or more points of view and by the synthesis of a great many diffuse, discrete, more or less present and occasionally absent *concrete individual* phenomena, which are arranged according to those one-sidedly emphasized viewpoints into a unified *analytical* construct. In its conceptual purity, this mental construct cannot be found empirically anywhere in reality.... [Yet,] when carefully applied, those concepts are particularly useful in research and exposition.[20]

As Weber makes clear, an ideal-type is a logical construct; it may or may not be found (with all its attributes) in empirical reality. It represents reality in a *more-or-less* fashion.

Definitional coherence is fairly easy to achieve in a minimal definition, since the list of attributes is likely to be quite small and all contradictory elements are necessarily excluded. Coherence must be self-consciously cultivated in an ideal-type definition, however, for here many attributes vie for inclusion. We must choose, for example, between "abstraction" and

---

20. Weber (1905/1949: 90).

"specificity." As we make such choices, we must consider not merely the frequency with which different attributes appear (in everyday usage or social scientific usage), but also the *strength* of the association. Ideal-type definitions seek to describe a perfect (unalloyed) type. Thus, although attributes such as distortion, conviction, and dogmatism are not always found in formal definitions, we might agree that persons or groups who embody these traits are perfect specimens, or "paradigm cases," of ideology. Thus, Sartori's definition of ideology, "A typically dogmatic, i.e., rigid and impermeable, approach to politics,"[21] which would be absurd as a minimal definition (since it excludes so many phenomena that we currently classify as ideology), is more appropriately viewed as an ideal-type.

Ideal-type definitions tend to be quite long and are of a less definite nature, since any number of attributes might be said to contribute in some small way to an ideal portrait of a phenomenon. Our definition, listed in Table 4.3, adds the following attributes to the minimal definition: about politics (implied: also about relationships of power), constraining (causally significant), programmatic (action-oriented), shared (within a group or community), abstract as well as specific (coexisting traits), hierarchical (in its arrangement of parts), dogmatic, conscious, manifest, explicit (but perhaps with unconscious, latent, implicit elements as well), and finally, not reducible to external (nonideological) structures. A phenomenon having all these characteristics is more ideological than a phenomenon with just a few; this is ideology's ideal-type definition in common parlance and in social science.

Of "Min-Max" Definition

By combining minimal and ideal-type definitional strategies we engage a well-known feature of concept formation – the inverse correlation existing between intension and extension. More than a century ago, Stanley Jevons pointed out that when the definitional attributes of a word are expanded (e.g., "war" becomes "foreign war"), its empirical breadth is narrowed. In other words, more focused definitions generally refer to fewer phenomena.[22] The relationship is diagrammed in Figure 4.1.

This is an interesting regularity. Even so, we should note that a short definition may be quite constricted in empirical range. It is the attributes

21. Sartori (1969: 402).
22. Jevons (1877/1958: 26). Weber also noticed that "concepts with ever wider scope [have] ever smaller content" (quoted in Burger 1976: 72). See also Cohen and Nagel (1934: 33), Frege, *The Foundations of Arithmetic* (quoted in Passmore 1961/1967: 184), and the now-classic treatment, Sartori (1970: 1041).

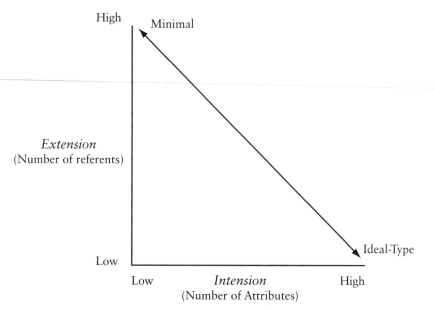

Figure 4.1. "Min-Max" Definition.

chosen as definitional, not simply the number of attributes, that determines the extension of a concept. The inverse relationship between intension and extension is perhaps better understood, therefore, as a product of different definitional goals – one aiming to identify the ideal properties of a concept (and hence its smallest extensional range) – the other aiming to identify minimal properties (and hence its broadest possible extensional range). The "min-max" approach to concept formation is not a mathematical law. However, properly applied we can expect that the addition and subtraction of attributes will have the desired effect on a concept's extension.

The utility of this approach to general definition may now be briefly enumerated. First, it identifies the meaning of a term within a broad linguistic context. Minimal and ideal-type definitions are well-suited for definitions that will be required to travel through time and space. They are hardy: in the one case because the definition is highly inclusive, in the other because it takes a lenient view of operationalization (attributes are manifest *more or less*).

Second, the min-max strategy trespasses lightly on ordinary usage. Indeed, ordinary usage – both in everyday language and, more important, within the social science community – provides the basis for this strategy of definition. In this sense, it may be seen as an adaptation of ordinary language techniques for reconstructive purposes, a marriage of the two contrasting schools of thought outlined at the beginning of this chapter.

(3)　Third, it specifies the parameters of a concept, a minimum and maximum of attributes and entities. This is the frame within which all contextual definitions should fall (otherwise, they are idiosyncratic). It does so by situating all definitional options within two-dimensional space, as diagrammed in Figure 4.1. Perhaps, one might object, social science concepts are not all two-dimensional; perhaps some require three or four dimensions. Or perhaps some concepts present *several* minimal-to-ideal-type continua. Justice, for example, may be interpreted as a matter of rights, needs, or deserts. It may be aggregative or distributive. It may refer to equality or to the advantage of the least advantaged (Rawls's "difference principle"). And equality itself is open to many interpretations. Concepts of this complexity do not seem to fit neatly into two-dimensional space. Even so, we may construe two attributes of a minimal definition within this morass of principles and interpretations: (a) treating equals equally and (b) giving to each her (or his) due. Aristotle's maxims are consistent with virtually all formal definitions of justice and virtually all nonidiosyncratic uses of the term. It establishes a floor to stand on as we contemplate further meanings. It should also be possible to construct an ideal-type of justice by adding further attributes. Thus, an action or condition is *most* just when it satisfies all qualities traditionally identified as just. Other concepts, equally fraught, can be subjected to the same min-max procedure. *Democracy,* for example, might be defined minimally as rule by the people and maximally by all the attributes traditionally associated with this word (including social, political, and civil dimensions of democracy).

Clearly, the provision of minimal and ideal-type definitions does not exhaust the work of definitional analysis. Indeed, most of this work occurs *prior* to our final definitions – in the canvassing of definitions and usages, in the differentiation of ordinary and idiosyncratic usages, in the identification of common attributes, and in the formulation of a typology to comfortably arrange those attributes. In certain respects, the approach to general definition outlined here is no different from that practiced by careful writers everywhere. Yet, by formalizing this ad hoc process, and by insisting upon the reduction of semantic plenitude into a reasonably compact form, this method offers certain advantages.

(4)　Fourth, the min-max strategy identifies a relatively stable meaning around which contextual definitions revolve. This provides a basis for mediating definitional disagreements, and a reasonably firm scaffolding for the social science lexicon. It is not a classificatory scaffolding, in which terms are arranged in a hierarchical fashion, defined by always-and-only attributes, and establishing a one-to-one correlation between words and things. Rather than a pyramid of terms, we envision a three-dimensional space anchored by minimal and maximal definitions. The one establishes an outer ring, the other an inner core, for each concept. Between these two extremes a concept's meaning will fluctuate, as we have said. Whenever contextually defined, these general meanings continue to resonate. (We cannot shut out the general sense of a term simply by stipulating a narrow definition.) Min-max nodes should allow us to navigate easily through semantic space.[23]

To clarify, the min-max vision of concept formation is not intended to dispose of definitional disputes. Work on ideology, justice, democracy, and other broad-gauged concepts usually involves an argument for how we *ought* to perceive these notions. As emphasized in Chapter 3, work with concepts is also work *on* concepts. Even so, these "normative" debates must be bounded; otherwise they make no sense. In order to argue about justice we must have some minimal level of agreement about what justice currently means. Without this base-level consensus we lose commensurability among the contending camps. Dissent is meaningless outside of some broader framework of consent. Minimal and ideal-type definitions specify this underlying consensus.

Naturally, even these boundaries are subject to change from time to time. Ideal-type attributes undergo continual revision. (Minimal definitions are usually more stable.) As new properties are suggested for a concept – for example, social equality as a characteristic of democracy (as in "social democracy") – our conception of the original concept changes. But these changes are incremental, occurring over many decades, and exhibit a high degree of subsequent stability. They do not challenge the utility of minimal and maximal definition as bounding strategies. Progress in social science depends on conceptual development; the intention of min-max definition is to structure this ongoing debate over terms and meanings so it can proceed more efficiently. We hope to have narrowed the scope of contention with respect to "ideology" with this inclusive, consensual approach. We now know what it is that we are talking about, at least in a general way, when we employ this complex and multivalent term.

(5)   Finally, the min-max strategy of lexical definition provides a ready framework for the formation of contextual definitions. A minimal defini-

---

23. This paraphrases Kaplan's metaphor. Concepts, he writes, "mark out the paths by which we may move most freely in logical space" (Kaplan 1964: 52).

tion offers a short set of attributes to which others may be added, while the ideal-type offers a long list of attributes from which attributes may be subtracted. Somewhere in between lies the terrain of (nonidiosyncratic) contextual definition. We turn now to a further consideration of contextual definition (definitions-in-use).

From General to Contextual Definition

For some research purposes, a general definition (either minimal or ideal-type) will be suitable. In other cases, we may require greater attention to operationalization, validity, and analytic utility. (General definition, we said, privileges resonance and contextual range. Coherence and parsimony are equally important for both styles of definition.) The task of defining ideology contextually we must leave to the individual writer, ensconced in a particular problem, region, time-period, and method. Suffice to say, different definitions will be useful for different purposes. Those studying political behavior at the individual level may require a different concept of ideology than those studying political organizations. Political parties may call forth a different set of accompanying attributes than revolutionary cells. Ideology may be a fundamentally different phenomenon in modern and premodern societies, western and nonwestern societies, religious and secular societies, at mass and elite levels, and so forth. These are matters for empirical investigation. No single definition of ideology could adequately perform all these functions. We usually need greater specificity when we descend from the lofty realm of minimal and ideal-type definition to the nit and grit of empirical work. Concepts inevitably take on local color.

Contextual definition, we have argued, is achieved by adding properties to a minimal definition or subtracting properties from an ideal-type definition. Suppose, for example, that an empirical study of public opinion finds that voters with highly coherent, differentiated, stable, and nonexpedient attitudes toward politics tend to defend their positions in a dogmatic fashion (while other voters are less dogmatic). One could argue that ideology causes dogmatism, thus separating the two concepts and maintaining a definition for "ideology" much like our minimal definition. Or, depending upon the further objectives of the study, one could decide that these various attributes ought to be combined in a single definition of ideology. (Perhaps one is interested in the effect of these ideological patterns of belief on political behavior.) In this case, one rightly adds dogmatism (7a) to the minimal definition.

The addition of "dogmatism" suggests, hypothetically, that this might also be an empirical regularity in other contexts, and certainly something that future investigators should be aware of in their own research. If researchers begin to discover dogmatism everywhere they find coherent, differentiated, stable, and nonexpedient attitudes toward politics then, over time, one might justify a new minimal definition of this term (since dogmatism has now become an accepted – virtually universal – attribute connected with use of the term ideology). But most contextual definitions are not attempting anything so far-reaching. Their work may be understood as a case study in the vast literature devoted to the general topic of ideology (understood by its general definitions). Contextual definitions, to choose another metaphor, are planets circling around min-max suns.

We have said that the distinction between general and contextual definitions is a matter of contextual range, and hence a matter of degree. But the distinction is critical. Just as propositions must specify their empirical breadth, so must concepts specify their contextual scope. Consider, X begins her discussion of ideology with a definition. *Ideology,* she stipulates, *is* Y. . . What is the status of this definition? Does it pertain to this study only? To all cross-national studies of ideology? To *all* studies of ideology? Writers are rarely clear on this point. (One suspects that they have not considered the matter at all.) The result is unfortunate. Studies that employ the same term for specific research tasks propose different meanings when, in fact, the only point at stake is what it might mean *in these particular research contexts.*

This is the somewhat artificial character of much debate over terms like ideology in the social sciences. Schematically, Adam begins to associate a given set of personality traits with an individual named Eve, and henceforth finds it a breach of conceptual adequacy to call other persons (with different personality traits) by that name. Thus is debate manufactured, and conceptual disarray propounded. The problem of "ideology" is, to some extent, the problem of Adam and Eve. Every author has a pet referent with which she associates a set of defining characteristics, giving little thought to other contexts that might require other definitions. This sort of poly-semic, poly-referent problem could be mitigated if writers clarified whether they are aiming for a general or contextual definition, and – in either case – what contextual scope is envisioned for that definition. This may be regarded as the definition of the definition, and no definition is complete without it.

PART II
Propositions

5

Propositions: General Criteria

The logic of historical thought is not a formal logic of deductive inference. It is not a symmetrical structure of Aristotelian syllogisms, or Ramean dialectics, or Boolean equations. Nor is it precisely an inductive logic, like that of Mill or Keynes or Carnap. It consists neither in inductive reasoning from the particular to the general, nor in deductive reasoning from the general to the particular. Instead, it is a process of *adductive* reasoning in the simple sense of adducing answers to specific questions, so that a satisfactory explanatory "fit" is obtained ... History is, in short, a problem-solving discipline. A historian is someone (anyone) who asks an open-ended question about past events and answers it with selected facts which are arranged in the form of an explanatory paradigm.

– David Hackett Fischer[1]

The foregoing passage, drawn from Fischer's classic, *Historians' Fallacies,* proposes that history is a problem-solving exercise. Why did the Roman Empire fall? What factors accounted for the industrial revolution in Europe? Who assassinated John F. Kennedy? History is the study of such questions, just as sociology is the study of a rather different (though not unrelated) set of questions. Arguably, every field and subfield within the social sciences takes its cue from a set of core questions. Anthropology, economics, history, political science, psychology, and sociology are *all* problem-solving disciplines, in this minimal sense.

But where do these questions come from? What distinguishes a good question from a bad or uninteresting one? How do we distinguish between good and bad *answers* to these questions? I will argue that a limited set of criteria apply to all empirical propositions in the social sciences. This is to say, over and above field-specific desiderata we invoke certain common claims when judging goodness (adequacy, utility, truth) among arguments,

---

1. Fischer (1970: xv).

explanations, generalizations, hypotheses, inferences, laws, predictions, theories, theses, and other sorts of propositions.[2]

Let us consider some of the possibilities. Propositions should be true, rather than false. They should be clearly stated and theoretically informed. They should be lawlike, rather than ad hoc. They should be explanatory, and perhaps predictive, rather than merely descriptive. And so forth. Evidently, a much longer list of desiderata could be compiled. Surprisingly, no one has looked systematically at the question of propositional adequacy.[3] I will argue that all such claims can be resolved into ten criteria: *specification, accuracy, precision, breadth, depth, parsimony, analytic utility, innovation, intelligibility,* and *relevance,* as summarized in Table 5.1. Additional criteria apply to predictive and causal propositions, as explained in Chapters 6 and 7.

To be sure, writers will choose to privilege some criteria over others. Forming a proposition involves making choices among competing goods. But such choices involve costs, and it is in this sense that we may describe the framework as inherent to, and constitutive of, the enterprise of social science. A writer striving for breadth, who thereby compromises precision, is still liable to accusations of imprecision. Thus, although writers must reach accommodations among these demands in the context of a particular research agenda, the criteria themselves transcend these contextual concerns. With propositions, as with concepts, the terms of this negotiated tradeoff are persistent and irreducible.

Specification

One must know what a proposition is *about* in order to evaluate its truth or falsity. As Durkheim remarked a century ago, "a theory ... can be checked only if we know how to recognize the facts of which it is intended to give an account."[4] The first step down the road to empirical truth, therefore, is *specification.*[5]

---

2. A single work, therefore, will contain many small-order propositions, together with one or two umbrella-propositions that compose the main argument.
3. But see Eckstein (1975: 88), Hempel (1991: 81), King et al. (1994: ch 3), Kuhn (1977: 322), Lakatos (1978), Laudan (1977: 68; 1996: 18, 131–2), Levey (1996: 54), Przeworski and Teune (1970: 20–3), Simowitz and Price (1990), Stinchcombe (1968: 31), Van Evera (1997: 17–21), and Wilson (1998: 216).
4. Durkheim (1895/1964: 34).
5. One might also label this criterion *falsifiability,* and certainly the Popper oeuvre (e.g., Popper 1934/1968) is relevant to our discussion. As we noted in Chapter 1, however, this concept is too big for the job; it refers to a wide range of desiderata. We should take note of the fact that "specification" carries a different meaning in statistical analysis, where it refers to the problem of identifying the appropriate causal factors in a general model (see Chapters 8 and 9).

Table 5.1   *Propositions: General Criteria*

---

1. *Specification* (clarification, operationalization, falsifiability). (a.) What type of argument is being made (e.g., descriptive, predictive, causal)? (b.) What are the positive and negative outcomes (the factual and the counterfactual, or the range of variation) that the proposition describes, predicts, or explains? (c.) What is the set of cases (the population, context, domain, contrast-space, frame, or baseline), that the proposition is intended to explain? (d.) Is the argument internally consistent (does it imply contradictory outcomes)? (e.) Are the key terms operational?
2. *Accuracy* (truth, facticity, consistency, validity) (*antonyms:* bias, prejudice). Is the proposition accurate across the set of cases it purports to describe?
3. *Precision.* How precise is the proposition?
4. *Breadth* (scope, range, generality, population, explanatory or descriptive power). How many cases, and potential cases, are covered by the proposition?
5. *Depth* (richness, thickness, detail, evocativeness, completeness, configuration, holism). How many features of the case(s) are accounted for by the proposition?
6. *Parsimony* (economy, efficiency, simplicity, reduction, Ockham's razor). How parsimonious is the proposition?
7. *Analytic utility* (theoretical utility, consilience, logical economy in a field) (*antonyms:* idiosyncrasy, "adhocery"). How useful is the proposition in broader analytic contexts?
8. *Innovation.* How innovative is the proposition?
9. *Intelligibility.* How intelligible is the proposition (to a lay or academic audience)?
10. *Relevance* (societal significance). How relevant is the proposition (to a lay audience)? Does it matter? (So what?)

Specification begins with a clarification of the kind of argument, or mix of arguments, that the writer is intending to demonstrate or prove. In Chapter 6, we divide such propositions into three basic categories: description (comprising generalization and classification), prediction, and causal explanation. Granted, most work combines arguments of different sorts. Yet, this combination of propositions should be transparent; we ought to know, as readers, when an argument shifts ground. Regrettably, causal arguments are sometimes smuggled in under the guise of description (or vice versa). Consequently, we are left guessing as to the writer's intended argument. There is no excuse for this sort of subterfuge; the writer should tell us what she means to say.

Adequate specification also involves the clarification of a positive and negative outcome – a Y and a not-Y, a factual and a counterfactual – or a *range* of variation on Y (high-low, weak-strong) that the proposition is intended to describe, predict, or explain. Without such variation, the statement cannot be disproven. Usually, these counterfactuals are obvious from the context of an utterance. If I say "roses are red," then it is fairly clear that the negative outcome I am envisioning is blue, white, and all the other colors of the spectrum. Which is to say, if roses are found whose color is *not* red, then my statement has been proven false (at least, one hastens to add, in this particular case). But intuiting outcomes is not always so easy.

Suppose it is argued that the United States is a "liberal" society. What does this mean? What are the hallmarks of liberalism? What are the hallmarks of *non*-liberalism? It will be evident that the second question is often more revealing than the first. Louis Hartz, who authored the classic contemporary work on this subject, seems to have envisioned only two outcomes that were obviously and irrevocably nonliberal – socialism and feudalism.[6] Thus, a vast range of outcomes, including the New Deal and the expansion of the American state that it inaugurated, are considered fodder for Hartz's argument. This is not cause for rejecting the argument, but it may be cause for reevaluating its relevance. In any case, we have provided a more specific *content* for the familiar Hartzian thesis.[7]

Let us consider some other examples. When the legendary bank robber Willie Sutton was asked why he robbed banks he is supposed to have responded "because that's where the money is." Here, we have a situation in which the Y – and hence, the not-Y – is unclear. The questioner, a priest, understood the possible outcomes in terms of (a) robbing and (b) not robbing. For Willie Sutton, however, the possible outcomes were (a) robbing a bank and (b) robbing something else. Needless to say, a

---

6. See Hartz (1955).
7. Arguably, Hartz has stacked the deck in favor of his proposition; there are very few (and more to the point, very unlikely) contemporary conditions under which the liberal hypothesis might be refuted. Popper would call this sort of proposition "barely falsifiable," and so it is. This does not seem grounds, in and of itself, to rebuke Hartz. After all, we can think of many propositions that are pretty obviously true – and which it would be difficult to prove false – but which nonetheless seem important: "Racism is deleterious to the health of a community," "Mass attracts mass," "Japanese culture is group-oriented." The virtue of a proposition, I argue (pace Popper), derives not from whether it identifies a scarce set of confirming facts, or an abundant set of confirming facts – whether it is difficult or easy to confirm or falsify. It derives, rather, from whether these facts are well-specified (and of course, from various other desiderata, as discussed later).

proposition cannot be verified until the terms of this *Y*/not-*Y* relationship are established.[8]

Another way of stating this basic point is to say that in order to be meaningful a proposition must explain why one thing happened and other things did not. Otherwise, we are are not really explaining anything at all. Suppose I am trying to explain the causes of social inequality, but I claim to find inequality everywhere: in primitive societies and advanced industrial societies, in the West and the East, in contemporary eras and in ancient times. Nowhere do I find instances of equality, and I do not find useful ways of distinguishing between societies that possess variable degrees of equality. I might propose a number of causes of inequality but I will not be able to explain anything, since all my outcomes are the same (inequality). The only way this argument becomes viable as a causal inference is if I *imagine* variation on this dependent variable. I might say, for instance, that equality would appear if a society outlawed all forms of private property. Thus, the ubiquity of private property becomes the cause of inequality. The important point to note, for present purposes, is that the causal argument depends on this presumed variation in the outcome. Variation may be great, or it may be slight. It may be real or imaginary, as we have discussed. Variation, finally, need not occur in the case actually under study. If one is studying equality one may choose to focus one's efforts on *in*egalitarian societies. Similarly, a study of revolution might focus on nonrevolutionary societies. In all cases, however, outcome-variation is essential to determining what the explanation is actually explaining.[9]

Suppose, to take yet another example, we are trying to explain "government." Many possible ways of defining this term may be imagined. Consider three: (1) size of government, divided into two categories, big and small; (2) size of government, specified as a continuous variable (say, government expenditures); (3) existence of government, classified into two categories, government and no government. These three ways of conceiving the topic pose very different questions, and probably very different answers. The point is, we will not have any idea what we are explaining until we understand the range of outcomes the causal inference is expected to take into account.

One further example is pertinent to the vagaries of "outcome." If I ask why *A* died, one might answer: (a) *A* died because she was mortal; (b) *A* died because she had cancer; or (c) *A* died because her heart gave out. We

---

8. This example is discussed in Garfinkel (1981).
9. "Variation" is used in another – closely related – sense in Chapter 8, where it refers to properties of a *sample*.

can understand these different responses as answers to differently understood outcomes. In the first case, our possible outcomes are (a) die or (b)
not-die. We are asking, in other words, what are the necessary and sufficient reasons for *A*'s death *in general*. In the second case, we conceive of
A's eventual death as inevitable, and hence conceptualize outcomes as (a)
cancer or (b) all other possible causes of death. In the third, our outcomes
are (a) heart failure or (b) all other *immediate* causes of death.

This is complicated enough. But we must also consider our definition of
cases. A proposition is not fully specified until it has identified a set of
cases (a context, background, baseline, or contrast-space) that it purports
to explain. Thus, we might also understand these varying responses as
constituting the same outcome (life/death) within different temporal contexts. The first answer would make sense if we were asking about *A*'s death
at any point in time, or within some very long period of time (say, 500
years). The second answer would make sense if we were inquiring why *A*
died before the age of sixty (well before the life expectancy of someone in
her part of the world). The third answer might be correct if we are asking
why she died on some particular Thursday in the afternoon. Again, all
three answers are correct, but for different temporal contexts.

Confusions regarding temporal context embroil academic work.
Debate over the causes of the French Revolution, for example, reveal that
some writers are considering the question of why the French Revolution
(or something like it) occurred, period. Others are interested in the question of why it occurred in the eighteenth century. Still others speculate
about why it occurred in July of 1789.[10] Evidently, each temporal context sets the stage for different sorts of explanations. Similarly, a study of
warfare that places its subject within the larger context of western civi-
lization will reach quite different conclusions about the sources of mili-
tarism than one focused narrowly on the twentieth century. The subject
is nominally the same, but the answers suggested by these two radically
different contexts are likely to be quite different. A cause in one domain
may not be a cause in another.

Next, let us consider several spatial contexts: comparative reference
points at roughly the same points in time that form the background for
an explanation. Let us do so by returning to *A*'s unfortunate demise. Our
first hypothetical answer (she died because she was mortal) sounds silly
in most contexts that we are likely to encounter. Yet, suppose we are discussing a work of Greek literature, where mortals and immortals inter-
mix. In this context, answer (a) makes perfect sense, for it explains

10. See Kafker and Laux (1983).

variation across relevant cases. Similarly, if we are trying to explain *A*'s death to a child we might find ourselves saying that *A*, unlike the child's doll, is mortal. If our context consists of animate and inanimate objects, then the clarification "mortal" is explanatory.

The more usual-sounding second answer (she died because she had cancer) makes sense if we are comparing *A* to the general population, only some of whom have cancer. Again, the explanation works because it explains variation across a set of understood cases; once again, the sense of the explanation is dependent on a tacit agreement about this spatial context. If, however, we were reviewing the medical histories of patients in a cancer clinic it would be nonsensical to say, by way of explanation, that *A* died because she had cancer. When all patients are suffering from cancer, we do not explain any variation by pointing to this common factor. Rather, we assume cancer to be part of the generalized background against which a proper explanation takes place. For explanation, we will look for a factor that differentiates *A* from others within this particular context. Answer (c) – her heart gave out – will do service in this more restricted context.

One does not have to look far to discover social science examples of arguments over spatial context. Consider the numerous possible contexts provided by studies of social mobility. One might choose to explore the life-chances of a single individual – say, "Marge." In this sort of study, the most obvious context is probably her family, friends, or immediate community. One is asking, in effect, why Marge has achieved a particular socioeconomic status in comparison with others around her. Since her family, friends, and immediate community are likely to be of similar race, ethnicity, region, educational background, and social class, these are not likely to provide useful explanations for Marge's rise or fall (as the case may be). Rather, we will look to personal qualities, or personal influences (a well-connected grandfather, a mentor...), that differentiate Marge from those around her. Alternatively, we might decide upon the entire U.S. population – or the world's population, for that matter – as our benchmark in judging Marge's success/failure. This will produce a very different set of probable causes. Personal qualities and connections are unlikely to explain variation across this set of cases. Here, within this very different context, we will rely on broader demographic and geographic sorts of explanations.

All arguments work by separating a foreground from a background. The author of a proposition accomplishes this by constructing a particular context – spatial and temporal – within which an explanation is proffered. This central fact has been variously labeled the background, baseline, breadth, contrast-space, counterfactual, domain, frame, population, or scope of an explanation.[11] The problems posed by context arise when it is realized that there are many events occurring around any single outcome, any one of which might provide a context for explaining that outcome. In short, a writer's definition of context is often problematic. Explanation depends on context, but contexts are usually multiple. Indeed, when we find ourselves in debates over causation it is often because we have either failed to be clear about our context, or because two writers disagree about the most appropriate context for a given proposition (see discussion of "boundedness" later).

To rephrase: the description, prediction, or explanation of an outcome cannot be understood without contemplating the events that go on around it. My examples have focused mostly on causal analysis because this is usually the most confusing. Yet, clarity of context is necessary for *all* propositions to achieve specification. Consider the Hartz thesis as a purely descriptive proposition – America is liberal (leaving aside *why* it might be liberal). We have discussed why it is important to specify the nonliberal outcome, or outcomes. The proposition is *still* vague unless we have also specified the set of cases it is *implicitly* intended to describe – the background or contrast-cases. Usually these cases (formally, the population of the inference) are understood to be "Europe," or perhaps the OECD. Thus, Hartz's thesis might be restated: "America is uniquely liberal in the Anglo-European world." Indeed, if the context is broadened – to include the entire world – it is unlikely that the United States would still appear so unique vis-á-vis its European counterparts (with whom it might be said to share a common "liberal" political culture).

Clearly, the context that a writer chooses to provide the background for her explanation is critical to that explanation. Different contexts will provide varied explanations for the same phenomenon. About all we can say *in general* about the relative utility of different contexts is that the chosen context should fit the object of explanation *(Y)* in some plausible fashion. Marge is part of her immediate community, so this community provides an obvious context for explanation. Marge is also, albeit much more distantly and less distinctly, a member of the United States and of

---

11. See Collier and Mahoney (1996: 67), Garfinkel (1981), Goodman (1965: ch 1), Hawthorn (1991), Putnam (1978: 41–5; 1987: 3–40), Ragin and Becker (1992), and van Fraassen (1980: 115–57). For most intents and purposes, context is also equivalent to the breadth of a proposition. To inquire about the context of an explanation is to inquire about the class of cases – real or imagined – to which it applies. Yet, the context of a proposition is rarely understood in this technical and precise manner (as a set of cases); usually, it is a more informal understanding about the background to a particular explanation.

the world, so these contexts are also meaningful. Which context is best? There is little one can say, in general, about this question. It all depends on what one is trying to explain (indeed, it *is* what one is trying to explain). Here, we touch upon other desiderata, including breadth, depth, analytic utility, and relevance (discussed later). Contexts, we might say – with a full sense of the ambiguity of our statement – must be *appropriate* to the outcome under consideration.

Specification also demands *internal consistency* in the proposition. If the argument shifts (e.g., from a descriptive to a causal proposition), if the outcomes are unstable, or if the definition of the population changes, then we cannot consider a proposition to be properly specified. Effectively, we have not one proposition, but several. These several propositions must be reconciled before we can identify the truth or utility of any one of them.

Specification, finally, demands that key concepts be fully *operationalized*. Since we have already discussed operationalization at some length (in Chapter 3), there is no need to expatiate further, except to note that propositional goodness and conceptual goodness are inextricably intertwined. One cannot have a fully specified proposition without fully operational key concepts; the one is an extension of the other.

The specification criterion belabors the obvious. No one is likely to challenge the importance of clarifying arguments, outcomes and cases, maintaining internal consistency, and operationalizing key concepts. Yet, these desiderata are often honored in the breach, particularly in more popular styles of social science writing. The following passage is drawn from Francis Fukuyama's well-known *The End of History and the Last Man,* a national best-seller in the 1990s:

> Desire and reason are together sufficient to explain the process of industrialization, and a large part of economic life more generally. But they cannot explain the striving for liberal democracy, which ultimately arises out of *thymos,* the part of the soul that demands recognition. The social changes that accompany advanced industrialization, in particular universal education, appear to liberate a certain demand for recognition that did not exist among poorer and less educated people. As standards of living increase, as populations become more cosmopolitan and better educated, and as society as a whole achieves a greater equality of condition, people begin to demand not simply more wealth but recognition of their status. If people were nothing more than desire and reason, they would be content to live in market-oriented authoritarian states like Franco's Spain, or a South Korea or Brazil under military rule. But they also have a thymotic pride in their own self-worth, and this leads them to demand democratic governments that treat them like adults rather than children, recognizing their autonomy as free individuals. Communism is being superseded by liberal democracy

in our time because of the realization that the former provides a gravely defective form of recognition.[12]

Here is a theory that evidences none of the requirements of specification (at least, none that we might intuit from this enigmatic passage). What is the outcome the author is describing? It would appear to be "liberal democracy"; how, then, is this concept operationalized? More important, what is the causal mechanism that explains the victory of liberal democracy? Is it *thymos* – a universal part of the soul? If so, why do some parts of the world experience more liberal democracy than others? Perhaps it is because of "the social changes that accompany advanced industrialization, in particular education." If so, we may wonder about the necessity of *thymos* in this causal argument. Under this interpretation, does Fukuyama mean to say that democracy follows wherever industrialization occurs? What level of industrialization is necessary for democracy to be installed (and how should we measure "industrialization")?

The reader can probably think of many other propositions that are so vaguely constructed as to be virtually useless in interpreting the world around us. For many years, Marxist and New Left writers spoke of a "capitalist crisis" or a "crisis of the state." It was never particularly clear whether the crisis had already begun, would soon be upon us, or how we would know if either was the case. Conservatives, by contrast, are fond of notions like "moral crisis," and "crisis of law and order." Of all these statements we must ask (with appropriate consternation) *how do we know it when we see it?*

The latter examples are quasi-popular. Yet, even within the hard core of social science (in work written by academics for specialized academic audiences) a surprising quantity of work is underspecified. Indeed, wherever causal arguments draw on large paradigms (e.g., marxism, weberianism, modernization theory, deterrence theory, dependency theory, resource-mobilization theory, evolutionary theory, structural-functionalism, equilibrium theory, rational choice, and cultural theories of all stripes) writers are prone to specification problems. It is possible, and desirable, to convert a broad theoretical framework into a set of fully specified propositions. Even so, the problem of specification is not easily overcome, since other analysts may specify outcomes, cases, and concepts in different ways. If the theoretical framework is sufficiently broad and abstract, virtually *any* study can claim viability. Writer *A*'s study of modernization theory is fully specified, and so is Writer *B*'s; yet they argue differently when faced with the same general empirical data. Broad theoretical frameworks cannot escape this

12. Fukuyama (1992: xviii–ix).

basic-level conundrum; everything is "definitional." Enormous breadth and adequate specification are often at odds.

Similarly, a theory with only a few referents is *also* difficult to specify. This is the well-known "degree of freedom" problem discussed in Part III of the book. Again, the problem stems from the wide range of choice available to the writer in defining cases and outcomes. The topic of revolution is bedeviled by the pliability of this key term. Some restrict it to social revolutions; some broaden the topic to include coups d'etat. Evidently, each definition of outcome is likely to identify a somewhat different set of precipitating causes. Even more complex is the identification of background cases (nonrevolutions).

This, in a nutshell, is the Scylla and Charybdis that "middle-range" theory is designed to avoid.[13] Theories of the middle range should be broad enough to identify a more or less obvious set of referents as cases and outcomes, but not so large as to cause formidable problems of specification. As an ideal, we can all subscribe to the virtues of middle-range theory. Yet, it is not clear how one could avoid broad theoretical frameworks, since we require large analytic bundles to tie our middle-range theories together, as well as to suggest what those middle-range theories might be. The problem of specification, therefore, is intrinsic to the enterprise of social science.

Accuracy

We should like propositions that are fully specified, but not merely specified. We should also like them to be true. Since truth is usually a matter of more or less, rather than yes or no (few propositions in the social sciences are completely and entirely false), I will refer to this quality as *accuracy,* or lack of bias.

Oddly enough, the criterion of accuracy requires some preliminary justification. For several generations, historians and philosophers have been reacting against what we now view as a naive inductivism: that the social scientist's task is "simply to show how it really was *(wie es eigentlich gewesen)*."[14] Ranke's infamous words are so evidently wrong that it is easy to dismiss their rightness. It is easy to forget, in other words, the extent to which the facticity of events acts as a worthy constraint on scholarly debate.

As Marc Bloch sat down to write *The Historian's Craft* in or about 1941 (we do not know precisely), he dealt at length with a subject that

---

13. See Merton (1949/1968).
14. Ranke, quoted in Carr (1961: 5).

was being actively, and for a time, successfully, suppressed all around him. In careful and painstaking prose Bloch set down what he called a "critical method" of using and interpreting evidence so as to be sure that one's conclusions are in accordance with *wie es eigentlich gewesen.* Hannah Arendt, who was fortunate enough to live through the horrors of the Holocaust (Bloch was imprisoned for his role in the Resistance, tortured, and murdered shortly before the end of the war), also experienced firsthand the efforts of collaborators and participants in the Nazi regime to write history in ways that were not recommended by Bloch's manual. "Facts inform opinions," writes Hannah Arendt, "and opinions, inspired by different interests and passions, can differ widely and still be legitimate *as long as they respect factual truth.*"[15] Where these factual truths are not respected – as in Nazi Germany or Soviet-era Russia – social science cannot thrive.

The facts of a case are not always apparent. But where they *are,* the existence of these facts is a healthy tonic for the imagination. Arendt relates a conversation between Clemenceau and a representative of the Weimar Republic over the question of Germany's guilt in the outbreak of World War I. "'What, in your opinion,' Clemenceau was asked, 'will future historians think of this troublesome and controversial issue?' He replied, 'This I don't know. But I know for certain that they will not say Belgium invaded Germany.'"[16] There is a certain hardness, a facticity, to facts like these. Caesar, we are certain, crossed the Rubicon; it was not the Amazon. All but the most passionate conspiracy theorists believe that Neil Armstrong landed on the moon on July 20, 1969. (It was not a studio stage set up to look like the moon.) Arendt notes that it would take something like world domination to suppress, or even significantly revise, such matters. In Gunnar Myrdal's words, "Facts kick."[17]

One would like to think that matters of fact are usually respected in scholarly circles. Alas, as Richard Hamilton has demonstrated, errors of a factual nature are alarmingly common. The medieval world was *not* unanimous in believing that the world was flat; this was a myth propagated by nineteenth-century writers seeking to convince themselves of their enlightenment (relative to the "medieval" beliefs of preceding centuries). Mozart did *not* die poor, forgotten, and forlorn. Wellington, so far as we can tell, did *not* say "The Battle of Waterloo was won on the playing fields of Eton." Hitler's electoral support in the Weimar elections

15. Arendt (1968: 238); emphasis added.
16. Arendt (1968: 239).
17. Myrdal (1970: 20).

of 1932 did *not* come primarily from the lower middle class. Weber's theory connecting the rise of capitalism to Protestantism was based, in part, on faulty statistics from another work, which Weber copied into a table. (The resulting column adds up to 109%.)[18]

These are fairly easy cases. As we have observed, most propositions are not so obviously true or false. Consider Hamilton's portrayal of Foucault's controversial work *Discipline and Punish*. Foucault, Hamilton writes:

> has provided an account of a shadowy "power" that successfully imposed a system of discipline and control on all aspects of modern society. This portrait is a misconstruction involving serious errors or, more precisely, gross misrepresentation of the events discussed. His account of the panopticon and its influence is a whole cloth fiction. As seen, his depiction of modern institutional history is based on Bentham's rejected plan. The Prussian infantry of the eighteenth century was certainly no fiction but, contrary to Foucault's bold declaration, it was not imitated by the whole of Europe. Military practice, within decades, was to follow an entirely different course. The Foucault "constructions" come with an appearance of scholarly support – that is, with footnotes, references, and the suggestion of documentation – but his own references tell another story. The most striking example, the day-to-night transformation, is his use of Bentham's *Works*.[19]

What we have here, it seems, are not so much factual *errors* (although, Hamilton thinks, there are some of these as well) as the misrepresentation of a historical record, a biased account of what happened and what it meant. Indeed, it is easy to see that most of the propositions that cause trouble in the social sciences are somewhere between facts and interpretations of facts.

However it is that we distinguish between truth and falsehood (a matter taken up in Part III of the book), it seems clear that it is the former that we are interested in obtaining. Any proposition that is factually untrue is less useful on this account. Recording errors, computing errors, partial evidence, and willfully altered evidence, do not conform to standards of truth in the social sciences (or anywhere else, one might add). Although we may never be able to specify a general procedure for distinguishing between truth and falsehood, we should never forget the importance of defending this imaginary line in the sand. "To leave error unrefuted," wrote Marx, "is to encourage intellectual immorality."[20]

---

18. See Hamilton (1996). See Fischer (1970) and Winks (1969) for additional examples in the field of history.
19. Hamilton (1996: 194).
20. Quoted in Thompson (1978: epigraph).

Precision

A proposition may be fully specified and factually accurate, but still not satisfy our intuitive sense of saying something interesting or useful. Consider the plight of the Cape Cod bourgeoisie:

> On Cape Cod where the pace of life is unhurried and casual you may ask a craftsman in June when he will come to repair your fence. If he answers, "Sometime in autumn," he is being accurate, but not precise. If he answers "Ten a.m., October 2," he is being precise, but not accurate – it is almost certain that on October 2, the fish will be running and he will be out on his boat.[21]

Comte, along the same lines, offers the example of a statement – "the sum of the angles of a triangle is equal to three right angles" – which is extremely precise, but lacks something in the accuracy department.[22] Evidently, propositions may be extremely precise ("Tomorrow, at 3:450030003 P.M., there will be 83.555% humidity, and the temperature will be 25.33443 degrees Celsius, at the corner of Bleecker and Sixth") and false. Indeed, as our previous example demonstrated, accuracy and precision are often at odds with one another. Nor is it clear that we need such extreme precision even if we could reliably obtain it.[23] Clearly, there is more to inferential goodness than the achievement of precision. But the general point still holds: precise statements tell us more; they contain more information than general, approximate, or "perhaps" statements.

Economists, for example, are supposed to tell us how the economy will be performing at various points in the future. Yet, as McCloskey points out, such forecasting is often fairly vague. "Forecasting the end of prosperity ... in the next 19 months is ... little better than saying that if it is August then southern Florida has a fair chance after a while of getting a hurricane."[24] We would like to know, more precisely, when that downturn is going to hit. Otherwise, the information is not very useful. Economists, noted Sidney Webb, "are generally right in their predictions, but generally a good deal out in their dates."[25] Precision matters.

The importance of precision can be seen in the distinction among *nominal, ordinal,* and *interval* measures, as laid out at the beginning of Chapter 7. Interval measurements, as most readers will know, are the

21. Kamarck (1983: 2), quoted in Mayer (1993: 23).
22. Comte (1975: 97).
23. This speaks to the *relevance* and *analytic utility* criteria discussed later. See also Adams (1965), and Adams and Adams (1987).
24. McCloskey (1992: 33).
25. Quoted in McCloskey (1992: 33).

most precise (followed by ordinal and nominal measurements), which is to say, they contain the most information about the subject at hand. A continuous measure tells us not only how *A* differs from *B*, but also by how much. To be sure, interval measures are not always accurate, particularly when nominal or ordinal measures are converted into interval variables for use in statistical analysis – another example of tradeoffs among different criteria.[26] The larger point remains: ceteris paribus, we will prefer indicators that are precise.

Breadth

If the fundamental purpose of social science is to tell us about the world, then it stands to reason that a proposition informing us about many events is, by virtue of this fact, more useful than a proposition pursuant to only a few events. I will refer to this desideratum as *breadth,* or generality. One wishes, when forming propositions, to capture as many events as possible. The more events one can describe, predict, and/or explain with a given proposition (ceteris paribus) the more powerful that proposition. Propositions of great breadth tell us more about the world by explaining larger portions of that world.

"There is no value in isolated facts for science, however striking and novel they might seem," Malinowski writes in his anthropological classic, *The Argonauts of the Western Pacific.* "Genuine scientific research differs from mere curio-hunting in that the latter runs after the quaint, singular and freakish – the craving for the sensational and the mania of collecting providing its twofold stimulus. Science on the other hand has to analyse and classify facts in order to place them in an organic whole, to incorporate them in one of the systems in which it tries to group the various aspects of reality."[27] Science generalizes.

Of course, different disciplines are differently enamored of breadth as an analytic goal. Historians commonly develop propositions whose range encompasses only a single event: the Spanish Civil War, the decline of the English aristocracy, the French Revolution, or the lives of individuals (biography). Economists, political scientists, and sociologists, by contrast,

---

26. As King et al. (1994: 151) point out, "quantitative research produces more precise (numerical) measures, but not necessarily more accurate ones." For classic work on measurement theory, see Fishburn (1985), Marks (1974), Mitchell (1990), Roberts (1976), and Stevens (1946) – all cited in Collier (1998).
27. Malinowski (1922/1984: 509). See also Easton (1953: 55), Kincaid (1990/1994), Lakatos (1978: 33), Laudan (1977), Levey (1996), McIntyre (1996), Przeworski and Teune (1970: 4), Scriven (1962), Skyrms (1980), and the work of other naturalistically inclined scholars like Carl Hempel and Ernest Nagel.

are wont to talk about larger subjects: revolutions, wars, the behavior of social classes, and the like. This is one way to describe the difference between work that is "idiographic" and that which is "nomothetic."

Yet, it would be a mistake to conclude that the traditional historian is utterly unconcerned with breadth. To begin with, any statement at all about the empirical world involves considerable abstraction from reality. Summarizing an individual's life, even in the context of several volumes (the most idiographic of all historical genres), necessitates many generalizations. Breadth, like our other desiderata, is obviously a matter of degree. Moreover, although we are wont to speak of events like revolutions constituting (individually) a single "case" or event, it may be more accurate to understand these large events as encompassing hundreds, if not thousands, of micro events (cases within cases) (see Chapter 8). From this perspective, the idiograph's breadth is just as capacious as the nomothet's: both sustain generalizations over scores of cases. For the moment, it is sufficient to observe that the traditional historian or anthropologist has not entirely absolved herself of the quest for analytic reduction.

Indeed, what idiographically inclined writers cringe at in work of great breadth is not really breadth per se, but rather the sacrifice such breadth may bring along other criteria (accuracy, precision, depth, and so forth). We conclude, therefore, that a proposition with a larger explanandum is *always* better, with the usual ceteris paribus qualification.

Depth

Perhaps the primary antagonism to breadth in a proposition is *depth*. While a broad proposition explains something across many cases, a deep proposition explains a lot about a single case, or a small set of cases. Depth fulfills a central goal of social science – to tell us as much as possible about the empirical world – by peering deeply into a small portion of that world. One might also call it informativeness, completeness, richness, thickness, or detail.[28]

"America is a country of individualists." "George is an observant Jew." "The Civil War was a bitter contest over identity, property, and sovereignty." These propositions, and others like them, qualify as deep. There is a lot more we could say about them. They are evocative, and being

---

28. The virtues of depth have been trumpeted under many names – for example, "thick description" (Geertz 1973), "configurative analysis" (Heckscher 1957: 46–51, 85–107; Katznelson 1997b), "contrast of contexts" (Skocpol and Somers 1980), or "holistic analysis" (Ragin 1987). See also Almond and Genco (1977/1990), Collier (1993), Eidlin (1983), Feagin et al. (1991), and Hirschman (1970b).

evocative, are likely to translate into studies of some length. Historical work, anthropological work, case studies of any variety – indeed, most work that takes descriptive proposition as central to its mission – are likely to provide accounts with great depth. It is no wonder that books are prized over articles in these fields. There are few shortcuts to depth.

The absence of depth is perhaps most noticeable in statistical studies, where large areas of human activity may be reduced to a single indicator: the complex subject of ethnicity becomes an index of ethnic fragmentation, the subject of public health is indexed through mortality rates, and so forth. Propositions based on statistical indicators often do not tell us very much beyond the parameters of the quantitative indicator. What does it *mean* if an index of ethnic fragmentation is high? What difference does it make to people in those societies? What sense do they make of it? How, if at all, does it constrain their behavior? A statistic may mean quite a lot; all these questions may be answered. In this case, we will refer to the proposition as deep. But if we do not know, or have reason to doubt, that this index indicates anything beyond a raw number, then we rightly call it *thin*.

These are the sorts of questions that scholars in the interpretivist tradition have been asking of social science for many years. And they are good questions. Social science cannot evade the call for rich, evocative analysis. Thick description offers advantages over thin description, and thick theories over thin theories: they tell us more about a particular case. Thin description, of course, may be able to tell us more about a *range* of cases. Here we see a struggle at the heart of many academic disputes. Some writers find it more satisfying to explain a little about a lot; others prefer to tell us a lot about a little. In statistical terms this conflict may be phrased as the choice between explaining 10% of the variance across 100 cases or 90% of the variance across 10 cases. Weber notes, "the more comprehensive the validity, – or scope – of a term, the more it leads us away from the richness of reality since in order to include the common elements of the largest possible number of phenomena, it must necessarily be as abstract as possible and hence *devoid* of content."[29] Because both breadth and depth are rightly prized, there is no easy solution to this conundrum. Indeed, social science is continually plagued by the question of whether it is better to tell the reader a little about a lot

29. Weber (1905/1949: 80). Weber's conclusion is that "in the cultural sciences, the knowledge of the universal or general is never valuable in itself" (ibid.). Yet, we might also note that Weber's work is replete with propositions of vast scope. Thus, rather than placing Weber entirely in the interpretivist camp it makes more sense to see him as exemplary of a struggle at the heart of social science – between breadth and depth.

of things, or a lot about one thing. Perhaps no other conflict does more to differentiate the fields of cultural anthropology and history from political science, sociology, and economics.[30]

It is important to recognize that narrative in and of itself does not ensure deep analysis, just as statistical work does not lead inexorably to thin, or reductive, analysis. One can think of many prose artists whose forte is the sweeping generalization. One can think of an equal number of statistical studies that are extraordinarily rich in detail.[31] The trend toward in-depth, open-ended interviewing – often side by side with standardized survey formats – may be viewed as an attempt to increase depth in studies of public opinion.[32] In any case, the demand for "analysis," "understanding," or "explanation" is, among other things, a call for depth.

Parsimony

Like a lever, a good proposition lifts heavy weight with a moderate application of force. It is powerful, and its power derives from its capacity to describe, predict, or explain a lot with a minimal expenditure of verbal energy. Such a proposition is *parsimonious*. If, on the other hand, a proposition is not summarized, if it is necessary to wade through several hundred pages of prose in order to obtain the meaning, and if that meaning (once the wading is finished) cannot be reduced to shorter form, then the impact of the proposition has been muted. Such a proposition is turgid.[33]

Some clarification is in order. First, one ought not think of parsimony as being at war with the length of a given work. Evidently, a long work may be constructed so as to provide evidence for a pithy proposition. Here, one might consider the work of Charles Darwin, Karl Marx, Adam Smith, Herbert Spencer, and Oswald Spengler. None of these men were known for their shortness of breath. All, however, are known for their parsimonious theories. In short, parsimony does not preclude length, though it does call for some sort of summary statement so that the larger proposition at-hand is apparent to the reader.[34] Similarly, if a

---

30. For discussions of this conflict, see Eidlin (1983), Gottschalk (1963), Kiser and Hechter (1991), Lipset and Hofstadter (1968), and Ragin and Becker (1992).
31. See, for example, Campbell et al. (1960), and Verba et al. (1995).
32. See, for example, Lane (1962) and Mansbridge (1983).
33. For work on the interrelated questions of reduction, simplicity, and parsimony, see Friedman (1972), Glymour (1980), Hesse (1974), King et al. (1994: 20), Popper (1934/1968), Quine (1966), and Sober (1975, 1988).
34. Contemporary examples of parsimony coexisting with plenitude can be found in Collier and Collier (1991) and Fischer (1989). Some long books, however, offer virtually no attempt at synopsis at all. See, for example, Gay (1984–98), Kantorowicz (1957), and Pocock (1975).

given work is pursuing a multitude of propositions, rather than one single argument, as is common in history and anthropology, then it seems appropriate to judge parsimony in reference to the particular propositions in question rather than the length of the book or article itself.

Parsimony is good *not* because we assume that simplicity conforms to the natural order of things, and is therefore more "true," as some have argued for the natural sciences.[35] It is for pragmatic, rather than ontological, reasons that we invoke Ockham's razor. We need to bring knowledge together in reasonably compact form in order for that knowledge to serve a useful purpose. Reduction is useful. A 3,000-page treatise on Belgian beer does not reduce one's information costs appreciably. One could go there and research the subject oneself in the time it would take to master such a tome – a far preferable option where many of us are concerned.

Analytic Utility

Propositions, even those basic truths we refer to as "facts," do not stand alone. They relate to a broader field of propositions. Comte's observations on this score, while basic and perhaps obvious, deserve reiteration:

> If it is true that every theory must be based upon observed facts, it is equally true that facts cannot be observed without the guidance of some theory. Without such guidance, our facts would be desultory and fruitless; we could not retain them: for the most part we could not even perceive them.[36]

Insofar as a given proposition proves useful within a broader theoretical context, we may say that it possesses *analytic utility,* or logical economy. Thus, conditions, observations, and variables generally take their place within the broader rubric of an argument, hypothesis, law, theory, or thesis. And the latter may fit within a research tradition or paradigm, or a theory of a higher order of magnitude. Propositions are useful insofar as they fit within other propositions. The proposition that sits by itself in a corner is likely to be dismissed as "ad hoc," or "idiosyncratic." It does not fit with our present understanding of the world. It refuses to cumulate. It has little analytic utility.

Of course, deviant propositions may be extremely useful in the long run. Indeed, the first sign of breakdown in a broad theory or paradigm is the existence of observations, or small-order theories, that cannot eas-

35. King et al. (1994: 20, 104) take this view of parsimony and reject it on those grounds. If interpreted as a *pragmatic* norm, however, it might not be rejected by the authors. See, for example, their discussion of the importance of leverage ("explaining as much as possible with as little as possible" [1994: 29]).

36. Comte (1975: 73).

ily be made sense of. Yet, until such time as a new theory or paradigm can be constructed (one that would gather the new proposition together with the old in a single overarching framework) it may truly be said of the wayward proposition that it is not useful, or less useful.

Analytic utility might be thought of as a demand for parsimony, but at a broader scale. Rather than referring to the qualities of individual concepts and propositions (both of which, I argue, respond to demands for parsimony), we are concerned with the way in which two or more propositions relate to one another. To what extent does a given proposition contribute to parsimony *in the social sciences at-large?* Ernst Mach saw the fundamental project of science in the effort to produce "the completest possible presentment of facts with the *least possible expenditure of thought.*"[37] Einstein, several decades later, endorsed "the effort to reduce all concepts and correlations to as few as possible logically independent basic concepts and axioms."[38] More recently, Edward O. Wilson has argued that "there is only one class of explanation. It traverses the scales of space, time, and complexity to unite the disparate facts of the disciplines by *consilience,* the perception of a seamless web of cause and effect."[39]

We are likely to experience considerably less success in this endeavor in the social sciences than Mach, Einstein, and Wilson envision for the natural sciences. Logical economy must be considered a matter of degrees. But this should not blind us to the need for logical economy, and the utility of such economy as we already enjoy. We are accustomed, for example, to categorizing works into various traditions – Durkheimian, Weberian, Marxist, Freudian, rational choice, behavioralist – and into smaller niches defined by particular subfields. This sort of grouping makes the academic enterprise manageable, to the extent that it is manageable at all. (Imagine if we had no such pigeonholes!) Whether we can do better at this, whether we can create something closer to what Einstein had in mind for the physical sciences, remains an open question. As with other criteria, we may simply conclude that were it possible, ceteris paribus, it would surely be desirable.

Innovation

"An author is little to be valued," says Hume in his characteristically blunt fashion, "who tells us nothing but what we can learn from every

37. Mach (1902/1953: 450–1).
38. Einstein (1940/1953: 253). See also Mill (1843/1872: 143–4), Homans (1967; cited in Rule 1997: 176), and King et al. (1994: 15–7). What I refer to as analytic utility or logical economy is similar to "coherence" approaches to truth, as that term is employed in epistemology and philosophy of science. See Kirkham (1992) and Laudan (1996: 79).
39. Wilson (1998: 291), emphasis added.

coffee-house conversation."[40] Indeed, we should like a proposition to be not just true, but also new, or reasonably so. Having discussed various meanings for truth, what about *innovation*?

It is difficult to know what to say about such an obvious desideratum. We do not want to be forever reinventing the wheel. To be sure, we need to know if things that were once true are still equally so. There *is* a point to retesting old hypotheses on new data, or in different situations. But there is less point to such a study if the result is entitled *Plus ca change...* The more a study (or a single proposition) differs from present views of a given subject – either in empirical findings or in theoretical framework – the greater its level of innovation. Marx was more innovative than Plekhanov, Weber more innovative than Parsons, and so forth.

Claims for innovation are traditionally established at the outset of a work, where the writer clarifies how her approach to the subject at-hand differs from previous efforts. The unfortunate tendency is to exaggerate one's claim to innovation by denigrating those who came before. Even so, this species of intellectual one-upmanship speaks to the general desideratum of innovation, which we are all obliged to strive for. A study that does *not* innovate – one that merely rearranges what we already know – rightly begins with an apology. Most telling of all is the study that refuses to engage the existing literature. Such a study leaves the reader in the dark as to its level of innovation, a highly unsatisfactory state of affairs.

Innovation is occasionally in conflict with analytic utility, for it is difficult to be different and assimilable in the same gesture. Yet one can make efforts in this direction by specifying how a proposition reorganizes existing work on a subject. Einstein, to take an extreme example, took the physical world apart and put it back together again. Something of this sort, though of a much lesser order, is required of all writers whose claims to innovation leave them at odds with existing analytic structures.

Both analytic utility and innovation prompt us to consider the extent to which propositions take form and meaning from their place within a broader scholarly tradition. In this, social science follows the way of all language communities: what is said at one juncture depends very much on what is said at previous junctures.[41] Call it cumulation, progress, evolution, or simply *change*. It is nonetheless clear that analytic utility and innovation cannot be established – indeed, are meaningless – without considering a proposition's contribution to a *canon* of work on a subject. Social science, to the extent that it achieves

40. Hume (1985: 254).
41. See Gadamer (1975).

coherence and unity at all (a matter discussed in Chapter 2) does so by continual reference to itself. Thus, although we have taken concepts, propositions, and research designs as our primary unit of analysis in this book we must be conscious that these building blocks of social science can be evaluated only in light of the larger, ongoing project that is social science.

Intelligibility

It is difficult to imagine a relevant work that is not also, at least minimally, understandable. Indeed, *intelligibility* may be one of the chief criteria distinguishing social science from the humanities and the natural sciences. Let us consider this argument briefly.

Within the humanities some writers are fairly easy for the general reader to digest. One thinks, for example, of essayists like George Orwell, George Steiner, E. B. White, and Edmund Wilson – all masters of lucidity and enemies of pretense. Continuing an old and venerable tradition of arts and letters, these writers saw their work as an extension of critical thinking and cultivated living, not as a specialized product of academic endeavor. In the past half-century, however, the most influential figures in the humanities, writers such as Theodore Adorno, Paul DeMan, Jacques Derrida, Michel Foucault, Jurgen Habermas, Fredric Jameson, and Jacques Lacan, have chosen to depart from the common tongue. In its place they have substituted their own idiomatic lexicons and locutions, which readers must master before a text becomes (at least minimally) comprehensible. (Even so, legions of critics and supporters argue over the meanings contained in writings produced by these masters of literary intrigue.) Under the spur of "theory," the fields of the humanities have moved with great verve and determination to sever lines of communication once connecting them to the broader culture. Culture, in the academy of today, is neither high culture nor popular culture; it is *academic* culture.[42]

Partisans of deconstruction may reasonably protest that it is not the primary goal of the humanities to achieve a readily accessible format. If denizens of the academy maintain principled positions outside the norms and conventions of popular culture, perhaps they are serving their

---

42. See Jacoby (1987). The point is also made by Karl Popper in his debate with Adorno and colleagues, whom he accuses of practicing a "cult of un-understandability" (quoted in Gellner 1985: 5). The irony is greatest among those critics of bourgeois intellectual life, the presumed champions of a more open and democratic academy, who are themselves obscure to the point of hilarity.

purpose better than if conforming slavishly to the status quo. It is perhaps not altogether a bad thing if the academy serves as a bastion of high culture in a world taken over (so it sometimes seems) by vulgar, commodified forms of art and entertainment.

I have presented this debate in rather stark terms precisely because it does not seem to me to be easily resolvable. It is a debate at the heart of the humanities, where the call of aesthetic excellence is so often at war with the call for general acclaim. In short, there would seem to be no a priori demand for intelligibility in the fields comprising the humanities.

In the social sciences things are different. If social science is to have any effect at all other than achieving job tenure for its practitioners it must find ways of translating its wisdom into the vernacular.

The special need for intelligibility becomes clearer still if we contrast the social sciences with their cousins on the other end of the academic spectrum. Natural science may also influence a broader public, as, for example, in debates over evolution, global warming, and genetics. But it need not, and usually does not. One does not need to know much about climatology in order to make use of the weather report, of medical science in order to make use of radiation therapy, or of computer science in order to use a computer. Arguably, natural science has had the greatest effect over human lives in areas where ordinary men and women have been most ignorant of the science involved.

The subjects of social science are different in that they require decisions on the part of the lay public. It is no use discovering the benefits and drawbacks of an electoral system if one cannot influence public debate on electoral reform. Knowledge about the effects of public and private investment do not bring any benefits at all if economists are the only holders of that knowledge.[43] Whatever sociologists may learn about the sources of racism will not help anyone overcome this condition if sociologists are the sole repositories of this truth. A tree felled in the social science forest makes no sound.

Of course, bureaucratic policymakers are often specialists and may be expected to understand a more technical level of discourse than the mass public. Even so, the top of the governmental pyramid is populated by decision makers who do *not* generally possess the requisite time and training to follow complex technical arguments. Politicians would like to know how to keep inflation under control without

---

43. "The economist who wants to influence actual policy choices must in the final resort convince ordinary people, not only his confreres among the economic scientists," notes Gunnar Myrdal (1970: 450–1).

having to master the dismal science. Generally, they do not hold degrees in social science disciplines, nor are they in the habit of reading scholarly journals.

All of this does not mean that specialized journals should be shut down in preference for mass-circulation magazines and Web sites. It *does* mean that whatever arguments are developed in those journals must, eventually, filter down to a broader audience. In order to make sure that this occurs, or at least has some chance of occurring, social science must be intelligible.

The problem of intelligibility, we might note, applies equally in democratic and nondemocratic settings. Kings, oligarchs, and generals, like the people they rule over, are disinclined to school themselves in the wiles of multiple regression and path analysis. Bringing social science to the people, in this sense, is directly analogous to bringing social science to the prince. Machiavelli, like Mill, must speak in a language that can be generally understood.

What, then, makes a work intelligible? Perhaps the most important criterion is something that I shall call (albeit vaguely) good writing. A work should be coherently organized, so as not to endlessly repeat its points; writing should employ standard English and a minimum of jargon; and so forth.[44] In contrast to writing in other venues, good social science writing should privilege clarity and simplicity. Writers should state their arguments explicitly, rather than leaving matters hanging. Readers should not have to guess at an author's intended meaning. When reading works of certain writers (e.g., Bourdieu, Foucault, Parsons, Pocock, Unger, Wuthnow) one feels that skills of interpretation worthy of a biblical exegete are required in order to decipher the passages. Subsequent debate over an author's argument is a sign that a writer has not paid sufficient attention to the criterion of intelligibility. Unclear writing, even if wonderfully elegant and entertaining at the level of the sentence or paragraph, is bad social science. Indeed, social science's greatest failing may have little to do with "methodology," as conventionally understood, but rather with the more mundane problem of effective communication.

Insofar as social science strives for intelligibility, we are well-advised to stick as closely as we can to the terms of everyday discourse. "Fetishism of the Concept," as C. Wright Mills calls it, obscures what we already know by renaming it, and obscures genuinely new insights by cloaking

---

44. For further pointers, see general manuals of style (e.g., Strunk and White), or manuals focused on social science writing (e.g., Becker 1986).

them in a novel vocabulary.[45] To construct social science in abstruse theoretical or mathematical languages subverts the goal of communicating the truths of social science to a broader audience.

Of course, communication failures are not always the fault of the social scientist. Social science methods are sometimes irreducibly complex. One cannot expect the average lay reader to understand multiple regression. Yet, we *can* expect the social scientist to summarize her findings in plain English, perhaps relegating technical discussion to footnotes, tables, methods chapters, or appendices. If the logic of an argument cannot be communicated in everyday language, it is not likely to be very logical at all. Walt Rostow once noted, by way of excuse for a rather nontechnical essay in economic history, "there are devices of obscurity and diversionary temptations that are denied the teacher of undergraduates."[46] I think we can take this justification more seriously than Rostow perhaps intended. Writing for a lay audience requires a clarity of exposition that we often overlook in specialized academic work, where the invocation of key buzzwords and citations to the literature may substitute for clear argument. If some writers look upon the task of communicating with a lay audience as burdensome, perhaps it is just the sort of burden they should be required to carry.

To clarify: I am not arguing that all social science must be conducted in everyday language. Rather, I am pointing out that all propositions, in order to impact the lives of citizens, must *at some point* be translated into the vernacular. A theory that cannot be understood, is for that reason alone, less useful. A theory that has a wider range of comprehensibility, whose argument can be grasped by greater numbers of the general public, is (ceteris paribus) a better theory.

Relevance

"One of the perplexing commonplaces of the university lecture hall," wrote Robert Lynd in 1939, "is the fact that whole courses and batter-

---

45. Mills (1959: 35). I discuss this subject in Chapter 3. We might conclude, with Bentham (1834/1952: 11): "Let the workshop of invention be shut up forever, rather than that the eardrum of taste should be grated by a new sound!" See also Connolly (1974/1983), Mahon (1998), Oppenheim (1975), and Pitkin (1972). At the same time, it should be remembered that there are occasional cases of legitimate neologism (where no existing word says precisely what the author has in mind). Indeed, every word we now possess, in social science and in ordinary language, was born of an act of neologism; so we must retain a half-open mind about such matters.

46. Rostow (1960: x).

ies of courses leading to advanced degrees are 'passed' and dissertations are written without the question's ever being raised as to what is to be done with all this knowledge – other than to give more lectures and to supervise the writing of more dissertations. A student may sit through an entire year of admirably analytic lectures on the structure and function-ing of an important current institution – e.g., our economic productive system – without the lecturer's once raising the direct question: What do we human beings want this particular institutional-complex to do for us, what is the most direct way to do it, and what do we need to know in order to do it?"[47] Lynd raises an important – some would say obvious – point. No matter how virtuous a proposition may be on other criteria, if it cannot pass the *so what?* test it is not worth very much. Propositions, large or small, have various levels of *relevance*. There are some things that, however much we may sympathize with the author, we are not bothered to argue about.

Here, I am not talking about relevance within a theoretical or classifi-catory framework (which I have called analytic utility), but rather rele-vance to the lay public. "In human affairs," writes Barrington Moore,

> the mere fact of uniformity or regularity, expressible in the form of a scien-tific law, may often be quite trivial. To know that Americans drive on the right hand side of the street is to know something that permits predictions about American behavior and meets all the formal requirements of a gen-eralizing science. Such knowledge does not, however, meet the criterion of significance.[48]

There are many ways one might claim relevance for a proposition or a study. One could claim to be addressing a point of general interest, a point of general need, or a question that *should be* considered a point of general interest. One need not attach a policy recommendation to a study in order to claim relevance (although, to be sure, policy recom-mendations always enhance the relevance of a study).

It seems fair to judge the proposition that possesses relevance superior (ceteris paribus) to one that does not. And it seems fair to ask writers to justify the reader's potential expenditure of time, effort, and money with some sort of payback. This is traditionally handled in the preface of a book or article, where the author tries to find a hook (a point of general interest) to hang her argument. Whether the author's hook catches its fish (i.e., compels the reader to delve further into the text) may be con-

---

47. Lynd (1939/1964: 129).
48. Moore (1958: 129). See also King et al. (1994: 15) and Van Evera (1997).

sidered the practical test of relevance. Readers are not likely to be carried very far on the strength of a writer's method or prose if they do not feel that there is something important at stake in the investigation. They must care about the outcome.[49]

But the relevance of relevance is not limited to one's choice of topic. This criterion also helps to identify salient factors in causal argument. Consider the following example, courtesy of Patrick Gardiner. "When the causes of war are being investigated," writes Gardiner, "it may be decided that both economic factors and human psychology are relevant to its outbreak; yet since we deem it to be within our power to influence or alter the economic system of a society, whereas the control of human psychology seems, at least at present, to be beyond our capacity, we are likely to regard the economic rather than the psychological factors as the 'cause' of war."[50] Similarly, in discussions of social policy, causal arguments that rest upon deep-seated political-cultural factors are less interesting than arguments resting on particular events and decisions. The notion that Clinton's health care initiatives failed because of American individualism is (ceteris paribus) less interesting than the argument that it failed because of poor judgment on the part of the Clinton administration. The former implies that there is not much that we can do about health care reform, like it or not; the latter implies that the right political decisions on the part of an administration might lead to health care reform in the future. Of the two arguments, the latter is likely to attract more attention, for it is more relevant to the needs and concerns of American citizens, conservatives and liberals alike. Thus, although many writers have spoken of "manipulability" as an attribute identifying causal factors, I think it may be seen that the underlying factor at work is the *relevance* of such causes. A cause that can be manipulated by the investigator or by society at-large is likely to be more relevant for the simple reason that it is contingent, rather than structural.[51]

49. For further discussion of the importance of relevance, see postscript.
50. Gardiner (1952/1961: 12). See also Collingwood (1940: 296), discussed in Garfinkel (1981: 138).
51. This follows Collingwood's (1940) analysis. We generally identify a causal factor which states "it is in our power to produce or prevent, and by producing or preventing which we can produce or prevent that whose cause it is said to be" (cited in Garfinkel 1981: 138). See also Gasking (1955), Harre and Madden (1975), Suppes (1970), von Wright (1971), and Whitbeck (1977) – all cited in Cook and Campbell (1979: 25).

Appendix: Relevance, Neutrality, and Normative Argument

To some readers, the foregoing arguments will suggest a social science composed of zealous advocacy, where writers embrace particular policies or draw moral/ethical conclusions about historical actors and actions: where the past becomes, in Michael Oakeshott's apt phrase, "a field in which we exercise our moral and political opinions, like whippets in a meadow on Sunday afternoon."[52] Nothing could be further from my intent.

It is vital that we distinguish between work that is *relevant,* on the one hand, and work that is normative, evaluative, prescriptive or even polemical, on the other. One may be relevant without being normative, and normative without being relevant; they are independent properties. The former, I maintain, is a general criterion applying to all social science work. The latter may or may not be appropriate, and in any case does not enhance the social scientific status of a work. Let us consider the matter further.

A normative proposition about something we (the hypothetical readers) do not care about is evidently irrelevant. A normative proposition about something that is self-evident ("Avoid falling objects" "Practice virtue") may also be irrelevant. By the same token, nonnormative propositions may be extremely relevant. ("The revolution will occur sometime in the next two years.") In each case, I think it can be seen that relevance, not moral evaluation, is what we ought to be striving for in the social sciences.

Similarly, we ought not take a dismissive attitude toward work that expresses an explicit point of view on the goodness or badness of an event, institution, or policy. Indeed, normative concerns are often difficult to avoid. Imagine writing about the Holocaust or slavery in a wholly dispassionate manner. What would an "even-handed" treatment of these subjects look like? Everyday language is not morally neutral, and social science must accept this affectively charged vocabulary as a condition of doing business.[53] Leaving aside such extreme examples, it is difficult to conceive of important statements about human actions and human institutions that do not carry some normative freight. At the very least, one's choice of subject is likely to be guided by some sense of what is right and wrong. "In theory," writes E. H. Carr, "the distinction may ... be drawn

---

52. Quoted in Fischer (1970: 78).
53. See, for example, Collier (1998), Gallie (1956), Freeden (1996), Hollis and Lukes (1982), MacIntyre (1971), Pitkin (1972), Searle (1969), Strauss (1953/1963), and Taylor (1967/1994).

between the role of the investigator who establishes the facts and the role of the practitioner who considers the right course of action. In practice, one role shades imperceptibly into the other. Purpose and analysis become part and parcel of a single process."[54] Indeed, I cannot fathom why anyone would choose to invest years (typically decades) researching a subject if it did not have some normative importance to her.

Normative statements need not be categorically avoided, therefore. Arguably, truth-claims are *enhanced* when a writer frankly proclaims her preferences at the outset of the work. This way, possible inaccuracies in evidence or presentation are easier to detect, and to evaluate. Hidden prejudices probably do more harm than those that are openly avowed. Yet, it must be stressed again that the value of a work of social science derives from its relevance, not its normative point of view. To say, "Y is good" or "We should do Y" is to say extraordinarily little. Few are likely to be persuaded by such a statement. Indeed, social science is probably most powerful when the normative angle of a work is handled more delicately. The most compelling arguments for social welfare, for example, are those that are able to demonstrate that such programs (a) aid in alleviating conditions of poverty and (b) do not have distressing economic or social side-effects. Such studies do not proclaim baldly "Poverty is bad," or "We should increase social welfare spending," although there is no question that these views undergird most research on poverty and social policy. So long as the author's research is sound we are not likely to be particularly concerned with her normative position on the matter.

Otherwise put: the persuasiveness of any normative argument is itself dependent on the persuasiveness of whatever descriptive, predictive, and causal propositions compose that argument. Descriptive, predictive, and causal propositions serve as the meat of any prescriptive statement. Similarly, whether or not the researcher is motivated by some vision of a better society, or only by personal or material interests, is rightly immaterial to our judgment of the quality of her work. There are idiots and geniuses of every persuasion. We should prefer to read the geniuses and leave the idiots alone, leaving aside their personal views and ethical codes.

Finally, it seems appropriate to observe that the vast majority of social science analysis has little to do with what is good or bad. No one – or virtually no one – argues against the virtues of peace, prosperity, democracy, and self-fulfillment. What is relevant, therefore, is any knowledge that might help us to achieve these desiderata.[55] Here is where social science matters, or ought to matter.

---

54. See Carr (1939/1964: 4).
55. See Friedman (1953/1984).

6

Description and Prediction

What the devil is going on around here?

– Abraham Kaplan[1]

In Chapter 5, I argued that all empirical propositions are liable to ten general criteria of adequacy – specification, accuracy, precision, breadth, depth, parsimony, analytic utility, innovation, relevance, and intelligibility. It is readily apparent that most propositions have more work to do, even once they have satisfied these basic criteria. Indeed, the main purpose of some propositions is not even broached in the foregoing desiderata. In order to understand these additional demands we must differentiate among four types of assertion: *generalization,* which seeks to describe, and perhaps interpret, an event or class of events; *classification,* which seeks to place diverse events within a related set of categories; *prediction,* which seeks to tell us something about a future state of affairs, or a past state of affairs which is not yet known (post-diction); and *causal inference,* which seeks to explain why something occurred, or will occur. The first two categories will be referred to as *descriptive.* These five key terms, together with illustrative examples, are arrayed in Table 6.1.[2] This chapter deals with descriptive and predictive propositions. The following chapter takes up the more complex question of causal inference.

Description

Generalization

The simplest sort of proposition we can make about the world is factual. Caesar crossed the Rubicon in 49 B.C.; Columbus sailed the ocean blue

---

1. Kaplan (1964: 85).
2. Of course, most studies combine arguments of several propositional types (few arguments are *solely* descriptive, predictive, or causal). This is unproblematic so long as the reader is able to discern what sort of empirical claims are being made at various points in the narrative.

Table 6.1   *A Typology of Empirical Propositions*

Description		Prediction	Causal inference
Generalization	Classification		
"Social welfare spending in the United States is lower than in most other rich nations."	"There are three types of welfare regime: comprehensive, targeted, and sparse."	"U.S. social welfare spending will stagnate when the Republican party takes power."	"The cause of low social welfare spending in the United States is the weakness of organized labor."

in 1492; the Japanese attacked Pearl Harbor on December 7, 1941. I do not mean to imply that such statements are unproblematic. Indeed, historians, anthropologists, and other social scientists spend a good deal of time debating questions of factual accuracy. Nonetheless, specific factual statements involve fewer logical complications than propositions referring to a cluster of events or a more general process or condition. We might refer to such factual statements as pure description.

The more a proposition abstracts from the immediate and observable facts of the case – the more, that is, it *generalizes* – the more inferential in nature the proposition becomes. Perhaps the simplest sort of generalization is the labeling generalization. "The literati," "the Chinese Empire," "the time of troubles": these are statements meant to cover a large range of phenomena.[3] Another sort of generalization consists of longer statements about a class of phenomena: "The literati embraced a modern code of ethics during the May 4th Movement," and so forth. No work of social science is without some type of generalization. It may be scarce, as in the work of ethnomethodologists, and it may be implicit, as in the work of many nineteenth-century historians, but it is present nonetheless.

As I use the term, generalization refers to all manner of descriptive propositions, running the gamut from reportage to highly speculative interpretations. What, then, makes a generalizing proposition fruitful? There is nothing I can think of to add to the criteria discussed in Chapter 5. Generalization does not aspire to do more than describe, so its list of desiderata ends at ten. This does not make it *easier* than propositions of other sorts, except in the obvious sense that it has fewer criteria to juggle.

3. See Wright (1963: 36).

Table 6.2 *Classification: Additional Criteria*

---

11. Mutual-exclusivity. Are the categories mutually-exclusive, or do they overlap? (Can relevant phenomena be sorted into one or another category without difficulty?)

12. Exhaustiveness (comprehensiveness). Do the categories account for all phenomena of a given type?

13. Comparability (uni-dimensionality). Are the dimensions of the classification comparable? (Are they logically-compatible parts of a larger whole?)

Classification

If generalization describes a class of phenomena, then a *classification* (aka typology or taxonomy) describes a class of generalizations, a class of classes. Weber, for example, divided authority into three types: traditional, legal-rational, and charismatic. Some culturalists, following Douglas and Wildavsky, divide human activity into five orientations: autonomy, hierarchy, egalitarianism, individualism, and fatalism.[4] The representation of political interests may be deemed pluralist, corporatist, monist, or syndicalist.[5] The relationship obtaining between an individual (or smaller group) and a larger group may be understood in terms of exit, voice, or loyalty.[6] Such classifications inform all fields and subfields of the social sciences.

In order to best perform the classificatory function – in order, that is, to most efficiently order a large field of diverse phenomena – a classification strives for categories that are *mutually-exclusive, exhaustive,* and *comparable,* as explained in Table 6.2. Otherwise put, one seeks to avoid a schema that (a) comprises categories with overlapping boundaries; (b) describes some, but not all, of a set of related phenomena; or (c) where categories are selected according to heterogeneous principles.[7]

The aforementioned typologies do not entirely satisfy all three desiderata. We might wonder, for example, about the mutual-exclusivity

---

4. Thompson et al. (1990).
5. Schmitter (1974).
6. Hirschman (1970a).
7. See Bowker and Star (1999: 10–11), and Neuman (1997: 152–3). These three criteria may be viewed as a stricter, more formal, version of *field utility,* a general criterion applying to all concepts (see Chapter 3). On classification generally, see Bailey (1994), Blalock (1969: 30–5), Bowker and Star (1999), Chafetz (1978: 63–73), Hempel (1952: 52–4; 1965: 137–9), Jones (1974), Mill (1843/1872), Reynolds (1971: 4–5), and Stinchcombe (1968: 41–7).

of Weber's trichotomy (in many ancient and contemporary civilizations – Rome, China, England, Prussia – these three forms of authority seem to coexist) or Douglas and Wildavsky's five-part schema (writers employing the schema often describe individuals as *mixtures* of two or more orientations). Similarly, we might question whether all types of authority are captured in the three-part Weberian typology; we might question, that is, its exhaustiveness. Finally, we might question the comparability of at least one of the foregoing typologies. (Is loyalty the same type of phenomenon as exit and voice?)

All typologies, or at least all those that rest at a fairly high level of abstraction, are likely to encounter difficulties of these sorts. The humanly created world does not always fit neatly into pigeonholes. Yet, insofar as it *does* fit into pigeonholes, we will want to correctly identify and label the holes.

Generally, we think of classifications as comprising several categories. Yet, dichotomous categorizations also produce classifications that strive for mutual-exclusivity, exhaustiveness, and comparability. Thus, one finds ascription/achievement, community/society, individualism/collectivism, particularism/universalism, pluralism/corporatism, and many other dichotomous typologies of a more or less formal nature. Dichotomous terms achieve exhaustiveness almost automatically. If defined by the presence or absence of an hereditary monarch, all polities are either monarchies or republics; they cannot be otherwise. Of course, the same phenomena will often be amenable to *different* classificatory schema. One might, for example, typologize persons by religion, social class, or any number of other criteria.[8] Many classificatory schema combine several dimensions, such as the 2 × 2 matrix beloved by political scientists.

Classificatory schema are not useful for all analytic purposes. But they are possible, and perhaps even requisite, in others. Consider the task facing the biologist or zoologist, or the anthropologist studying communities around the world. Consider the analogous task facing the historian who wishes to tell a long story – one, say, stretching over several centuries. Some sort of classification, however loose, would seem necessary in order to place this wealth of material into a reasonably concise form.

Typically, historians resolve events into discrete periods (a periodization). Anthropologists tend to classify things according to structure and function. Sociologists are attuned to social roles. Indeed, each discipline

---

8. See Jevons (1877/1956: 677, 722), cited in Adams and Adams (1987: 437).

has characteristic ways of seeing the world, and hence of classifying events in the world. The point remains: *any* writer with a large and heterogeneous topic on her hands will have recourse to categories, and with those categories will come demands for mutual-exclusivity (don't place a single thing in more than one category), exhaustiveness (don't leave anything out), and comparability (don't classify *A* by one principle and *B* by another).[9]

Of Description Generally

To many in the social science community, good work is causal or predictive in nature. Work that seeks only to describe is "*merely* descriptive." According to the prevailing view in nomothetic disciplines like economics and political science, descriptive work is at best preliminary to higher-order analysis. Descriptive studies are the plankton of social science. They float about, waiting to be consumed by theories.

Several objections may be laid against this view. First, there should be no shame in description where such analysis is (a) lacking, (b) needed, and (c) highly complex (hence, requiring the exclusive attention of the scholar). It will be readily granted that good descriptions are necessary to causal analysis of any sort. In order to state a relationship between *X* and *Y*, it is necessary to *describe* a *Y*. "First, specify the dependent variable," goes the adage. This means, figure out what it is that you are trying to explain or predict *before* trying to explain or predict it.

But description is not merely a precursor to further analysis. It is also important in its own right. We should like to know, for example, who killed John F. Kennedy and Martin Luther King, Jr. – *whether or not* such knowledge helps us to predict future assassinations or explain the course of the Vietnam War and the civil rights movement. It is inherently useful and interesting. The same could be said for less flashy subjects. We would like to know, for instance, what life was like during the colonial period of American history, or among the Bushmen of the Kalahari. Indeed, many classics in the social science canon are primarily (though not exclusively) descriptive. One thinks, for example, of Benedict's *Patterns of Culture,* Fenno's *Home Style,* Goffman's *Frame Analysis,* Lévi-Strauss's *Elementary Structures of Kinship,* Liebow's *Tally's Corner,*

---

9. We might note that, strictly speaking, a generalization is also a comparative statement – it says that *X* is true for *Y,* and implicitly that *X* is less true of not-*Y*. Therefore, the line between generalization and classification, as described in this chapter, is not hard and fast.

the Lynds' *Middletown,* Malinowski's *Argonauts of the Western Pacific,* Mayhew's *Placing Political Parties,* Pocock's *Machiavellian Moment,* Thompson's *Making of the English Working Class,* or Whyte's *Street Corner Society.*[10]

We are prone to think of description as a virtue attached to work of an "interpretive" nature, such as might be produced by historians, anthropologists, and cultural sociologists. Rich, contextual narratives are likely to be primarily descriptive in nature. Yet, description may also be statistical. Some years ago, Jean Dreze and Amartya Sen brought attention to the phenomenon of "missing women" by counting the ratio of men and women in various societies around the world. They discovered that some societies, particularly those located in South Asia and the Middle East, had markedly higher male:female ratios.[11]

Of a more complicated nature (statistically speaking) are recent arguments over increasing global income inequality. Until quite recently, the consensus among scholars was that between-country inequality had increased dramatically over the past half-century.[12] However, Glenn Firebaugh has shown that if one weights each country in the dataset by its population, and if one uses purchasing-power parity (PPP) measures of income to calculate each country's per capita income (rather than current exchange rates), changes in global inequality over the 1960–89 period are negligible.[13]

This result is not beyond challenge. The point is, we are fascinated by the argument. We should also like to know their causes, and the future course of these phenomena; but such further study (bound to be of a highly tentative nature) will not detract from the intrinsic importance of these findings. Description matters.

We might also point out that *natural* science, still the paragon of virtue for many scholars in the social sciences, contains many areas of research that one would have to consider primarily descriptive in orientation, such as biology, physiology, geology, geography, and astronomy. The descriptive typologies developed in these fields are linked to causal arguments; but they are not *reducible* to causal relationships. Similarly, disciplines such as physics, which are more oriented toward causation,

10. See Benedict (1935/1961), Fenno (1978), Goffman (1974), Lévi-Strauss (1969), Liebow (1967), Lynd and Lynd (1929/1956), Malinowski (1922), Mayhew (1986), Pocock (1975), Thompson (1963), and Whyte (1943/1955).
11. The initial finding was reported in Dreze and Sen (1989). For subsequent work, see Dreze et al. (1995).
12. See, for example, Korzeniewicz and Moran (1997).
13. Firebaugh (1999).

respond as well to descriptive demands. We want to know what is there, not merely how it relates to something else.

Finally, one ought to point out that descriptive propositions can be every bit as broad and parsimonious as predictive or causal propositions. Generalization and classification generally achieve both, or at least strive to do so. There is a world of difference between reportage and descriptive analysis. Thus, insofar as scholars favor a nomothetic ("lawlike") vision of social science, descriptive propositions may be just as satisfying as predictive and causal inference. (Indeed, some logical positivists favored jettisoning causation as a mode of apprehending the world, preferring the apparently greater objectivity of description.) Causal and predictive work, similarly, may be extraordinarily narrow in focus or lengthy in form, so as to fail the criteria of breadth and parsimony. The point is that description may be pitched at any level. We ought not, therefore, confuse arguments over breadth, parsimony, accuracy, precision, and depth (matters taken up in the previous chapter) with arguments over descriptive versus nondescriptive inference.

We need good descriptive work. We would also like to know why things happened and what things are going to happen, but few studies manage to adequately fulfill all three goals at once. Arguably, description is more sure, more nuanced, and more impressive generally when not confounded by the expectation to predict or explain. Intuitively, I have greater faith in a descriptive analysis where description is the summum bonum. Such accounts are less likely to be skewed by the analyst's search for a knockout causal or predictive theory. If the analyst is concerned only with Y, and is not burdened with discovering an X:Y relationship, perhaps she will get Y right.

Regrettably, long-standing preferences for causal or predictive work may have discouraged researchers from taking up descriptive questions, even in areas demonstrably in need of study. For example, while an enormous literature addresses the question of why America is exceptional, relatively few studies address (in a rigorous and empirical way, that is) the antecedent question: *Is* America exceptional, and if so, in what ways? Similarly, while economists devote themselves to finding the causes of growth, few bother with the menial task of collecting data on indicators and correlates of growth. It should be obvious that causal models, no matter how sophisticated, cannot transcend bad data.

A second deleterious effect can be seen in case of the scholar who dresses up her argument in causal or predictive garb when its significance is primarily descriptive. In this latter case, the derogation "merely descriptive" *is* apt. A better appreciation of the legitimacy of descriptive work could alleviate both pathologies.

Prediction

"All sciences aim at prevision," wrote Comte. "For the laws established by the observation of phenomena are generally employed to foretell their succession in the interests of human action.... Determination of the future [is] the direct object of political science, as of the other sciences."[14] Perhaps. However, we need not take a positivist view of social science to realize the significance of prediction for the human sciences.

We cannot operate at all in the present without making innumerable assumptions about the future. Indeed, from a certain philosophical angle the notion of a "present" makes no sense at all without a future that follows it. In any case, and without begging venerable philosophical debates, we have no choice but to prognosticate. And we are surely on firmer ground when we do so in an explicit and self-conscious manner, with all the wisdom that social science can offer, rather than relying on intuition or a "continuation of present trends."

One might think of prediction as an instantiation of the breadth criterion; a proposition that extends into the future is, ceteris paribus, more relevant than a proposition limited to the past. We should add that knowledge of future events is generally more useful than knowledge of the past, fulfilling the relevance criterion (see Chapter 5).

Let us begin this discussion by distinguishing between soothsaying and social science prediction. In soothsaying, one merely states what is going to happen – in the manner of prophets or crystal-ball gazers. In predictive propositions, one stipulates a set of circumstances – a *predictor* – that is held to correlate with the outcome. "As Maine, goes the nation" is an old (and no longer valid) proposition to the effect that voting in Maine will prefigure voting behavior across the country in presidential elections. (It was of some utility in the era before the advent of accurate exit polling.) Here voting in Maine is the predictor *(X)*, and voting across the country the outcome *(Y)*.

Prediction, like causal inference, seeks to establish an $X:Y$ relationship. In the case of predictions, we are saying simply that where X appears, Y will also appear; no causal relationship is assumed (though it may exist). Occasionally, the term will be employed in the context of predicting *past* events whose outcome we are ignorant of ("post-diction" or "retrodiction"). In any case, goodness in prediction involves two criteria in addition to the ten general criteria discussed in Chapter 5: *covariation* and *priority*, as laid out in Table 6.3.

---

14. Quoted in Brown (1984: 209).

Table 6.3   *Prediction: Additional Criteria*

11. Covariation. Does X (the predictor) co-vary with Y (the outcome)? (Is the prediction correct?)
12. Priority. How far does X precede Y in time?

Covariation (or correlation) is the essence of predictive inference. The higher the covariation between X and Y (in the predicted direction) the better the prediction. If I say it will rain tomorrow because the dew point is high today, and it does, then the prediction has succeeded: the posited covariation (between the previous day's dew point and the next day's precipitation) is true. If, over the course of ten days my dew-point predictor indicates rain every day, but it rains for only two days, then the success rate is .2, or 20% – not an outstanding rate, even where weather is concerned.[15]

One is also concerned, however, with *priority*. For predictive theories, priority refers to temporal distance: the amount of time separating the X and Y variables (the prediction and the predicted outcome). A theory that is able to predict election results six months in advance of an election is superior (ceteris paribus) to one that can predict results only a week ahead. Economic forecasts that can see forward a decade or longer are superior to those that concern themselves only with the next quarter. The closer one moves to the outcome of interest, the less useful a prediction is likely to be. Earthquake warnings that arrive seconds before the earthquake itself are scarcely predictions at all, in the normal sense of the term. Comets, eclipses, and other natural occurrences, on the other hand, have been predicted decades, sometimes even centuries, in advance of their occurrence. These are better.

Prediction and Causal Explanation

Thankfully, predictions are usually fairly simple to prove or disprove. Having stated what one thinks is going to happen, one has only to wait to see if it actually does. Assuming that the proposition is fully specified, predictions offer something akin to a laboratory test of a proposition's

---

15. So important is covariation (or correlation) to prediction that we often employ the two terms interchangeably. This is confusing in work oriented toward causal explanation, where an author might write of predictors that have causal weight. What she means is that (a) certain factors are highly correlated with the outcome of interest, and (b) they have (or might have) a causal relationship with that outcome.

veracity. It is important to remember, however, that in successfully predicting an outcome we have not necessarily explained the *cause* of that outcome. Consider an election. If one is interested in predicting its winner on the eve of the election our best predictor will probably be a random-sample poll asking respondents whether they plan to vote and, if so, for whom. But the prediction resulting from this poll, however accurate, does not explain the result. Similarly, although a great many propositions could be brought to bear on the question of what might cause *A* to win (*A*'s party has enjoyed increasing support in the electorate, *A* represents the largest ethnic group in the country, etc.), none of these are likely to be more effective in predicting the result than the poll itself. Thus, one's purpose in approaching a particular dependent variable often determines which *X*s are most useful. That which best explains may not best predict, and vice versa. Causal propositions usually have some predictive merit, but we had best keep these two logical relations separate in our heads and in our work.

Generally speaking, whenever one has sufficient observations of a given type, and whenever the outcome of interest has happened in the same fashion many times before, accurate predictions can be obtained without reference to causal mechanisms. Such events are *predictable*, as we say. Night and day are examples of events that can be accurately predicted by the simple device of a timepiece, and for which we are in need of no causal explanation. Causal relationships, however, often provide a better glimpse into the future when convenient indicators of that future event are lacking, or when covariational relationships are indeterminate. Most predictions of a social science sort (e.g., macroeconomic forecasting) are likely to mix causal *X*s with purely correlative *X*s.

The point remember, in any case, is whether one's goal is predictive or causal. If the former, then one need only be concerned with covariation and priority in the *X:Y* relationship. If the latter, a number of additional concerns arise, as discussed in the following chapter.[16]

---

16. One should also note the potential for confusion when predictions function, at the same time, as causal variables. Wherever events are open to human manipulation a good predictor variable is liable to become either self-fulfilling or self-negating if it is made public. A prediction about the stock market, if published and if issued from a reputable source, may have an effect on the performance of the stock market – and hence on the accuracy of the prediction itself. Alan Greenspan's analysis of future economic trends will not *merely* predict. Conversely, if experts predict a population explosion, human beings may thwart that prediction by taking action against this eventuality. Indeed, this is the primary purpose of such predictions. These are obvious points, but worth keeping in mind as we progress to a discussion of the most complicated proposition of all, causation.

7

Causation

Surely, if there be any relation among objects which it imports to us to know perfectly, it is that of cause and effect. On this are founded all our reasonings concerning matter of fact or existence. By means of it alone we attain any assurance concerning objects which are removed from the present testimony of our memory and senses. The only immediate utility of all sciences, is to teach us, how to control and regulate future events by their causes. Our thoughts and enquiries are, therefore, every moment, employed about this relation: Yet so imperfect are the ideas which we form concerning it, that it is impossible to give any just definition of cause.

– Hume[1]

We have looked, thus far, at propositions that are descriptive or predictive, and we have defended their utility. It seems clear, however, that we will not be content to rest social science only, or even primarily, upon propositions of these sorts. We wish to know not only what happened, and (where possible) what is going to happen, but also, and perhaps more critically, *why* these things happened or will happen.[2]

Causation is the principal means by which we are able to order and make sense of the humanly constructed world. It is the central explanatory trope by which relationships among persons and things are estab-

---

1. Hume (1960: 220).
2. See Homans (1961; quoted in Berelson and Steiner 1964: epigraph) and MacIver (1942/1964: 5–11). Moreover, causal analysis of a phenomenon will also enhance confidence in our ability to *predict* that outcome, even if explanation and prediction hinge on different variables. A prediction that rests solely on past experience – without any supporting causal explanation – is a highly tentative prediction. Without some notion of *why* a predictor and an outcome are highly correlated it is impossible to say how long, or under what circumstances, this relationship is likely to hold up. History does not always repeat itself. Our only recourse for understanding these apparent irregularities is causal analysis.

lished. Hume, whose words are quoted previously, called causation the cement of the universe.[3] Without some understanding of who is doing what to whom we cannot make sense of the world that we live in, we cannot hold people and institutions accountable for their actions, and we cannot act efficaciously. We need to know, for example, not only what racism is, where it is, and where it might appear, but also what *causes* racism. Even where causal understanding does not lead to social change (for not all causal analysis is policy-relevant, and more to the point, not all policy proposals are implemented) we are likely to be reassured when we can order events around us into cause-and-effect relationships. "When we have such understanding," notes Judah Pearl, "we feel 'in control' even if we have no practical way of controlling things."[4]

We begin with a clarification of key terms. This will pave the way for a discussion of the concept of causation. After reviewing the most common attributes of this difficult term, I will argue for the following minimal definition: "causes" are factors that raise the (prior) probabilities of an event occurring. In the second section, the heart of the chapter, I apply the criterial approach to the question of causation. Here, I argue that four criteria (in addition to the ten criteria applying to all empirical propositions) define goodness in a causal inference: differentiation, priority, independence, and contingency. The chapter concludes with a brief discussion of how different criteria compete with one another in arguments over causation.

Key Terms

Relationships assumed to be causal involve at least two elements, a cause and an effect. We employ various near-synonyms for both. A cause may be referred to as a causal factor, an input, an explanatory variable, a predictor variable, an independent variable, or simply *X*. An effect may be referred to as an outcome, a dependent variable, or *Y*. It is important to stress that by specifying an *X* we are simply asserting that such-and-such a factor *may* have caused *Y*. To prove or demonstrate this allegation is another matter altogether.

Both *X* and *Y* are assumed to vary, even if only hypothetically. Hence, they are referred to generically as *variables*. Although this term is normally used in the context of statistical work I employ it broadly for the *X* or *Y* element of any explanatory proposition. *Categorical* (aka dis-

---

3. Hume (1888).
4. Pearl (2000: 345).

Table 7.1 *Variable Types*

Variable types		Different categories?	Ranked categories?	Distance b/w categories measured?	True zero?
Categorical	Nominal	Yes			
(aka, discrete)	Ordinal	Yes	Yes		
Continuous	Interval	Yes	Yes	Yes	
(aka, scalar)	Ratio	Yes	Yes	Yes	Yes

crete) variables distinguish among phenomena by placing them in a limited number of categories. If these categories do not suppose a rank-order (e.g., male/female), they are considered *nominal*. If they are ranked (e.g., high/low, present/absent), they are considered *ordinal*. The foregoing are examples of *dichotomous* (aka binary or dummy) variables, because the universe of potential cases is divided into only two options. But categorical variables are commonly subdivided into multiple categories, such as the Likert scale ("strongly agree," "agree," "disagree," "strongly disagree"). *Interval* variables offer a range of options ordered along a continuous numerical scale. Since a temperature gauge does not possess a true zero (the designation of zero degrees varies by temperature systems, such as Celsius and Fahrenheit), it is referred to as an *interval* variable. A currency gauge, however, will have a true zero (where no money is present) – zero dollars is equivalent to zero yen – qualifying it as a *ratio* scale. These points are presented schematically in Table 7.1.[5]

What Does Cause Mean?

Arguments over the concept of causation have exercised writers since ancient Greece and show no sign of abatement today. Indeed, causation is complex, much more complex from a logical point of view than descriptive and predictive propositions. In order to come to terms with this complexity we will have to enter territory that social scientists usually consider philosophical or linguistic, rather than empirical. I hope it will be clear by the chapter's conclusion why this discussion is essential for any empirical consideration of causal inference. At the same time I should clarify that I am not attempting to settle the question of what cause means *in general* (the task of philosophy), but merely what it might

---

5. Adopted from Neuman (1997: 147).

mean in the context of social science. If the question is narrowed down in this fashion it is possible to reach reasonably firm conclusions on this age-old question without a book-length treatment of the subject.[6]

My approach in dealing with this complex, but unavoidable, concept will be analogous to that pursued in Chapter 4 (with reference to "ideology"). I begin with a collection of attributes, organized in Table 7.2.[7] This typology, while by no means comprehensive, includes the most common definitional attributes of "cause" in social science contexts.

Aristotle conceived of four, quite different, types of causation: formal (that which an effect is made, thus contributing to its essence), material (the matter out of which an effect is fashioned), efficient (the motive force that made an effect), and final (the purpose for which an effect was produced). Since Aristotle, discussion has centered on the third type, the efficient cause, and I will follow this well-established precedent here. The efficient cause, according to Aristotle, is "the primary source of the change or coming to rest; e.g., the man who gave advice is a cause, the father is

6. A focus on social science allows one to sidestep a number of venerable brain ticklers. Consider, for example, the five "fundamental issues" raised in a recent, widely cited, philosophical work on causation: "(1) What relationship is there between causal laws and causal relations? In particular, are causal relations between events logically supervenient upon causal laws together with the totality of non-causal states of affairs? If not, do causal relations at least presuppose the existence of corresponding, covering laws, or, on the contrary, is a singularist account of causation correct? (2) Are causal states of affairs logically supervenient upon noncausal ones? (3) If not, is an a posteriori reduction of causal states of affairs to noncausal ones possible? Or is a realist approach to causation correct? (4) Is it possible for causal relations to be immediately given, either in perceptual experience, or introspectively? (5) Do causal concepts need to be analyzed, or can they be taken as analytically basic? If they do stand in need of analysis, should the analysis be one that reduces causal states of affairs to noncausal ones, or should it treat causal terms as theoretical, and offer a realist account of the meaning of those terms?" (Sosa and Tooley 1993: 5). Whatever interest such questions might have for philosophy, they have very little, I think, for social science. For additional work on causation in philosophy and philosophy of science see Bohm (1957), Bunge (1959), French et al. (1984), Gellner (1973), Hart and Honoré (1966), Mackie (1974), Toulmin (1970), and van Fraassen (1980: 125). For work on causation in statistical inference, see Blalock (1964, 1971), Davis (1985), Glymour et al. (1987), Holland (1986), McKim and Turner (1997), Nowak (1960), and Suppes (1970). One exception to philosophers' general neglect of social science is Marini and Singer (1988), which I draw on extensively. See also Bennett (1999).

7. For a sampling of definitions, I consulted prominent work on the subject in social science and, to a lesser extent, in philosophy (see previous footnote). The scaffolding erected in Table 7.1 should be regarded as preliminary, because I have not attempted a comprehensive review of the subject. Nonetheless, it may be sufficient to indicate a usable minimal definition. (It is unlikely that additional – nonidiosyncratic – usages of the word "cause" would leap the boundaries of this capacious definition.)

Table 7.2 *Outline for a Definitional Typology of "Cause"*

Near-synonyms:

Affect, condition, control, effect, generate, influence, produce, structure.

Causal factors and outcomes (X and Y) may be...

Binary (dichotomous) or scalar (continuous).

Events (dynamic, swift, and discrete), processes (dynamic and slow), or
conditions (static).

Positive (something that happened) or negative (something that did not)

Causes may be classed as...

Deterministic:

Necessary: X is necessary to Y, but X does not always cause Y (at least not
by itself). In covariational terms, one may find X without Y, but one
does not find Y without X.

Sufficient: X always causes Y, but Y has other causes. In covariational
terms, one may find Y without X, but one does not ever find X without Y.

Necessary and sufficient: X always causes Y and is the only cause of Y. In
covariational terms, X and Y go together; one never finds one without
the other.

Probabilistic: X sometimes or usually causes Y, or some portion of Y,
perhaps in combination with other Xs; but there may be other causes of Y.
In covariational terms, X goes with Y more often than some other Xs (but
not necessarily all others).

Specific types of causes include...

Conjunctural causes (aka, compound cause, configurative cause, combinatorial
cause, conjunctive plurality of causes; a particular combination of causes
acting together to produce a given effect).

Multiple causes (aka, a disjunctive plurality of causes, redundancy, equifinality,
or overdetermination; where several causes act independently of each other
to produce, each on its own, a particular effect).

A cause in fact (that which explains a specific event, rather than a class of
events).

Nonlinear causes (e.g., causes with takeoff or threshold levels).

Irreversible causes (e.g., ratchet effects).

Constant causes (a cause operating continually on a given effect over a
period of time).

Causal chains or causal paths (with many intermediate causes lying between
the fundamental X and the ultimate Y).

Critical-juncture causes (a multiple cause at a particular moment in time that
has enduring effects).

Path-dependent causes (a causal chain where the probability of Y increases
over time; a sequential causal relationship with self-reinforcing properties).

cause of the child, and generally what makes of what is made and what causes change of what is changed."[8] In Mario Bunge's words, the efficient cause is "the *agent* producing some change in" something else.[9] This replicates the first definition of cause in the *American Heritage* dictionary, which defines a cause as "the producer of an effect, result, or consequence." A cause *generates, creates, produces, effects.* It is the *agent,* upon which an outcome *depends* – hence, the designation of causal factors as independent variables and effects as dependent variables.

Causation in its strongest sense is *deterministic.* Thus, for Mill, a cause is "the sum total of the conditions positive and negative taken together ... which being realized, the consequent invariably follows."[10] The crispness of deterministic causation means that we can understand this concept in terms of "counterfactual conditionals." If the removal of a condition prevents the occurrence of an outcome, then it must be considered a cause of that outcome. If its removal has no such effect (if the outcome still occurs), then it cannot be considered a cause. A cause, in this interpretation, is the sine qua non of an effect. Deterministic causation, as the term will be used here, refers to causes that are conceptualized as necessary and/or sufficient.[11]

Even among deterministic causes, however, important questions remain. For example, is the outcome in question produced only by these conditions, or are there other causes? Traditionally, we observe a tripartite formula, according to which deterministic causes are either (a) necessary, (b) sufficient, or (c) necessary *and* sufficient to produce a given result.[12] These familiar terms are defined in Table 7.2. As an example, consider Jones's close victory in a congressional election. Pundit *A* argues that Jones owes her victory to her political experience. Pundit *B* says it was her well-managed campaign. Pundit *C* says it was her family ties in the district that proved key. And so on and so forth. In a close election, dozens of factors might be cited. If one is considering *necessary* causes, all pundits might be considered correct. If, on the other hand, one is considering

8. Aristotle, *Physics,* book II, ch. iii, 194b, quoted in Bunge (1959: 33).
9. Bunge (1959: 33). This something else was known for centuries as the 'patient,' terminology that seems rather odd today.
10. Mill, quoted in Davidson (1993: 76).
11. See Mahoney (2000) and Sobel (1995: 5).
12. The necessary/sufficient distinction harks back to Mill (1843/1872: 222). The association between causation and *necessity* is even older, harking back to Aristotle, and finding echoes in Spinoza, Hobbes, Hume, Kant, Mill, Russell, and many others (Anscombe 1971/1993: 89–90). For discussion of causation as founded on counterfactual conditionals, see Lewis (1973/1993). For criticism of this understanding of causation, see Mackie (1974), Miller (1987), and Scriven (1966/1993).

sufficient causes, all pundits are definitely wrong, since none of these factors, by itself, could have caused Jones's election. If, we are considering necessity *and* sufficiency, we will probably have to include all of the foregoing arguments, and perhaps many more besides. Much the same logical difficulty inheres in discussions of other particular events, historical and contemporary (e.g., revolutions, crimes, depressions). Arguments will be clarified to the extent that writers articulate their causal claims explicitly in terms of necessity, sufficiency, or necessity and sufficiency.

At this point, we must observe that most causal relationships under investigation in social science are not captured by the necessary/sufficient distinction. If, for example, an outcome is a matter of degrees (e.g., turnout rates), it is somewhat confusing to speak of necessity or sufficiency. To be sure, one could categorize the outcomes as "high" and "low," thereby arriving at a categorical outcome. But this vastly reduces the precision of our observations. If we wish to preserve all the information conveyed by variable turnout rates, we will have to speak of different Xs causing *degrees* of variation in the outcome. Thus, we might say that automatic voter registration procedures increase turnout in a state or country (all other things being equal). Registration procedures are neither necessary nor sufficient causes of turnout; indeed, these words make sense only when one is dealing with dichotomous outcomes (either/or, yes/no, 0/1). Yet, even with dichotomous outcomes we often find, or suspect, that whatever cause or causes we have managed to identify are not *invariably* associated with the outcome. They are, therefore, neither necessary, nor sufficient, nor necessary and sufficient. (We could talk about *degrees* of necessity and sufficiency, but this strains the normal meaning of these terms and dilutes their analytic utility, premised on binary logic.)

When faced with continuous variables (X or Y) or inconsistent causal relationships (perhaps with estimated probabilities) we speak of causal relationships as *probabilistic,* rather than *deterministic.* Most causes are related to their purported effects in a probabilistic manner – at least, so far as we can tell.[13] We look, therefore, for degrees of causation, degrees of likelihood, or we speak of one cause as *better* than another. As John Dupre points out, "the basic idea behind probabilistic theories

---

13. Perhaps, if we knew more about the causal relationship we would be able to interpret it in a deterministic fashion, as some philosophers have speculated. But we are unlikely to achieve that level of causal knowledge – at least not in the social sciences. Moreover, it remains to be settled (and probably never will be settled) whether causation in the universe is fundamentally probabilistic (a matter, at least in part, of sheer chance) or deterministic (ultimately a product of what happened before, or of fundamental causal laws). We need not take a position on this age-old debate.

of causality is ... that the cause should raise the probability of the effect."[14] This does *not* mean that a purported cause cannot be dismissed as entirely false. If someone asserts that the average height of a population is related to voter turnout rates we can still say (within a probabilistic framework) that the causal argument is false. It simply means that we can accommodate degrees of power, strength, or consistency in an *X:Y* relationship without sacrificing the notion of causation.

Although deterministic claims are more useful where we have reason to believe that causal relationships are in fact deterministic, most social science research is based on the more flexible parameters of probabilistic causation. Thus, we would say that *X* accounts for a certain part or percentage of *Y*, causes *Y* in a certain percentage of cases, or is, in varying degrees, likely to cause *Y*. (The outcome need not be continuous; it may also be dichotomous, so long as the causal relationship is couched in terms of probabilities.) The extent to which any given *X* contributes to *Y* may be thought of as the degree of variance on *Y* that a particular *X* is able to explain (with all other factors taken into account).

We may treat the variation implicit in all causes and outcomes as *binary* (0/1, either/or) or *scalar* (matters of degree). To ask why Jones won the election is to pose the question in binary terms (win/lose). To ask why Jones obtained 55% of the vote is to pose the same general question in scalar terms. Similarly, causal variables for either result may be binary (she won/lost the endorsement of the local boss), or scalar (local unions supported her by a 2:1 margin). Consequently, we often deal with mixtures of binary and scalar variables in a causal relationship. (Deterministic causes and effects must be in binary form.)

Causes and outcomes may be characterized as events (dynamic, swift, and discrete), processes (dynamic and slow), or conditions (static). Causes and outcomes may be positive (something that happened) or negative (something that did not).

We may now return to causal relationships, this time with attention to complex forms of causation. Causal relationships may be linear – the same when values of *X* or *Y* are low as when they are high – or nonlinear. Concepts such as takeoff and critical mass are metaphorical ways of expressing nonlinear relationships between a cause and an effect. Nonlinear relationships may take many forms, of course (in principle, they are infinite). Causal relationships, similarly, may be reversible or irreversible – for example, "ratchet" or "threshold" effects. [15]

---

14. Dupre (1984: 170).
15. See Lieberson (1985).

A cause may operate continually on a given effect over a long period of time (a "constant cause"). A cause may establish a connection with an outcome through a set of intermediate causes, each more or less the product of the previous cause (a causal chain or path). A cause with enduring effects may be established during a brief period of time, as with a "critical juncture" and its aftermath.[16] If, once established, an arrangement that had no initial advantage over other alternatives begins to have self-reinforcing properties ("increasing returns"), we may refer to this causal structure as one of path dependence.[17]

Causal arguments may explain a single outcome (sometimes referred to as token or singular causation), or multiple outcomes (a class of outcomes). Causes themselves may be singular, or plural. When an outcome is due to a particular combination of causes acting together we call it a conjunctural cause, compound cause, or conjunctive plurality of causes (they are synonymous). If these multiple causes act independently of each other to produce an outcome it is termed a disjunctive plurality of causes, causal redundancy, equifinality, or overdetermination.[18] If, for example, a hail of bullets from a firing squad reach the victim at the same time and each is by itself sufficient to cause his death we cannot distinguish among these various causes. Each is sufficient; none is necessary.

We refer to a *cause in fact* in the following scenario. A gunshot from assailant #1 inflicts what would be, under any circumstances, a fatal injury to *A*'s heart. But she is not dead yet. Along comes another shot from assailant #2, which goes through her head and kills her instantly. Both shots must be considered sufficient to cause *A*'s death; neither is, by itself, necessary. In any case, we may be interested in identifying the *actual* cause of death. Which assailant actually disposed of *A*? (It is of course assailant #2.) More ponderously, we define a cause in fact as "a necessary and sufficient cause *for a particular event* (an event taking place at a particular time and place)."[19] Thus, we can say that assailant #2 was the necessary and sufficient cause of *A*'s death at time *T* (were it not for assailant #2, she would have lived a few moments longer).

The foregoing options represent the most common and most important varieties of causal argument that we are likely to encounter in the social sciences. But they are certainly not comprehensive. Indeed, the

16. See Collier and Collier (1991).
17. This definition relies on Pierson (2000). See also David (1993), Goldstone (1998), and Mahoney (1999b).
18. See Braumoeller (1999), Bunge (1959), George and Bennett (in press), Mackie (1965/1993), Marini and Singer (1988: 354–5), and Scriven (1966/1993).
19. See Marini and Singer (1988: 353) and Pearl (2000: ch 10).

field is limitless. One has only to discover a new causal relationship in time and space, or a new method of ascertaining such a relationship, to coin a new causal concept (e.g., "INUS" causation, discussed in the appendix to this chapter).

It should be pointed out that there are two basic varieties of causal questions. One focuses on the outcome in question, and the other on a particular cause, or causes. I will refer to the first as *Y*-centered causal analysis and the second as *X*-centered analysis. In the first case, one asks What causes *Y*? (i.e., what are the various *X*s that contribute to *Y*?). In the second case, one asks Does *X* cause *Y*? or alternatively, What does *X* cause? (What are the various effects of *X*?) These two sorts of questions suggest somewhat different research designs, as we will see in Chapter 8.

Finally, we should note the difference between a cause and a causal *framework*. A causal framework, like evolutionary theory, suggests a general model for explaining a wide variety of outcomes without naming either a specific cause or a specific outcome. Thus, when we say that a particular feature of an animal or plant can be explained by evolution, we are indicating a general mechanism by which a specific cause might be (given the requisite empirical work) identified. Other causal models, including general equilibrium theory, game theory, "realism" (in international relations), and systems theory are similar in this respect. They are not *X*s (causes), but rather frameworks or mechanisms within which an *X:Y* relationship might be explained.

Having surveyed the field, albeit in a hurried and incomplete fashion, we may now return to the question of definition. How are we to reduce this extreme polysemy to a single general definition? There are, I have argued, two definitional strategies available: minimal and ideal-type (see Chapter 4). Both have important ramifications for our discussion. An ideal-type approach encourages us to seek out the most pure, most extreme, vision of causation. Deterministic causes comprised of necessary *and* sufficient conditions fit this bill admirably. Here is a cause *par excellence*. Every time *X* appears *Y* also appears, and *Y* does not appear under any other circumstance. This is probably the oldest and most well established understanding of cause and is deeply rooted in everyday intuitions.

Yet, an ideal-type definition may not be the most useful jumping-off place for our very general discussion. It would exclude from the outset any consideration of probabilistic causes, scalar variables, causal conditions, and many forms of causal complexity. To be sure, we could reserve other words for these peripheral phenomena (e.g., "conditions"). However, if these peripheral phenomena are difficult to separate from the ideal phenomena, if they evidence many of the same characteristics, if they are investigated in much the same manner (a topic taken up in

Table 7.3   *Causal Explanation: Additional Criteria*

---

*11. **Differentiation** (exogeneity) (antonym: endogeneity).   Is the X differentiable from the Y? Is the cause separate, logically and empirically, from the outcome to be explained?*

*12. **Priority** (exogeneity) (antonym: endogeneity). How much temporal or causal priority does X enjoy vis-à-vis y?*

*13. **Independence** (exogeneity, asymmetry, recursiveness) (antonyms: endogeneity, reciprocality, symmetry, feedback). How independent is X relative to other Xs, and to Y?*

*14. **Contingency** (abnormality). Is the X contingent, relative to other possible Xs? Does the causal explanation conform to our understanding of the normal course of events? Does it establish appropriate boundary conditions?*

Part III of the book), and if they are commonly referred to as causes, then it makes sense to group them together under the same rubric. Our purposes are probably better served with a permissive minimal definition than a restrictive ideal-type definition.

Without tediously examining all the possibilities (see Table 7.2), I will simply stipulate what seems to me a sensible and workable minimal definition: *X may be considered a cause of Y if (and only if) it raises the probability of Y occurring.* In shorthand, causes raise prior probabilities.[20] Here is a definition that is perfectly substitutable; it covers deterministic and probabilistic causes, variables of all sorts, and any kind of complex cause. So defined, cause may be considered the general concept and near-synonyms – such as factor, influence, affect, control, and condition – special subtypes of causation.

Criteria of Goodness

We are now in a position to address our primary question: what distinguishes *good* causal arguments – those useful for the conduct of social science – from those that are less good? I argue that four criteria, in addition to the ten general criteria pertaining to all propositions, characterize a good cause: *differentiation, priority, independence,* and *contingency,* as set forth in Table 7.3. I now turn to a detailed discussion of each.

---

20. This is a very informal way of expressing the notion that causes may be understood in terms of prior and posterior probabilities, which in Bayesian work is usually couched in a mathematical expression (so that such probabilities can be calculated). See, for example, Dupre (1984: 170) and Pearl (2000: 5).

Differentiation

Everyone knows that tautological reasoning is a terrible, terrible sin. This one little word will send your research proposal back without funding, your article back without publication, and your theory back to the drawing board (*where it belongs!* we can all cry in unison). But why? Tautology – along with its near-synonyms circularity and endogeneity – is a somewhat confusing notion, as it turns out. It can refer to any one (or a combination) of three shortcomings in causal argument: differentiation, priority, and/or independence. Let us begin with the most obvious of these, *differentiation*.

A cause must be differentiable from the effect it purports to explain. This seems self-explanatory, and wholly unobjectionable. Yet, even here, we must admit that differentiation is often a matter of degrees. To begin with, Xs and Ys are always *somewhat* differentiated from one another. A perfect tautology (e.g., "The Civil War was caused by the Civil War") is simply nonsense, and never encountered. One occasionally hears the following sort of argument: "The Civil War was caused by the attack of the South against Fort Sumter." This is more satisfactory. Even so, it is not likely to strike readers as a particularly acute explanation. Indeed, there is very little explanation occurring here, because the X is barely differentiated from the Y (the attack against Fort Sumter was of course part of the Civil War). Equally problematic is an argument that links the Civil War to a warlike relationship between North and South, one that persisted from the 1850s to the outbreak of the conflict in 1961. Again, one is at pains to distinguish between cause and effect.

Consider a second example, this one classical in origin. To say that this man *(X)* is father to this child *(Y)* is to infer that the father *caused* the child to exist; he is a necessary (though not, of course, sufficient) cause of the child. (We might speculate that present-day notions of causation are rooted in the primordial question of legitimacy.) We are less impressed, however, by the argument that a *fetus* is the cause of a child, or a child the cause of an adult. There is something wrong with these formulations, even though X is clearly necessary for Y (and prior to Y). What is wrong is that there is no demonstrable differentiation between these Xs and Ys; they are the same object, observed at different points in time. In short, we have stipulated a causal relationship to a "continuous self-maintaining process," and this violates the precept of differentiation.[21] (We might accept the argument that an adult is the product of

---

21. Marini and Singer (1988: 364).

her *childhood*, however, because the notion of a childhood is separable from the adult.)

We should be clear that differentiation is not the same as *priority*. It is possible for a cause to be quite close to an effect – spatially or temporally – and still be clearly differentiated. Causal arguments hinging on human motivations usually have this quality. So long as we have an adequate indicator of a person's motive, and a separate indicator of her actions, we will be satisfied that differentiation between X and Y has been achieved.

Priority

Causes, Hume thought, must be prior to their effects. Certainly, one might say, a cause may not arrive *after* its effect.[22] Yet, it is not clear that causes are always, or necessarily, prior. It seems apparent that some causes are coterminous with their outcomes. If two cars collide, it is not clear that either car came "first"; and even if it were the case, it is not clear that this would give the prior car greater claim to causality.

Even so, from a social science perspective we can say that it is more *useful* to identify factors that are prior to the event to be explained.[23] Consider the following path diagram:

$$X_1 \Rightarrow X_2 \Rightarrow X_3 \Rightarrow X_4 \Rightarrow Y$$

We are likely to consider X_1 to be *the* cause, and causal factors X_{2-4} intermediate (and less important) causes, all other things being equal. Of course, all other things are rarely equal. We are likely to lose causal power (accuracy and depth, in the terms of Table 5.1) as we move farther away from the outcome. Yet, if we did not (e.g., if the correlations in this imaginary path diagram were close to perfect) we would rightly grant precedence to X_1. Causes lying close to an effect are not satisfying as causes precisely because of their proximity. Rather, we search for causes that are ultimate or fundamental.

Consider a quotidian example. To say that an accident was caused because A ran into B, is not to say much that is useful about this event. Indeed, this sort of statement is probably better classified as descriptive,

22. The apparent exception to this dictum – the anticipated cause – is not really an exception at all, I would argue. If A alters her behavior because of the expected arrival of B, one could plausibly claim that B was causing A's behavioral change. However, it would be more correct to say that B was already present in some sense, or that A's behavior change was stimulated by an expectation that was, already present. (This sort of question is debated with respect to functionalist arguments in social science.)

23. See Miller (1987: 102–4).

rather than explanatory. An *X* gains causal status as it moves back farther in time from the event in question. If, to continue with this story, I claim that the accident was caused by the case of beer consumed by *A* earlier that evening, I have offered a cause that has greater priority and is, on this account at least, a better explanation. If I can show that the accident in question was actually a reenactment of a childhood accident that *A* experienced twenty years ago, then I have offered an even more interesting explanation. Similarly, to say that the Civil War was caused by the attack on Fort Sumter, or that World War I was caused by the assassination of the Archduke Ferdinand at Sarajevo, is to make a causal argument that is trivial by virtue of its lack of priority. Indeed, proximate causes are often referred to as "occasions" for specific outcomes, rather than causes.[24]

Priority considerations lie beneath many of our most virulent arguments over rival causal explanations. It is widely recognized, for example, that ideational approaches to explanation are problematic. This is so partly because it is difficult to separate the *X* (the attitude or ideas said to exert causal force) from the *Y* (the action or event to be explained) – a problem of differentiation. Ideational explanations also tend to suffer from a lack of priority. Consider the argument that Americans do not fund welfare programs because they do not like welfare, and they do not give their government more power because they do not like government. There is every reason to suppose that a strong correlation exists between what people think and desire and what they do. Cultural theories are *generally* true for this anodyne reason.[25] Similarly, leadership theories of politics exemplify a form of argument that is almost invariably true. Leaders make policies. (It is difficult to imagine "masses" doing so.) Again, there is little distance between the purported cause and effect, such that (even if true) it is not clear how useful the theory is as an explanation. In other words, we are wont to ask *why* leaders acted in a certain way, and *why* members of the public expressed a given set of preferences. Prior causes are more analytically useful, ceteris paribus.

The ongoing debate over gun control offers another example of priority at work in causal explanation. NRA bumper stickers used to carry the slogan "Guns don't kill people; *people* kill people." What is being implied

---

24. See Hook (1946: 115).
25. As usual, there are exceptions. Hanson (1997), for example, argues that philosophical questions worked out in the 1840s affected economic institutions constructed in the Soviet Union during the 1930s. But most cultural interpretations lie much closer to the outcome they are intending to explain. My own work (Gerring 1998) would be an example of this.

here? The gun control opponent wishes to call attention to the fact that although guns are the immediate cause of death, the "real" (i.e., prior) cause of death is the person squeezing the trigger. Of course, this argument constructs a straw man opponent. Gun control advocates are not arguing that guns themselves are the cause of the high murder rate in America. Rather, they claim that the absence of effective gun control *legislation* is the cause of this unfortunate outcome. At this point, gun control advocates may claim to have gained the edge in priority. Yet, the astute gun control opponent will counter that we are better off directing legislation against crime, rather than against gun possession. Both advocates and opponents of the issue therefore move to capture the position of greatest priority, and end up (logically) at about the same spot: statute.

The further away we can get from the outcome in question, the better (ceteris paribus) our explanation will be. This explains some of the excitement when social scientists find "structural" variables that seem to effect public policy or political behavior. It is not that they offer fuller (deeper) explanations; indeed, the correlations between X and Y are likely to be much weaker than with cultural or leadership theories. It is not that they are more relevant; indeed, they are less relevant for most policy purposes, since they are least amenable to manipulation (usually). And it is not that they offer more accurate explanations; as we move away from an outcome of interest to causes that have greater priority, our explanation is likely to become more difficult to prove. Thus, priority often imposes costs on other criterial dimensions. Yet, such explanations will be better insofar as they offer us more power, more leverage on the topic. They are nonobvious.

Independence

The search for causal explanation is also a search for causes that are *independent*. Two species of independence must be distinguished. The first refers to the independence of a cause relative to other causes.[26] A cause that is codependent, one might say – a cause whose effect is dependent upon the existence of a range of other factors – is less useful than a cause that acts alone. (Of course, all causal arguments depend on a background of necessary conditions, but these may be fairly obvious

---

26. The research design analog would be collinearity (discussed in Chapter 8). Here, however, we are dealing only with the formal properties of causes – that is, with causal relationships as they really are (ontologically) – rather than with matters of proof or demonstration.

and ubiquitous. If so, we can afford to ignore them and can claim independence for the cause that acts alone.)

The second, and more usual, meaning of independence refers to the independence of a cause relative to the outcome that is being explained. Dependence, in this sense, means that Y has a reciprocal effect on X, and is often referred to as symmetry, feedback, circularity, or endogeneity. This is also the origin of the familiar independent and dependent variable notation. The former is the cause because (or insofar as) it is independent of the effect; the latter is an effect because (insofar as) it depends upon X.[27]

Causal differentiation, priority, and independence are likely to co-vary. An X that is high on one dimension is likely to enjoy similar status on the other: the farther away X is from Y the easier it may be to distinguish X from Y, and the less likely it is that Y will affect X. But there are plenty of exceptions. One often looks to socioeconomic variables like the density of labor union organization to explain social welfare policies. (The more densely organized the labor force the more this labor power is likely to be felt in the political arena – via social democratic parties and egalitarian policies.) However, we also know that many government policies affect the ability of labor unions to organize. Thus, not only does labor affect state-level policymaking, but also the reverse. Labor union organization, in our terms, is not entirely independent vis-à-vis the effect that it is purported to cause, even though it enjoys great priority.

Contingency

One final consideration weighs upon all causal arguments. Consider the many possible causes of a particular car accident. We list: car A, car B, driver A, driver B, the road, the intersection, the decision of driver A to turn right at the previous intersection, the failure of driver A to pack her lunch before leaving home (a detour that would have delayed her and, hence, avoided the accident). In a case such as this, where the smallest change of detail would alter the outcome, just about anything that driver A and B did, or did not do, or that their cars did, or did not do, could be considered important to explaining why this particular car crashed at this particular place and at this particular moment in time.

Why, to take an equally perplexing example, did the AIDS patient die (before reaching life expectancy)? Because (one might say): she was unlucky; she contracted pneumonia; she was not taking drug treatments; she could not afford to pay for these treatments (and had no insurance);

---

27. See King et al. (1994: 94, 108, 185) for a mathematical treatment of this problem, and Mackie (1974: ch 7) for a philosophical treatment.

she was working part-time and so was not covered by her employer; she was engaging in unsafe sex; she was engaging in unsafe sex because of some early-childhood experiences that led her to disregard the value of her own life; no cure for AIDS had been yet discovered. Many other causes could be manufactured, but the point is by now clear.

Let us pursue the car accident a little further. If someone argues that the accident was caused because both cars were working, which is to say hurtling through space at some forty miles per hour, one would call this person a fool (or perhaps, a philosopher). But why? What grounds do we have for calling her a fool? It will not do simply to point out that this causal property is necessary but not sufficient – for, as we have seen, an infinite number of factors could be similarly labeled. The point is that we *assume* that cars hurtle through space. This is what they are designed to do, and this is what they do, in actual fact, with great regularity. To say that cars collided because they were moving would be like saying the man tripped because he was walking. For cars, hurtling through space constitutes what Hart and Honoré call the "normal course of events."[28]

Charles Taylor gives the example of a bridge that collapses.[29] To be sure, a car was going over it at the time, and had the car not been there the bridge would not have collapsed. However, we are inclined to expect cars to go over bridges. As cars are made to hurtle over bridges, bridges are made to sustain them. Thus, when they fail to do so we are not likely to blame the car.[30] Suppose that we had not completed the building of a bridge, and a car unexpectedly appeared on top of said bridge, causing its collapse. Under these rather different circumstances it will be more correct to say that the car caused the accident.

Similar principles of selection apply to the analysis of causation in social science contexts. If we are interested in explaining why *A* won the election, we are probably not going to be happy with the explanation that *A* won because people decided to vote. It is true, of course, and could be considered a necessary condition of *A*'s victory. But it is not a causal factor we are likely to dwell upon – unless, of course, there are some unusual features of this polity or this election that would cause us to consider mass abstention as a realistic possibility. (Here, the distinction between a condition and a cause seems apt.)

I call the selection factor that helps us separate critical from noncritical factors the *contingency* criterion. Proper explanations seek out the

---

28. Hart and Honoré (1966: 225).
29. Taylor (1970: 53).
30. Causation, of course, need not have anything to do with blame in the moral sense; I use the term loosely here.

most contingent cause from a field of possible factors; the so-called cause is distinguished from background circumstances or boundary conditions. Those explanations that violate our sense of the normal course of events within a given context by identifying a *non*contingent cause are judged to be poor explanations.[31]

One can think about the logic of this selection criterion in the following way. A causal argument necessarily assumes a good deal about the world – namely, that it continues to revolve in about the same way over the temporal scope of the inference. This is often referred to as the ceteris paribus assumption. Within this structure of what happens normally, repeatedly, one or two things seem unusual, unexpected. These are the contingent factors to which we assign causal status.

We do much the same thing when we make plans for the future; we assume, that is, that the world as we know it will continue to exist, and we will continue to exist, until the plan we have made comes to fruition. This requires a certain degree of faith, one might say, but such faith has been borne out by experience. And so it is with causation. Without normality assumptions we would be unable to attribute causal status to anything – even events that we directly observe.

Things are even more complicated when we ascend from these everyday examples to examples of causal analysis in social science. Here, the contingent element of a causal relationship is not always so clear. Even so, we depend on some judgment of normality and contingency (which are, of course, two sides of the same coin) to assess all causal arguments.

Consider the proposition, common among journalists and well-known commentators, that we do not have better government in Washington because politicians are more interested in getting reelected than in solving problems of public policy. In other words, self-interested behavior is the cause of our current mess. This may be true, in the sense that a wholesale change of perspective on the part of the Washington establishment with regards to their reelection might lead to significant policy changes. But does this explanation identify the most contingent element with respect to this outcome of interest? Can advocates of this position think of other examples where members of a legislature have

31. The concept of contingency reiterates the same basic idea expressed by other writers under a variety of rubrics – "abnormality" (Hart and Honoré 1959: 32–3), the "normal course of events" (Hart and Honoré 1966: 225), "in the circumstances" (Marini and Singer 1988: 353), a "causal field" (Mackie 1965/1993: 39), and "difference in a background" (Einhorn and Hogarth 1986). See also Holland (1986). All point to the task of differentiating a foreground (the cause) from a background (the structure against which the causal relationship can be understood) by identifying that causal feature that is most contingent.

decided, as a group, to ignore their reelection prospects and pursue *only* those policies that, personally, they consider to be in the national interest? As a causal proposition, "self-interest" violates our sense of normality; it confuses a more or less permanent background condition with a contingent cause.

Consider, as a second example, a range of arguments about the cause of income inequality in the United States. (1) "Inequality is caused by the selfishness of the rich. If rich people shared their wealth with the poor, the rate of inequality would decline." (2) "Inequality is caused by counterproductive behavior by the poor. If they worked hard, saved their money, invested in education, avoided criminal activity, and limited drug and alcohol consumption, glaring income inequalities would be substantially reduced." (3) "Inequality is caused by capitalism." (Implied: preindustrial and communist societies are more egalitarian.) All these causal propositions are true. They imply sufficient conditions for the lessening of wealth inequalities in America. Are they *useful?* It is probably clear to the reader that there is something funny about these arguments. They all violate assumptions of normality; they ask us to accept as plausible a set of circumstances that is so different from the state of circumstances actually existing in the United States as to be somewhat unreal. By contrast, one might consider a fourth proposition: "High levels of inequality are the product of government policies." This is equally true, and more to the point, it is relatively contingent. It is more likely, in other words, that the U.S. government will change policies (e.g., establishing work-friendly social policies, increased child support, better health insurance coverage, higher minimum wages...) than it is that (a) the rich will voluntarily donate vast sums of money to the poor, (b) that the poor will be Horatio Algerized, or (c) that capitalism will be exchanged for a preindustrial or communistic economic system. Government policy is the most contingent cause among this set of proposed causes.

The principle of contingency applies equally to counterfactuals. If we are interested in the outbreak of the Civil War, we do not want to hear about the possible poisoning of Abraham Lincoln during his 1860 campaign. (Had he been poisoned, we might speculate, the Republicans might not have won the presidential campaign, which might have averted the secession of the South from the Union.) This is so far outside the normal course of events (*normally* people are not poisoned), that it would be downright silly of any historian to mention it. One can think of numerous other examples of things that, were they to have occurred (or *not* occurred), would have "altered the course of history," as the phrase goes. Similarly, to say that the course of Reconstruction was altered by Lincoln's assassination is an inference that seems very real, and very useful. Precisely, one might add, for the same reasons: because assassination is such an *unusual* event.[32]

"All possibilities for a world," writes Geoffrey Hawthorn, "should ... start from a world as it otherwise was. They should not require us to unwind the past. And the consequences we draw from these alternatives should initially fit with the other undisturbed runnings-on in that world. Neither the alternative starting points nor the runnings-on we impute to them should be fantastic."[33] Thus, we arrive at the following formulation: in identifying causes we seek those inferences that do least violence to the normal, expected course of events. The more normality a given inference assumes (in light of what we know of the world and of a given era or context), the more readily we bestow causal status on that inference. This means that for actually occurring events, *contingency* is prized: we want to identify the contingent event amid the broad current of noncontingent events that constitute the normal course of history and human behavior. Lincoln's assassination is such an event. So are structural flaws in the design of the bridge, or the drunkenness of one of the drivers in the car accident. By contrast, with counterfactual events – events not actually occurring – we want to find those that are *least* contingent (most normal). Thus, causal arguments based on Lincoln's actual assassination (1865) are more meaningful than causal arguments based on his nonassassination (1860).

Criteria-Jockeying: A Brief Example

I have discussed many examples of tradeoffs among the fourteen formal criteria of causal inference presented in this section. But I have done so with reference to only two or three criteria at a time. It may be useful, therefore, to examine how a larger number of criteria interact within a particular research site. I will explore the subfield of voting behavior, a field with a fairly simple, and easily specified, dependent variable ("How did you vote?"), but one that encompasses a wide variety of independent variables. Arguments within this field, as within most fields of social science, have a great deal to do with the criteria of causal explanation that writers choose to prioritize. It is a good case study of criteria-jockeying. The causal factors of interest – demographic characteristics, party identification, ideology, issue-positions, and so forth – will be familiar to most readers. Most can be traced back to the landmark *American Voter* studies of the 1950s and 1960s.[34] What, then, can we say about the cri-

32. See Lieberson (1985: ch 3).
33. Hawthorn (1991: 158).
34. Campbell et al. (1960).

terial merits of these different explanations in this important question of causal inference?

With respect to *specification,* a clear advantage can be seen for "hard" demographic categories like sex and age. Other characteristics, including race, ethnicity, and religion, pose problems. What is a person's race, if she is not "pure-bred"? What, indeed, is pure-bred (how far back should one trace a lineage)? Are Hispanic Americans a race, or a variation of "white"? What is a person's religion, if she is not actively practicing a religion? Party identification is also problematic from this perspective. Although we have a standard set of survey questions to draw upon, there is ongoing debate about how to classify those respondents who call themselves independent but lean toward one or the other party. Ideology poses even greater challenges to specification because it can be operationalized in so many ways – for example, according to the respondent's self-placement on a left-right scale, according to their self-placement among a set of ideological categories (liberal, conservative), or according to their positions on specific issues.

With respect to *differentiation, priority,* and *independence* the vices and virtues of different explanatory frameworks are similar. Demographic variables, particularly sex and age, are most satisfactory, being easily differentiated, prior, and independent relative to other causal variables and to the outcome of interest (voting behavior). They are least liable to problems of circularity, tautology, and endogeneity (we have discussed the nearly synonymous meaning of these terms). With issue-positions, in contrast, we may easily establish differentiation, but we may have trouble establishing priority and independence. Indeed, some studies indicate that the voting choice influences voters' positions on the issues (they wish to achieve congruence between their views and the views of their favored party or candidate).[35]

With respect to the *depth* of an explanation, on the other hand, we find ideology to be one of the most attractive frameworks. Generally speaking, ideology manages to explain the voting decision in a more complete and nuanced fashion than other approaches. In statistical terms, one would say that ideology explains a greater portion of the variance in the outcome. Party identification is also fairly successful in this regard. Demographic explanations, by contrast, are generally rather thin. With some exceptions, they do not explain a large portion of the voting decision.

35. See Page and Jones (1979).

When it comes to *breadth,* the positions of these rival causes are again reversed. Those with the greatest range of applicability (through time and across the world of democracies) are variables like social class, gender, and party identification. Other sorts of explanations, such as race, ethnicity, and issue-positions, do not travel comfortably from one context to another. Even social class may be difficult to compare across countries with different class structures.

There is little to say about *parsimony* except the obvious. Each rival explanation, taken on its own, is equally parsimonious (unless, of course, the handling of the topic is unwieldy). Yet, those writers striving to *combine* different causal factors in the same general explanation will be forced to sacrifice this virtue for others.

Most standard explanatory frameworks can make strong claims to *analytic utility,* but we can imagine many explanations that would not. Incidents specific to a given campaign, for example, unless placed within a broader rubric, will not score well on analytic utility; they don't help us to understand anything other than that particular election.

Relevance, similarly, can be established for most explanations. But some writers will have to work harder than others. Any explanation rooted in race, class, or gender is likely to claim the immediate attention of the general public. These are things that most of us care about; they are intrinsically interesting. Explanations drawing on party identification, political structures, or more obscure demographic categories have higher hurdles to clear.

Of other criteria – *accuracy, precision, innovation, intelligibility,* and *contingency* – it is difficult to say anything in the general case. Particular inferences may be accurate or inaccurate, for example, but we cannot say that particular *classes* of causal explanation are more likely to produce accurate inferences than others with respect to this outcome of interest (voting behavior). The general point still holds. What makes a causal inference persuasive or nonpersuasive, useful or unuseful, is in part determined by the specific criteria that the writer seeks to satisfy. And to satisfy one criterion is often to neglect others. There is no avoiding the business of tradeoffs.

Appendix: "INUS" Causes

Our framework may also help to make sense of some of the more complicated philosophical issues surrounding causation. When we use the terms *necessary* and *sufficient,* John Mackie correctly points out, we usually mean a cause that is neither necessary nor sufficient to produce a result. He explores the example of a house fire that is caused, according to the analysis of insurance experts, by an electrical short-circuit in a certain section of the building. The short-circuit, however (i.e., this particular short-circuit) is neither necessary nor sufficient to produce a house fire on this property. Rather, it indicates a cause that is an insufficient but necessary part of a condition that is itself unnecessary but sufficient for the result – an INUS condition, in Mackie's well-known terminology. He explains: "The experts are saying, in effect, that the short-circuit is a condition of this sort, that it occurred, that the other conditions which conjoined with it to form a sufficient condition were also present, and that no other sufficient condition of the house's catching fire was present on this occasion."[36] But other causes *could* have caused the fire (or a similar fire), so this cause was clearly not "necessary." Moreover, many other conditions had to have been present in order that the identified cause, an electrical short-circuit, could have its actual effect (e.g., flammable material, oxygen...), so this cause was clearly not sufficient.

The exposition is faultless. But is the INUS condition a useful way of thinking about causation in the social sciences? What Mackie exposes is the inability of the necessary/sufficient distinction, long a hallmark of thinking about causation, to distinguish causes from non-causes. We have already remarked upon this. (For any single event, the "necessary" causes are *innumerable*. Since that event, or something like it, could probably be produced in other ways, these causes are not even necessary.) Yet, I contend, the necessary/sufficient distinction is a highly useful one. The caveat is that a writer must be aware of additional criteria that are applicable to the formation of causal inferences. She must be aware, in particular, of the fact that causes take shape against a background; without such a context, a causal proposition is underspecified. In the case of the fire, we are taking for granted certain things like oxygen, flammable material, and so forth. They form the context that makes the insurance experts' analysis – indeed, any analysis – possible. We usually do not need to specify such contexts because they are clear, as it were, from context. But we could do so if pressed to defend our causal reasoning (as Mackie urges us to do) by pointing to the greater *contingency* of our chosen cause, relative to other possible causes.

Similarly, in order for a causal inference to be fully specified we must clarify the positive and negative outcomes we envision – in other words, what it is precisely that we are trying to explain. In this case, the relevant

---

36. Mackie (1965/1993: 34).

question is whether we are trying to explain the cause of this particular fire at this particular point in time, the cause of a fire occurring at this address over some longer period of time, or some other outcome. In the former case, our task is presumably the same as the insurance experts' – to assess the "cause in fact." So stated, and with the understood background context, we can identify the electricity short-circuit as *the* cause – that is, the necessary and (perhaps) sufficient cause – of the fire in question. The common idiom is vindicated; we need not resort to Mackie's awkward acronym.

Nor would it help us to do so, for simply to call a cause INUS says nothing about whether we have made a good causal argument. (Is one INUS cause better than another, or better than a non-INUS cause?) Mackie's work has made us more aware of the ambiguities involved in our use of the word cause. Yet, as with much philosophical work, one finds that once we have taken our language apart we feel a strong need to put it back together. In other words, although we *could* start to talk about "INUS conditions" rather than causes, I think we would find this terminology unnecessary and insufficient (not to mention tiresome).

PART III
Research Design

8

Research Design: General Criteria

But is it True?
– Aaron Wildavsky[1]

Social science methodology, I have argued, may be usefully divided into three broad tasks, concepts, propositions, and research design, corresponding to the three parts of the book. Concepts nest within propositions, since propositions must be stated with key concepts. And propositions nest within research designs, since all propositions must be demonstrated in some fashion.

Research design refers here to any investigation of the empirical world that bears upon a proposition's truth-value – its degree of truth or probability of truth, which we called accuracy in Chapter 4. How do we know that a given proposition is true or false? How will we go about demonstrating (i.e., verifying, falsifying, proving) its truth? These are the central questions of research design.

This chapter explores general criteria pertaining to all research designs. Chapter 9 discusses a variety of methods by which writers attempt to maximize these desiderata. Chapter 10 sets forth two polar strategies that all research designs navigate between – confirmatory and exploratory.

Since *causal* relationships are the most complicated sort, at least from a methodological point of view, these chapters focus primarily on research design in causal inference. Of course, causal analysis rests on descriptive analysis. We must be able to identify an X and a Y in order to determine their relationship. At a basic level, descriptive and causal analysis are inextricably linked, as we have emphasized (Chapter 6). Indeed, insofar as both sorts of inference rest upon comparative refer-

---

1. Wildavsky (1995).

ence points, they are quite similar (see next section). However, the problems posed by descriptive analysis involve few epistemological leaps of faith (except, of course, that leap of faith that supposes we can understand anything at all about the world). Descriptive analysis involves two empirical questions: (1) what is out there and (2) what will we call it? The first question is factual in nature. Historians have discussed the rules of engagement with respect to events occurring in the distant past, and many of the same rules could probably be applied to the analysis of contemporary events.[2] Yet, it seems likely that the techniques of factual verification will vary considerably according to the subject matter (even *within* the field of history). As for what to call these facts – how to group them, define them, and label them – we have discussed these questions in connection with concept formation (Part I) and description (Chapter 6). There is more to say about these subjects, but we will not attempt to do so here.

Much of our discussion will bear on research design problems in *predictive* inference, since both causal and predictive inference are correlative in nature. Indeed, causal inference might be considered – methodologically, that is – a complex form of predictive inference. In both cases we attempt to demonstrate covariation between X and Y. In causal inference, however, we assert that X *generates* Y.

Hume, one of the first philosophers to embrace a rigorously empirical approach to human understanding, struggled with the quandary of how causation is apprehended. There is nothing, he perceived, about a conjunction of events that would lead us to assume a *causal* relationship between the two. Even so, "after a repetition of similar instances, the mind is carried by habit, upon the appearance of one event, to expect its usual attendant, and to believe that it will exist. This connexion, therefore, which we *feel* in the mind, this customary transition of the imagination from one object to its usual attendant, is the sentiment or impression from which we form the idea of power or necessary connexion."[3] The metaphysical nature of causation has led some writers to conclude that causation has no useful place in scientific or philosophical investigation.[4] I do not find this radically skeptical perspective very com-

2. See Bloch (1941/1953), Fischer (1970), Hamilton (1996), Thompson (1978: 30–1), and Winks (1969).

3. Hume (1960: 219). Otherwise stated, "our natural conception of causality derives from program in the brain that 'allows the forecast that sequences of events that have been repeatedly connected in the past will (probably) be connected in the future'" (Young 1978: 234; quoted in Marini and Singer 1988: 367).

4. See, for example, Russell (1917/1968: 174). See also statistical work from Karl Pearson to the present (discussed in Pearl 2000: 340–1).

pelling. (What would we replace causation with? Could we do without it?)[5] However, it is worth noting that causation faces problems of demonstration not shared by other inferences, and it prompts us to ask what sort of evidence and inference might allow us to make this leap of faith in some instances, but not in others.

We begin with the importance of comparative analysis, discussed in general terms. We proceed to a brief discussion of key terms – made necessary by the multiple, and often contradictory, uses of basic methodological terms. (Readers unfamiliar with this terrain are advised to read this section carefully.) Finally, we present the main argument – research design as a criterial venture.

Why Compare?

All knowledge is comparative. Or, as one writer puts it, "thinking without comparison is unthinkable."[6] In order to know one thing, we must know neighboring things, perhaps even things that are quite different from what we set out to talk about. In this, propositions are like concepts.[7] We understand trees in terms of forests and forests in terms of trees, brothers in terms of sisters and sisters in terms of brothers. No proposition is an island.[8]

Consider World War II. Why, to begin with, do we refer to this event as a war? Evidently, because it shares a family resemblance with other events that we have come to know as wars. If it did not share these characteristics, or fewer of them, then we should have to struggle for some other word to apply to this event. But whatever concept we arrived at would be grounded in the differences and similarities we find between the phenomenon of interest and other related phenomena. New knowledge is categorizable only in terms of old knowledge; what we learn is contingent on what we already know. Moreover, what we have to say about WWII will depend heavily on other cases of war. Having called it a war we have already said a good deal about the event in question – we have elucidated its generic features. This is the classificatory feature of language. The addition of the qualifier "world" links this event with one other, the "first" world war. It narrows the topic from the generic (or

---

5. As Hausman (1992: 297) notes, "the topic of causality is unfortunately not only a mess, but also unavoidable."

6. Swanson (1971: 145), quoted in Ragin (1987: 30–1).

7. "Terms both demarcate and connect," writes Dewey (1938: 349), "and hence no term has logical force save in distinction from and relation to other terms."

8. Indeed, as Campbell (1919/1957: 50) notes, the chain of knowledge is endless and virtually seamless. See also Bowen and Petersen (1999), Campbell (1975: 179–80), Durkheim (1897/1951: 41), Jevons (1877/1958: 1), Sartori (1991), and Taylor (1985: 22).

genus) "war" to a particular type of war and set of wars. Our comparative frame has become more focused.

Even when focusing on the unique features of World War II, even, that is, when writing in an idiographic mode, our commentary necessarily rests on a consideration of other wars. To put the point in the most general light: one cannot talk about World War II – and, by extension, of anything – without considering how it is like, and unlike, other phenomena. This is a feature of human language and human cognition.[9] Propositions that individualize are every bit as comparative as reductive propositions. Lumpers (those who like to put things together into big piles) and splitters (those who prefer to disaggregate reality into smaller piles), on some basic level, are both comparativists.[10]

Let us take this argument to its logical extreme. Biography, relating the life of a single individual, tends to focus on unique features of that individual. The underlying thesis of most biography is, "There is only one *Y* [Gladstone, Lincoln, Trotsky, et al.]." At the same time, however, biography thrives on comparison. How can one describe Gladstone without referring to Disraeli? Or Lincoln without referring to Douglas? What is it that made Gladstone Gladstone, and not Smith, Jones, or Tucker? If we wish to answer this question we must take a look at Smith, Jones, and Tucker. We want to have captured all those elements of *this* man's experience that made him different from, or similar to (depending on one's argument), other "cases" of man. Even proper nouns invoke comparisons.

If concepts and descriptive propositions are minimally comparative, causal proposition is particularly so, regardless of how many instances are being studied. Indeed, causal relationships cannot be perceived at all without a backlog of relevant experience.[11] Hume observes, "The first time a man saw the communication of motion by impulse, as by the shock of two billiard balls, he could not pronounce that the one event was *connected:* but only that it was *conjoined* with the other. After he has observed several instances of this nature, he then pronounces them to be *connected* [causally]."[12] We are able to label one thing a "cause"

---

9. As E. H. Carr (1961: 80) points out, "The very use of language commits the historian, like the scientist, to generalization."

10. For discussion of lumpers and splitters, see Chapter 2 and Hexter (1979: 141–3). When one utters the word comparative – as in comparative history – one is usually understood to be talking about comparison through space (i.e., America/Europe, North Dakota/South Dakota, Smith/Jones). These are cases observed at roughly the same points in time. However, comparative knowledge can be *temporal* as well, as in our previous discussion of World Wars I and II. Indeed, this is the sort of comparison that historical accounts generally exploit.

11. See Marini and Singer (1988: 351).

12. Hume (1960: 219).

and another an "effect" because we have seen many similar instances relate to one another in similar ways. It fits with experience. The point is, both kinds of causal knowledge, common sense and scientific, are premised on the identification of comparative reference points ("cases").

Key Terms

We have already emphasized the importance of concepts in the work of empirical social science (Part I). Regrettably, concepts are even more confused in social science methodology. No doubt, this confusion has something to do with the nonreferential character of methodological terms (they do not refer to things "out there" in the phenomenal world). But it is also because these terms are heavily implicated in each others' definitions. Thus, the minor alteration of a single definition has a house-of-cards effect on the semantic field. This is why we will attempt to define the entire field at once, rather than taking a term-by-term approach to definition.[13]

Let us begin with *case*, perhaps the most polysemic term in the social science lexicon. Here are six common definitions (there may be more!):

1. *argument for* ("the case for action is strong," "the prosecution's case is strong")

2. *circumstance or situation* ("in any case," "in all cases," "in the first case")

3. *example* ("a case of the flu," "a case of democracy at work")

4. *unit under study where within-case analysis is undertaken* ("a case study of France")

5. *observation that provides, or might provide, independent evidence of a proposition* ("Every case points to the same conclusion")

6. *observation* ("I checked that chart 44 times and in each case it indicated that India was a democracy")

I will refer to definitions 1–3 as everyday (nontechnical) definitions. They are quite distinct from each other and from definitions 4–6. We should be aware, however, that to say "Sweden is a case of ethnic strife" (sense 3) is to indicate something quite different from "Sweden is a case in my study of ethnic strife" (sense 4). The first is factually untrue (Sweden, a largely homogeneous country, has experienced little ethnic strife). The second is stipulative. Indeed, Sweden might be a terrific case

---

13. For additional terms and further clarification on the methodological lexicon, see Blackburn (1994), Durbin (1988), Mitchell (1979), Sartori (1984), and Vogt (1993).

(sense 4) in a study of ethnic strife. These different senses of the term are usually clear from context and need not detain us.

Definitions 4–6, however, bear directly on methodological discussions. Regrettably, they are often difficult to distinguish from each other; indeed, the definition of case often varies (legitimately) within a single study. This definitional ambiguity causes a good deal of methodological friction, as will become clear in the following discussion. Although this ambiguity will never be entirely resolved, we will choose sense 5 as our core meaning of case.[14] *Case,* then, as employed here, refers to any observation that is intended to provide independent evidence of a proposition. This is a minimal definition; the following sections of the chapter discuss the characteristics of a *good* (ideal-typical) case.

Every case comprises one or more *observations,* and is situated within a *sample* (all the cases chosen for study) and a *population* (including cases studied as well as those that remain unstudied) but fell into the purview of the causal inference). All cases must exemplify the same *unit of analysis.* Cases should generate variation within and/or across a given unit of analysis; hence, evidence may be either *within-* or *across-case.* All these terms, finally, gain meaning only within a particular proposition, or research question.

We now offer formal definitions for these additional terms (and several more besides).

> *Unit of analysis:* The sort of phenomena (e.g., countries, political parties, individuals) that constitute cases in a given research context.
>
> *Population:* (aka *breadth, domain, scope*): All the cases that an inference is said to apply to, or "cover."
>
> *Sample:* The case, or cases, chosen for study, referred to collectively.[15]
>
> *Observation:* An element of a case. (Cases are constructed from one or more observations.)
>
> *N:* The total number of cases or observations in a given context (usually comprising the sample).

Let us proceed to a concrete example. Suppose I am investigating turnout rates (measured as a percentage of the eligible population) in elections around the world. Table 8.1 demonstrates four ways one might go about investigating this research question (there are, of course, others). Research

---

14. This definition may be further justified on grounds of field utility (see Chapter 3): we have separate terms – *case-study* and *observation* – for senses 4 and 6, but not for sense 5.
15. My usage here deviates from those who use sample to refer only to random samples (cases chosen randomly from a population).

Table 8.1   *One Research Question, Four Research Designs*

Research question: What accounts for variable turnout rates throughout the
world?

1. **Cross-sectional Research Design**
   Evidence: across-case
   Unit of analysis: countries
   Temporal scope: synchronic (the 1990s)
   Population: all countries and semisovereign territories (210)
      Sample (N = 163)
         Case: mean turnout in a given country during the 1990s
            Observation: turnout for each country-election in the 1990s
      Unstudied cases (37)

2. **Single-country, Single-shot (United States) Research Design**
   Evidence: within-case ("case-study")
   Unit of analysis: individuals within a single country (the United States)
   Temporal scope: synchronic (1990)
   Population: all eligible voters in the United States (app. 260,000,000)
      Sample (N = 1,000)
         Case: one person's survey responses
            Observation: a response to an individual question (N = 50)
      Unstudied cases (259,999,000)

3. **Single-country, Historical (United States) Research Design**
   Evidence: within-case ("case-study")
   Unit of analysis: presidential elections (United States)
   Temporal scope: diachronic (1828–2000)
   Population: presidential elections (43)
      Sample: 20th-century presidential elections (N = 25).
         Case: aggregate turnout in a single presidential election
            Observation: votes in a single presidential election (N = various)
      Unstudied cases (18)

4. **Cross-sectional, Time-series Research Design**
   Evidence: across-case and within-case
   Unit of analysis: country-elections
   Temporal scope: synchronic and diachronic (1945–97)
   Population (2,100)
      Sample (N = 1,000)
         Case: turnout in each country-election in the period under study
            Observation: probably equivalent to "case" (unless several sources for
               the same election are considered)
      Unstudied cases (1,100)

methods will be discussed in Chapter 9; here, we are interested only in terminology, so as to situate this later discussion. The point to notice is that
our key terms all change according to the research design chosen.

Because different research designs define terms in different ways, and
because a given study may employ several research designs, there is
rarely a single and unequivocal answer to the apparently simple question, *What is your N?* Multiple and changing definitions are present, and
ineradicable, in our discussion of *any* empirical research topic in social
science. Thus, if I had chosen to employ research design #3, someone
might respond that my population is *really* countries, not presidential
elections. This is true in the broader scheme of things, for we have
already specified that the research question of interest involves variation
across countries, not merely within the United States. Yet, the logic of
our research design demands that we distinguish between the sample
employed (twentieth-century elections) and the larger set of elections
(1828–2000) that, we assume, illustrate the same causal relationships.
Thus, we cannot avoid the double-meaning of "population."

It will also be observed that every definition is hostage to a particular
way of framing the research question or hypothesis. Thus, if I had begun
my research by specifying that I was only interested in *twentieth-century*
elections, under the presumption that things worked very differently in
the nineteenth century, there would be no distinction between sample
and population in research design #3. But there would still be a difference between the definition of population as employed in this within-
case (United States only) analysis and the population of the inference.

If we make a further adjustment to the research question, specifying
that we are not interested in turnout at-large but only in variable turnout
rates in U.S. history, then *only* research design #3 will be relevant. The
population specified by the research design will then be the same as the
population of the inference.

To repeat, there is never a single true-for-all-times-and-circumstances
definition of these methodological terms. An author's original understanding of a study may be perfectly correct for purposes of her own
research, but not for other research. Indeed, it is common to see country
studies appropriated as "case studies" in the analysis of some broader phenomenon. Here, a high-N study is collapsed to a single data-point ($N = 1$).
This is what we observe occurring in research design #2. Nominally, the
$N = 1,000$; but in the context of a cross-national study of voting behavior,
it is a single case study ($N = 1$).

The distinction between across-case and within-case analysis is particularly fraught, as we have already observed. Another way of understanding this distinction is to say that within-case analysis is designed to prove

a minor proposition, which will then be mustered as evidence for the major thesis. Because every proposition rests on another proposition, this is a potentially infinite regress. Here we have only one layer – from across-case to within-case analysis – but we might also have explored within-case analysis for each within-case case. The point at which we cease to interrogate evidence and simply accept what is self-evidently true is the point at which cases become "observations." *Any* proposition of significance demonstrates this tiered quality: cases build upon cases build on cases build on observations. It is an endless regress if one chooses, in the manner of the curious schoolchild, to interrogate *why?* at each level of analysis. (Why the variance in cross-country turnout? Why the variance in U.S. turnout? Why the variance in turnout among American whites? Among blacks? Among residents of Ohio?...) At some point, a study will have to take something for granted. This is the point where the research design ends and general notions of plausibility kick in.

Other research design issues, such as temporal scope, are equally fraught. Most studies have some diachronic element; but few are self-conscious in the way that they construct cases through time. The important point to remember is that in order for a case to perform its function (providing independent evidence of a proposition), it must retain some degree of independence from other cases (see "independence" below).

General Criteria

Because causal knowledge is thoroughly dependent on comparison, our choice of temporal and spatial reference points is perhaps the most important decision we face in a study. The topics of case selection and research design are thus virtually indistinguishable, and so we will treat them.

Why, wondered Mill, is "a single instance, in some cases, sufficient for a complete induction, while in others myriads of concurring instances, without a single exception known or presumed, go such a very little way towards establishing an universal proposition?"[16] Ten factors, I argue, characterize goodness in case selection – and, more generally, in research design – *plenitude, boundedness, comparability, independence, representativeness, variation, analytic utility, replicability, mechanism,* and *causal comparison* – as summarized in Table 8.2. Here, as previously, I adhere to a criterial approach. Research design is governed by tradeoffs among different criteria, rather than fixed rules of procedure. Effective research design involves juggling these desiderata into the best possible fit.

16. Mill (1843/1872: 206).

Table 8.2 *Research Design: General Criteria*

═══

1. Plenitude (evidence). How many cases? How large is the sample (N)?

2. Boundedness (non-arbitrariness, coherence). Does the specified population include relevant cases and exclude irrelevant ones? Does the domain make sense?

3. Comparability (equivalence, unit homogeneity, cross-case validity) (*antonym:* uniqueness). (a) *Descriptive comparability* (conceptual validity): How comparable are the Xs and the Y? (b) *Causal comparability:* How similar are the cases with respect to factors that might affect Y, or the X:Y relationship of interest? (c), Can any remaining dissimilarities be taken into account (controlled, modeled)?

4. Independence (*antonyms:* autocorrelation, Galton's problem, contamination) How independent are the cases with respect to factors that might affect Y, or the X:Y relationship of interest? Can any remaining interdependencies be taken into account (controlled, modeled)?

5. Representativeness (external validity) (*antonyms:* sample bias, selection bias). Are the cases representative of the population with respect to all factors that might affect Y, or the X:Y relationship of interest? Can any remaining unrepresentative elements be taken into account (controlled, modeled)?

6. Variation (variance). Do the cases offer variation (a) on Y, (b) on relevant Xs, (c) without collinearity, and (d) within a particular case?

7. Analytic utility (theoretical utility). Do the cases enhance the analytic utility of the sample?

8. Replicability (reliability). Can the research design be replicated? Are the results reliable?

9. Mechanism (process-tracing, discerning, pattern-matching, causal narrative, congruence, contiguity, colligation, intermediate processes, causal framework). Is there a plausible mechanism connecting X to Y?

10. Causal comparison (hypothesis testing, specification problems, omitted variable bias). Does the research design allow us to test alternate hypotheses? Are there *better* explanations for a given outcome? Is the purported X superior (along criteria 1–9) than other possible Xs? Would the addition or subtraction of other variables alter the results?

═══

Plenitude

All knowledge is comparative, we have said. It follows that the more comparative reference points we have at our disposal the better we can test the veracity of a given proposition. The accumulation of comparative reference points constitutes "evidence," and more evidence is better (ceteris paribus). For this reason, *plenitude* in a sample is desirable; the more cases one has to demonstrate a posited causal relationship the more confidence we are likely to place in the truth of that proposition. Cases, we should remind ourselves, are simply observations that provide independent evidence of a proposition. One case is much better than none. Indeed, it is a quantum leap, since the absence of cases means that there is no empirical support whatsoever for a proposition. Two cases are better than one, and so forth. As Ray Wolfinger reminds us, the plural of anecdote is *data* (implied: anecdotes are better than anecdote). The same logic that compels us to provide empirical support for our beliefs also provides the logic behind plenitude in case selection.

A large sample may also help in specifying a proposition: clarifying a positive and negative outcome, a set of cases that the proposition is intended to explain (a context or contrast space), and operational definitions of the foregoing. In order to see why this might be so let us return to an example from Chapter 5. When the priest asks Willie Sutton why he robs banks he responds (by common report) that he does so because that is where the money is. Sutton and the priest have different ideas about what constitutes the positive and negative outcome at issue in this causal question. For Sutton it is banks versus other things (e.g., trains); for the priest it is robbing versus not robbing. Would this sort of disagreement be possible in a large-N study? It is difficult to imagine it being so, for in the act of creating additional cases one is more or less *obliged* to specify the outcomes at issue.

Does this fanciful (and perhaps apocryphal) example have echoes in social science? You bet it does. We explored the question of "big government." If our universe of cases includes only one country it is very difficult to evaluate the outcome in question. How do we know whether the government is big or small? Any number of perspectives are possible on this fraught subject. We might explore government spending in actual dollars, in constant dollars, as a fraction of the population, or as a fraction of the gross domestic product. We might use as our baseline (our contrast space) any number of different years. If we choose 1945, a war year, we will reach very different conclusions than if we choose 1960. The point is, we will have difficulty saying what, precisely, we *mean* by "government" if our cases are limited to one (examined over a short period of time). And without an adequate specification of outcome, any causal proposition will be essentially unfalsifiable.

Another example may be drawn from the Kurosawa classic, *Rashomon*. The central event of this film is a murder. The action of the film, however, concerns the replaying of that murder from a variety of different perspectives, according to the accounts of different eyewitnesses. In social science circles, *Rashomon* has become identified with the subjectivity of human perceptions and the importance of interpretation in endowing actual physical events with meaning. It is a case study in hermeneutics. For present purposes, what is interesting about this much-discussed example is that a "Rashomon effect" is likely to manifest itself whenever the N is small, but rarely when the N is large. If, let us say, the movie's investigators were attempting to research not a single murder but rather a large number of crimes, or if they were attempting to place this single event within the context of other crimes taking place in the region, under these circumstances it is likely that they would be able to distinguish adequately between more and less plausible accounts. Indeed, when one says that a problem has been "contextualized," or "put into perspective," this is another way of saying that a small-N perspective has been superceded by a large-N perspective. It is no wonder that we often feel more comfortable drawing conclusions from broader perspectives. In addition to distinguishing among possible causes (a point we will make shortly), large-N research designs have the effect of creating a clear context for the argument.

The same basic point may be put into statistical terms. As Harry Eckstein observes, "through any single point an infinite number of curves or lines can be drawn."[17] In other words, the causal relationships that one might intuit from a single case (data point) are, in principle, infinite. If I am constructing arguments about the French Revolution and my N is equal to 1 (the French Revolution), the context for my argument could be many things – the eighteenth century, the Old Regime, England, modern France, traditional societies, and so forth. It is very difficult to say. As Eckstein notes, "scarcely anything in the French *ancien regime* has not been blamed, by one writer or another, for the revolution, and all of their interpretations, however contradictory, are based on solid facts."[18] Part of this conundrum of apparent overdetermination stems from the $N = 1$ structure of these historical arguments. "Even with the widest imaginable knowledge of 'laws,'" noted Weber more than a

17. Eckstein (1975: 113).
18. Eckstein (1975: 101).

century ago, "we are helpless in the face of the question: how is the *causal explanation* of an *individual* fact possible – since a *description* of even the smallest slice of reality can never be exhaustive?"[19] In contrast, if I include in my study of the French Revolution a number of other cases (say, Anglo-European nation-states in the eighteenth century) then the background for my argument will be more clear, and likely explanations may be distinguished from less likely ones. Large-N studies, again, are more likely to succeed as fully specified propositions.

Large-N studies will also have an easier time identifying causal *contingency* in a research situation. (Noncontingent causes – those that are part of the normal course of events – have less claim to causal status, as discussed in Chapter 7.) To see why this is so, let us consider the $N = 1$ research design. With a single event under our microscope, any number of things might be considered part of the normal course of events. The writer has wide latitude to construct her own definition of contingency. However, if we broaden the number of cases under investigation we have *automatically* provided a way to distinguish between what is normal and what is abnormal. Whatever varies among these cases may be considered contingent; whatever does not may be considered part of the normal course of events. Thus, in the example of the fallen bridge, we do not need to ponder the relative normality of cars going over the bridge; we can simply examine our cases of bridges (fallen and standing) to see whether the passage of cars helps to explain variation on this outcome.

These are formal criteria pertaining to causal propositions (as discussed in Chapters 5 and 7). With respect to other criteria of case selection, the topic of this chapter, we should note briefly that plenitude usually enhances the boundedness, representativeness, and variation of a sample; it is, similarly, often at odds with the criterion of comparability. These points are discussed in the following sections.

Plenitude and Causal Types. Having argued for the utility of plenitude in a sample, we must take note of an important counterargument: that for sorting out *certain types* of causal relationships, those that are necessary or sufficient, a small sample may be appropriate, or even desirable.[20] I will argue that this is sometimes true, and sometimes not; in either case, we are on safer ground with more cases. I will argue, secondly, that plenitude is even more important when we are dealing

---

19. Weber (1905/1949: 78). It may be observed that the logical problems posed by INUS causes (see Chapter 7) are largely a product of the fact that $N = 1$.
20. See Dion (1998: 141), who argues for the utility of small-N analysis in considering necessary causes.

with causes of a probabilistic nature (a point that is not disputed). This section will bolster the case for plenitude; the reader should keep in mind, however, that we will temper this enthusiasm for large-N analysis as we proceed to discuss other desiderata.

Consider the following example. I observe A pick up a motorcycle by herself. I conclude from this that a single person is sufficient to carry a motorcycle. *Sufficiency* has apparently been proved; no other cases need be tested. Thus far, the argument for small-N research design seems warranted. Yet, let us note that the addition of additional cases (other persons trying to lift the motorcycle) will not in any way weaken our conclusion. More important, we should note that our sufficiency argument relies on the separation of foreground (causal) and background (noncausal) factors. Background factors, in this situation, are fairly obvious and unproblematic: gravity, a flat and stable surface for A to stand on, perhaps a light motorcycle, and so forth. In most social science settings it will not be so easy to differentiate foreground and background. Consider a revolution. If I observe that schoolteachers are manning the barricades in a revolution, may I safely conclude that schoolteachers are "sufficient" to produce a revolution? This is not a meaningful causal argument, and its deficiencies stem from the fact that we cannot really identify the sufficient cause (or causes) from those that are merely incidental without a broader range of cases.

If I wish to prove a *necessary* causal relationship, sample size is even more important. At the very least, I will need to test all cases demonstrating the outcome of interest. Thus, if I wish to explain the necessary cause or causes of revolution, I will need to examine all revolutions. One might feel warranted in ignoring negative outcomes (nonrevolutions). Yet, this corner-cutting approach is problematic. Suppose we find that all revolutions are accompanied by a rise in prices, leading us to propose – on the basis of our skewed sample – that inflation is a necessary condition of revolution. The argument seems plausible. On a whim, we decide to look at countries that did *not* succumb to revolution. Here, let us suppose, we find inflation to be just as common as in revolutionary regimes. Shall we still consider inflation a necessary cause of revolution? The argument is no longer so compelling. In any case, our study of additional cases has added relevant information to our initial analysis.

For causes of a probabilistic nature, the argument for plenitude is even stronger. Indeed, as a general rule, the more complex the causal relationship, the more cases we will need in order to test its intricacies.[21] We

---

21. This argument runs counter to Ragin (1987) and Rueschemeyer (1991). But see discussion later on within-case analysis.

should add that most causal relationships of interest to social science are probabilistic, not deterministic. Indeed, once we begin to measure the *rate* of inflation we have converted a categorical variable into a continuous variable – meaning that the causal relationship (if any) must be understood as probabilistic. Let us now examine some illustrations of complexity among probabilistic causes in order to see why these situations militate toward large-N analysis.

Consider the problem of variation (discussed at length below). If an outcome, or a causal factor of interest, varies only slightly from one case to the next we shall want to compensate for our lack of variation by extending the number of cases. Large samples, coupled with statistical analysis, are capable of detecting the presence of causal relationships even when the effects are slight. Generally speaking, the less the variance in outcome, the greater the number of cases that will be necessary to demonstrate a causal relationship. If we are investigating the effect of Catholicism on welfare spending, for example, it is likely that the contribution of this variable (if it is causal at all) will be minimal. One or two cases will be insufficient to prove this theory true or false. Yet, if we have 100 cases, our slight relationship may achieve causal significance (by standard statistical norms).

Similarly, if we face a situation in which a causal relationship is highly *irregular* – in which X sometimes causes Y, but not always – we prefer a large-N research design. Small samples are likely to mislead when X:Y relationships are unpredictable. The point may be clearer if we approach it from the other angle. For purposes of ordinary language analysis it is sufficient to interview a native speaker of a language (typically, oneself). The assumption underlying this research strategy is a reasonable one: everyone within a given linguistic group speaks the same language and has the same intuitive sense of correct usage. There is no need to draw a large sample of speakers, because they would all respond in more or less the same fashion. The salient feature about language usage is its *regularity*.[22] If, however, one's focus changes from language to political opinions one would expect a more irregular relationship between stimulus (question) and outcome (response). A survey of this sort that rested on a single respondent would be absurd. For this sort of research question the ordinary language philosopher must metamorphose into a survey researcher. We can imagine causal relationships of even greater irregularity. The general point, however, is clear: the more irregular the relationship between X and Y, the greater our need for additional cases.

22. See Pitkin (1972: 16).

For much the same reason, wherever an outcome of interest has several causes, operating in conjunction with one another or independently, we prefer a large sample. Suppose, for example, one suspects that the French Revolution was influenced by at least twenty different factors. Would this extraordinarily complex causal relationship be understandable (in any but the most impressionistic way) simply by studying one or two country cases? Problems of overdetermination are rife: many things appear to be a cause of this event and it is difficult to distinguish the causal weight carried by each one. It could be the burden of ongoing European wars, the corruption of the French administration, the landless state of the French peasantry – or any *combination* of the foregoing. (Consider, as well, various temporal *sequences* of these causal factors.) Unless exceptionally persuasive within-case evidence is available to solve this riddle, we will need a large number of cases (across-case cases) in order to increase our leverage on this complex problem. "High-X, high-N," is the relevant slogan here: the more factors (possible Xs) we must sort out, and the more complex and irregular their interaction, the more we desire additional cases to test all these possible causal relationships. In statistical language, this is often referred to as a problem of "degrees of freedom." There is little freedom in a small-N research design where many causal factors compete. One does not have much room to maneuver (or one has *too much* room to maneuver) where causal options are many and cases few. Without additional cases, all plausible hypotheses must be entertained, for none can be disconfirmed by the evidence. (This problem was discussed in Chapter 5 as a problem of specification.)[23]

Before concluding this discussion of causal complexity it should be pointed out that the viability of large-N samples is inextricably linked to the viability of statistical methods of analysis, on which the latter depend (see Chapter 9). This is not the place to undertake an evaluation of causal analysis as performed by statistical manipulation. However, it is important to note that common methods of quantitative analysis may privilege some sorts of causal relationships over others. Multiple regression, for example, generally treats causes as linear and additive: X_1, X_2,

23. See Collier and Collier (1991), and Lijphart (1971). Rueschemeyer and Stephens (1997: 60) report that at least sixty factors were identified as factors leading to the breakdown of democracy in interwar Europe by a recent study. Yet, the total number of cases in this study was limited to twenty – a daunting degrees-of-freedom problem. Campbell (1988: ch 15) also discusses the degrees-of-freedom problem. His conclusion on the viability of case-study methods (methods focused on a single unit) is somewhat more optimistic than that portrayed here. However, Campbell's guarded optimism stems from his recognition that a single unit, such as an indigenous culture, may offer numerous cases – that is, *within-case* variation (discussed later).

X_3, ... are inserted in a single equation and their effects are assumed to "add up" to explain some percentage of the total variance in Y. We know that some causes do not work in this fashion. Wherever multiple factors may cause a result *on their own* (multiple causation, as discussed in Chapter 7), or where varying causal sequences affect the particular interaction of causal factors, common regression techniques may give misleading results, or will have to be adjusted (e.g., by the use of interactive variables or nonlinear designs).[24]

Some of the difficulties discussed by writers critical of statistical analysis are probably best understood as problems of execution (where the wrong method is employed), or of interpretation (where the wrong results are inferred). We do not wish to damn a whole toolbox of methods because of their occasional misuse. What rightly concerns us are inherent limits, or intrinsic biases, of large-N methods of analysis. The issue is complicated by the fact that many quantitative techniques are actually quite new, or are just gaining currency within the social sciences. It seems premature to reach firm conclusions on this rapidly evolving set of methods. Indeed, scholars have been hard at work remedying the shortcomings of ordinary least squares regression analysis. Bear Braumoeller, for example, has proposed a method of analyzing multiple causal paths with large-N samples, thus potentially overcoming one of the problems noted previously.[25]

It seems likely that the menu of quantitative methods available to scholars will continue to grow in the coming years, so that – given the right choice of method – scholars will no no longer feel so constrained when playing the numbers game.[26] There is no reason, then, to suppose that numerical methods are *inherently* less capable than prose when faced with the task of analyzing causal complexity. More cases are still better.

24. Imputing causal relationships from correlational analysis is tricky business. See Abbott (1988), Achen (1977), Braumoeller (1999), Mahoney (2000), Marini and Singer (1988), McKim and Turner (1997), Ragin (1987), and Rueschemeyer (1991).
25. See Braumoeller (1999).
26. With this increased freedom of choice, however, come greater problems of use and interpretation. The more contextually-specific and flexible our methods, the more judgments are required by the analyst in choosing and deploying her method. Indeed, we need to have a good idea of the sort of causal relationship we are expecting to find before we begin to apply statistical models of analysis. Moreover, the more complicated a writer's method, the more assumptions are usually required to reach conclusions about causal relationships. In short, as the choice of methods becomes increasingly complex, the practice of "stats" is likely to become more like existing practices in qualitative methods (i.e., "squishy" and "interpretive"). But the general conclusion about this development should be optimistic, for this ambiguity has been present in our use of standard statistical techniques all along.

Boundedness

The foregoing argument for plenitude raises a fundamental objection, one often mustered in defense of case-study (small-N) methods. What if we are not interested in explaining the outcome of more than one or two cases? If the breadth of a causal inference is small, is sample-size still an issue? Suppose, for example, our sole concern is to explain the French Revolution, not other revolutions or revolutions in general. It is a vast and complicated subject and one might feel justified in ignoring multi-country comparisons. Suppose that on the basis of our single-case study we argue that this event was caused by the confluence of four factors: a monarchy, an overcentralized state, an exploited and landless peasantry, and costly military conflicts. (These are, of course, only several of a multitude of causal factors that might be explored.)

The trouble with resting a causal argument on a single case is that one cannot reasonably avoid comparative analysis *if there are comparable cases available.* Indeed, implicit in our causal inference is a comparative judgment: that other nation-states with the same general characteristics as France would also have undergone revolutions if they had experienced the confluence of these four factors. If, for example, we find monarchy, overcentralization, exploited peasants, and costly military ventures present in another country, and yet no revolution occurred, this case rightly calls into question our original argument.

One could choose to ignore this comparative case. Yet, anyone knowledgeable about this counterexample would quite rightly dismiss the original argument. Good causal analysis draws on relevant (i.e., comparable) cases. "An historical event which is regarded as absolutely unique or novel, that has no points of significant similarity with … other events, is outside the scope of historical understanding or explanation," observes Sidney Hook. "As soon as the historian formulates an hypothesis about the cause of an event, he converts that event into an instance of a more or less loosely constructed class of similar events from the recorded past or present experience."[27] Arguments about a single case (e.g., France) must be couched in such a manner that all other known cases with similar characteristics would evidence the same result. In this rather obvious sense, causal propositions must be "universal."[28]

The criterion of boundedness has nothing to do with plenitude per se; it has to do, rather, with the identification of *relevant* cases. Relevant

---

27. Hook (1946: 113). Otherwise stated, propositions with great breadth, if supported empirically, are more likely to be true than propositions with narrow breadth (see Mill 1843, discussed in Brown 1984: 240).
28. See Collier and Mahoney (1996: 63).

cases may be many, or few. Indeed, we can think of many situations in which increasing the N of a study would destroy its sense, since a proposition would be asked to cover cases that are fundamentally dissimilar (the apples and oranges problem). Whether a case is, or is not, relevant (comparable) is sometimes tricky. The point is, a sample that is improperly bounded will not make sense, or will make less sense (we will not be entirely clear about what the proposition means). There is a Goldilocks logic to the criterion of boundedness: the sample should be neither too big, nor too small, but just right.

Consider the well-worn observation that U.S. voters prefer low taxes and high benefits. We might chalk this up to political culture, since it seems to obtain everywhere in the United States. However, it might also be surmised that this is a universal feature of human nature, one we might locate in Cuba as well as Louisiana. A sample that studies only the United States in this instance will not be properly bounded.[29] Similarly, if we were focusing on elements of public opinion that are in evidence only among certain subsections of the American population (say, among Jewish voters) then a sample drawn from the general U.S. population would also be inadequately bounded – in this case, by virtue of being too large.

A larger sample will generally (though not invariably) help to clarify a study's appropriate population: the set of cases to which it properly refers. This is so because the criterion of boundedness requires that we look *beyond* the cases of primary interest, to those lying at the periphery of a study. Doing so requires a larger number of cases than are generally available in small-N studies. Yet, it should also be noted that if small-N work can rely confidently on existing studies to define the relevant population, then boundedness may be established without adopting a large-N research design. Thus, plenitude and boundedness in a study are often, but not necessarily, correlated.

Establishing boundedness in an inference is usually an empirical endeavor; a matter of testing the theory against the evidence to discover where it works, and where it does not. We should note that if the cases where the theory fails are *excluded* from the population of the inference we have managed to escape the problem of falsifiability entirely: we have "defined out" all cases that do not fit the theory. Studies in the rational choice genre have been accused of this sort of case-gerrymandering (in Green and Shapiro's terms, "arbitrary domain restriction").[30] Whether

---

29. It will be seen that boundedness is closely related to variation (see later); where we have achieved variation on our dependent variable we are likely to have also achieved boundedness.
30. See Green and Shapiro (1994: 45).

rational choicers are guilty of this sin is not important for present purposes. The point to remember is that the specification of the population is only the first step on the road to a meaningful empirical proposition. We must also make sure that our chosen population makes sense – is relevant to the inference. The sample must include (or be representative of) cases that we would normally expect the proposition to explain. If there are questions about the boundedness of a proposition, there are also serious questions about its accuracy.

Comparability

The problematic status of a case is that in order for it to serve its function, in order for it to be a case *of* something, cases must be similar to one another in some (though by no means all) respects. *Comparability* refers to three elements of a sample: (a) *descriptive comparability:* the comparability of the relevant *X*s and the *Y* (such that *X* and *Y* mean roughly the same thing across cases); (b) *causal comparability:* the comparability of the *X:Y* relationship (such that *X* and *Y* do not interact in idiosyncratic ways in different cases); and (c) *control:* the extent to which remaining dissimilarities (of both sorts) may be taken into account.[31]

Descriptive comparability is easiest to explain, albeit often difficult to determine. It is essentially equivalent to concept validity, which we discussed in Chapter 3. Consider the example of political parties. If I am arguing, following Duverger, that proportional electoral systems foster larger party systems than plurality electoral systems then *Y* may be measured by the number of political parties in a given party system. Party system is the unit of analysis; cases, therefore, comprise party systems, considered through time or across regions and countries. However, if it is discovered that two parties with different names in a single party system (e.g., the CDU and CSU in Germany) are acting as members of the same party, then we will probably want to make adjustments to our con-

31. Comparability is one of the main preoccupations of comparativists. Of course, we are all comparativists in some minimal sense (see above). The term "comparativist," however, implies the comparison of things that we do not ordinarily think of as comparable – that is, different countries or cultures. See, for example, Achen and Snidal (1989), DeFelice (1986), Dion (1998), Eidlin (1983), Ember (1991), Frendreis (1983), Geddes (1990), Hammel (1980), Holt and Turner (1970), Mahoney (2000), Meckstroth (1975), Munck (1998: 29), Przeworski and Teune (1970), Smelser (1976), Vallier (1971), as well as various work by David Collier, Stanley Lieberson, Arend Lijphart, and Charles Ragin listed in references. What I have called comparability has also been referred to as "equivalence" (Van Deth 1998; Vijver and Leung 1997: 7) and "unit homogeneity" (King et al. 1994).

sideration of the German case. (Not to do so would exaggerate the degree of fragmentation in the German party system.) If, on the other hand, in some imaginary world *all* parties had such tacit alliances, such that they went around in pairs, or if one was only interested in studying these sorts of parties, then one would want to treat the CDU and CSU in whatever way one treated parties in these other party systems (either as one unit or as separate units). In either situation, one is obliged to establish comparability among the chosen cases.

Evidently, in order to make comparisons we must transform our information about each of the phenomena to things that can be readily compared. We must reduce the plenitude of information that we have on individual cases into shorthand forms that can be handled among a sample, either statistically or through some other aggregating method. We should point out that given sufficient time and effort one can easily *describe* 200 cases in everyday prose, or even 2,000. (Compilations of case studies, either in edited volumes or in archive collections, are good examples of large-N descriptive analysis.) Yet, we cannot meaningfully compare this many cases without resort to numbers, or at least to simple categories (yes/no, high/medium/low). The more cases we wish to understand, the more we will have to reduce complex facts and expressions into datalike forms.

Is this information reduction a problem? Not necessarily. If one is interested in deaths caused by leukemia, it is hard to see how one could avoid a numerical representation of this phenomenon, or how a nonnumerical representation would be any more clear or accurate. However, many phenomena do not lend themselves readily to numerical form. This is where we run into problems of concept validity. For it is precisely those phenomena that are *not* amenable to arithmetic expression which are most difficult to compare across cases. Numbers function as a universal language: the Esperanto of the scientific community. If something cannot be translated into this language, chances are it cannot be translated at all. Or it must be poorly translated, in ways that suggest hidden ambiguities and which do not hold up nicely across our cases. Cultural properties are often difficult to categorize and are even more difficult to rank along a single dimension. Events of "historical" importance are often considered to be sui generis. Even where numerical representation seems appropriate, we may wonder about the validity of such measures across different cases. Do unemployment figures mean the same thing in France and the United States (which is to say, is this concept defined and measured in the same ways in these countries)? Does party identification mean the same thing in France as in the United States? Does labor density mean the same thing in Mexico as it does in Sweden? Much depends, of course, on our use of these variables (the inference within which they are employed). Even so, we encounter troubling issues of descriptive comparability.

Causal comparability is even more complex, because here we are attempting to judge a hypothetical relationship (while presupposing conceptual validity across our cases). Let us say, to choose a rather stark example, that I am interested in the causes of government growth in nation-states and I decide to study several national governments as well as several *student* governments. Are student governments comparable to the governments of nation-states? Perhaps, but not necessarily. Suppose that in response to this objection I decide to limit my analysis to national governments. Among those nation-states chosen for analysis are the United States and China. Again, one might wonder about case-comparability: factors leading to government growth in a communist system might be quite different from those affecting government size in a democratic-capitalist system. Suppose, finally, that my set of cases is further restricted to democratic countries; yet, among those countries are the United States and Liechtenstein. Once again, one might object that the criterion of comparability is not fully met: government growth in a mega-state might differ from government growth in a microstate.

Evidently, there must be some similarity between entities in order for phenomenon *A* to be able to tell us anything about phenomenon *B*. But perfect similarity (identity, uniformity) is not necessary. Indeed, strictly speaking it is not even possible, because every case (every apple, every person, every cell, every molecule) is, in some sense, unique.[32] In some situations, cases need only bear a distant resemblance to one another. If we are investigating the role of gravity a piano is as good a case as an apple. Either will do. The demands of comparability are quite loose when it comes to gravity since anything with mass is subject to this law of nature. However, if we are investigating something else, say, malleability, then a very different set of comparability requirements are in order.

Generally speaking, one can say that two cases are comparable, or "unit homogeneous," when they respond in similar ways to similar stimuli. Achieving causal comparability in a research design means choosing cases that are similar to each other in whatever ways might affect the *Y* or the posited *X:Y* relationship, *or whose remaining differences can be taken into account* by the analysis. All causal investigations attempt to hold certain features of the cases constant, even if this extends only to one very basic characteristic, such as having mass. Again, it is important

32. At the very least, it occupies a unique position in time and/or space.

to stress that the particular features (*X*s) we have to worry about are contingent on the particular causal relationships of interest. It is neither necessary nor possible for *all* features be similar. Indeed, as the criterion of variation suggests, we do not want identical cases.

The important point is that we be able to deal with whatever differences we find among cases insofar as they bear upon the *X:Y* relationship. If the differences are slight, or if we do not seek great precision in our results, then perhaps we can ignore such differences entirely (chalking them up to "accident"). If we have many cases, and the differences between cases can be captured in quantifiable form, then we may be able to control for these differences statistically. If we have only a few cases, we may be able to consider the possible effects of those differences in a qualitative way. We should not conclude that a heterogeneous sample of cases (perhaps even including national governments and student governments) is undesirable *unless* we have reason to believe that such differences (a) might affect the outcome (government growth), and (b) cannot be effectively controlled in the analysis.

Ceteris paribus, additional cases improve a research design, as argued earlier. But this is a crucial caveat, for it takes for granted something that is, in the event, usually at risk. It will not aid our efforts to sort out complex causal relationships if our additional cases are only minimally comparable. Indeed, the addition of barely comparable cases is likely to *weaken* our causal leverage. Strictly speaking, a noncomparable case adds nothing to an analysis. It is the familiar apples and oranges problem: if the Chinese Revolution is not comparable to the French Revolution then adding it to our study of the latter will only confuse matters. Of course, comparability is usually a matter of degrees. The Chinese Revolution is probably comparable on some dimensions, but not on others. Yet, in order to make it comparable we will have to take account of those noncomparable dimensions – the difference in time separating the two cases, the difference in class structure, the difference in political structure, and so forth. If we were handling these cases statistically, we would have to introduce a new variable for each noncomparable item in order (we hope) to "control" them in the analysis. The addition of noncomparable cases comes at a price. In this particular example, it seems rather costly.

This brings us to a central argument: complaints about large-*N* "reduction" or "oversimplification" are best understood as complaints about comparability. Large-*N* studies are viable only when the hypotheses that the researcher wishes to test can be transformed, without too much loss of information, to interval variables that are valid across the cases in the researcher's sample. Perhaps the most important defense of small-N research designs, therefore, is the practical impossibility of achieving a large sample of comparable cases.[33] It will be noticed that there are only so many nation-states to go around. Even if all the irredentist movements in the world were to succeed, we would still end up with a universe no larger than 300 or 400. More critically, we cannot use all these nation-states as cases in many studies – either because the data to do so are not available, or because additional nation-states do not meet the minimum requirements of a case. To put the issue in a more specific context, it is not clear how much we can learn about fascism from studying cases outside the developed world. What would fascism mean in an Indonesian context? Probably, the question is meaningless. At the very least, it dramatically alters normal understandings of the concept. This means that we have, at most, a dozen or so cases that we might interrogate. We are stuck with a small-N sample if we are studying fascism, whether we like it or not.

Wherever the units of analysis are scarce (e.g., in the study of social movements, revolutions, dramatic social-policy changes, cultural and ideological transformations, the birth and death of political parties, ethnic and racial groups, and so forth) we will be relegated to a small-N or medium-N research design. Indeed, the reader will find that many, if not most, of the things that social scientists would like to know about are scarce. Thus, there are good grounds on which to mount a practical defense of small-N methods of research. We simply don't have as many good cases as we would like. Plenitude and comparability are often at odds.

Independence

Comparability should be distinguished from a very similar criterion, *independence*.[34] "There is a story," reports David Hackett Fischer, "of a scientist who published an astonishing and improbable generalization about the behavior of rats. An incredulous colleague came to his laboratory and politely asked to see the records of the experiments on which the generalization was based. 'Here they are,' said the scientist, dragging a notebook from a pile of papers on his desk. And pointing to a cage in the corner, he added, 'there's the rat.'"[35] What this story illustrates is the problem of case-independence: testing a single rat over and over again does not provide independent evidence of a proposition; it only provides

---

33. See Collier and Mahoney (1996).
34. See, for example, Lijphart (1975a: 171), Przeworski and Teune (1970: 52), and Zelditch (1971: 282–3).
35. Fischer (1970: 109).

further confirmation of how a single rat responds to various stimuli. (Of course, if one was looking for variation across repeated observations of the rat – during which a treatment was administered – then these observations might rightly be regarded as independent cases in support of some proposition. This, however, is a different definition of case than Fischer has in mind.)

Moving to social science ground: suppose, in our study of government growth, that certain countries were influenced *by each other* (rather than deciding taxing and spending issues independently of one another). This could occur through the influence of an international agency like the World Bank, the IMF, or the EU, or through a simple process of diffusion. What, one might then inquire, is the logic of counting each as a separate case? Indeed, N is equal to precisely 1 if country policies are entirely the product of diffusion.[36] Of course diffusion, and the criterion of independence more generally, is usually a matter of degrees. (*All* cross-national studies suffer from some violation of the independence criterion.)

Another example of case dependence may be found in survey research. If various respondents are sharing information about a poll while it is being conducted, then considerable doubt is cast on the independence of each case. Even more ridiculous is the hypothetical poll in which a single respondent ("Smith") is polled twice. Smith's answers the first time are likely to be highly correlated with his answers on the second round. Thus, we have not gained any information in this second round. Otherwise put, Smith's responses on the second round do not provide an *independent* test of whatever hypotheses we wish to test. We are not likely to feel any more sure of our hypothesis after the second round than after the first.[37] The problem of Smith is the problem of Fischer's rat.

Douglas Rae's well-known study of electoral laws and their effect on party systems offers a third, and more subtle, example. The evidence for the analysis is drawn from 115 elections. Yet, as Arend Lijphart notes, these 115 elections are drawn from only 20 countries, and these units exhibit very little change over the period of observation with respect to variables that might impact party system size. (France, which alters its electoral system between the Fourth and Fifth Republics, is the notable

36. This has become known as "Galton's problem" (Ember and Otterbein 1991; Goldthorpe 1997; Hammel 1980: 147; Naroll 1965; Przeworski and Teune 1970: 51–2). See also Lieberson's (1985: ch 3) discussion of "contamination." An early discussion of this difficulty can be found in Durkheim (1897/1951: 130–1).

37. To be sure, if our hypothesis concerns the consistency of responses over time, then a "panel" format is appropriate and *all* our respondents will be polled twice. Here, as always, the definition of case hinges on the research design.

exception.) In effect, Lijphart is arguing, Rae has polled his respondents (countries) multiple times.[38]

The problem of case independence is stated in general terms by Zelditch: "If a unit is not independent, no new information about [a variable] is obtained by studying it twice, and no additional confirmation of [a theory] is obtained by counting it twice."[39] This refers to diachronic case-independence (serial autocorrelation) as well as synchronic case-independence (spatial autocorrelation). Usually, problems of case-dependence create problems of comparability as well. For example, if certain countries' government expenditures are influenced by membership in the EU, as in the foregoing example, then they may no longer be comparable to countries outside the EU. If certain respondents are talking to one another, or if a single respondent is polled twice, these presumed cases fail the comparability requirement. Comparability problems could be solved by assuring that all cases experience the same contextual effect (e.g., only countries in the EU are observed, or all respondents are polled twice). However, there are also genuine problems of independence illustrated by these examples – that is, cases where no additional information is obtained about an *X:Y* relationship.

With independence, as with comparability, these problems can *sometimes* be corrected. If one could find a viable indicator for international agency influence and simple diffusion, and if one had enough cases to include such variables in a statistical analysis, then one could effectively "control" for the problem of dependence in the first example – the same way, that is, one controls for comparability problems such as country size, GNP, ethnic heterogeneity, and so forth. Similarly, if one knew who was talking to whom in a given survey and one had plenty of respondents, one could introduce this into a statistical analysis in the same fashion. In the final example (Rae's study), one might choose to average results for each country or control for the varying number of observations taken on each country case, weighting the results accordingly. Even so, one would *prefer* perfectly independent cases, obviating the need for statistical controls (controls whose efficacy is likely to remain somewhat suspect).

---

38. Worse, he has polled these countries *different* numbers of times. Thus, "By presenting his results in terms of elections, Rae merely gives a greater weight to countries with frequent elections than to those where elections are less frequent. The United States, with ten elections in the 1945–1965 period, has twice the weight of Norway, where only five elections were held in the same period" (Lijphart 1975a: 171).

39. Zelditch (1971: 282–3), quoted in Lijphart (1975a: 171). Zelditch may be overstating the case somewhat. One *can* obtain new information by studying a nonindependent case, but this information gain will be less than if the case were wholly independent (Craig Thomas, personal communication).

Another qualification concerns studies *of* case-independence (e.g., of processes of diffusion). Here, case-independence constitutes the dependent variable and one looks for variation on this outcome. Even so, one is attempting to test *certain* hypotheses about diffusion (or non-independence), holding other factors constant. The latter factors constitute the sort of case-independence that one must retain if the study is to have any validity.

Representativeness

Comparability refers to the internal properties of the sample. *Representativeness* refers to comparability between the sample and the population (sometimes referred to as external validity). Specifically, are we entitled to generalize from a given case or cases under study to a larger universe of cases? Do we have reason to believe that what is true for the sample is also true for the population?

The distinction between comparability and representativeness becomes clear when one considers the use of laboratory experiments on rats as evidence about human physiology or behavior. There is no problem of comparability here; rats of a given type are usually quite similar to each other. But there are formidable problems of representativeness. What happens to a rat during an experimental treatment may or may not happen to a human. Attempts to shed light on contemporary western societies by examining societies in other parts of the world, small-scale human interactions (e.g., PTA meetings), or, for that matter, computer models of human societies, all meet with the same basic objection. Do the results of such studies illustrate a broader phenomenon, or are they limited to the cases under study?

Sometimes, we have the opportunity to test representativeness assumptions. Experiments conducted on laboratory rats may be repeated on human beings. Results from a computer simulation may be repeated in the real world. Polling results are put to the test of an election. In these circumstances, what is happening, methodology-wise, is that potential cases are transformed into actual cases. The point is, every time we make assumptions about a broader class of phenomena than we have directly studied we are raising questions of representativeness. No methodological procedure will overcome this basic assumption, which must be dealt with in light of what we know about particular phenomena and particular causal relationships.

It is apparent that representativeness, like other criteria, is a matter of degrees. If we are studying the response of billiard balls when struck by other billiard balls and they are all produced by some standard set of specifications, then we might safely assume that one billiard ball is, for all intents and purposes, the same as another. Yet, small defects will appear in certain balls (rendering them unfit as cases), and even among perfect specimens there will be minute differences of mass, volume, and such. If our measurements of the outcome are sufficiently precise, these differences might turn out to be quite significant; under these circumstances, one billiard ball may not be equal to another, which is to say, problems of representativeness become real. If our project is altered in a more elemental fashion – suppose we are now interested in the effects of differently colored balls on the responses of a rat – then a blue ball is no longer representative of a larger collection of (multicolored) balls. In short, here as elsewhere, everything depends on the intent of the research. There is no such thing as representativeness *in general*.[40]

Achieving Representativeness. There are two easy ways of achieving representativeness (aka avoiding bias) in a sample. First, one may choose cases randomly from the population of potential cases. Properly conducted, randomization procedures maximize the representativeness of a given sample. To be sure, obtaining random samples is not always easy. One has to know a good deal about the population one is studying and the causal relationship under investigation to determine what is representative, and what is not. Moreover, one must make sure to catch enough cases in one's sample to test the causal relationship of interest. If a relevant type is rare, but nonetheless of interest to the researcher, then it may be necessary to over-sample this specific type.[41] Randomization also presumes a large population to draw cases from, and a reasonably large sample. There is no sense in picking five cases randomly from a population of 10, or five cases randomly from a population of 10,000.[42]

Second, one might choose *all* possible cases, in which circumstance there is no problem of representativeness at all (since N = the entire population). If the events are not overwhelming in number, or data are easily available, this is a sensible approach, for it alleviates any problems of representativeness in the sample and maximizes the number of cases at one's disposal. (One still faces problems of case comparability and independ-

40. See Dewey (1938: 480). Problems of representativeness encountered in natural science are generally less acute than those usually encountered in social science. One billiard ball is likely to be representative of other billiard balls, for most intents and purposes. Similarly, with rats. Not so, however, for human beings and human institutions, which tend to vary enormously from one unit to another.
41. See Rosenberg (1968).
42. See Collier and Mahoney (1996: 57), and King et al. (1994: 125–6, 129, 139, 196–9).

ence, of course.) Research on topics for which there are a very limited number of potential cases are often forced to employ a comprehensive selection procedure. (Even if all these potential cases are not studied with equal intensity it is advisable to incorporate these potential cases in an informal manner.)

We should draw the reader's attention to another rather obvious point about representativeness. One may have a probabilistically representative sample (via random selection) or a perfectly representative sample (via comprehensive selection) and still not be able to say anything useful about events occurring in the future, or at some period in the past (prior to one's collection of data). Representativeness means representative of a given population. If the proposition is intended to cover events occurring in some other place or time, then one will have to work out the representativeness issue in a more speculative way. Actually existing cases may not be the best bet. One may be better off looking at *trends* among existing cases, at particular cases that seem to exemplify the sort of cases that will occur, or have occurred, at some other place or time. Counterfactual analysis (i.e., the speculative treatment of causes and effects under slightly different – other than factual – circumstances) may be particularly useful (see Chapter 9). Future-oriented causal analysis encounters formidable problems of representativeness. A large *N* may be meaningless, since it *cannot* include cases of primary interest.

Often, there are good reasons for adopting a small-*N* research design even where there are many more potential cases available for study. Yet, problems of representativeness are likely to be extreme in these circumstances because a few cases will be asked to carry the burden for a large number of unstudied cases – to "represent" that population in all ways that are relevant to the causal proposition. This is one of the most problematic features of small-*N* research designs. However, there is a way of coping with this problem. It involves making representativeness a primary criterion on which one chooses cases – either through typical-case or crucial-case methods, as discussed in Chapter 9.

Variation

In observing two billiard balls collide we observe that *A* and *B covary:* where *A* hits *B*, *B* responds by moving. Prior to *A*'s arrival, *B* was stationary, and after *A*'s departure, *B* becomes stationary once again. Covariation, as the term implies, means that where *X* appears, *Y* appears as well; where *X* does not appear *Y* is also absent; where *X* is strong so is *Y*; and so forth. It might also be called correlation (common in statistical work), constant conjunction (Hume), association (Neuman), congruity (Bennett), or concomitant variation (Mill).[43] All these terms convey a view of causation expressed by Galileo: "that and no other is to be called cause, at the presence of which the effect always follows, and at whose removal the effect disappears."[44] Of course, the precise relationship between X and Y may not be immediately proximate in time and space. It may be lagged; it may also be a matter of waning and waxing, rather than appearing and disappearing entirely. Many possibilities can be imagined. The central point is that, whatever the temporal and spatial relationship, it is *regular.*

Covariation is by no means the only consideration available to us in evaluating the complex subject of causation. For one thing, it may not be present in observable forms (though it must always be *potentially* present). Even if observable, it may not be indicative of a *causal* relationship. We have all heard the maxim that "correlation does not equal causation." The traditional example concerns night and day. Night follows day on a regular basis; the $X:Y$ correlation, if we were to calculate it over a period of years, would be perfect. Yet, we know that night does not *cause* day. As Rueschemeyer and colleagues point out, covariational evidence is sometimes weak when it comes to explaining *why* a particular X and Y are highly correlated.[45]

Even so, variation is good. It deserves to be considered a central element of causal demonstration. But what sort of variation should we seek, and *why* is variation good? Is variation *absolutely* necessary? What, indeed, *is* variation? These matters are less well understood.

As a firsthand approximation we might look at variation as the *range* of values registered on a given explanatory variable *(X)* or outcome *(Y)*. A higher range is better (for reasons that will shortly become clear). Yet, we must concern ourselves not only with the distance between the maximum

---

43. See Bennett (1999), Hume (1960: 219), Marini and Singer (1988), Neuman (1997: 50), and Mill (1843/1949: 263). These terms are not exactly synonymous (no two terms are). However, for my purposes the differences between them are slight.

44. Quoted in Bunge (1959: 33). Bowley, an early pioneer of statistical modeling, put it this way: "It is never easy to establish the existence of a causal connection between two phenomena or series of phenomena; but a great deal of light can often be thrown by the application of algebraic probability ... When two quantities are so related that ... an increase or decrease of one is found in connection with an increase or decrease (or inversely) of the other, and the greater the magnitude of the changes in the one, the greater the magnitude of the changes in the other, the quantities are said to be *correlated. Correlation* is a quantity which can be measured numerically" (quoted in Morgan 1997: 62). See also Frendreis (1983).

45. Rueschemeyer et al. (1992: 4). We discussed the distinction between covariation (correlation) and causation in Chapter 6.

and minimum scores but also with the distribution of values on our variables. If, let us say, all our cases cluster in one sector of an imaginary distribution *except one*, then we must rely on that single case to provide all the variation. Our analysis of the causal relationship of interest will depend critically on this influential case. This is problematic, because we can never be absolutely certain that this case is representative of the population (it may be deviant) or that we have correctly measured its value. In short, our level of uncertainty will be high if our sample is skewed.

The concept of *variance* incorporates the range of variation in a sample but refers to the distribution of *all* scores, rather than simply maximum and minimum values. It is a measure of overall dispersion. The larger the variance, the farther the individual cases are from the mean; the smaller the variance, the closer the individual scores are to the mean. Variance, rather than range, is what we are after when we speak of maximizing variation in a sample. However, because the term variation is more common, and more likely to be understood, I will follow everyday usage here.

With this conceptual issue under our belt, we may now proceed to discuss where variation (variance) is located. Specifically, (a) whether a sample offers variation on the outcome of interest (the most usual understanding of variation), (b) whether a sample offers variation on the relevant causal variables (including the variable of interest as well as other variables that might affect the X:Y relationship), (c) whether collinearity is avoided, and (d) whether variation *within* one or more cases can be analyzed. Once we have sorted these matters out it will be clear why arguments over variation are endemic to methodological debate, crucial to the effective practice of social science, yet often difficult to resolve.

Y-Variation. Let us say we are exploring our familiar question of government spending and we decide to focus on two cases with similar values on the dependent variable, Sweden and Norway. Why do these countries spend what they do? We notice that they are both characterized by small and heterogeneous populations, a northern European location, strong socialist parties and labor unions, strong agrarian traditions, a weak feudal past, late industrial development, proportional electoral systems, high voter turnout, Protestant religions, sparse populations (relative to land mass), isolation from the European continent, and intertwined ("Scandinavian") cultures. Doubtless, other similarities could be noted, but the point is already clear: because the outcome is the same (or similar) in both these cases, it is impossible to eliminate any of the foregoing factors as possible causes of government spending. Indeed, without a glance at other cases with different values on the dependent variable we do not even know whether Sweden and Norway have "high" or "low" government spending; in other words, we do not know what it is that we are trying to explain. With variation on Y, however – with the inclusion, let us say, of Switzerland, Japan, or the United States (all low-spenders) – we are now on much firmer ground. We can interpret similarities and differences between the high-spenders and the low-spenders and get a sense for what might be driving government growth.[46]

We are prone to think of variation as occurring across cases but it may also occur over time. Thus, an alternative approach to answering our original question would be to examine a single unit, or several units, over time to find out when spending waxed and waned. This is useful, of course, because we can then look at whatever was going on at that particular time, or previously, that might have affected these changes.

Can variation always be achieved? After all, there are some objects of study that are fairly constant and which we nonetheless would like to understand. American society has always been individualistic, according to some writers. The incest taboo appears virtually everywhere. All societies distribute valued goods unequally. Virtually every person with the physiological means to do so learns to use a language. Political parties of some sort are present in all democracies. Here are dependent variables apparently quite limited in variation. Indeed, it is the very *constancy* of these phenomena that we may be interested in explaining.

Several observations are in order. First, invariant dependent variables are much more common in natural science research than in social science. Nature is more predictable than nurture. Indeed, one of the foregoing phenomena – linguistic facility – is perhaps better looked on as a subject of natural science, rather than social science.

Second, even among fairly uniform phenomena one can usually find differences of degree, or exceptions. Indeed, some anthropologists claim to have found examples of societies where incest is *not* taboo, or at least less so. Enormous variation can be found in the degree of egalitarianism in human societies. Individualism, depending on how you choose to define it, has waxed and waned through American history and is found in varying intensity among different persons and different groups within

---

46. See Geddes (1990). There is one partial exception to the dictum that change in Y is always useful. This is the so-called most-different method, discussed at length in Chapter 9. However, I argue that this method is rarely used in social science, and of very limited utility when it is used. (At best, the most-different method prompts us to call into question a hypothesis; it cannot effectively prove a causal hypothesis.) It seems clear that some variation on Y is almost always better than no variation on Y.

American society. Of course, we may frame our research question in terms of constancy (why are incest taboos so widespread? why are human societies never perfectly egalitarian?). But, in order to reach firm conclusions about the reasons *for* constancy it is important to investigate variation. These rare moments of change, or exceptional outcomes, rightfully attract the attention of social scientists. The vast amount of work conducted on Sweden by political scientists and on Polynesian societies by anthropologists is motivated by the need to maximize variation on the distribution-of-wealth outcome. The vast amount of work devoted to deviance (by sociologists) and abnormal behavior (by psychologists) is similarly motivated. Historians, likewise, generally focus their work on moments of change rather than periods of continuity, even though the latter are, from a certain perspective, more important. It is when observing these rare moments of change – "events" – that longitudinal analysis is most revealing.

Consider the problem of growth. More particularly, why does economy A not grow? We can observe this economy over time, noting its absence of growth, and find that even though various factors were present that might have led to growth (e.g., increases in education, investment), they did not, in the event, do so. Without variation, our investigation is at an impasse, for any one of a wide variety of causes might be held responsible for this nongrowth. Citizens of country A are lazy, we hypothesize; they are burdened by an unfavorable climate and limited natural resources; they are oppressed by international investors; they are part of the economic "periphery"; their taxes are too high; their taxes are too low; and so forth and so on. If we turn to other economies that have also failed to grow, we may be able to cast doubt on the some of these possible reasons. But we will not reach these conclusions with a great deal of confidence. It is always possible, for example, that some combination of factors (rather than a single factor) is at the root of country A's nongrowth, or that different *levels* of a given factor are responsible. Suppose, for example, that country C, which did not grow either, obtained generous loans from the IMF. Does this mean that economy A (which did not obtain such loans) would *not* grow if granted an equivalent package of aid? All we can conclude with certainty is that this level of international aid is not a *sufficient* condition of growth. It could be that IMF loans *in combination with some other factors* would lead to growth.

Third, if there was absolutely no variation on a dependent variable of interest, and no variation could be mustered by the investigator in an experimental fashion, then one would have to conclude that the result in question is truly inevitable: it cannot be otherwise. This raises deep philosophical questions (are human actions predetermined? what does determination, and its correlate "free will" mean?). Without dipping our toes in this swamp it may be observed that in all situations social scientists are likely to encounter there is always a proviso, a caveat, a set of preconditions that set the stage for a supposedly inevitable outcome. Even where observable variation is minimal we may speculate on probable changes that would ensue if various factors were realigned (a counterfactual exploration of cases). Thus, one might say, "given *X*, *Y* will occur" – for example, given a long-standing democracy with competitive elections, political parties will establish themselves. These provisos constitute causal explanations. They also posit variation in the outcome.

Some writers claim that if one is interested only in causal *necessity*, variation is inessential.[47] Several points must be made in response to this objection. To clarify, I am not claiming that variation is absolutely essential; I am claiming that it is useful. A research design with variation is more useful than one without. I think this may be shown to be true even when investigating necessary causes. Suppose one is interested in the necessary conditions of revolution. One duly collects information only on revolutions, ignoring all nonrevolutionary societies and nonrevolutionary situations (a spatial *and* temporal limitation, one should note). Next, one catalogs the facts, looking for those conditions that are constant across all cases. Under this method *there is no way to identify possible causal factors*. If there are peasants present in all revolutionary situations – even if only a few – one must consider them "causes" (or conditions) of revolution. Similarly, for other factors that are likely to be incidental (rather than causal) – for example, motorcars, soda pop, miscegenation...

Of course, we could rely on general theories and intuitions about revolutions – that is, on general knowledge which is assumed to be true – to eliminate some of these nonsensical correlates. Here our investigation is no longer empirical; we employ deductive logic only. In sum, a no-variation research design is not as helpful in differentiating real and spurious causes as a research design that incorporates variation into its case comparisons. Indeed, I think it may be shown that when scholars defend no-variation research designs what they usually mean is a design in which (a) variation occurs through time, rather than across units of analysis, or (b) in which variation occurs outside the research design but is nonetheless taken into account by the researcher (implicitly). This is common in case studies, where the researcher is writing about her case, but with other cases firmly in view.[48]

---

47. See Dion (1998) and Most and Starr (1982).
48. For discussions of the importance of variation with particular attention to statistical analysis, see Hagood (1941), King et al. (1994: 108–49), and Stinchcombe (1968: ch 5).

The simple, and by now tedious, conclusion is that without *Y* variation – either synchronic or diachronic – we are at pains to reach firm conclusions. Even *with* such variation, of course, our conclusions may be tentative. Yet, they will be much firmer than otherwise. In most research situations one would gladly sacrifice 100 cases with similar outcomes for a single case exhibiting a different outcome. This is the virtue of variation on the dependent variable.

X-Variation. I have spoken thus far only about the importance of establishing variation on the dependent variable *(Y)*. The implicit question driving this sort of research design is *What causes Y?* If, however, one is primarily interested in *What X causes,* or *Whether X* causes a particular *Y,* then one must ensure that the research design incorporates variation on the independent variable of interest. In other words, whether or not X-variation should play a part in case selection hinges on the question that the researcher wishes to focus on.[49]

Consider government growth. In *Y*-centered analysis we need only ensure that our sample of cases contains variation in *Y.* But let us say that we are interested in the particular question of whether industrialization causes government growth. With this research agenda, we will want to seek out a sample in which there is some variation on the *X* of interest (industrialization). If we study *only* highly industrialized cases, for example, we will be unable to say very much about the effects of industrialization on government growth.

Choosing cases according to *Y*-variation is likely to garner cases with variation on the relevant *X,* so it is not always necessary to make X-variation an explicit criterion of case selection. Indeed, with a large sample, we are likely to be assured of variation on both *Y* and the relevant *X*s. The methodological point here remains: variation on both axes is important, and we may wish to sacrifice some representativeness in the sample to achieve this variation.

Finally, we must assure ourselves that variation on *relevant* *X*s, not simply those we are interested in, are included in the sample. By "relevant" we mean all those causal factors that might affect the primary *X:Y* relationship. Causal analysis, as we will discuss, rests on causal comparisons; the more thoroughly we have plumbed the *possible* causes of *Y,* the more confidence we have that a particular *X* is the true cause of this outcome. Cases should be chosen with an eye toward investigating rival hypotheses, not just our favored hypothesis.

---

49. We must appreciate that *Y* and *X:Y* are different research goals, as discussed in Chapter 7. The importance of X-variation is stressed in Collier and Mahoney (1996: 74), Dion (1998), and King et al. (1994: 146).

Table 8.3   *Collinearity*

case	X_1	X_2	X_3	Y
1	0	0	1	0
2	1	1	0	0
3	1	1	0	1
4	0	0	1	1
5	1	1	0	0
6	0	1	1	0
7	0	0	1	0
8	1	1	0	1
9	0	0	1	1
10	1	1	0	0
11	0	0	1	0
12	1	1	0	1
13	1	1	0	0

Avoiding Collinearity. The problem known in statistical circles as *collinearity* may be thought of as a corollary of the general search for X and Y variation, which we have just discussed. Here, the particular issue is the correlation of the *variables* in our sample (rather than the extent to which we can find variation on any single variable across cases). It is possible to have a great deal of X and Y variation, but still suffer severe collinearity.[50]

Let's see how this works in an example. Suppose all our variables are coded dichotomously, as "present" or "absent." And suppose that we have both positive and negative outcomes for each variable. This means that variation in the simple sense has been achieved. Yet, here we find a situation in which the values registered by two causal variables – X_1 and X_2 – are identical in all but one case, as illustrated in Table 8.3. This means that we cannot effectively distinguish the causal effects of these two variables from each other. Insofar as we are interested in the hypotheses measured by these variables, this will not be a good selection of cases for us to work with. Usually, problems of collinearity are less extreme; collinearity, like other criteria, is a matter of degrees. The point is, we should strive for samples that include cases whose relevant causal factors do not covary (and whose irrelevant factors *do* covary).

Within-Case Variation. The term variation usually indicates variation *across* cases. Thus, if I am trying to explain levels of welfare spending among nation-states (unit of analysis = nation-state) I will look for

---

50. See King et al. (1994: 122–4).

variation across nation-states. However, we might also look at a single nation-state – the case-study approach – for clues to this question. Indeed, it might be very useful to know more about how and why the United States increased its spending levels at certain times, why some American citizens favor social welfare policies and others do not, and so forth. This sort of variation is referred to as *within-case* (see Chapter 9 for further discussion).

Whether or not within-case analysis is useful for illustrating broader, cross-case relationships will depend on the case and propositions in question. American legislatures offer a great deal of useful variation about why legislators voted as they did. Legislatures in parliamentary regimes, however, generally offer evidence on one question only: which side of an issue did each party support. As a result, within-case analysis of legislatures in strong-party regimes is less useful, at least for most purposes.

In other situations we have plenty of within-case evidence, but the evidence is of dubious utility in explaining cross-case variation. Consider the classic question of why voter turnout in the United States is lower than in most other rich democracies. An exploration of within-case variation – who votes and who does not within the United States – identifies education levels as a principal factor in voter turnout. Educational attainment is the strongest predictor of turnout in the United States and there is every reason to think that this relationship is causal.[51] Yet, the United States has one of the highest educational attainment levels in the world, so within-case analysis offers a misleading cue if we are interested in explaining aggregate turnout rates between the United States and other countries. The general point holds: insofar as within-case variation is usefully applied to our causal question, we may wish to choose cases that offer this genre of evidence.

Achieving Variation. As a coda to this lengthy section we can remind ourselves of the ways in which variation might be achieved in a given research design. (Usually, this involves increasing the size of the sample, so this discussion bears on the criterion of *plenitude* as well.) The basic options are as follows. One can extend the analysis temporally, so as to create new cases through time. One can explore counterfactuals, as discussed in Chapter 9. One can oversample among a group that is poorly represented in a population. One can broaden the definition of the subject under study (the dependent variable), so as to create more cases. (Thus, a study of genocide might be changed into a study of racial/ethnic violence; fascism might be looked on as a type of authoritarianism; and

---

51. See Wolfinger and Rosenstone (1980).

so forth.)[52] Cases can also be generated – indeed, *must* be generated – by looking at "negative" examples of a given phenomenon. (Thus, a study of fascism might look at examples of nonfascism in order to better understand this phenomenon.)[53] Finally, one can look for *within*-case variation (effectively changing the definition of "case" in a particular study), as discussed earlier.

Analytic Utility

We must also consider the utility of a particular research design within a broader field – a theory, a theoretical framework, or a scholarly tradition. The purpose of a case, we might recall, is to demonstrate the accuracy (or inaccuracy) of a proposition. If this proposition is already strongly linked to a particular case, then we may want to include that case in our sample. It is difficult to study federalism without studying the United States. A study of fascism that makes no mention of Germany will be an odd, and uncompelling, study. One can think of many other examples of influential cases that drive theoretical reflection. To be sure, analytic utility is more likely to be a concern in small-N studies than in large-N studies, where propositions are generally not hostage to particular cases. Even in the latter situation, however, one might find a theory linked to a *set* of cases (e.g., a continent, a time period, etc.).

The tradeoff posed by analytic utility is perhaps already obvious: influential cases are not necessarily *representative* cases. Indeed, the fact that the world of social science is dominated by a few Big Cases is cause for some concern. I do not know, offhand, how the number of studies devoted to French politics compares with the volume of literature on Portuguese politics. But I suspect that the ratio is nowhere near parity. Studies of urban poverty in the United States have concentrated on Chicago and New York, with scarcely a mention of Pittsburgh, Philadelphia, and other cities. Economic and political science work *in general* has focused on the United States to the point of absurdity. More studies have been devoted to individual American cities and states, I imagine, than can be found on many *countries* around the world. If all European countries were like France, and all American cities like Chicago and New York, these regional biases would not be problematic

---

52. Naturally, this also runs the risk of "conceptual stretching" (Collier and Mahon 1993, Sartori 1970) – redefining a concept so that it loses much of its original meaning (by application to new and heterogeneous phenomena).
53. For further discussion of how to generate more cases, see Collier (1993), and King et al. (1994: 24, 47, 120, 123, 217–8).

(they would not be biases, in the technical sense, at all). But there is good reason to suppose otherwise. More to the point, we will not know for sure until sufficient study is devoted to other peoples and places.

All of this notwithstanding, we cannot afford to ignore the call for analytic utility. In fact, there is a counter argument to the foregoing: theoretical advance ("progress") may be most readily achieved when scholars are focused on the same object of study. So long as we can expect some minimal level of representativeness between the object chosen for intensive study and a wider field of cases, we can expect a more rapid and sure cumulation of knowledge than if our research efforts are dispersed over a wide range of cases. It is possible that England, France, and the United States have performed this hothouse function. Certainly, theories generated by studies of these countries have found application elsewhere in the world.

Replicability

A good research design is one that produces *reliable* results (results that do not vary from iteration to iteration) and *replicable* results.[54] Reliability and replicability may be viewed as two aspects of the same general goal – one applies to different results from a given study and the other applies to results obtained by different studies of the same subject. There is no hard-and-fast line separating these two terms, and we will use them almost synonymously. One might say that a study's findings have high intercoder reliability, or that they have been successfully replicated by different coders. There is no sense in parsing this distinction any further.

The key point is that if a finding is obtained under circumstances that are essentially unrepeatable (e.g., a "natural" experiment that comes around only once), then we rightfully entertain doubts about its veracity. We are cognizant that any number of factors might have interfered with the validity of the original study, including (among other things) measurement error and the willful misreporting of data. Verification involves repetition; claims to truth, therefore, involve assurances of replicability.

In order to achieve replicability two conditions must obtain. First, the procedures employed in a given study must be carefully laid out. A thorough accounting of "what I did" should allow someone else with the requisite research skills to follow in my tracks. Second, the cases chosen for study (or other cases like them in all relevant respects) must be available for future research.

---

54. See, for example, King (1995) and King et al. (1994: 23, 26, 51).

To be sure, some research is messy. A historian's work on a particular period may have no clear beginning date, and it would be difficult to specify her conclusions as the outcome of a particular procedure. The notion of keeping a research journal of hypotheses and tests is silly. Yet, the conscientious historian lists all sources, including whatever additional information might be necessary to locate those sources. This is the function of a bibliography or special appendix. Similarly, the anthropologist doing fieldwork is well advised to record her observations in a research diary. The notion, in both cases, is that later researchers ought to be able to replicate earlier findings.

The second element of replicability is problematic for the simple reason that some sorts of evidence are evanescent. We cannot retest a solar eclipse or a revolution. By contrast, it is fairly easy to reexamine a data set or revisit a research site – though the latter may have been altered by the previous intervention, or by subsequent events. In any case, the conscientious researcher should archive all evidence – quantitative or qualitative – that might allow future researchers to replicate her findings.

The goal of replicability prompts us to consider the extent to which social scientific research is parasitic on other social scientific research. In social science, as in the natural sciences, any single venture must be considered within the context of a larger collaborative effort. Indeed, it is impossible to evaluate the value or truth of a given study in isolation from other studies. It would not make any sense. Replicability is simply the formal acknowledgment of the ongoing collaborative project that is science.[55]

---

55. Although I have not attempted to cover the issue of *reportage* in this book, I cannot omit mention of one crucial point. Because social science is a collaborative project, researchers are obligated to report not only their "positive" results – those that verify their own arguments – but also those that do not. Regrettably, little credit is given for the latter. The cumulative effect of reporting only positive results is to give a highly skewed picture of a given causal problem. Suppose, let us say, nine out of ten analyses of the welfare state show labor unions to have a strong effect on outcome. The first of the nine analyses will be considered to have made an original contribution to the field. The others merely confirm standard wisdom, and are unlikely to be published, or otherwise reported. The tenth analysis, *dis*-confirming the causal influence of labor unions, will also be published, probably amid great fanfare. The naive reader, who has not conducted her own analysis of the question, is likely to conclude that studies of the welfare state are mixed on the question of labor unions. We rightly prize innovation over redundancy (see Chapter 5). But we do not want to sacrifice accuracy for an account that is biased toward novelty. Accuracy requires a full reporting of results – those arguments that worked, and those that did not. Otherwise, we are unable to judge the *relative* importance of different factors bearing on the same outcome.

Mechanism

In addition to covariational evidence (either within-case and/or across-case), we will want to specify a causal *mechanism* of some sort connecting the putative cause with the effect. In the hypothetical example of night and day we lack such a mechanism (we cannot explain how night can "cause" day). Many correlative relationships in social science mirror this problem. For example, a fairly strong association can be found between British colonies (current and former) and lower levels of corruption around the world; yet, the causal mechanisms linking this putative cause and effect are opaque.[56] Until these causal processes can be delineated we are likely to regard this causal hypothesis with some degree of skepticism.

To be sure, the distinction between a "mechanism" and a "cause" is a blurry one. All mechanisms might also be regarded as causes. Otherwise stated, an infinite number of mechanisms link any cause with its effect (the regress is infinite); as soon as these mechanisms are identified, they may be regarded as "causes," or "intermediate causes."[57] However, we choose to explore this infinite chain of causation only so far as is necessary to prove the plausibility of a given causal relationship. (Certain things are always taken for granted in any causal explanation, as we have discussed.) It is at this level that we identify intermediate causes as mechanisms and thereby cease to pursue the infinite causal regress. Thus, *within the rubric of any causal argument* there will be a causal mechanism (explicit or implied).

The identification of a causal mechanism is often associated with the technique of *process tracing* – eyewitness accounts and other more or less direct evidence that *X* has influenced *Y*. The classic example concerns a billiard ball colliding with a second (heretofore stationary) ball. One knows for sure (as sure as one can be about anything, that is) that Ball *A* has caused Ball *B* to move, for one has seen it with one's own eyes. Similarly, to the extent that we could trace a connection, through time, between British colonialism and anticorruption efforts we would have achieved the demonstration of a causal mechanism between these correlated variables. Process tracing itself has many near-synonyms, including discerning, process analysis, pattern-matching, microfoundations, causal narrative, congruence, colligation, contiguity, and intermediate

---

56. Gerring (2000a).
57. King et al. (1994: 86).

processes.[58] All concern the ways in which we attempt to elucidate a clear causal path between X and Y.

We noticed that the infinite regress of causal investigation between X and Y stops at the point at which we arrive at a generally accepted process or mechanism. Thus, to explain why a ball dropped we might say simply "gravity." Since gravity is a widely accepted mechanism, this may satisfy the requirements of an explanation. To those who dispute the existence of gravity, or its workings, we will have to inquire further into the mechanisms by which gravity itself operates. The point, then, is that although the concept of a causal "mechanism" implies a specific and highly targeted level of explanation (we imagine ourselves crawling into the space between X and Y to observe their interaction), it also implies a larger theoretical framework, or a taken-for-granted sense of how the world works. When explaining human behavior, the appropriate mechanism often takes the form of a motive. Why did so-and-so do such-and-such? Covariation among human actions is senseless until we have provided a plausible motivation for these actions.

A causal mechanism like gravity or evolution suggests a general model for explaining a wide variety of outcomes without naming either a specific cause or a specific outcome. Thus, when we say that a particular feature of an animal or plant can be explained by an evolutionary process, we are indicating a general mechanism by which a specific cause might be (given the requisite empirical work) identified. Other causal frameworks, including general equilibrium theory, game theory, realism, and systems theory are similar in this respect (and were discussed briefly in Chapter 7).

The search for causal mechanisms thus operates with a double-movement – inward toward the event to be explained (identifying intermediate variables between the independent and dependent variables), and outward toward a causal framework that might explain these interactions. It is both highly specific and highly abstract. Marini and Singer note that a causal inference is strengthened "if there is a carefully rea-

---

58. Terms and associated works are as follows: process-tracing (George and McKeown 1985: 34ff), discerning (Komarovsky 1940: 135–46), process analysis (Barton and Lazarsfeld 1969), pattern-matching (Campbell 1975), microfoundations (Little 1998), causal narrative (Abbott 1990, 1992; Abrams 1982; Aminzade 1992; Bates et al. 1998; Griffin 1992, 1993; Katznelson 1997; Kiser 1996; Mink 1987; Quadagno and Knapp 1992; Roth 1994; Rueschemeyer and Stephens 1997; Sewell 1992, 1996; Somers 1992; Stone 1979; Stryker 1996; Watkins 1994), congruence (George and Bennett, in press), colligation (Roberts 1996), intermediate processes (Mill 1843/1872). For general discussion see Bennett (1999), Brown (1984: 228), Collier and Mahoney (1996: 70), and Goldstone (1997). For philosophical discussion, see Bhaskar (1975/1978), Harre (1972), McMullin (1984), and Salmon (1984).

soned explanation (*theory*) that provides details of a mechanism by which the cause is related, often *step-by-step,* to the effect."[59]

Nonetheless, the utility of mechanisms in causal explanation has not gone unchallenged. B. F. Skinner, who articulated behavioralism at its most militant phase, looked upon mechanisms as unscientific distractions. If one wished to explain an outcome, Skinner argued, one need only look at the inputs that caused that outcome (e.g., hours of deprivation). Discussion of unobservables such as drive, habit, and frustration served only to confuse matters. Few take this position today.[60]

Still, we should acknowledge that the identification of a causal mechanism is not absolutely essential to causal explanation. In certain experimental situations one can be fairly certain that a given *X* caused a given *Y* without being able to specify the mechanism connecting the two. (Skinner, of course, was the product and principal booster of the experimental tradition within psychology. These "pure" experimental situations are more common in natural science than social science. Skinnerian psychology itself focuses primarily upon the natural properties of human behavior – those conditioned by genetic factors – not those that are learned through human association. As such, it does not fall into our definition of social science.) Even so, most philosophers of science seem to agree that an experiment *supplemented* by a plausible mechanism connecting *X* and *Y* is preferable to an experiment that links these two factors in a purely associational fashion. "Black-box" explanations are intrinsically suspect; one wishes to see inside the box. Mechanisms matter.

Causal Comparison

We ought not lose sight of the fact that causal demonstration is conducted, to some extent, by a process of *comparison.* A causal argument is verified to the extent that inductive and deductive evidence indicates that one causal story is superior to others which might be constructed to explain the same event. In other words, we have little faith in a causal conjecture based on the investigation of a single cause. Nor have we much faith in a causal argument that eliminates other possible causes but does not give these causal hypotheses a fair shake – the "straw man"

59. Marini and Singer (1988: 379), emphasis added. See also Blalock (1964), Hedstrom and Swedberg (1998), Little (1998), Mahoney (2000), Salmon (1984), and Stinchcombe (1992). This double-movement helps to explain the attraction of "mechanism" to scholars in the rational choice tradition, who are concerned with individual-level behavior as well as macroframeworks of analysis (e.g., Elster 1989a; Petersen 1999).
60. See D'Andrade (1995: 9).

argument (where the explanations the writer wishes to discredit are posed in such stark or unrealistic terms that they could not possibly be true). If, however, the writer has scrupulously investigated other possible causes for the event – as indicated by common sense, by secondary work on a subject, or the writer's own best guess – and none of these causes seem as secure, then we will be much more confident in proclaiming X to be truly a cause of Y.[61]

The reason we look to other possible causes, rather than focusing entirely on our favored cause, has something to do with the assumption of *regularity* in the universe of human behavior. We assume that most human actions occur for a reason; they are not random. This assumption is even stronger when considering the sort of actions that are generally of interest to social scientists – actions of organizations, groups and leaders, and actions relating to matters of great importance. The cause of someone's misstep while climbing a stairway may not be fathomable. The cause of someone's vote, by contrast, is more apprehensible for it is intentional, and intentional actions are likely to have a specifiable cause. Moreover, social science usually focuses on actions that are iterated, either over time or through space; here again, the regularity assumption seems warranted. Things that happen again and again in roughly the same way are likely to have a cause (or set of causes).[62] If we can conclude that the parts of the world with which we are most concerned are causally ordered, then the task of assigning a particular cause to each event, or set of events, is vastly simplified: we can proceed by elimination. Knowing something about how the world works, we identify possible causes and then try to assess their relative influence on a particular effect.

But it is not simply the search for new and different causes that makes causal analysis a comparative venture. One is also interested in ways in which causes *interact*. Indeed, the lock, stock, and barrel replacement of one cause by another is rare; more commonly, one finds that a causal relationship is altered, not destroyed, by the introduction or subtraction

---

61. The criterion of *comparison,* as I have called it, might also be labeled inference to the best explanation (Harman 1965), the method of residues (Mill 1843/1872: 259), abduction, the method of hypothesis, hypothetic inference, the method of elimination, eliminative induction, or theoretical inference (most of the foregoing are discussed in Harman 1965). See also Campbell (1988: ch 6), Campbell and Stanley (1966), Cook and Campbell (1979: 23), Marini and Singer (1988: 386), Miller (1987: ch 4), Neuman (1997: 51), Popper (1969), and Stinchcombe (1968: 20–2).

62. In saying this we are once again begging a number of ontological questions. Is the world really determinative, or is it instead stochastic? Again, I will sidestep this (I believe, unanswerable) conundrum. All we need say is that we can identify causes (factors that operate in the manner described by the word "cause") in many human actions.

of additional factors. Thus, one cannot state with confidence that X_t is a cause of Y unless one has examined the possible effects of other variables on this relationship. Without comparative analysis one's initial causal argument is likely to be flawed, or "spurious." In statistical jargon, one's analysis is suffering from "omitted variable bias," or "specification" problems.[63]

Nonempirical Factors in Causal Analysis

It is time to repeat the obvious: no causal argument of any sort could be made without assuming a good deal about how the world works (see Chapter 7). Some of these assumptions are commonsensical. Others may be of a highly sophisticated sort (e.g., carbon dating). Others may be drawn from a sense of plausibility honed over many years of work on a specialized topic. All writers, in any case, put their inductive evidence together with their deductive knowledge (knowledge that might have been inductive at some point in time but which is now considered true beyond question). The point is simple: causal arguments are never entirely empirical matters, and may be challenged by an endless regress of empirical questions (since each causal argument rests, necessarily, upon other descriptive and causal arguments), along with some questions of a philosophical nature that are assuredly not empirical. Causal arguments, therefore, rest delicately upon a skein of existing truisms and theories. It is this background knowledge, the knowledge that makes causal explanation possible at all, that composes the nonempirical part of any causal argument. This goes without saying, but – as Sartori once put it – deserves saying nonetheless.

---

63. See King et al. (1994: 170–4). There are, of course, many different ways of testing rival arguments against one another, a matter that we take up in the next chapter.

9

Methods

The scene is an inn. Pickwick and some young friends are dining when Editor Pott comes upon them. Some preliminary chatter of a delightful sort and Pott is convinced that Pickwick's young friends are waverers – they do not follow the blue. To set their opinion on solid foundations, he urges them to read a series of articles that appeared in his paper in the form of a review of Chinese metaphysics. "An abstruse subject," says Pickwick. "Very," says Pott, but my writer "crammed for it ... he read up for the subject, at my desire, in the Encyclopaedia Britannica." "I was not aware that this valuable work carried anything on Chinese metaphysics," responds Pickwick. "He read, Sir," rejoins Pott, looking round with a smile of intellectual superiority, "He read for metaphysics under the letter M and for China under the letter C, and combined his information, Sir."

— Martin Landau/Charles Dickens[1]

A good research design, I have argued, is characterized by plenitude, boundedness, comparability, independence, representativeness, variation, analytic utility, replicability, mechanism, and causal comparison. To the extent that we can draw accurate conclusions about causal relationships in the sphere of human actions we do so with studies that embody these ten features. This is the simplest and most parsimonious way of summarizing the complex task of research design in causal analysis.

As we have already noted, these criteria are often in conflict with one another, such that we *cannot* fulfill all ten (at least not to an equal degree). Here is where a research design must reach beyond generalities and toward specific, and often very hard, choices. Since each choice – of cases, of treatments, and of analysis – implies a somewhat different method, there are, in principle, an infinite number of social science methods. Most of these, however, can be understood as variants of nine

1. A scene from Charles Dickens' *Pickwick Papers*, as related by Landau (1972: 218–19).

basic approaches to case selection, treatment, and analysis: *experimental, statistical, QCA, most-similar, most-different, extreme-case, typical-case, crucial-case,* and *counterfactual,* as summarized in Table 9.1.[2]

The chapter begins with a review of these nine methods, most of which will be familiar to the reader. A second section explores the relative utility of two dimensions of analysis – synchronic and diachronic – implicit within each of the nine methods. A third section discusses the issue of sample size in research design. A final section discusses the utility of methods-driven social science.

Large-N Methods

We begin with two methods that characteristically employ large samples – the *experimental* method and the *statistical* method. We should note that the notion of a "large" sample size is open to considerable interpretation. Experiments in social science are likely to generate fewer cases than experiments in the natural sciences; and many fewer than the average nonexperimental ("statistical") research setting. Nonetheless, by reference to the other methods reviewed here, and keeping in mind a plastic notion of sample size, we may lump these two types of research design together in a single basket.

Experimental

The experimental method is revered as one of the hallmarks – perhaps *the* hallmark – of scientific method. Those who look to the natural sciences to provide methodological direction to the social sciences are likely to base their claims on the formidable accomplishments of this approach to knowledge gathering. What, then, makes the experimental method so special?

---

2. Readers may wonder why there has been scant mention of narrative explanations, process-tracing, pattern-matching, ethnography, the historical method, structured, focused comparison (George 1979), grounded theory (Glaser and Strauss 1967), and triangulation. Each of these (and many more!) might be regarded as methods. Yet, none are very specific. Griffin (1992: 405), for example, describes narrative as "the portrayal of social phenomena as temporally ordered, sequential, unfolding, and openended 'stories' fraught with conjunctures and contingency." This is not a method in the sense that we are using the term here. More important, most of what is understood to be desirable in the foregoing approaches is encapsulated in the ten general criteria pertaining to research design (Table 8.2) or in the methods delineated in this chapter. Other approaches, such as event-structure analysis (Griffin 1993; Heise 1988, 1989) and simulation modeling (Johnson 1999), are specific enough, but have not yet demonstrated their utility for social science research.

Table 9.1 *Methods and Dimensions of Analysis*

Methods	Pleni-tude	Bounded-ness	Com-para-bility	Inde-pend-ence	Repre-senta-tiveness	Variation	Analytic utility	Mechan-ism	Repli-cability	Causal Compar-ison	Treat-ment	Analysis	Causal logic
Large-N													
Experi-mental	+	+	+	+	–	+	–	+	+	+	experi-mental	stat	proba-bilistic
Statistical	+	+		+	+	+		–	+		none	stat	proba-bilistic
Small-Medium-N													
QCA	–					across-case					none	boolean	deter-ministic
Most-similar	–		+	–	–	across-case					none	non-stat	deter-ministic
Most-different	–		–	+	–	across-case					none	non-stat	deter-ministic
Case study (N = 1)													
Extreme-case	–				–	within-case		+			none	non-stat	proba-bilistic
Typical-case	–				+	within-case		+			none	non-stat	proba-bilistic
Crucial-case	–					within-case	+	+			none	non-stat	proba-bilistic
Counter-factual	–					within-case		+			speculative	non-stat	proba-bilistic
DIMENSIONS													
Synchronic	–	+	–	+									
Diachronic	+	–	+	–				+					

+/–: Indicates whether the method is generally strong or weak on that dimension. Empty cells indicate that there is no defining characteristic.

Let us begin with an example. A researcher wishes to discover the effect of racial cues on the evaluation of political issues among members of the majority racial group. To do so she sets up an experiment in which randomly sampled respondents of the majority race are split into two groups, a test group and a control group. The test group is read a series of passages from recent news reports about the involvement of minorities in politics. (These are "positive" news stories, but they highlight the involvement of minorities in politics.) They are then asked a battery of questions about current political issues. The control group is asked the same set of questions, but without the prior reading of news reports. Results can then be directly compared so as to determine whether the framing of the issue has demonstrable effects on respondents' issue-positions.

Definitionally, the experimental method involves two essential features: the arbitrary manipulation of the causal factor (or factors) of interest and the control – usually by random selection – of all other factors that might plausibly affect the causal relationship of interest. Usually, this research design produces the following wonders. Its cases are plentiful, or can be multiplied easily so as to become plentiful.[3] Its cases are well-bounded (since one is able to study the universe of possible cases it is fairly easy to decide what constitutes a *relevant* case). Its cases are comparable – one subject is similar enough to the next subject with respect to the causal relationship of interest to offer useful evidence. (We should note that case-comparability is achieved by assigning subjects randomly to control and treatment groups. It is the randomization of the sample, not the a priori qualities of this sample or the treatment itself, that achieves high levels of case-comparability in experimental research.[4]) Its cases are independent of one another, such that each test is considered to offer independent evidence on the question of interest to the researcher. Its cases demonstrate sufficient variation to prove the relationship of interest. The treatment of cases allows the researcher to isolate the mechanism at work in the causal relationship. The experiment is replicable. And finally, alterations of the experiment allow one to test a wide range of alternate hypotheses.

Clearly, there is much to be said for an experimental design. In Mario Bunge's memorable words, "The best grasp of reality is not obtained by

3. Experimental methods are associated with large samples because there is usually little marginal cost to testing additional cases. We may retest the same unit, or we may find other units that are virtually identical. We occasionally encounter circumstances in which retesting is costly, or even prohibitive, so there is no *necessary* connection between experimental study and large samples.

4. Another way of expressing this virtue is to say that randomization allows for the control of all but one (or several) variables of interest by maintaining comparability on all other dimensions.

respecting fact and avoiding fiction but by vexing fact and controlling fiction."[5] Indeed, the *only* problematic feature of the experimental method is its narrowness of application – hence, its poor scoring on representativeness and analytic utility. In the social sciences, experimental methods are generally limited to questions about the attitudes and behavior of the mass public, since members of the public can be interviewed individually or observed in group experiments. We have considerably less access to elites. More important, it is difficult to replicate the *circumstances* of elite behavior in ways that would answer meaningful questions. For example, suppose one is interested in figuring out the influence of campaign contributions on the decision making of legislators. Even if access to these political elites could be arranged, an experimental setting would probably be inappropriate for testing this hypothesis. We cannot test hypotheses about many events in an experimental setting because we cannot construct a reasonable facsimile of that event for our participants to experience. Revolutions, to take an extreme case, are difficult to simulate. Moreover, we are not entitled, for reasons of ethics and law, to manipulate our subjects' behavior in ways that might elucidate questions we would like to know about. (Nor, I might add, are we funded sufficiently for this purpose.) It is difficult to see, humanitarian and financial concerns aside, how one might test a society. Finally, many of the phenomena we try to explain are rooted firmly in the past. If we could travel through time to replay the French Revolution 100 times, each under slightly different conditions, we could discover – with a level of certainty comparable to that found in the natural sciences – whether the Enlightenment, royal misjudgments, corruption, foreign wars, or any other factor was the necessary or sufficient cause of that event. But we cannot.

A glimpse of the complications inherent in experimental research design is afforded by a well-known film, *Groundhog Day,* which offers a wonderful illustration of the experimental method as it might be applied to human subjects. In this film, a single day is repeated over and over again under identical initial circumstances. Each day functions as a case, and each case is entirely independent of the next. Only the protagonist (Bill Murray) – or, as we might say, the experimenter – has knowledge of the previous day's events. Thus, he is able to systematically test various hypotheses related to his goal (winning the heart of the heroine, Andie MacDowell), while controlling other factors. Appropriately, the method proves successful; his policy designs are realized.

It could be that experimental methods are underutilized in the social sciences today.[6] In the future, we may discover ways to simulate various

5. Bunge (1959: 129).
6. See, for example, Kinder and Palfrey (1993).

social, political, and economic contexts so that we can test, in an experimental fashion, individual and group responses. Even so, I suspect that most of our current concerns cannot be tested experimentally, or at least raise serious questions of representativeness. Consequently, nonexperimental methods will probably continue to dominate social science research. The rest of this chapter is concerned, therefore, with *natural* research designs – where cases are taken more or less as they present themselves (i.e., without experimental manipulation).[7]

Statistical

Wherever cases are nonexperimental and one wishes to integrate a large number of them into an analysis, one is more or less forced to reach causal conclusions with *statistical* methods. Strictly speaking, "statistical" refers only to a method of analysis; it tells us nothing about case selection, except that the sample will be relatively large. Experimental results, of course, may be analyzed statistically – and usually are. We will employ the term here to refer to any large-N research design that uses statistical, rather than experimental, methods to differentiate among ("control for") causes.

Even so, "statistical" is an embarrassingly large term, covering a wide range of analytic methods – from simple correlation to multiple regression, path analysis, structural equation modeling, and so forth and so on (the menu continues to grow). What one can do with this bundle of methods in a particular research context is determined by the sort of variables, the number of variables, the number of cases, and the sort of causal questions that one has at hand. The critical element, for our purposes, is that one is using statistical, rather than experimental, methods to control for confounding factors.[8]

As described by Vaughn McKim, the most frequently employed features of statistical analysis follow this pattern.

> The observation (and measurement) of values of two or more properties distributed variably within a population is the raw material... In order to apply

---

7. Mill was well aware of the limitations of the experimental method in the study of social phenomena (see Mill 1843/1872: 298). It is worth noting that not all natural sciences are based on experimental research. Scholars of theoretical physics and astronomy, for example, rarely find themselves in laboratory situations.
8. The term "statistical method" is employed elsewhere (e.g., Lijphart 1971). It is similar, though not identical, to what Mill described as the method of concomitant variation (see Mill 1843/1872; DeFelice 1986; Mahoney 2000). Introductions to the general topic of statistics can be found in virtually all methods textbooks. Achen (1982), Freedman et al. (1991), Hamilton (1992), and Kennedy (1998) are good points of departure.

standard techniques for revealing the relationships that hold among properties whose values can vary, a procedure for measuring the distribution of the
values of each variable must be selected. This will typically involve both a representation of central tendency, e.g., a variable's mean value, and a measure
of the dispersion of its values, commonly represented by the average deviation of individual values from the mean, i.e., its variance.[9]

As McKim notes, this association between variables can be established
visually – for example, through scatterplots. If the association is strong,
there are only two variables of interest, and one does not seek great precision, this may be sufficient. However, "the critical breakthrough made
by statisticians late in the nineteenth century [drumroll please] involved
capitalizing on the idea that the *degree* of association among variables
represented in a scattergram could be represented algebraically" – clas-
sically, by drawing a "best fit" line that minimizes the distance between
each (actual) data point and the (projected) line.[10] The slope of the line
in a simple linear relationship then functions as a measure of the "degree
of association" between the two factors (X and Y), and the total dis-
tances of all the data points from the line as a measure of the goodness
of fit – that is, the extent to which variation on Y is "explained" by X (if
it is truly a causal relationship).[11]

This is a brief and schematic description of one of the most common
forms of statistical analysis, ordinary least squares (OLS) regression.
Here, we have simply measured the association of two variables. Usually,
statistical analysis is asked to sort out the causal implications of many
variables at once. In an experimental design, of course, we would have
been able to control for all but one or two of these variables, thus vastly
simplifying the task of causal comparison. Inferring causation from correlations is tricky business, but it is not categorically distinct from what
goes on in experimental, small-*N*, or case-study research designs.
Because one cannot observe a cause – causation is an inference, not an
observation – all causal conclusions build upon covariational evidence.

Small- and Medium-*N* Methods

A second class of methods is often referred to as "Millean" (since they
stem from J. S. Mill's *System of Logic*) or simply as "the comparative
method" (because they are commonly employed by comparativists in

9. McKim (1997: 5–6).
10. Ibid.
11. For qualifications of this rather crude account, see Achen (1982).

political science and sociology). These methods employ small or medium-size samples and generally focus on variation across the primary unit of analysis. There are three primary types: *qualitative comparative analysis (QCA), most-similar,* and *most-different.*

QCA

Qualitative comparative analysis (QCA), pioneered by Charles Ragin, offers a midway station between large- and small-*N* analysis.[12] Here, the ideal *N* lies somewhere between a handful and 50. Beyond 50, the method begins to lose its distinctiveness and merges with statistical methods; below 10, it merges with the small-*N* methods discussed below. QCA has nothing particular to say about case selection (all the usual caveats, as specified in Chapter 8, apply), but a great deal to say about how causal factors should be coded and analyzed.

The hallmark of QCA may be found in three features.[13] First, causes and outcomes must be coded dichotomously (present/absent, strong/weak, etc.) so they can be represented as 0 or 1 in a truth table. Ragin offers the imaginary example of regime failure – represented by 1 in the column under *Y* in Table 9.2 (0 indicates that a regime has endured). The causal factors in the table are (1) conflict between older and younger military officers, (2) death of a powerful dictator, and (3) CIA dissatisfaction with the regime. Second, cases are combined into common sequences (combinations of variables), noting the number of cases in each sequence in the initial column *(N)*. There are nine examples of the first sequence, two of the second, and so forth. Thus, a complex set of causes and consequences may be reduced to a parsimonious table. Finally, one arrives at causal conclusions through Boolean logic. While statistical logic generally approaches causal relationships in an "additive fashion" – X_1 is correlated with *Y*, holding the other *X*s constant – Boolean logic allows us to examine the possibility that X_1 has a different effect on *Y* when combined with the presence or absence of other variables. Each causal sequence, as specified by the presence or absence of relevant *X*s and the *Y*, is looked upon as a unique causal relationship.

The table indicates that all three causes are sufficient (but not necessary) causes of *Y*. Regimes will fail if there is conflict between older and younger military officers, the death of a powerful dictator, *or* CIA dis-

---

12. See Drass and Ragin (1992), Hicks (1999: 69–73), Hicks et al. (1995), Ragin (1987, 2000), and several chapters by Ragin in Janoski and Hicks (1993). I offer a greatly simplified version of this method here.
13. Ibid.

Table 9.2   *QCA*

N	X₁	X₂	X₃	Y
9	O	O	O	O
2	I	O	O	I
3	O	I	O	I
1	O	O	I	I
2	I	I	O	I
1	I	O	I	I
1	O	I	I	I
3	I	I	I	I

Adopted from Ragin (1987: 90).

satisfaction with the regime. With more cases, and more complex inter-actions (e.g., multiple causal paths), a more formalized procedure is nec-essary in order to discern this conclusion. But the logic of the analysis remains the same.

We should keep in mind, however, that reaching this conclusion involves several assumptions. Most important, we must assume that the causes and outcomes in question are adequately handled with dichoto-mous coding procedures. This may involve significant loss of informa-tion. What if there is moderate conflict between older and younger military officers? How will we code this in-between state? If differences of degrees are sufficiently extreme, we can afford some loss of exactitude (i.e., we do not need to register the precise measurements demanded by most statistical analyses). But many factors in social and political con-texts occupy this in-between realm. More generally, we may note that QCA presupposes deterministic causation. At home with necessity and sufficiency, QCA is at pains to analyze probabilistic relationships (but see discussion in footnote #15).

The utility of QCA in discerning causal *paths* – either conjunctural cau-sation or multiple causation (see Chapter 7) – is a primary selling point, necessitating the introduction of a more complex example. A recent study of income-security programs in fifteen industrialized nations employs QCA to reach the following conclusion. Extensive social security policies appear in these nations by 1920 when "(1) patriarchal statism and working-class mobilization are present and Catholic government and unitary democracy are absent ..., (2) Liberal government, working-class mobilization, and uni-tary democracy are present while Catholic government is not..., *or* (3) Catholic government and unitary democracy and patriarchal statism are present but Liberal government is absent." Thus, the authors conclude, there were three distinct paths to social security in the World War I era.[14] Where causal paths are well defined (i.e., deterministic), QCA is well constructed to explore these relationships – a major advantage over small-N methods (as usually employed) and statistical analysis (as usually employed). However, where causal paths are probabilistic – another sort of complexity – QCA falters. If there had been exceptions to any of the foregoing paths, for example, the Boolean logic of QCA would have eliminated that path as a causal hypothesis.[15]

Relative to small-N approaches, the larger samples made possible by QCA are likely to include greater variation, and hence are more likely to be adequately bounded and correctly representative of a larger population. Because there are few restrictions on the type of cases and variables that can be included (as is the case in most small-N strategies) QCA is considerably more flexible and can interrogate a larger number of possible causal hypotheses in a single research design (an advantage shared with large-N methods). Relative to large-N methods (experimental or statistical), the contrast is reversed; here, the method is deficient in plenitude, boundedness, variation, and representativeness, and more limited in the testing of alternate hypotheses. Consequently, QCA receives no scores at all in Table 9.1, signifying its middling status on our range of methods. It should be noted that the deterministic assumptions of QCA echo the assumptions of small-N methods, but not those of case studies and large-N studies, which are likely to take a probabilistic view of causation.

QCA is a significant addition to our arsenal of social science methods (arguably, the first since 1843!), even though its range of application is likely to remain limited. Most research situations will fall more naturally into a small-N, case-study, or large-N research designs.

Most-Similar

Preeminent among small-N methods is the *most-similar* method discovered by J. S. Mill (which he called the "method of difference"). Briefly

14. Hicks et al. (1995: 339).
15. In later work, Ragin (2000) incorporates probabilistic elements into the QCA procedure. These pertain to (a) the degree of membership of a case in a category (which can be scored, and correspondingly weighted) and (b) the frequency with which a designated causal path is found (one or two exceptions, where the N is fairly high, may not be sufficient to eliminate a hypothesis). These revisions move QCA closer to a probabilistic style of reasoning that is more in sync with the statistical methods explored earlier. As the N increases, probabilistic techniques become possible; but QCA then loses its distinctiveness as a method and Boolean logic breaks down.

stated, the most-similar research design looks for a few cases that are as similar as possible in all respects except the outcome of interest, where they are expected to vary.[16]

This will be clearer if we look at an example. Suppose we are interested in explaining the French Revolution. There are many possible comparative cases we might choose to study. However, the closest country – culturally, economically, politically – to France, and the one with the most different outcome (i.e., the most *non*revolutionary heritage) is probably England.[17] Thus, we construct a two-country comparison. Next, we look to survey all *possible* causes of the outcome in question (revolution) – the existence of a repressive monarchy, the willingness of the regime to exercise violent repression to quell internal dissent, the existence of a nonpropertied agrarian proletariat, expensive foreign wars, and so forth. With each hypothesis, let us say, we find a rough equivalence between France and England during the eighteenth century. Each of these hypotheses can then, by the logic of most-similar analysis, be discarded. If the presence of this factor did not lead to revolt in England, we reason, it probably cannot be considered a cause of revolt in France (see X_{2-5} in Table 9.3). Yet, one possible factor *is* different between the two cases – X_1. This, of course, is our probable cause, for we have eliminated all others.

Several possible difficulties should be noted at this point. First, we have stipulated a perfect most-similar research design. Things in the real world are rarely so neat. Suppose that our two cases are so similar that, although the outcome is different, we cannot specify any obvious cause (there is no X_1, in the terms of Table 9.3). In this situation we must either look at other countries, or at more subtle differences of degree in the England/France comparison. It will be noted that we have treated each hypothesis, as well as the outcome itself, as a dichotomous variable: Xs are either present *(y)* or absent *(n)*. Since most social science hypotheses

16. Most work on comparative methods, and virtually all methods textbooks, include some discussion of the most-similar method, though terminology varies. Przeworski and Teune (1970) invented "most-similar." Alternate names (for approximately the same thing) include the method of difference (Mill 1843/1872), the method of controlled comparison (Eggan 1954: 748), specification (Holt and Turner 1970: 11), and the comparable-cases strategy (Lijphart 1975a). See also DeFelice (1986), Goldstone (1997), Lieberson (1991; 1994), and Ragin (1987). It is important to note that *all* methods of analysis are based on the selection of comparable cases, as indicated by the criterion of comparability. However, only the most-similar method (a) seeks to eliminate *all but one* of the many differences that might be discovered between cases and (b) eschews the experimental treatment of cases.

17. Assume, for heuristic purposes, that the so-called English Revolution is not comparable in any way to the French Revolution.

Table 9.3   *The Most-Similar Method*

Cases	X_1	X_2	X_3	X_4	X_5	Y
England	y	y	y	y	y	stability
France	n	y	y	y	y	revolution

are matters-of-degree, we might try to incorporate these finer distinctions into our analysis. Thus, we might substitute for our dichotomous categories a tripartite scheme (high, medium, low), or an even more subtly graded calibration. Perhaps we will find nonquantitative adjectives (violent/peaceful) more useful. Naturally, such subtlety imposes a cost. The more complex our operationalizations the more difficult it may be to incorporate additional cases, or even to compare England and France.

The only restriction on our operationalization of variables and outcomes is that the variation measured by such operationalizations must be fairly significant. In a trichotomy of high, medium, and low, for example, the difference between cases exemplifying "high" and "medium" levels on a particular causal factor may not be significant enough to suggest firm causal conclusions. This problem was discussed earlier, in connection with QCA.

If no single cause jumps out of the analysis (as it does in Table 9.3), we will also want to consider the possibility that the causal factors at work in producing revolution are *multiple,* and work in conjunction with one another. But this sort of complexity is unlikely to come to light in a small-N research design. All we can do is to observe variation on individual variables; we do not have sufficient cases to analyze sequences – unless of course country-cases are also observed diachronically, as suggested by the comparative-historical tradition of Barrington Moore and Theda Skocpol. (Diachronic analysis is discussed later.)[18]

It is important to point out, finally, that whatever conclusions we reach on the basis of small-N analysis may not be very useful in illuminating the phenomenon of revolution, as applied to other (un-studied) cases. If the most-similar research design works perfectly, we may argue that X_1 is necessary to the occurrence of revolution *in France* and at that point in time. Stated more generally, the proposition runs thus: If a country is England or France in the eighteenth century, it will not experience revolution unless X_1 is present. We do *not* know, however, whether X_1 is sufficient, unto itself, to cause revolution. Nor can we speculate wisely

18. Skocpol (1979, 1984).

Table 9.4   *The Most-Different Method*

Cases	X_1	X_2	X_3	X_4	X_5	Y
France	y	y	y	y	y	revolution
China	y	n	n	n	n	revolution

about the causes of revolution in other countries. At best, we have managed to explain only two cases, with some speculation about how the causal argument might apply to a broader population.

Our perspective on the utility of the most-similar method is likely to hinge on how we interpret this method. Narrowly interpreted – as a two-case comparison with only one variable differing between the two cases (as illustrated in Table 9.3) – the most-similar method has a limited range of applicability, its ability to decipher complex and probabilistic causes is virtually nil, and it will probably have to operationalize variables dichotomously (resulting in a considerable loss of precision in many contexts). In this light, the criticisms of Stanley Lieberson and others seem justified.[19] If we take a more permissive attitude toward the parameters of this method – extending the number of cases (spatially and/or temporally) – we find that it has a better chance of overcoming some of these difficulties. On the other hand, this permissive rendering jeopardizes its distinctiveness as a method of case selection and analysis.

Most-Different

Most-different analysis (in Mill's terminology, the "method of agreement") is the reverse image of most-similar analysis: variation on X values is prized, and variation on Y eschewed. Ideally, one discovers a single X that remains constant across the two cases, signaling a causal relationship (see Table 9.4). Thus, to continue with our previous example, we might decide to compare France with China, another country with a revolutionary outcome. Differences of time-period (roughly two centuries) are, in principle, no problem for the most-different research design; indeed, they are enhancements, because they constitute another difference that can be analyzed with reference to the common outcome. The more such differences we can identify the more handily these cases fit the requirements of the most-different method.

There are formidable difficulties with this method, however, accounting for its general scarcity in social science. First, as Mill recognized,

---

19. See Lieberson (1991, 1994) and Goldstone (1997). But see also Mahoney (2000).

most-different research designs are more useful in eliminating possible causes than in providing positive proof of a causal argument. Thus, in the France/China comparison we might be able to eliminate religion as a necessary cause of revolution, since our two cases had widely varying religions. We might also be able to eliminate the bourgeoisie as a cause of revolution, since they played no prominent part in the Chinese revolution. Yet, without variation on *Y* any *positive* conclusions about causation are particularly vulnerable to the problem of causal comparison (aka "omitted variable" bias). Although we might be able to eliminate, or at least cast doubt on, possible causal factors it will be difficult on the basis of this logic to conclude that the one remaining constant variable is the sole cause of *X* simply because it is the only hypothesis left standing (all the others having been discarded). It is always possible, for instance, that some other factor has been ignored – either because it is not apparent to the researcher or because it is too difficult to measure – and that this omitted variable holds the key to our inquiry.

Second, it is a general feature of most-different research designs that one will be *unable* to eliminate all-but-one possible cause. This is so because cases that demonstrate the same outcome are likely to be similar in other respects as well. Thus, France and China both experienced financially draining foreign wars; both had discredited elites with serious internal divisions; both had a large and landless peasantry; and so forth. None of these possible causes can be safely eliminated. Thus, the most-different research design may indicate which of a number of arguments are wrong (insufficient), but it probably will not tell us much about which argument is right.

Otherwise put, we are very unlikely to find situations where cases have similar values on *Y*, but highly divergent values on relevant *X*s. Another example may clarify this point. Suppose we are looking at government spending. It will be noticed that big spenders tend to look alike; they tend to have strong labor movements, strong left parties, centralized governments, long-established welfare programs, and so forth. If, let us say, Switzerland, had a big government (measured monetarily by government receipts or government spending), then we would be able to eliminate many probable causes. Of course, Switzerland has a very frugal (central) state. If we are extremely lucky, we may find one or two cases that exemplify the most-different case design. But it is asking a lot to rest a theory on two cases.

This leads to a third critical point: although we can eliminate necessary causes, we cannot come to firm conclusions about relationships of a probabilistic nature. Suppose, that is, that high government spending is *usually* (even though one of our high-spending cases has a weak labor movement) correlated with a strong labor movement, and this is a plausible cause. We would be quite wrong to eliminate this variable as an explanation of government growth, even though the $X:Y$ relationship is not perfect. Since most causal relationships in human societies are of a probabilistic sort (the relationships are not perfect), we must hold the results of most-different analysis at arm's length.[20]

This doubt is enhanced by the following consideration. When a case that is *radically* different from our other case, or cases, shows a similar outcome, there are prima facie grounds for rejecting this case as deviant. Precisely *because* the Xs vary so greatly, this research design strains the assumption of comparability that underlies all comparative analysis. Cases that are so different in their X characteristics (social, economic, political, historical) may not respond in the same fashion to similar stimuli. They may be "outliers."

Finally, we must assume – if the logic of most-different analysis is to tell us anything at all – that Y is the product of one and only one cause. If, let us say, high social welfare spending can be produced by more than one cause, or by a combination of causes, this method of analysis will not help us to solve the riddle. Indeed, it may be fundamentally misleading insofar as it encourages us to discard causal factors that are not constant across the two cases.[21]

For all these reasons I think it is fair to conclude (along with most other writers who have examined this question), that most-different case comparisons are rarely found in the empirical world of social science and, where found, are of limited utility.[22] The only circumstances I can conceive of in which most-different analysis might be useful is when (a) one is interested in eliminating putatively "necessary" causes,[23] or (b) there is no variation whatsoever in the dependent variable. Then, indeed, one is thrown back on more primitive expedients. But in all other circumstances – which is to say, in the vast majority of research scenarios – we are better off choosing cases so as to achieve variation in the phenomenon we wish to explain.[24]

---

20. To be sure, one can modify the most-different method to take account for "almost-necessary" causal relationships (Dion 1998). However, within a small-N framework it is difficult to know when an exception proves a rule, and when it disproves a rule.
21. This point is made at some length in Ragin (1987: 36–9).
22. This appears to be the general opinion of Mill (1843/1872: 258; and elsewhere), who invented the method. But see DeFelice (1986).
23. See Dion (1998) and Mahoney (2000).
24. The strongest evidence against the most different method is that writers who claim to be following it usually smuggle-in variation on the dependent variable. Karl (1997), for example, in her excellent study of petro-states, frequently compares these states to other (non-petro) states. To the extent that she does so, her most-different design is compromised. (We are grateful for these compromises.)

Case-Study Methods

We turn now to methods where the sample is, in some formal (but perhaps misleading) sense, equal to 1. There are four common ways of choosing a case study: *extreme-case, typical-case, crucial-case,* and *counterfactual.* The terms are a bit confusing, since they designate a type of case (e.g., "extreme") as well as a method of analysis (e.g., extreme-case analysis). No harm is done so long as we keep this terminological ambiguity in mind.

As a research design, case studies offer one generic virtue and one generic vice. Their virtue is their ability to elucidate mechanisms connecting a particular *X* with a particular *Y.* By watching the progress of a single unit (a country, a city, a person) over time and by paying attention to variation within that case we can often observe, or at least intuit, a complex causal relationship at work. The corresponding vice is that case studies focus on a single case; they lack plenitude. The extent of this vice is often unclear. Indeed, it is often unclear whether so-called case studies deserve this appellation. Formally (i.e., definitionally), case studies rely on within-case variation in order to parse larger causal relationships. However, we should notice that three of these methods (extreme-case, typical-case, and crucial-case) are defined by their across-case characteristics (their characteristics relative to a larger set of cases). Indeed, while the formal analysis may be limited to within-case evidence (cases within the case), most case studies devote some attention to across-case comparisons as well – usually by reference to the secondary literature, or to well-established features of the other cases. Thus, there is a formal (within-case) as well as an informal (across-case) element to most case studies.[25]

Arguments over the adequacy of case studies often hinge on clarifying this distinction. Regrettably, work in the case-study genre is not always clear on what sort of variation is being analyzed. We can understand this problem as stemming from an ambiguity of purpose. Formally, a case study of Kenya focuses on Kenya; this is where the writer has conducted her field research (or whatever sort of research is required). Yet, the Kenyan case is not likely to make much sense unless there is some consideration of other countries – countries which, in light of the author's causal argument, constitute good cases (see previous chapter). Typically, these will include neighboring countries. The same problem is encountered in historical work focused on a particular era: while the ostensible topic might be Kenya in the 1930s, it will be difficult (and in

---

25. See Collier and Mahoney (1996: 67), Lijphart (1975a: 160), and Smelser (1973: 56).

all likelihood impossible) to explore this topic without some consideration of the 1920s and 1940s.

Case-study writers feel an understandable discomfort when forced to theorize beyond the bounds of their own primary research. However, they cannot avoid, and should not avoid, some consideration of relevant additional (unstudied) cases; otherwise, the study is poorly bounded. Whether the N is single, or multiple, hinges on this issue. By the same token, when other cases are brought into consideration they are unlikely to bear the same weight as the case that has been extensively studied. They are not "cases" in the same sense.

This methodological difficulty is by no means limited to case-study research. Indeed, cases are often assigned variable weights in large-N research, and this weighting procedure responds to the same sort of criteria (e.g., we have better, more secure, observations for one country than another). The remedy is clear: case-study researchers must devote the same self-conscious attention, and careful elucidation, to their weighting schemes as large-N researchers. Although this weighting procedure cannot be carried out in a quantitative fashion (unless of course the researcher employs a large-N dataset to situate her case study), we can at least distinguish between *formal* cases (the case or cases that a writer has in-depth knowledge about) and *informal* cases (cases occupying a peripheral position in the research design). This distinction clarifies the sense in which the N of a case study may be both single *and* multiple.

The first N issue is therefore the extent to which a case study employs cross-case analysis. The second N issue is equally fraught, and equally difficult to explain. We have said that case-study work (by definition) relies primarily on within-case variation (i.e., variation within the primary case). We have also noted that within-case variation often employs a multitude of cases (the N is high). Here is a second sense, then, in which the N of a case study is unclear, for the definition of "case" (and hence the N of a study) can only be understood by reference to a particular causal proposition, and a single study contains multiple propositions. A proposition about Kenya (at-large) defines country as the unit of analysis. Here, the N is 1 (except insofar as *informal* cases are brought in to bolster the analysis). A causal proposition about variation *within* Kenya (e.g., why the Mau-Mau rebellion emanated from Nairobi and the Central and Rift Valley provinces) defines subnational units as the primary unit of analysis. Here, the N might be equal to the number of regions in Kenya. If, to choose a third option, the causal proposition concerns why some people in Kenya (and not others) participated in the rebellion, then the unit of analysis becomes individuals. The N of this study may number in the thousands.

We have already noted these points (in Chapter 8) but it is important to emphasize that the N of a study – and particularly of a case study – is often indeterminate. An author is likely to advance different propositions in the course of such a study, each of which defines a different primary unit of analysis, and she is likely to exploit both across-case and within-case evidence to demonstrate these propositions. Consequently, the N question is not easily settled.

Whatever the complexities, the general point stands. Comparisons that are to bear scrutiny must be laid out in an explicit fashion. The problematic status of N within case studies should not be regarded as an invitation to ambiguity, or to "intuitive" methods. Indeed, it imposes a special (albeit oft-neglected) burden on case study researchers. Case issues should be vetted as thoroughly and explicitly as possible. It should be clear to readers, in particular, what sort of variation is being mustered for what sort of causal claims. With these general matters under our belt, we may now turn to the variety of case-study methods.

Extreme-Case

While the most-different method seeks to minimize variation on the outcome of interest, the *extreme-case* method seeks to maximize such variation. Indeed, it exalts the criterion of variation to the point of being the principal feature of research design. Thus, France or Switzerland might be chosen for a study of state strength; Sweden or Japan for a study of government spending; North Korea for a study of totalitarianism; and so forth.[26]

In addition to great variation (the virtues of which are discussed in Chapter 8), an extreme case is likely to offer advantages in elucidating the mechanism at work in a causal relationship. Moments of extremity, as William James noted, often reveal the essence of a situation.[27] Consider cases A, B, C, D, E, F, and G, which vary along dimension X. Let us say that A, B, C, D, E, and F, vary minimally, whereas G exemplifies an extreme value (either "positive" or "negative"). Ceteris paribus, G will be the most useful case for in-depth analysis. Naturally, we will want to keep the other cases in mind as we conduct our analysis, since these cases provide the variation we are seeking. But we can justify focusing our attention on this particular unit as an exemplar.

Extreme cases are particularly useful when a phenomenon is difficult to operationalize. If we cannot measure X with accuracy and precision,

---

26. See Durkheim (1947), Eckstein (1975), Harris (1978, 1985), Jackman (1985: 167), Ragin (1987: 23), and Smelser (1976: 158–9).
27. William James, *Varieties of Religious Experience*, paraphrased in Dower (1999: 29).

we are on particularly unstable ground in examining cases *A, B, C, D, E,* and *F*. With *G*, however, we can assert with some assurance that something happened. It is a clear "yes" or "no," and therefore worthwhile contemplating for underlying causal relationships. Extreme cases offer an informal method for dichotomizing a continuous variable. Since we cannot accurately measure "degree of fascism," we look to the most extreme cases of this phenomenon – Germany and Italy – to tell us about what fascism meant, or would have meant, in other places. Since we cannot accurately measure "degree of business regulation," we look to socialist countries, on the one hand, and Hong Kong, on the other, as revelatory cases (of high regulation and low regulation, respectively). These are the virtues of the extreme-case method.

There may be some sacrifice in representativeness, of course. A case exemplifying an extreme outcome is less likely to be representative of a broader population of cases than a midrange case. It is, by definition, extreme, and what is true at one extreme may not be true at the middle, or at the other extreme. But this is not *necessarily* so. Remember, we are interested in *X:Y* relationships. If those relationships exhibit similar within-case relationships then an extreme case is just as representative as any other. Let us say that we are investigating the relationship between labor organization and government spending and we decide to focus only on a high-spending case (e.g., Sweden). Our within-case analysis tracks the changing strength and consolidation of the Swedish labor movement and its relationship to welfare-state spending. (There are, of course, other sorts of within-case evidence that one might wish to investigate.) If the relationship between labor power and government spending operates in much the same way across the other cases of concern to us, then our sample ($N = 1$) may be considered representative of the population. If, however, the relationship is *not* uniform – if, for example, the labor power and government spending relationship functions differently in parliamentary and presidential political systems – then we will have reached a set of findings that is *not* generalizable to a larger population.[28]

Typical-Case

The *typical-case* method is quite similar to its cousin, the extreme-case method, except that here representativeness, rather than variation, is maximized. A typical-case approach seeks to find the most usual case in a particular population – which is to say, that case which is likely to be

---

28. For further discussion, see Achen (1986), Achen and Snidal (1989), Collier (1995b); Collier and Mahoney (1996), Geddes (1990), and King et al. (1994).

most representative on whatever causal dimensions are of interest.[29] This involves choosing a case that exemplifies the median, mean, or mode (it is hoped they are not too far apart) on relevant causal dimensions. Thus, in investigating American public opinion, Robert and Helen Lynd looked for a community that was closest to their conception of America (Muncie, IN). In investigating ideology in America several decades later, Robert Lane turned to men who, he thought, exemplified the "American urban common man."[30]

Just as the extreme-case method can be adjusted so as to choose cases from both extremes, so the typical-case method can be adjusted to choose typical cases from different *subgroups* of a general population so as to better represent that population. It is a question of stratified sampling (to use the stats jargon), but on a small-N scale and with more informal methods.[31] In a population that is assumed to vary considerably from subgroup to subgroup one naturally strives to find typical cases from each of the subgroups, which can then be added together to form a composite picture of the population.

Crucial-Case

Cases are rightly chosen for reasons of analytic utility, I argued in Chapter 8. When this governs case selection in a small-N sample we are identifying *crucial* cases – cases that are, for one reason or another, critical to a concept or to a broader body of theory.

There are two basic versions of a crucial case. In the first, a case is chosen because it has come to define, or at least to exemplify, a concept or theoretical outcome. France is a crucial case in the study of revolution; Sweden a crucial case in the study of big government; the Soviet Union a crucial case in the study of communism; Switzerland a crucial case in the study of democratic longevity, and so forth. These are "paradigm-cases," one might say. Because of their importance (theoretically, conceptually), whatever we know about them matters more than what we know about other cases. How could one study revolution *without* studying France?

---

29. We should remind ourselves that representativeness is not a matter that can be tested empirically in a small-N study; for, by definition, we are only examining one or a few cases out of a larger population. Hence, when we use the term "typical case" we mean typical *insofar as we can ascertain* from other sources or from general knowledge.
30. See Lynd and Lynd (1929/1956) and Lane (1962: 3).
31. On stratified sampling, see Neuman (1997: 212).

A second sort of crucial case reveals a result that is unexpected in light of the causal inference under investigation – either a *least-likely* case is shown to be positive (with respect to the predicted outcome) or a *most-likely* case is shown to be negative.[32] Both are "deviant" cases, with respect to some theory. Let us take Duverger's law as an example. Duverger surmised that a simple-majority single-ballot system favors a two-party system.[33] Disconfirming crucial cases would therefore be of the following sort: a country with single member districts and first-past-the-post rules (a "most-likely" scenario) that does *not* have a two-party system, or a country with multimember districts (a "least-likely" scenario) that *does* have a two-party system. Confirming cases would be of the following sort: a country with single-member districts and first-past-the-post rules that, *in other respects,* seems an unlikely candidate for a two-party system (e.g., it is heterogeneous, riven by internal conflict, barely democratic, with weak party structures, and so forth). It is the latter, non-electoral characteristics that make this case "least-likely" to evidence the outcome predicted by Duverger's theory. One might also choose to study a country with a proportional electoral system which, along other dimensions, seems ripe for two-party control but whose outcome is multiparty. The crucial-case method may be used therefore to confirm or disconfirm an existing theory, or to suggest modifications in that theory.

Statistical analysis is often helpful in identifying which cases might be crucial for a given theory. If a case lies far away from its predicted value, it would appear (on the basis of the statistical model) that this case does not fit the theory very well. It poses an anomaly. Either the theory is wrong, the measurement is wrong, or some additional factor (heretofore unaccounted for) is causing the case to fall away from the regression line. It should be noted that cases with high residuals are quite different from cases with extreme values. An extreme case may fit

---

32. One may quibble with definitions here. One could define a crucial case simply as a case that "must closely fit a theory" (Eckstein 1975: 118). Thus, Great Britain would be a crucial case in the study of Duverger's law. Yet, it will not be a very useful case if it ends up fitting the theory to a T. No researcher is advised to undertake a crucial-case analysis – or any analysis, for that matter – without having a pretty good idea of what she will find in that analysis. In other words, a crucial case does not become a crucial-case *method* until one considers the results of such study (vis-à-vis some theory of interest). Examples and discussion of the crucial-case method can be found in Allen (1965), Gourevitch (1978), Lijphart (1975b), and Rogowski (1995). On the "deviant" case study, see Emigh (1997).

33. Duverger (1963: 217).

a theory perfectly; a high-residual case, which we refer to as "deviant," does not.

The weaknesses of this otherwise splendid method are perhaps obvious from our chosen example: there may not *be* a crucial case, and even when there is it may be possible to explain its existence without compromising the major premise of the theory. Thus, one might say with reference to a single disconfirming case that this is, after all, just a single case in a large universe of cases. Indeed, even when operating in the disconfirming mode, crucial-case studies usually end up by reformulating the theories under investigation so as to account for newly discovered anomalies, rather than rejecting those theories out of hand. Modification, not falsification, is the usual purpose of studies focused on a crucial case.

Counterfactual

Up to this point, we have discussed methods that analyze "real" cases – cases that actually exist, or existed. Equally important to much social science work, and particularly to work of a historical nature, is *counter-factual* analysis – the exploration of things that did not happen, but (conceivably) could have. Counterfactuals are thought-experiments. Carried out in our heads, they nonetheless allow us to test various hypotheses against the available evidence.[34]

Counterfactual analysis is implicit, we have observed, in all causal reasoning. To be sure, some counterfactuals are more useful for testing causal arguments than others. The general rule, set forth in Chapter 7, is that counterfactuals which do the least damage to the historical record as we know it – the normal course of events – are the most useful. If I argue that the United States won World War II because of its decisive invasion of Europe in 1944, this argument is bolstered by a counterfactual: had we waited, giving Germany time to develop its own nuclear device, the outcome might have been different. This is a reasonable argument, given what we know of Germany's efforts in this direction. It is not necessarily conclusive (few counterfactuals are), but it is helpful in analyzing the truth of our initial proposition.

Properly constructed, counterfactual analysis thus conforms to the logic of most-similar analysis. One looks to find that counterfactual which creates two cases that are as similar as possible in all respects except for the outcome and the presumed cause (which will of course

---

34. On counterfactuals generally, see Fearon (1991), Hawthorn (1991), Lewis (1973), Mill (1843/1872: book III, ch 8), Moore (1978), Tetlock and Belkin (1996), and Weber (1905/1949: 173).

vary). Indeed, the notion of a "counterfactual" is perhaps a bit of a misnomer. Because causal arguments are themselves matters of interpretation (they are not facts, in the usual sense of this term), a counterfactual merely plays out the logic of the initial hypothesis. Every "factual" hypothesis suggests a counterfactual hypothesis.

Some have blamed the fact of the American Revolution on unwise policies pursued by the British in the wake of the French and Indian War. Would the colonists have revolted in the absence of ("harassing") taxes, the billeting of British soldiers, the uncompromising and scornful statements emanating from the Crown and the Cabinet? This seems a fruitful line of inquiry, a useful set of questions to pose to the historical record. A useful counterfactual is a thought-experiment that allows us to replay history in a somewhat different fashion than the actual course of events. It is no more counter to the facts than the argument it is intended to test – in this case, that British policy *was* responsible for the Revolution.

The technique of counterfactual reasoning allows us to create additional cases (albeit hypothetical ones) where cases are scarce. It is not clear that there are any other cases *at all* that one might interrogate for evidence on the two propositions discussed here (the effect of the American initiative in ending World War II and the role of British policy in the American Revolution). Certainly, these situations would be difficult to replicate in an experimental research design. There is nothing unscientific about a counterfactual, therefore. Wherever actual cases are scarce and a single outcome (rather than a general outcome) is of interest, one may be obliged to calculate *what-if* scenarios in order to form, and test, causal hypotheses.

Two Dimensions of Analysis

Comparisons, we have noted, may be across space or through time. I will refer to the former as *synchronic* (or cross-sectional), and the latter as *diachronic* (aka temporal, longitudinal, or historical). I have emphasized the synchronic elements of the nine basic methods introduced in this chapter because comparisons through space are easier to understand on a conceptual level. However, it should be clear to the reader that all of these methods may also be employed diachronically.

Indeed, some are *irreducibly* diachronic. Experiments, we have said, have before-and-after components, thus creating at least two cases for analysis.[35] They may, of course, produce many more diachronic cases,

---

35. We may not always count those two cases separately (they may conflated into a single case).

as when an experiment is conducted over a long period of time or when frequent observations (each constituting a separate case) are taken over a limited period of time. Panel polls (where the same subjects are polled at various times) serve as longitudinal experiments. Counterfactual methods are also inherently diachronic, since one is analyzing a given unit over time under various hypothetical conditions.

Any study that looks at a single unit over time – and where some variation in Y and/or X is observed over that period of time – may be understood as employing a "most-similar" method of analysis (this includes the counterfactual method). Thus, rather than comparing France and England, as in Table 9.3, one might compare France with itself over time – creating two cases, France at T_1 (prior to the Revolution) and France at T_2 (after the Revolution). This is the approach normal to case-study research, and to historical research more generally. The historian of the French Revolution typically looks carefully at changes in French society during and prior to the event of interest. Ideally, all but a few factors are held constant in this diachronic research design, and can therefore be eliminated as probable causes. (They do not change; therefore, they cannot have caused the revolution.) The historian's focus is drawn to the one or several factors that did alter in form prior to the event, and this becomes the primary causal suspect.

This is what makes the natural experiment so attractive. Here, the willful manipulation of inputs is simulated by the natural occurrence of events, creating a near-perfect most-similar research design (observed through time). For example, when the Netherlands abolished compulsory voting, just prior to the 1970 election, analysts could observe changes in turnout before and after the innovation. Because these changes were dramatic, and because no other explanation could account for them (alternative causal factors were controlled), this quasi-experiment offered strong corroboration for the argument that voting regulations affect turnout levels.[36]

What can be said, then, about the utility of diachronic and synchronic analyses? What are the characteristic advantages and disadvantages of longitudinal comparison in different research situations?[37]

---

36. See Irwin (1974), discussed in Verba et al. (1978: 7–8). On the importance of natural experiments in economics, see Miron (1994). Of course, one must always be wary of judging the significance of temporal changes in nonexperimental settings – particularly when the number of cases on either side of the "treatment" is limited (Campbell 1988: ch 8).

37. For helpful comments, see Jackman (1985: 173–5).

One advantage of diachronic analysis is that it usually manages to establish at least two cases that satisfy the comparability requirement. A single country, party, institution, or individual at T_1 is liable to be quite similar to that entity at T_2, so long as the two time periods are fairly close together. Thus, diachronic analysis is particularly useful when we wish to hold cultural factors constant in a research design. Cultural factors involve problems of comparability, we have noted, because it is difficult to reduce across-unit differences to a standard metric. Diachronic research designs have a somewhat easier time dealing with cultural differences since country A at T_1 is likely to be, culturally speaking, quite similar to country A at T_2 – thus holding culture constant across the two cases.

To be sure, the further we separate our cases in time the more tenuous comparability becomes. Historians are rightfully suspicious of attempts to compare contemporary England with Elizabethan England. It all depends, of course, on the proposition one is attempting to sustain. If one is arguing that the strength of party is determined by the strength and independence of parliament, then a comparison between weak-party/weak-parliament Elizabethan England and strong-party/strong-parliament contemporary England could be quite useful. If one is arguing that growth in government is the product of a competitive bidding war between political parties, it is probably not wise to use Elizabethan England as a case. Parties were so different in that era (more like what we would today refer to as factions) that they are not likely to tell us anything useful about the sources of government taxing and spending.

A reciprocal situation is encountered in the problem of case-independence. The closer two diachronic cases are in time, the less likely it is that these two cases are fully independent of one another. If not, they cannot be regarded as independent sources of evidence (cases) for whatever proposition is being advanced. Although synchronic analysis also faces problems of case-independence, such problems are rarely so severe as those experienced in diachronic analysis: More important, they are usually more *apparent*, and therefore easier to control for. Since the problem of case-independence was discussed at some length in Chapter 8, I will not dwell on the matter here.

The most important advantage of diachronic research designs comes into play whenever the purported X and Y are thought to be closely linked, or at least *regularly* linked, in time. In these circumstances, we need only trace the outcome to see when, precisely, it occurred (or when some precipitate increase or decrease occurred), and then figure out which of the possible causes was also changing at that point (or just prior).

If, on the other hand, we have reason to believe that the $X:Y$ relationship is more complicated, or if we wish to find causes that lie at further remove from the actual outcome of interest, then a diachronic research design is likely to be inconclusive. Matters of timing will be less critical, and perhaps even irrelevant, since we imagine long and perhaps irregular periods separating cause and effect. Changes in land-tenure arrangements, for example, are unlikely to have a close temporal relationship to revolutionary uprisings, even though they might be quite important in setting the stage for such events.

Alternatively, the X or Y variables may be of such a nature that they cannot be tracked precisely through time. We may have observations at twenty-year intervals only, a gap which is perhaps too large to provide useful evidence on the $X:Y$ relationship. Because events are easier to mark than processes – they happen at fairly well-defined moments in time – outcomes that take the form of events are more amenable to a diachronic research design.

It is fairly obvious that if one's primary interest is in explaining the *timing* of an event, a diachronic research design is likely to be more useful. Usually, when one attempts to explain a specific event one is interested in explaining why it occurred, or why it occurred within a fairly long period of time (say, the eighteenth century), not why it occurred precisely when it did. Yet, for those who wonder why the French Revolution occurred in 1789 (and not in 1788 or 1790), a diachronic research design is de rigueur.

Diachronic analysis can mean many things, therefore, depending on the type of method employed, the type of evidence encountered, and the type of causal inference one is attempting to prove. In *most* research situations, diachronic analysis offers a chance to look at proximate causal connections – at who did what to whom – which I have referred to as the causal mechanism. Its disadvantage is equally evident: there is a single unit of study (a country, party, individual). Unless that unit offers a great deal of variation over time, the N will be limited. Even if there *is* great variation over time, one may question the representativeness of this informant vis-à-vis a wider population (of countries, parties, or individuals). In sum, the breadth of a proposition based on a diachronic study is likely to be smaller than the breadth of a proposition based on cases considered synchronically.

The N Debate: Small versus Large

Throughout this chapter and the previous chapter runs a fundamental, recurrent, and often dogmatic debate about research design: how many cases should we study? Specifically, should we divide our attention among many examples of a phenomenon, or focus in on a few?[38] We may speculate on the reasons for the intransigence of the two camps in this long-standing debate, which has vexed social science from the very beginning. Surely, it is related to the habits, proclivities, and capabilities of practitioners in these camps. Those unfamiliar with statistical methods are perforce restricted to relatively small samples. Those uncomfortable with a narrative format generally prefer large-N approaches, where tables and graphs take center stage. Expediency and temperament should not concern us here. What we *should* be concerned with are methodologically grounded reasons for preferring one approach over the other.

Cases are good and more cases are better; we established this much in Chapter 8. It is worth noting that there is no parallel argument for small-N research designs: smallness per se is not a virtue. But plenitude is only one criterion among ten governing research design (see Table 8.1). Although plenitude may enhance the boundedness, representativeness, variation, and causal comparison of a sample, it often has deleterious effects on case comparability. Because comparability is perhaps the most important feature of a sample, and because there is often no obvious way of overcoming case-incomparabilities (by "controlling" noncomparable factors), we must be very careful in championing large-N research designs. A large sample with heterogeneous cases is likely to prove something about nothing, or nothing about something.

We should also note that for many propositional criteria (Table 5.1) there is no clear advantage to small or large samples. Consider *precision.* If one is examining the precision of an inference with respect to a given sample of cases (cases actually studied by the investigator), it seems clear that small-N analysis has the edge. The relative precision of a study often suffers when additional cases are added. Measurement issues are compounded whenever highly contextual factors must be operationalized across a large number of cases. And if qualitative judgments (e.g., weak,

---

38. For helpful discussions, see Campbell (1975), Collier and Mahoney (1996), Coppedge (1999), Eckstein (1975), Feagin et al. (1991), George and Bennett (in press), Goldstone (1997), Goldthorpe (1997), Jackman (1985), Lieberson (1985; 1991), Mahoney (2000), McKeown (1999), Ragin (1987), Ragin and Becker (1992), and Rueschemeyer (1991). Opinions are divided over whether small-N and large-N research embody different "logics" of inquiry. McKeown (1999), Munck (1998), Ragin and Zaret (1983), and Skocpol (1984) emphasize the differentness of these two styles of research; King et al. (1994) emphasize their similarity (some would say, at the expense of small-N analysis). My argument on this front reiterates the argument of the book: although it would be foolish to deny any differences among scholars pursuing case-study and small-N analysis and those working with large samples, we would be even more foolish to emphasize these differences. To do so is to create incommensurabilities among the social sciences and encourage the ghetto-ization of scholarship.

medium, strong) must be converted into quantitative form, it is likely that precision has been sacrificed for the purpose of achieving greater breadth. A matter that takes several pages of prose to explain cannot be captured in a single indicator without some loss of precision. However, if we are interested in the precision of an inference relative to a larger population – an issue of *representativeness* – then it is clear that large-N analysis will be favored. A random-sample poll with more respondents will achieve a higher level of precision (as measured by the smaller margin of error), indicating that we are more sure that results reached among our sample are, in fact, reflective of the true results in our population of interest. This is axiomatic. I raise the point only to illustrate that when small- and large-N partisans argue over the problem of precision they are often arguing over different issues – precision within a sample versus precision relative to a population.

We might also note that small- and large-N methods of analysis are not all of a piece; thus, the terms of this usual contrast can be highly misleading. For example, while most small-N methods of analysis employ a deterministic view of causation (causes are necessary and/or sufficient, and all variables understandable in unequivocal, categorical terms), both case-study (where $N = 1$) and large-N methods tend to take a probabilistic view of causal relationships.[39] Thus, it is difficult to generalize about the N issue.

The most important ambiguity concerns the definition of *case*, and hence of sample size. Small-N researchers are likely to look for within-case variation, large-N researchers for across-case variation. Assuming that one recognizes the legitimacy of within-case analysis, it will be realized that case-study research may not be a single case at all. Indeed, within-case analysis often offers a much larger N than across-case analysis, as we have noted. Although there may be problems of representativeness when one seeks to generalize from this case to others (not studied), *sometimes* stronger evidence is available from within-case analysis than from across-case analysis. In sum, the perennial small-N/large-N debate admits no simple resolution, for the size of a sample is only one of many features that characterizes good research designs.

Is There a Best Method?

Arguably, there *is* a best method for social science analysis, and it is the experimental method. Indeed, the experimental method mimics the definition of causation in terms of counterfactual conditionals. It is definitionally true, one might say. As we have also noted, however, the pure

---

39. See also Mahoney (2000).

experiment is rarely applicable to social science problems – or, if peripherally applicable, rarely illuminating. Experimental situations, it turns out, are rarely representative of social phenomena that we care about (wars, depressions, elections, legislative roll calls, etc.). Consequently, they are likely to have limited analytic utility and relevance. They are either trivially true, or nontrivially doubtful.

Unfortunately, the nonexperimental character of social science has led certain members of the academy to declare their emancipation from science. The logic appears to be "If we cannot conduct experiments, we cannot do science." This dichotomous logic is not very helpful. Dewey remarks, "The idea that because social phenomena do not permit the controlled variation of sets of conditions in a one-by-one series of operations, therefore, the experimental method has no application at all, stands in the way of taking advantage of the experimental method *to the extent that is practicable.*"[40] If social science is not an experimental science it is at least a *quasi*-experimental science, since it mimics the aims and the methods of experimental analysis. Indeed, one often hears of the virtues of the "natural" experiment – an experiment that tests a hypothesis in much the same way a researcher would do so *if* she could manipulate the inputs of a society. Statistical, most-similar, most-different, extreme-case, typical-case, crucial-case, and counterfactual methods might all be looked upon as quasi-experiments.[41]

The reasonable and useful lesson to be drawn from this discussion is not that we should revel in our nonexperimental status but rather that we should attempt to retain as many of the virtues of the experimental method as we reasonably can, given our research agendas. If we must take the evidence as it presents itself (rather than creating it for our own purposes), this does not mean that the scientific ideal is dead. What it means is that social scientists have to work harder, and think longer, about research design than the average natural scientist. There is rarely an easy answer to the question of which research design is best. Yet, rarely will one design be just as good as another. Given a particular research situation and a particular hypothesis of interest there will probably be one or two "best" (most appropriate, most illuminating) methods of analysis. Whether these methods are good compared to methods that might be, or have been, applied to *other* research situations is irrelevant. What matters is that we have taken care to select the most appropriate method for the question of interest. Some questions are more easily proven than others.

40. Dewey (1938: 509), emphasis added.
41. See Achen (1986) and Campbell and Stanley (1966).

Once again, we see the importance of *relative* standards of adequacy (see Chapter 2).

We must resist the temptation to study only the easy questions (ones, for instance, that can be answered with experimental methods). Methods-driven social science often ends up proving conclusively what we already knew before we started, or what we care little about. Research design matters, and our careful consideration of various methods and cases matters all the more because the answers are complicated and not easily summarized in a pithy phrase or equation.

Finally, we should note that most research designs *combine* various elements of the nine methods and two dimensions presented in this chapter. Experimental designs in the social sciences are probably more accurately labeled *quasi*-experimental (they are often quite different from experiments in the natural sciences), thus merging with the vices and virtues of the other eight methods. Most-similar methods often favor cases with extreme values on the *X* or *Y* of interest, thereby merging with the extreme-case approach. Wherever the *N* is small, writers look to incorporate "crucial" cases, even if the writer is not explicitly following a crucial-case research design. Most methods of all sorts, as we have said, include synchronic and diachronic elements and – to confuse matters further – these may compose separate research designs (e.g., the synchronic analysis may be most-different and the diachronic analysis most-similar). Counterfactual analysis, as we have also noted, is a species of most-similar analysis – as, for that matter, is most traditional narrative history. Even *within* each stipulated method there is enormous variation. The statistical method, in particular, houses an enormous variety of approaches. Indeed, the closer one examines the typology set forth in Table 9.1 the less adequate it appears. It is a good first approximation, but a very poor summation of research design as it is carried out in the social sciences.

10

Strategies of Research Design

I shall distinguish sharply between the process of conceiving a new idea, and the methods and results of examining it logically... [With respect to the latter,] certain singular statements – which we may call "predictions" – are deduced from the theory; especially predictions that are easily testable or applicable. From among these statements, those are selected which are not derivable from the current theory, and more especially those which the current theory contradicts. Next we seek a decision as regards these (and other) derived statements by comparing them with the results of practical applications and experiments. If this decision is positive, that is, if the singular conclusions turn out to be acceptable, or *verified*, then the theory has, for the time being, passed its test: we have found no reason to discard it. But if the decision is negative, or in other words, if the conclusions have been *falsified*, then their falsification also falsifies the theory from which they were logically deduced.

– Karl Popper[1]

Our discussion of research design has ranged from general criteria (Chapter 8) to particular methods (Chapter 9). This final chapter takes up general considerations of *strategy*. How should we formulate and test our propositions and what, specifically, should be the relationship between theory and evidence?

According to one view, exemplified by Karl Popper, the best test of an empirical proposition is provided when the acts of theory generation and theory testing are segregated in time and space, so that the analyst is prevented from adjusting her favored explanation to suit the facts of a given case. Such "post hoc" theorizing renders a theory unfalsifiable, since most theories – and particularly those of a general and abstract nature –

---

1. Popper (1934/1968: 32–3).

can be suitably adjusted after the evidence is in so as to prove the writer's point. Unless we have specified *in advance* the terms by which a given theory can be proven false, we have not stated our theory in falsifiable terms. I call this vision of proper scientific method *confirmatory* because it envisions empirical analysis as a process of confirming or disconfirming a previously stipulated hypothesis. (One might also call it deductive, although this raises problematic epistemological issues.)[2]

Opposed to this vision is an *exploratory* model of research, according to which theory and evidence are closely intertwined. Hypotheses may be suggested by prior theories, intuitions, or the evidence itself, and should be adjusted to reflect the evidence at-hand. Moreover, the evidence itself (i.e., the scope of the research) may be redefined as the project evolves. An exploratory strategy of research is perhaps best understood as a process of mutual adjustment such that – by the end of the process – concepts, theories, and evidence are properly aligned.[3]

The strategies employed by confirmatory and exploratory research designs are thus directly contrary to each other. In the first tradition – the one usually favored by those with an experimental or theoretical bent – the best research is conducted on autopilot; important decisions about evidence and analysis are specified beforehand. Here, one answers specific questions in a yes/no fashion. In the second tradition – one usually favored by those with a behavioralist or interpretivist orientation – the best research is of the "soaking and poking" variety. One is advised to *leave open* issues about conceptualization, theorization, and investigation so as to be sensitive to the evidence at-hand. Evidence should be allowed to "speak for itself," not shoved into ill-fitting a priori categories. Here,

2. Goldthorpe (1997: 15) writes: "If a theory is formed entirely inductively – without, so to speak, any deductive backbone – ... it is hard to see how it can be genuinely tested at all ... [I]f a theory amounts to no more than an assemblage of inductions, the possibilities for 'saving' or 'patching' it in the face of contrary evidence are virtually limitless." King et al. (1994) also seem to prefer confirmatory research designs. This is evident from the sort of advice that they offer, for example: "Ad hoc adjustments in a theory that does not fit existing data must be used rarely" (21), "always ... avoid using the same data to evaluate the theory [you] used to develop it" (46); original data can be reused "as long as the implication does not 'come out of' the data but is a hypothesis independently suggested by the theory or a different data set" (30). See also Eckstein (1992: 266) and Friedman (1953/1984: 213).

3. For methodological work supporting an exploratory mode of analysis, see Collier (1999), Fenno (1978: appendix), Glaser and Strauss (1967), Ragin (2000), and Rueschemeyer and Stephens (1997). See also discussion in Williamson et al. (1977: ch 1). Earman's (1992: vii) distinction between a "context of discovery" and a "context of justification" roughly parallels the exploratory/confirmatory dichotomy, though his concern is with broader philosophy-of-science issues.

the process is one of discovery, rather than confirmation, with the goal of enhancing the fit between theory and evidence.

Each approach has claims to greater accuracy, claims that rest on different understandings of empirical knowledge. Confirmatory approaches are consonant with a *falsificationist* epistemology; here, the process of gathering knowledge (or apprehending truth) consists of "conjectures and refutations."[4] The explorationist, on the other hand, is an *inductivist* – not necessarily of the naive Baconian sort, but an inductivist nonetheless. She supposes that knowledge arises in interaction with the data, that conjectures are never independent of refutations, and that, therefore, we ought to get our hands dirty as quickly as possible. The confirmationist asks whether a theory is (a) true or (b) false. The explorationist asks *under what circumstances,* or *to what extent,* a theory is true or false. Truth, for the explorationist, is a matter of degrees. The falsificationist looks to theory to provide a sturdy framework for knowledge; the explorationist looks to the empirical world. "Data-fitting" is thus the bane of the former camp and the boon of the latter.

What is interesting about the confirmatory/exploratory dichotomy is the different ways these two research traditions attempt to establish truth. Indeed, it would appear that writers in the two camps conduct research in entirely incommensurable ways. However, there may be less disagreement *in practice* than in theory. (Epistemological debates are often misleading in this respect.) I shall argue that most social science research falls somewhere in between the confirmatory and exploratory ideals. What we witness in this ongoing debate, therefore, are two heuristic models, *neither* of which provides firm grounding for questions of research design.

The shortcomings of explorationism are fairly obvious. Soaking and poking research *is* difficult to falsify; invariably, the favored theory finds facts that confirm (or appear to confirm) its veracity. The limitations of confirmationism are less clear, so I will spend some time deconstructing this (generally favored) mode of analysis.

Marxist theory predicts that the progressive immiseration of the working classes will lead to revolution. Here, we have a theory safely ensconced in a text – safe, that is, from contamination with actual empirical results. It would seem to approximate (at least in this respect) the confirmationist ideal. Yet, the theory is so vaguely stated in Marx's oeuvre that we cannot easily test its truth or falsehood. Indeed, *all* macro-theories in social science demand many particular research decisions along the road

---

4. Popper (1969). See also Popper (1934/1968).

to confirmation/falsification. We must decide how to define and operationalize key concepts, which outcomes and cases the theory explains (specification), which cases to test the theory on, and which method of analysis to employ. Evidently, each of these decisions is likely to affect whether, or to what extent, Marx (or Durkheim, Weber, et al) is vindicated. There is simply no way to avoid a certain degree of authorial meddling and empirical fiddling. In operationalizing the key concept "working class," for example, we might rely on a Marxian definition (e.g., those who work for a living but do not own the means of production), or on definitions that have predominated in the sociological literature (e.g., members of the manual trades) or the economic literature (e.g., those with low-to-moderate wages). Or one might extend one's purview to include peasants and the rural proletariat. Other key terms (e.g., progressive, immiseration, and revolution) must also be operationalized. In general, the broader the theory the more we are forced into an exploratory relationship with the data.

Prediction, as Popper tells us, is the ideal of the confirmationist. Good theories should render accurate predictions, and the temporal separation of theory and evidence provides a secure safeguard against ex post facto data fitting. Milton Friedman, a faithful Popperian, writes:

> theory is to be judged by its predictive power for the class of phenomena which it is intended to "explain." Only factual evidence can show whether it is "right" or "wrong" or, better, tentatively "accepted" as valid or "rejected." ... [T]he only relevant test of the *validity* of a hypothesis is comparison of its predictions with experience. The hypothesis is rejected if its predictions are contradicted ("frequently" or more often than predictions from an alternative hypothesis); it is accepted if its predictions are not contradicted; great confidence is attached to it if it has survived many opportunities for contradiction. Factual evidence can never "prove" a hypothesis; it can only fail to disprove it, which is what we generally mean when we say, somewhat inexactly, that the hypothesis has been "confirmed" by experience.[5]

The logic seems compelling. Let us examine the matter more closely, however. Suppose we are testing a theory of economic growth, and suppose that this theory, unlike Marx's, issues specific predictions for future economic performance. The theory, let us say, predicts 3% growth for an economy over a five-year period. The economy grows, in fact, at a rate of 5% (as judged by standard GDP measurements, adjusted for inflation). Do we toss out the theory? Or do we adjust it to fit the facts (as we now know them to be)? I presume that the latter course of action is more usual among

---

5. Friedman (1953/1984: 213).

economists. Yet, to assume the latter course we must sacrifice the priority of the confirmationist model; we are now in conspiracy with the facts.

Moreover, every adjustment in a theory is, in a very real sense, a new conjecture, and every new conjecture a new hypothesis. Precisely because we do not know the future, what matters *at any given point in time* is that theory which best explains the data that are currently available. This is an obvious point but it seems to have been lost on some methodologists. We are always limited to past events; otherwise stated, there is no such thing as a true or false theory of the future. It may *turn out to have been true* (in retrospect). But in retrospect, we will always have the liberty of constructing theories that are even better. This ex post facto theory, if superior to the ex ante theory, rightfully replaces it. (A theory is not necessarily more accurate for having been concocted before the fact.) Again, the confirmationist model is compromised.

In short, although it would be very easy for philosophers to conclude that the exploratory/confirmatory debate constitutes epistemological incommensurability, there may be less difference between these research strategies than meets the eye. Arguably, there are no purely confirmatory or purely explanatory research designs.

Tradeoffs

Having argued that the confirmatory/exploratory argument is a misleading dichotomy, I shall now try to show that this ongoing argument can be understood as a classic example of methodological *tradeoffs*. Some research projects tend toward a confirmatory research design, and others toward an exploratory design; what matters in this decision is the context of the research situation. A confirmatory mode of investigation is appropriate in situations: (a) where the research (including relevant concepts and propositions) is relatively formulaic; (b) where experimental or statistical methods can be employed; (c) where questions and answers can be (or, for various reasons, must be) in binary form; (d) where Type 2 errors are of greater concern than Type 1 errors (i.e., where we would prefer to miss a true causal relationship than to mistakenly identify a false causal relationship); (e) where we are concerned about the possible biases of researchers; and (f) where research can be overseen by a neutral body. To the extent that a given research situation deviates from this scenario, we will be forced (or allowed) to adopt a more exploratory research design – that is, we will compromise the rigid separation of theory and evidence.

Where relevant concepts and propositions are already well defined, and where there is little reason to doubt these definitions, it makes sense to follow the orthodoxy when conducting research. Where questions of research design are similarly well defined and unproblematic, we rightly apply the standard research design to the question at hand. Where, finally, we are unconcerned with broader questions, cases, or causal relationships lying outside the specified research design we rightly leave these in abeyance. In short, the more formulaic the research situation the more justified we are in resolving such questions *prior* to our interaction with the data. Deviations from this formula – in the exploratory mode – will require a good deal of justification. Readers of our study will rightly question why we have chosen to approach a standard subject in a heterodox manner. They will be particularly curious about what sort of results the standard approach would have provided. Indeed, wherever a problem and a corresponding method are well defined, a researcher is well advised to follow the formula first, and *then,* if results are for some reason unsatisfactory, proceed to an exploratory mode of analysis.

The flip side of this coin is that wherever a research situation is *un*formulaic, or where the existing formula is flawed, the researcher will be forced to adopt an exploratory strategy. It will *not* suffice to prescribe an orthodox research design drawn from some vaguely related study on another subject. Nor can concepts, propositions, and research designs be satisfactorily worked out in a deductive fashion, prior to all encounters with the evidence.

Consider our previous example, "the immiseration of the working classes." I know of no standard way of operationalizing this concept. Yet, the researcher who adopts a confirmatory stance vis-à-vis the evidence must decide how to operationalize the concept first, before messing around with the data. Suppose she says that immiseration means the loss of 10% of real income by the bottom two quintiles of any national community within the space of a single decade. Revolution she interprets, in turn, as the overthrow of the ruling institutions of a government, whether democratic or nondemocratic. Now, let us suppose that workers get much more restive when they lose 15% of their real income; or that this must happen within the space of five years (rather than ten) in order for the working class to reach a revolutionary state; or that revolutions are contingent on immiserating factors other than wages. Many other suppositions might be added. The point is, any one of these alternate scenarios begs the question of whether we have adequately tested the general theory of interest. To investigate only one hypothesis out of many possible hypotheses (each more or less compatible with the general theory of interest) is *arbitrary.* It does not shed much light on the question and may be downright misleading.

Consider as a second example, *ethnic heterogeneity,* a commonly discussed cause for a wide range of political and sociological outcomes. Evidently, one can operationalize this item in many different ways. One might measure the size of the largest ethnic group in a given community; one might employ a measure of fractionalization; and one might measure ethnic affiliation itself in various ways (some give priority to linguistic identity, others to religion or to race). Surely, it would be arbitrary to choose only one of these operationalizations as a conclusive test of the influence of ethnic heterogeneity on a particular outcome of interest.

The trouble, then, with a confirmatory view of social research is not that it is wrong per se, but rather that it is sometimes inappropriately applied – that is, in situations where no existing formula can resolve questions of concept formation, proposition formation, and research design. What is really happening here is that the analyst is testing *one particular specification* of the theory at hand. If the specification or research design is improper in any respect (a matter we cannot know because it is off-limits to the investigator) the theory has not been properly tested.

In unorthodox research situations, therefore, an exploratory approach to theory and data is fully appropriate and should not require apology. Otherwise stated, insofar as justification is required – and of course, all methods must be justified – it ought to be required of confirmatory and exploratory research designs alike. There is no reason, a priori, to be more suspicious of one approach than the other. Indeed, we are as likely to be hoodwinked by the naive confirmationist as by the naive explorationist.

This much seems fairly axiomatic, at least in the general case. The problem, of course, is that we do not always know, or cannot always agree, when we are in a formulaic or unformulaic research situation. We may not know for sure whether an existing formula – including relevant concepts, propositions, and research designs – is sufficient to guide present research, and when it is not. Indeed, we *cannot* answer this question without entering into an exploratory relationship to the data. A version of Heisenberg's principle is in play: we cannot confirm the viability of our method without compromising the falsifiability of our initial proposition.

All I will say in conclusion to this interesting dilemma is that *most* research situations in the social sciences include some nonformulaic elements. All pathbreaking research, by definition, is nonformulaic. For this reason alone we may be on safer ground when conducting research in an exploratory mode.

The second point to make is that some methods are more amenable to confirmatory research than others. The experimental method, in particular, fits nicely with a confirmatory vision of social science. Here, the analyst manipulates independent variables in order to test specific hypotheses.

Each test confirms or disconfirms a distinct hypothesis. To be sure, the repetition allowed by most experimental designs allows for a subtle adjustment of theories and evidence as experimentation proceeds (perhaps over the course of many years). Yet, the inputs and outputs of an experiment are separated from each other in time. Thus, an analyst cannot easily tamper with the evidence to fit a particular theory, or vice versa. Statistical methods (see Chapter 9) are slightly messier. Still, one can formulate hypotheses and then "run" them on the data, in confirmatory fashion.[6] With nonquantitative research designs, by contrast, it is almost impossible to fully segregate theory and evidence. No sooner has one conceived a theory than one is forced to think about how the theory fits a particular context. Indeed, the latter may come first, thus reversing the confirmationist's expected order (first propose, then confirm/reject).

Whether we prefer a confirmatory or exploratory research design depends, as well, on the sort of answers that we wish to receive at the end of our research. Sometimes, it is important to answer questions in a yes/no fashion. For example, when pondering the initiation of new drugs the FDA likes to know whether the new drug is (a) safe or (b) not safe. It is interesting, but perhaps not policy-relevant, to discover that Drug *A* is "pretty safe." Of course, research is likely to result in a probabilistic sort of answer initially – few drugs kill on contact, and all will kill if consumed in sufficient quantity. The point is, the FDA specifies levels of consumption which it considers "healthy" so that researchers can answer these sorts of questions in a dichotomous fashion (yes/no). Once these outcomes are specified, research can be conducted in a confirmatory mode. (We should also note that this sort of a priori specification by the FDA also creates a more formulaic research situation.) By contrast, if our initial research question is more generally posed (i.e., the variable effects of Drug *A* on a variety of human functions) it will be difficult, and perhaps impossible, to conduct our work in a purely confirmatory style.

Similarly, much depends on the nature of the evidence (i.e., the causal relationships) that we are investigating. We have already discussed a natural-science example, the physiological effect of a drug. Social science research, by contrast, is likely to be less clear and specific in outcome, and consequently less amenable to a confirmatory research design. If we are interested in the effects of living in a high-crime neighborhood, let us say, it is difficult to conceive of specifying all such effects *prior* to our

---

6. Even so, as Rueschemeyer and Stephens (1997: 69) observe, "It is rather naive to think that a similar back and forth of data examination and theory adjustment does not go on in quantitative work [as it does in qualitative work]. Precisely because of the textbook injunction, however, research is simply written up as if that did not happen."

encounter with the evidence. A purely confirmatory research design would be virtually impossible. We can, and *should,* construct hypotheses prior to beginning our research. However, it is unlikely that we will be able to anticipate all the relevant causal relationships that will arise from this research question. Or alternatively, we will be obliged to issue so many a priori hypotheses that we are, for all intents and purposes, back in an exploratory mode of research. (No purpose is served by a study that specifies, in advance, 300 empirical hypotheses; this sort of pseudo-confirmatory approach is indistinguishable from exploration.)

Our previous medical example is of interest for another reason as well. With the issuance of new drugs, we are likely to be more concerned about the approval of a dangerous drug than the rejection of a safe drug. (This is, of course, not invariably the case; where a disease is of epidemic proportions we may be willing to tolerate a greater degree of risk.) In methodological jargon, we are more worried about Type 2 errors than Type 1 errors. The confirmatory approach allows one to construct a research design in just this fashion, so that the bias is in one direction or the other. If we allowed our researcher full play to explore the data, we would be unable to judge the difficulty of the empirical tests she used to obtain her results. Wherever the results of social science have important policy repercussions we may wish to bias our research in what is usually called a "conservative" direction. We may not get the positive results we would like, but if we do we can have confidence that they are accurate. Again, we should emphasize that these sorts of research situations are much less common in the social sciences than in the natural sciences.

Similarly, the benefits of a confirmatory mode of analysis are enhanced wherever a neutral body of observers is on-hand to monitor the research in question. Thus, the FDA monitors the initial proposal for drug testing, the final results, and perhaps even the research itself. In doing so, it can enforce the stipulated rules of a (confirmatory) method. (When researchers travel to Washington to present their results, overseers from the FDA may interrogate them to see whether they deviated from their initial research design.) If, however, this research is conducted in an exploratory manner, then the overseers have considerably less oversight capacity. They must trust their investigative team to make the right decisions as they go along, and they must trust that these decisions are being properly executed. In short, a confirmatory research design allows a good deal more centralized control over the conduct of social research. This may be a good thing, and it may be a bad thing. In either case (as David Mamet would say) it is a thing. Funding agencies, organizations, and individuals are more likely to hand out money to those they can properly supervise. An exploratory research design, by contrast, creates principal-agent dilemmas that are difficult to overcome.

Our next observation follows closely on this dilemma. Wherever we have reason to doubt the abilities or good faith of investigators we are likely to prefer a confirmatory research design. If, let us say, the research on our new drug is being paid for by the pharmaceutical company that developed it, a neutral board of experts charged with overseeing the research rightly insists on a confirmatory research design. If, to take an example from social science, we are researching an area that is fraught with "ideological" disagreement (e.g., school vouchers), we might prefer the comfort of a confirmatory research design since it gives a biased researcher less opportunity to manipulate results.

The final point to make is that confirmatory research is generally a lot less productive than exploratory research. What confirmatory research discovers is "Yes, a given hypothesis is true," or "No, it is not." Research conducted in an exploratory manner can lead us to a much richer set of questions and answers. We will find out, for example, under what circumstances, or to what extent, our initial hypothesis is true, and when it is false. We will be able to explore related questions. Indeed, we will expect to explore a wide variety of inferences suggested by prior research, our own interests, and the data itself. If productivity is important (i.e., the knowledge-return on a given investment of time and effort), one is likely to adopt an exploratory approach to one's research. Indeed, the developer is likely to have employed an exploratory mode of analysis in the initial discovery of Drug *A*.

Conclusions

This leads us to a commonsense resolution to our initial debate: when developing new theories, conduct research in an exploratory mode; when attempting to confirm existing theories, conduct research in a confirmatory mode. Fair enough, and certainly useful enough in a natural-science context. Yet again, we must observe that social scientists rarely find themselves with the luxury of so much funding, and so much attention to a single causal relationship, that they can afford to separate exploratory and confirmatory exercises in this manner. Nor, as we have seen, would this way of framing the research help us to resolve situations in which the theory and the data are soft and pliable. Theories are likely to be connected to other theories, so that the testing of an isolated hypothesis (ignoring the effects of neighboring factors) makes little sense. Could one pry one hypothesis loose from Barrington Moore's *Social Origins of Dictatorship and Democracy* and test it, by itself?

Certainly. But this isolated empirical endeavor would probably not be considered a fair test of Moore's general theory.

As we have seen, there *are* situations where a confirmatory procedure is warranted. Wherever our research interests are relatively narrow, where questions of research design are formulaic, where theory may be separated from evidence through an experimental design or temporal disjunction (prediction/outcome), where questions and answers allow for dichotomous (yes/no) testing, where we have reason to be concerned with problems of researcher accountability, where we are particularly concerned with Type 2 errors, and where funding is generous and man-power abundant – in these cases hypothesis-generation and hypothesis-testing are appropriately segregated.

As I have tried to show, these situations are rare, and never *purely* confirmatory. Testing theories in a dichotomous fashion (theory confirmed/theory disconfirmed) resembles a child at play with a spatial-relations toy. The child pokes her dowel into one opening after another until the appropriately shaped hole is discovered. If the world of human relations had holes that could be poked in this fashion, we could formulate laws of human behavior of the same certitude as those reached by a reasonably intelligent child after some diligent poking: square pegs fit in square holes; round pegs fit in round holes; and so forth. It should not be necessary to point out that the humanly created world is rarely so simple. Yet, the scholarly community seems more inclined to bestow honorifics on work that bears the hallmarks of confirmatory research design.

It is rather pointless and misleading for journals to insist upon the presentation of a priori hypotheses ("suggested by the literature"), which will then (the writer characteristically moves into the future tense) be "tested against the data" when the data at-hand are soft and pliable. This is appropriate *only* insofar as the research situation meets the aforementioned confirmatory criteria. When it does not (i.e., in the vast majority of social science research), we do a disservice by dressing-up exploratory data analysis in confirmatory language. Nothing is gained – and a great deal may be lost – by presenting our findings in these scientist terms.

Against Method-ism; For Methodology

I have argued implicitly in this section of the book that social science is often led astray by a too-strict adherence to method. Most research designs, as we saw in Chapter 9, cannot be reduced to single method. Each of our nine core methods has serious flaws; none is a sure guide to methodological success. Thankfully, they are rarely adhered to in a scrupulous fashion. This is perhaps why the ongoing debate over Theda Skocpol's study of revolution is essentially irresolvable. Skocpol did not rely on a single method, but rather on a mix of methods – some formally adopted, and some of a more informal nature.[7] This, indeed, is the nature of most good research, qualitative and quantitative. A nonmethodical method is a marked improvement over a methodical one that imposes unjustifiable restraints.

Moreover, even to the extent that one *could* restrict oneself to the strictures of a single method we should take note of the fact that because a study is of a "most-similar" variety does not bestow a seal of methodological approval on that study. It merely describes a writer's general approach. We have seen how even the "best" method, the experimental method, often comes up short when attempting to address problems of theoretical and practical relevance. Thus, although it may impress some people to say that a study is experimental, readers will do well to check to see, among other things, whether this study is representative of the population it claims to represent, or whether the findings matter at all.

Regrettably, having a method – a single, specifiable, and recognizable procedure of case selection, treatment, and analysis – has become a hallmark of methodological respectability. Ironically, the pressure toward method-ism may be even more pronounced among qualitative researchers than among their quantitative peers. The former are generally considered to be methodologically suspect, and thus are prone to seek methodological ballast wherever they can find it.

For researchers of *all* stripes a narrow, formulaic conception of method often leads to an unhappy choice. The researcher may suppress all deviations from the strictures of the method, thus compromising the broader methodological adequacy of the study. Or, she may pretend to follow the method but sidestep its strictures wherever convenient, thus misrepresenting her actual research design (and making replication difficult). These are the twin dangers of methods-driven social science.

---

7. Mahoney (1999a: 1156–7) summarizes the current state of this long debate. I paraphrase: Skocpol (1979) claims to be employing most-similar and most-different comparisons. Various writers have debated the utility of these methods, as applied to the analysis of revolutions, and more generally (e.g., Burawoy 1989; Lieberson 1991, 1994; Nichols 1986; Savolainen 1994; Sewell 1996; Skocpol 1986). Goldstone (1997) finds that Skocpol is not using Millian logic, but rather a different logic altogether. Sewell (1996) concedes the use of Millian methods, but sees them as ineffective. The truly effective part of the analysis, he argues, relies on historical narrative ("the discovery of analogies on which new and convincing narratives of eventful sequences can be constructed" [1996: 262]). Mahoney's own interpretation is that Skocpol employs a variety of methods, which he calls nominal, ordinal, and narrative.

Obviously, wherever a clear and obvious method exists for a given research problem, it should be employed. However, these situations are rare in the social sciences, as argued earlier. Although it might seem that experimental and statistical work is more methods-driven – and more rule-bound – than qualitative work, this probably exaggerates the true state of affairs. We have noted that the ongoing proliferation of quantitative methods means that there are now at least several ways of performing virtually every statistical task. And varying approaches often yield different results. Arguably, the realm of statistical analysis has moved closer in recent years to the methodological conundrums usually associated with qualitative research. Of both realms we might say that the methods are myriad and choices among them difficult. Indeed, it is common to observe that correct choices among different statistical methods can only be made in light of correct – and often untestable – assumptions about the nature of the reality that the statistical study is designed to test. Both small-N and large-N cross-national comparisons rest on assumptions about which set of countries constitute appropriate cases (i.e., which are truly comparable with respect to the causal inference at issue). Such assumptions are not easily tested. Similarly, methods of correction for autocorrelation in a time-series analysis usually hinge on assumptions – again, usually untestable – about underlying causal relationships.

For all these reasons method-eclecticism, rather than fixed rules of procedure, is likely to remain – and should remain – the dominant mode of inquiry in the social sciences. Norman Campbell's well-chosen words, from a founding text in scientific methodology, deserve pondering:

> If the discovery of laws could be reduced to a set of formal rules, anyone who learnt the rules could discover laws. But there is no broad road to progress. Herein lies the most serious objection to much that has been written on the methods of science. There is no method, and it is because there is no method which can be expounded to all the world that science is a delight to those who possess the instincts which make methods unnecessary.[8]

To the unwary reader, the foregoing might appear to be an argument for Feyerabendian anarchy.[9] It is not. It is, rather, an argument for a larger, more capacious – and, I think, more realistic – conception of method. It is an argument against method-ism, and *for* methodology.

Adequacy in research design, as in concepts and propositions, should be judged by reference to *general criteria*, not by their adherence or non-adherence to a recognized method. Plenitude, boundedness, compara-

8. Campbell (1919/1957: 112).
9. See Feyerabend (1975).

bility, independence, representativeness, variation, analytic utility, replicability, mechanism, and causal comparison are the hallmarks of good research design, not whether a study utilizes an experimental or most-similar method. Methods describe options. Whether they succeed or not, and if not how they might be adjusted, is a matter that can only be determined by returning to the broader goals that research is designed to achieve – that is, methodological criteria.

We should view methods as a jumping-off point, a way of thinking about research design in its initial stages. Following a method cannot provide a foolproof approach for constructing good social science. Fools will still be foolish. Being wise entails understanding the underlying purpose, or purposes, of one's method. With these desiderata clearly in view we ought to be able to take a pragmatic and pluralistic approach to the task of research design without losing ourselves in highly subjective preferences.

Postscript
Justifications

Surely, in a world which stands upon the threshold of the chemistry of the atom, which is only beginning to fathom the mystery of interstellar space, in this poor world of ours which, however justifiably proud of its science, has created so little happiness for itself, the tedious minutiae of historical erudition, easily capable of consuming a whole lifetime, would deserve condemnation as an absurd waste of energy, bordering on the criminal, were they to end merely by coating one of our diversions with a thin veneer of truth. Either all minds capable of better employment must be dissuaded from the practice of history, or history must prove its legitimacy as a form of knowledge. But here a new question arises. What is it, exactly, that constitutes the legitimacy of an intellectual endeavor?

— Marc Bloch[1]

I have argued that the various disciplines of the social sciences may be conceptualized as elements in a single quest – to understand the world of human action in a scientific manner (Preface). I have argued, further, that there are good reasons for seeking greater methodological unity among the social sciences (Chapter 1). I have argued, finally, that this goal is best served by a criterial framework (summarized in Chapter 2 and set forth in Parts I, II, and III of the book). This framework, I claimed, better accounts for what social scientists do – or at least for what they try to do – than other extant methodologies. It is broad enough to encompass all the social sciences, specific enough to make sense of what practitioners do, and concise enough to be useful. If it will not resolve our strife – not a course I would recommend, in any case – it should help to clarify what it is we are arguing about, thereby paving the way for a sharing of findings and resources among an increasingly balkanized set of disciplines. A narrow focus on methods and models will not

1. Bloch (1941/1953: 9).

perform this mediating function; nor will a wide-angle focus on philosophy of science.

The criterial framework may strike some readers as commonsensical. Indeed, none of the criteria presented in previous chapters were invented by the author (though I have chosen labels for things that did not have well-established names), and most have been discussed extensively by other writers. From this perspective, the book qualifies as a compendium of truisms – a function shared, one might note, by any integrative work on methodology.[2] Thus, the first and perhaps most important justification for the criterial framework is that it represents a formalization of what we already know, and can therefore generally agree upon.

Nevertheless, readers are bound to have qualms about some elements of the argument. They might take issue with the criterion of operationalization, for example. They might like what I have to say about concepts, but not about research design. On what grounds can we adjudicate this sort of dispute? It is not sufficient, even were it possible, to resolve these disputes by counting heads. If four of five social scientists accept operationalization as a basic criterion of social science concepts this is not necessarily a good reason for the fifth to fall into line. There must be some *reason,* some underlying rationale, that one can appeal to in this sort of meta-methodological debate.[3]

A second line of defense (beyond majority opinion) may be found in the definitional attributes of our key term, *social science.* "Social," we have said, specifies the subject matter (society), and "science" the methodological goal. I argued in the Preface for a broad interpretation

2. Mill's (1843/1872: iii) opening words, in a work that might be called the Old Testament of scientific methodology, deserve repeating: "This book makes no pretence of giving to the world a new theory of the intellectual operations. Its claim to attention, if it possess any, is grounded on the fact that it is an attempt not to supersede, but to embody and systematise, the best ideas which have been either promulgated on its subject by speculative writers, or conformed to by accurate thinkers in their scientific inquiries."

3. The questions addressed in this postscript are generally avoided by social science methodologists, who appeal to specific goods – fertility, productivity, analysis, and so forth – but do not clarify the ground on which these goods might rest. Evidently, without addressing the question of grounding in some fashion we are utterly unable to defend one methodological approach against another, or to defend the enterprise of social science (writ large). Some recourse to broader "philosophical" questions is essential, therefore, even though we do not have the luxury of covering this complex terrain in the detail and nuance that it deserves. For recent introductions to epistemology and philosophy of science, see Bohman (1991), Boyd et al. (1991), Fiske and Shweder (1986), Kirkham (1992), Martin and McIntyre (1994), Miller (1987), Murphey (1994), Rosenberg (1988), and Trigg (1985).

of science, rather than the restrictive model of natural science. Even so, the implications of science are much the same, including attributes such as coherence, consistency, clarity, cumulation, empirics, evidence, falsifiability, generality, knowledge, objectivity, progress, reason, rigor, system, and truth. The criterial framework, I would argue, instantiates these general goals in more specific terms. It is science, fully specified.

But what will we say to those who question the very idea of science, who have different ideas about how this science ought to be put together, or who reject the apparently circular nature of this argument? Here, I fall back on a *pragmatic* line of argument. Pragmatism suggests that in order to resolve issues of adequacy we must have some notion of what functions, purposes, or goals an institution is expected to achieve. If our purpose is normative – if we wish, that is, to improve the state of affairs in a given area of human endeavor – it is logical to begin with a pragmatic interrogation. What do we expect social science to accomplish?[4]

4. My argument parallels pragmatic arguments within contemporary philosophy. In a landmark set of essays from several decades ago, Quine pointed out that since the universe impinges upon human consciousness only at the margins of human cognition we cannot reasonably use "objectivity" as the guide for reforming our language. Rather, Quine (1953: 79) counsels, "Our standard for appraising basic changes of conceptual scheme must be, not a realistic standard of correspondence to reality, but a pragmatic standard. Concepts are language, and the purpose of concepts and of language is efficacy in communication and in prediction. Such is the ultimate duty of language, science, and philosophy, and it is in the relation to that duty that a conceptual scheme has finally to be appraised." Laudan (1996: 140) writes, along similar lines, "Methodology, narrowly conceived, is in no position to make [teleological] judgments, since it is restricted to the study of means and ends. We thus need to supplement methodology with an investigation into the legitimate or permissible ends of inquiry." Yet, my approach is not the same as that advocated in most of Quine's and Laudan's writings. It should also be distinguished from the "pragmaticism" of Peirce (see Kirkham 1992: 80–7) and – to some extent – from the pragmatism or "instrumentalism" of William James and John Dewey. James and Dewey tended to apply the pragmatic test to individual utterances. Thus, "the meaning of any proposition can always be brought down to some particular consequence in our future practical experience, whether passive or active" (quoted in Ogden and Richards 1923/1989: 198), whereas I am applying pragmatism to the enterprise of social science, at-large. Similarly, James and Dewey tended to look upon truth as an essentially undifferentiated realm, including quotidian truths, whereas I am marking out social science as a distinctive realm with its own (more or less) standards of appraisal. With "truth," and other topics of similar abstraction, it is rather problematic to specify a general goal, as James and Dewey suggest. It is all very well to define truth as that which accommodates our interests, but this begs a series of questions – whose interests? over what period of time (short-term or long-term)? and so forth. In the end, we have not clarified very much at all when a pragmatic approach is applied at this very general level. When applied to a specific *institution* (e.g., social science), however, the pragmatic/consequentialist approach gains traction.

This teleological question may be posed of any discipline, or of any human activity where the consequences of human actions may reasonably be assessed. If, let us say, we are investigating the stock market to see how its operations could be improved we might begin by asking what "improvement" would mean. What functions do we expect a stock market to perform? What would a "good" stock market look like? The consequentialist's most basic question can also be posed in the form of a counterfactual: Where would we be without it? Implied in this question are the following additional questions: Is there another institution that might perform these functions more effectively? Do its costs outweigh its benefits? In the case of the stock market I imagine an inquiry such as this leading fairly quickly to several conclusions: (a) its main purpose is to raise capital; (b) we can't do without it (no other institution does this as effectively); (c) its relative success in doing so can be judged by the amount of money that it raises. All of this is more or less taken for granted, nowadays, so a pragmatic perspective on stock markets does not turn out to be very interesting. In the case of social science, however – a much more complicated case, by all accounts – a pragmatic perspective is quite revelatory.

The purpose of social science, I maintain, is to help citizens and policymakers better understand the world, with an eye to changing that world. Social science ought to provide useful answers to useful questions. Robert Lynd has made this argument at greater length, and with greater acumen, than anyone else. Social science, he writes, "is not a scholarly arcanum, but an organized part of the culture which exists to help man in continually understanding and rebuilding his culture. And it is the precise character of a culture and the problems it presents as an instrument for furthering men's purposes that should determine the problems and, to some extent, the balance of methods of social science research."[5]

This is not a new idea, of course. Lynd made this argument in 1939, and many others have echoed the general sentiment.[6] Indeed, the pre-

5. Lynd (1939/1964: ix).
6. See, for example, Bloch (1941/1953), Bok (1982), Haan et al. (1983), Lerner and Lasswell (1951), Lindblom and Cohen (1979), McCall and Weber (1984), Mills (1959), Myrdal (1970: 258), Popper (1936/1957:56), Rule (1997), Simon (1982), Wilensky (1997), and Zald (1990). *Prior* to the rise of the modern scientific ideal, the connection between the study of society and its reform (or preservation) was even stronger. Aristotle writes, "since politics ... legislates as to what we are to do and what we are to abstain from, the end [of political science] must be the good for man" (*Nicomachean Ethics*, in Aristotle 1941: 936). This "normative" sentiment did not die with the rise of social science, therefore; it merely went underground.

sumed connection between social science and social progress has been present from the very beginning of the disciplines we now label social science. The Statistical Society of London, one of the first organized attempts to develop the method and employment of statistics, proposed in 1835 to direct their attention to the following question: "What has been the effect of the extension of education on the habits of the People? Have they become more orderly, abstemious, contented, or the reverse?"[7] Whatever one might think about the perspectives embedded in this research question it is clear that early statisticians were interested in *society,* as well as technique. They were eager subscribers to Karl Marx's famous thesis: the point of scholarly reflection is not merely to interpret the world, but also to change it.

Social scientists and philosophers have not fully grasped the potential deliverance that this simple thesis presents. Bluntly put, whatever species of social science methodology seems most likely to produce useful knowledge ought to be embraced; whatever does not should be eschewed.[8] To be sure, "usefulness" is not self-evident. Much depends upon one's time horizons (what is useful today may not be useful tomorrow, and vice versa). And utility functions vary. I do not wish to imply that everyone should agree on a precise metric by which the utility of social science should be measured. A vulgar version of pragmatism implies that a single telos, universally agreed upon, should guide all our actions. For Dewey, however, pragmatism meant "that it is good to reflect upon an act in terms of its consequences and to act upon the reflection. For the consequences disclosed will make possible a better judgment of good."[9] In this spirit, it is more important to *ask* the question of social science's purpose, in a serious and conscientious way, than to provide a specific answer. The answers will surely vary from place to place, from time to time, and from person to person. What does seem certain is that if we ignore the question entirely – hunkering down in our insulated academic bunkers to perform "basic research" – we are likely to fall far from the mark.

At the present point in historical time we might nominate prosperity, peace, democracy, individual freedom, human rights, and social justice as generally agreed-upon goals. More agreement will be found at this teleological level, in any case, than at methodological levels. Thus, the

---

7. Quoted in Turner (1997: 25–6), originally quoted in Porter (1986: 33). See also Collins (1985: 19).
8. Rule (1997) argues along similar lines. See also Rescher (1977).
9. Dewey (reprinted in Rorty 1966: 283–4).

pragmatic exercise, whatever its ambiguities, *does* provide common ground. And we can go further.

The most obvious methodological conclusion to be drawn from pragmatism is that social science should be *relevant* to present-day problems and concerns. This is captured in the tenth criterion pertaining to all propositions (Chapter 5), and is discussed at greater length below. At the same time, I wish to argue that the pragmatic ground is not exhausted when relevance is achieved. Any fool can be relevant; and most are. Pragmatism relates not only to the content of social science, but also to its *form*. This is the broader sense in which the appeal to social utility might help resolve debates over methodology and constitutes the second portion of the chapter.

This raises a more fundamental objection: if social utility is our goal, perhaps this goal might be more readily achieved by abandoning social science for other occupations, rather than fiddling with methodological niceties. This is a sound argument for those with the right aptitudes and inclinations. But as a general proposal, it does not hold water. In the final section of the chapter I defend the notion that the utility of social science stems from its status as science, a status that hinges on methodological niceties such as those explored in the previous chapters. Thus, while we may discover many other ways to serve the common good, we will not do so by producing bad social science. The utility of social science lies in its *distinctiveness* as a mode of apprehending reality; improving social science involves recognizing these distinctive traits, and cultivating them.

"Relevance"

Social science, in all its guises, is *practical* knowledge. "Any problem of scientific inquiry that does not grow out of actual (or 'practical') social conditions is factitious," Dewey writes. "All the techniques of observation employed in the advanced sciences may be conformed to, including the use of the best statistical methods to calculate probable errors, etc., and yet the material ascertained be scientifically 'dead,' i.e., irrelevant to a genuine issue, so that concern with it is hardly more than a form of intellectual busy work."[10] If social scientists cannot tell us something useful about the world, then they (we) are serving very little purpose at all.

The argument becomes clearer if we contrast the social sciences with the natural sciences and the humanities. To be sure, the natural sci-

---

10. Dewey (1938: 499).

ences may have greater social utility than the social sciences. Certainly their utility is more readily apparent. Most of the great technological advances of the twentieth century (e.g., satellites, fertilizers, computers, pharmaceuticals) have built on the discoveries of academics working in the sciences. (This was, of course, less true in previous eras.) Yet, the *greatest* advances of science often do not have immediate practical repercussions for humankind. Were we better off after Einstein's discovery of the theory of relativity, or Watson and Crick's discovery of the double helix structure of DNA? The point here is that natural science may do its best work when *not* focused directly on the interests and needs of lay citizens. Scientists engaged in basic research generally do not ask citizens and policymakers for guidance on what sorts of questions they should be working on. And rightly so. Whatever it is that guides natural scientists, these rules and rewards are quite removed from everyday concerns and everyday ways of thinking. Laudan writes,

> Much theoretical activity in the sciences, and *most of the best of it,* is not directed at the solution of practical or socially redeeming problems. Even in those cases where deep-level theorizing has eventually had practical spin-off, this has been largely accidental; such fortuitous applications have been neither the motivation for the research nor the general rule. Were we to take seriously the utilitarian approach to science, then a vast re-ordering of priorities would have to follow, since the present allocation of talent and resources within science manifestly does not reflect likely practical priorities.[11]

Paradoxically, one could apply the same argument to the humanities. It is not clear to me what guides, or should guide, academics exploring the regions of art, language, literature, music, religion, and philosophy.[12] But it is probably not – or at least only partially – social utility. This is not to say that the humanities are irrelevant. It is to say that they are probably not doing their best work when in hot pursuit of relevance. Indeed, it may be that they are of greater relevance when pursuing truth, beauty, and knowledge in a less "interested" fashion.

What I am suggesting is that although all segments of the academy can lay claim to social utility, only social science pursues that goal in a fairly direct and unmediated fashion. *Art for art's sake* has some plausibility, and *science for science's sake* might also be argued in a serious vein. But no serious person, I think, would adopt as her thesis *social science for*

11. Laudan (1977: 224–5), his emphasis. See also Zald (1990: 175–6).
12. For thoughts on this question, see Delbanco (1999), Ellis (1999), and Kernan (1997).

social science's sake.[13] Social science is science for *society's* sake. These disciplines seek to provide answers to questions of pressing concern, or questions that we think should be of pressing concern, to the general public. We seek to pursue issues that bear upon our obligations as citizens in a community – issues related, perhaps, to democracy, equality, justice, life satisfaction, peace, prosperity, violence, or virtue, but in any case, issues that call forth a sense of duty, responsibility, and action.

This is not to say that social science should be preoccupied with *policy* relevance. One would be hard-pressed, for example, to uncover a single policy prescription in work by David Brion Davis, Edmund Morgan, and Orlando Patterson on the institution of human slavery.[14] Yet, arguably, no one ignorant of these writers' work can fully comprehend *any* contemporary social policy debate in the United States. Similarly, although work on the American Revolution, the Constitution, the Civil War, and various other historical topics is undoubtedly important for understanding where we are today, it would be difficult to derive policy implications from each of these events. The same could be said for many subjects of study in the various fields of the social sciences. The point, then, is not that every study should have a policy "lesson," but that every study should reflect upon something that citizens and policymakers care about, or might care about.

It should be stressed that relevance, like other criteria, is a *relative* virtue. The study with a feasible policy suggestion can probably claim greater relevance, ceteris paribus, than one that does not. But policy relevance is not the only sort of relevance available. The telos of social utility, therefore, encompasses work in history, anthropology, and other interpretive fields whose relevance to public affairs is bound to be more diffuse. Indeed, one of the strongest arguments *against* a naturalist model for the social sciences is that such a model would prevent us from writing about things that matter. Too preoccupied with its status as a science, Barrington Moore thought,

---

13. At a dinner for scientists in Cambridge, someone is supposed to have offered the following toast: "To pure mathematics, and may it never be of any use to anybody!" (Merton 1949/1968: 597). It is difficult to imagine the same toast being given at a dinner of *social* scientists. Laudan (1977: 32) remarks that "certain problems [in the natural sciences] assume a high importance because the National Science Foundation will pay scientists to work on them or, as in the case of cancer research, because there are moral, social, and financial pressures which can 'promote' such problems to a higher place than they perhaps cognitively deserve." One cannot imagine somebody arguing against funding a social science problem because, although socially and politically important, it was not "cognitively" so.

14. See Davis (1988), Morgan (1975), and Patterson (1982).

social science overlooks more important and pressing tasks. The main structural features of what society can be like in the next generation are already given by trends at work now. Humanity's freedom of maneuver lies within the framework created by its history. Social scientists and allied scholars could help to widen the area of choice by analyzing the historical trends that now limit it. They could show, impartially, honestly, and free from the special pleadings of governments and vested interests, the range of possible alternatives and the potentialities for effective action. Such has been, after all, the aim of inquiry into human affairs in free societies since the Greeks.[15]

"One may still hope," Moore concludes portentously, "that the tradition can survive in modern society."[16] At the same time, we ought to remind ourselves that a wholesale *rejection* of the goals of science will not necessarily help anthropology, economics, history, political science, psychology, and sociology become more useful – a matter taken up below.

Beyond Relevance

Relevance means addressing concerns that people – citizens and policymakers – care about, or might care about. It is an important criterion, and one that is bound to be neglected if our only epistemological foundation is *science*. But relevance is only one dimension of social utility.

Consider: many of us would like very much to know why Rwandans were killing each other off with such zeal in the mid-1990s. All work on Rwanda, or on genocide more generally, is therefore relevant. But obviously, not all work on these subjects is equal in value. What is it, then, that makes one work more useful than another?

Let me suggest a few desiderata. We would prefer a work that is accurate to one that is misleading, or downright wrong. We would prefer a work that describes the situation in depth, rather than one that passes over the subject in a superficial manner. We would prefer a work that tackles the question of causation (who or what started this mess?), and perhaps even the speculative question of prediction (when will it end?). In approaching causal problems, we will feel more comfortable with the argument if it applies to more than one event – if it is generalizable to many cases. And so forth. In short, *all* the criteria presented in the foregoing chapters can be justified as pragmatic expedients, helping us to understand the world in ways that are useful to us as citizens and policymakers. Pragmatism, not an a priori conception of what we ought to be doing, is the proper ground for adjudicating these basic-level debates.

15. Moore (1958: 159).
16. Ibid.

Consider, second, the challenge to social science posed by poststructuralism (including its analogs, postmodernism and deconstruction) and other radically skeptical perspectives on truth and science.[17] Most practitioners within the social sciences today would dispute these challenges. But on what grounds? What is one to say to those who deny the goals of science, truth, or knowledge (as conventionally understood)? The only viable response, I think, is the consequentialist one. Where would we be if we dispensed with social science and, instead, approached these sets of problems with the tools of poststructuralism? What would a poststructuralist social science look like? Would it tell us about things that we want to know? Would it allow us to reach societal consensus on important problems? Could it be integrated into a democratic politics? If the answer to any one of these questions is in the negative, what would be consequences of that negative? (It will be clear, without playing out these alternate scenarios, which side of the methodological fence I am on.)

Other methodological disagreements with the criterial framework are more difficult to resolve, if only because the disagreements are more subtle. Interpretivists, for example, may be frustrated with the degree of emphasis placed on causal and predictive analysis. Rational choicers may feel that the criterion of analytic utility deserves more attention. Behavioralists in the experimental tradition might argue that the possibilities of experimental research in the social sciences are unjustifiably downplayed. These sorts of disagreements may be understood as disagreements of emphasis, rather than of principle. Perhaps there is nothing to say *in general* about this sort of dispute except that different research questions and research situations call for emphasizing different tasks and criteria.

Yet, if we *are* to engage these debates at a general level, we will have to resort to a pragmatic line of argument. We can then pose the series of questions we have just applied to poststructuralism to other schools of social science. Would such a vision tell us things we want to know? Would it allow us to reach societal consensus on these matters? Which vision of social science is likely to prove, in the long run, most useful to society?

The Distinctiveness of Social Science

We must remind ourselves that however mightily social science strives for social utility, solving problems such as racism, poverty, and the spread of AIDS requires much more than good social science. It requires, among

17. On poststructuralism et al. and their relevance for social science, see surveys by Norris (1997) and Rosenau (1992). See also Feyerabend (1975), Latour and Woolgar (1979), and Winch (1958).

other things, good polemic and compelling dramatizations. The cause of civil rights, for example, was advanced more by visual images – of peaceful protesters being sprayed with water cannons and beaten by police – than by social science. The sermons of Martin Luther King, Jr., resounded with greater force than the lengthy and detailed analysis of Gunnar Myrdal's *An American Dilemma*. Beyond rhetoric, social change requires *power,* as the role of social movements, voters, and national political elites during the 1950s and 1960s attests. This is not an argument, therefore, for the primacy of social science.

The point, rather, is that whatever its relative impact on policy, politics, and public opinion (a matter I leave to others to decide), the work of social science is best carried forth by remaining true to standards proper to its domain.[18] It will not aid citizens and policymakers to have a field of anthropology that is differentiable from theology, or a field of political science indistinguishable from party ideology. If Christopher Jencks, a noted social policy expert, approached problems in the same manner as Edward Kennedy – or Ronald Reagan, for that matter – then we would have no need whatsoever to consult the views of Professor Jencks. What academics like Jencks have to *add* to the political debate is premised on their expertise. And what are the grounds for expertise, if not the practice of good social science? One may disagree about the norms that constitute good social science – none of the criteria advanced in the preceding chapters are sacrosanct – but it is difficult to deny the necessity of norms. There is some utility to good social science, and none at all to bad social science.

Again, we must avoid misleading analogies to natural science, where "expertise" and "science" are easier to define and more generally respected. There will always be some contention on these matters within the social sciences, and rightly so. Yet, there remain important differences between social science and party politics, and social science and journalism, which justify the use of these loaded terms in the context of serious academic work in anthropology, economics, history, political science, psychology, and sociology.

It should also be pointed out that the willful avoidance of methodology has doleful long-term consequences for social science, and for those who would like social science to play a role in the transformation of society. To the extent that social scientists forego systematic analysis in favor of polemic they compromise the legitimacy of the enterprise of which

---

18. See Eckstein (1992: ch 2), who invokes Weber in support of this limited and differentiated role for social science (vis-à-vis the public sphere).

they are a part, and from which they gain whatever prominence they enjoy. As judges walk a fine line between their assigned constitutional roles and their desire to affect public policy, so must social scientists walk a line between science (methodological rigor) and society (sociopolitical relevance). The day when this line disappears is the day when social science no longer has a calling.

Throughout this book the reader will have discerned a double-edged argument. I am opposed, on the one hand, to a post-positivist stance which says there is little except academic pretense separating social science from other modes of discourse and argumentation. I am equally opposed to a vision of social science modeled on the natural sciences – or perhaps, on an older view of the humanities – in which the conduct of social science is viewed as essentially autonomous from the concerns of ordinary people. Let us explore this tension in greater detail.

The pulls and tugs – sometimes financial, sometimes personal, sometimes partisan – that social scientists experience from the "real world" are usually looked on as detriments to properly scientific work. "A social scientist has no place, qua scientist, as a party to power-politics," Lynd writes. "When he works within the constricting power curbs of a Republican or of a Communist 'party line,' or when he pulls his scientific punch by pocketing more important problems and accepting a retainer to work as an expert for the partisan ends of a bank or an advertising agency, he is something less than a scientist." However, Lynd adds perceptively, "when the social scientist hides behind the aloof 'spirit of science and scholarship' for fear of possible contamination, he is likewise something less than a scientist."[19]

Social scientists occupy positions of class and status in society, just like everybody else. They have personal and professional interests at stake in what they do, just like everybody else. It is folly to suppose that anyone could entirely dispense with these positional influences while conducting research on precisely these same questions. Indeed, investigations informed by personal experience may be *more* insightful than those that begin with a theoretically derived, or laboratory-style, hypothesis. It is neither possible nor desirable for academics studying human behavior to strip themselves of all notion of self, isolating themselves in a cocoon of scienticity. As scholars in the hermeneutic tradition have pointed out, involvement with society is the stuff out of which any understanding of that society must evolve. No knowledge is possible in the abstract. (Here, again, we find a striking contrast between the conduct of natural and social science.)

19. Lynd (1939/1964: 178).

Worldly pressures, then, are both the bane and the boon of social science. Sometimes, it appears that one cannot live scientifically with the world. But it is equally true that one cannot live scientifically without the world. Thomas Bender puts it nicely: "To say that the university ought to be connected to society is not to say that it might properly be a synecdoche for the world. But neither should it claim a position of transcendence."[20] No *general* resolution is possible to this problem; each must strike her own bargain. The proper conclusion is therefore agnostic: a scholar's involvement with the state, with business, with the university administration, or with other non-social science institutions is neither inherently good nor inherently bad.

This is about all we can say, as well, for the stance of social science vis-à-vis the status quo. To be sure, as Durkheim remarks, "if there is to be a social science, we shall expect it not merely to paraphrase the traditional prejudices of the common man but to give us a new and different view of them; for the aim of all science is to make discoveries, and every discovery more or less disturbs accepted ideas."[21] Lynd seconds the notion of a "disturbing" social science: "To the extent that social science accepts more or less uncritically the definition of its problems as set by tradition and current folk-assumptions, and views its role as the description and analysis of situations so defined, it forfeits thereby, if these problems are wrongly defined, its chief opportunity to contribute to the 'emancipation from error.'"[22]

At the same time, however, it would be folly to make *rejection* of the status quo – or of standard wisdom – the premise of social science research, as is seemingly advocated by writers in the critical theory mold. Brian Fay, for example, suggests that social science should lead the way for future transformations in society "by assuming a particular form, namely, one that isolates in the lives of a group of people those causal conditions that depend for their power on the ignorance of those people as to the nature of their collective existence, and that are frustrating them. The intention here is to enlighten this group of people about these

---

20. Bender et al. (1997: 47). For further observations on these matters, see Karl (1982).
21. Durkheim (1895/1964: xxvii). Plenty of "disturbances" can be found in Durkheim's own work. With respect to racial theories of human behavior – then quite popular in the Anglo-European world – Durkheim (1895/1964: 108) makes the following observations: "The most diverse forms of organization are found in societies of the same race, while striking similarities are observed between societies of different races. The city-state existed among the Phoenicians, as among the Romans and the Greeks; we find it in the process of formation among the Kabyles." His conclusion: "No social phenomenon is known which can be placed in indisputable dependence on race."
22. Lynd (1939/1964: 122).

causal conditions and the ways in which they are oppressive, so that, *being enlightened, these people might change these conditions and so transform their lives* (and, coincidentally, transcend the original theory)."[23] Are we to assume, as a point of departure, that existing consciousness is false, that existing knowledge "reifies" a structure of oppression? This seems about as senseless as its conservative counterpart, the glorification of the status quo.

The proper recourse, it seems to me, lies in maintaining the norms of social science – "methodology," broadly speaking – rather than in cultivating a particular attitude toward society or the status quo. This should not prevent academics from acting in other capacities – as polemicists, politicians, activists, or bureaucrats. It should, however, dissuade us from labeling these activities in a misleading fashion. The line between activism and social science is a real one, and worth preserving. It is possible, I believe, to be a first-rate activist and a first-rate scholar, but probably not in the same breath or on the same page.

In other words, we ought to begin with a recognition that social science constitutes an independent – although never entirely autonomous – realm of endeavor. The trick is to make social science speak to problems that we care about *without* sacrificing the rigor that qualifies it as a science. It is not an easy trick, but it is the trick of the trade.

23. Fay (1983/1994: 108), his emphasis. See also Fay (1976).

References

Abbott, Andrew. 1988. "Transcending General Linear Reality." *Sociological Theory* 6:2, 169–86.

Abbott, Andrew. 1990. "Conceptions of Time and Events in Social Science Methods: Causal and Narrative Approaches." *Historical Methods* 23:4, 140–50.

Abbott, Andrew. 1992. "From Causes to Events: Notes on Narrative Positivism." *Sociological Methods and Research* 20, 428–55.

Abrams, Philip. 1982. *Historical Sociology.* Ithaca: Cornell University Press.

Achen, Christopher H. 1977. "Measuring Representation: Perils of the Correlation Coefficient." *American Journal of Political Science* 21:4, 805–15.

Achen, Christopher H. 1982. *Interpreting and Using Regression.* Beverly Hills: Sage.

Achen, Christopher H. 1986. *The Statistical Analysis of Quasi-Experiments.* Berkeley: University of California Press.

Achen, Christopher H. and Duncan Snidal. 1989. "Rational Deterrence Theory and Comparative Case Studies." *World Politics* 41 (January).

Adams, Ernest W. 1965. "Elements of a Theory of Inexact Measurement." *Philosophy of Science* 32, 205–28.

Adams, Ernest W. and William Y. Adams. 1987. "Purpose and Scientific Concept Formation." *British Journal for the Philosophy of Science* 38, 419–40.

Adams, Ian. 1989. *The Logic of Political Belief: A Philosophical Analysis of Ideology.* Savage, MD: Barnes & Noble.

Adams, R. M., Neil Smelser, and D. J. Treiman (eds.). 1982. *Behavioral and Social Science Research: A National Resource.* Part 1. Washington, DC: National Academy Press.

Adcock, Robert. 1998. "What Is a 'Concept?'" Paper presented at the annual meeting of the American Political Science Association, Boston, MA (September).

Adcock, Robert and David Collier. 2000. "Connecting Ideas with Facts: The Validity of Measurement with Examples from Comparative Research on Democracy." Paper prepared for the annual meetings of the American Political Science Association, Washington, DC (August–September).

Adjdukiewicz, Kazimierz. 1969. "Three Concepts of Definition." In Thomas M. Olshewsky (ed.), *Problems in the Philosophy of Language* (New York: Holt).

Adorno, Theodore, Else Frenkel-Brunswik, Daniel J. Levinson, R. Nevitt Sanford. 1950. *The Authoritarian Personality.* New York: Harper.

Algeo, John (ed.). 1991. *Fifty Years Among the New Words: A Dictionary of Neologisms, 1941–1991.* Cambridge: Cambridge University Press.

Allen, William Sheridan. 1965. *The Nazi Seizure of Power: The Experience of a Single German Town, 1930–1935.* New York: Watts.

Almond, Gabriel A. 1990. *A Discipline Divided: Schools and Sects in Political Science.* Newbury Park: Sage.

Almond, Gabriel A. and Stephen J. Genco. 1977/1990. "Clouds, Clocks, and the Study of Politics." In Gabriel A. Almond (ed.), *A Discipline Divided: Schools and Sects in Political Science* (Newbury Park: Sage).

Almond, Gabriel A. and Sidney Verba. 1963. *Civic Culture: Political Attitudes and Democracy in Five Nations.* Princeton: Princeton University Press.

Althusser, Louis. 1971. *Lenin and Philosophy and Other Essays.* New York: Monthly Review Press.

Aminzade, Ronald. 1992. "Historical Sociology and Time." *Sociological Methods and Research* 20, 456–80.

Ammerman, Robert R. (ed). 1965. *Classics of Analytic Philosophy.* New York: McGraw-Hill.

Angeles, Peter A. 1981. *Dictionary of Philosophy.* New York: Barnes & Noble.

Anscombe, G. E. M. 1971/1993. "Causality and Determination." In Ernest Sosa and Michael Tooley (eds.), *Causation* (Oxford: Oxford University Press).

Arendt, Hannah. 1968. *Between Past and Future: Eight Exercises in Political Thought.* New York: Viking.

Aristotle. 1941. *The Basic Works of Aristotle,* ed. Richard McKeon. New York: Random House.

Aronson, Jerrold. 1984. *A Realist Philosophy of Science.* New York: St. Martin's.

Austin, John L. 1961. *Philosophical Papers.* Oxford: Clarendon.

Austin, John L. 1962/1975. *How to Do Things with Words.* Cambridge, MA: Harvard University Press.

Ayer, Alfred Jules. 1936/1950. *Language, Truth and Logic,* 2d ed. New York: Dover.

Babbie, Earl. 1973/1983. *The Practice of Social Research,* 3d ed. Belmont, CA: Wadsworth.

Bailey, Kenneth D. 1994. *Typologies and Taxonomies: An Introduction to Classification Techniques.* Thousand Oaks: Sage.

Ball, Terence. 1988. *Transforming Political Discourse: Political Theory and Critical Conceptual History.* Oxford: Basil Blackwell.

Ball, Terence, James Farr, and Russell L. Hanson (eds.). 1989. *Political Innovation and Conceptual Change.* Cambridge: Cambridge University Press.

Barnard, H. Russell. 1988. *Research Methods in Cultural Anthropology.* Newbury Park: Sage.

Barnes, Barry and David Bloor. 1982. "Relativism, Rationalism and the Sociology of Knowledge." In Martin Hollis and Steven Lukes (eds.), *Rationality and Relativism* (Oxford: Basil Blackwell).

Barnes, Harry Elmer (ed.). 1925. *The History and Prospects of the Social Sciences.* New York: Knopf.

Barry, Brian M. 1988. *Sociologists, Economists and Democracy.* Chicago: University of Chicago Press.

Bartels, Larry M. 1995. "Symposium on *Designing Social Inquiry, Part 1.*" *Political Methodologist* 6:2 (Spring).

Barth, Fredik. 1999. "Comparative Methodologies in the Analysis of Anthropological Data." In John R. Bowen and Roger Petersen (eds.), *Critical Comparisons in Politics and Culture* (Cambridge: Cambridge University Press).

Barton, Alan H. and Paul F. Lazarsfeld. 1969. "Some Functions of Qualitative Analysis in Social Research." In George J. McCall and J. L. Simmons (eds.), *Issues in Participant Observation* (Reading, MA: Addison-Wesley).

Bates, Robert H., Avner Greif, Margaret Levi, Jean-Laurent Rosenthal, and Barry Weingast. 1998. *Analytic Narratives.* Princeton: Princeton University Press.

Beard, Charles A. 1934. *The Nature of the Social Sciences in Relation to Objectives of Instruction.* New York: Scribner's.

Becker, Gary S. 1976. *The Economic Approach to Human Behavior.* Chicago: University of Chicago Press.

Becker, Howard S. 1986. *Writing for Social Scientists: How to Start and Finish Your Thesis, Book, or Article.* Chicago: University of Chicago Press.

Bender, Thomas, Carl E. Schorske, Stephen R. Graubard, and William J. Barber (eds.). 1997. *American Academic Culture in Transformation: Fifty Years, Four Disciplines.* Princeton: Princeton University Press.

Benedict, Ruth. 1935/1961. *Patterns of Culture.* London: Routledge.

Bennett, Andrew. 1999. "Causal Inference in Case Studies: From Mill's Methods to Causal Mechanisms." Paper presented at the annual meetings of the American Political Science Association, Atlanta, GA (September).

Bentham, Jeremy. 1834/1952. *Bentham's Handbook of Political Fallacies*, ed. Harold A. Larrabee. New York: Thomas Y. Crowell.

Berelson, B. R. and G. A. Steiner. 1964. *Human Behavior: An Inventory of Scientific Findings.* New York: Harcourt.

Bergmann, Gustav. 1951. "Ideology." *Ethics* 61 (April) 205–18.

Berkhofer, Robert F., Jr. 1969. *A Behavioral Approach to Historical Analysis.* New York: Free Press.

Bhaskar, Roy. 1975/1978. *A Realist Theory of Science.* Sussex: Harvester Press.

Bierstedt, Robert. 1959. "Nominal and Real Definitions in Sociological Theory." In Llewellyn Gross (ed.), *Symposium on Sociological Theory* (Evanston, IL: Row, Peterson).

Birnbaum, Norman. 1960. "The Sociological Study of Ideology (1940–60): A Trend Report and Bibliography." *Current Sociology* 9:2, 91–117.

Blackburn, Simon. 1994. *Oxford Dictionary of Philosophy.* Oxford: Oxford University Press.

Blalock, Hubert M., Jr. 1960. *Social Statistics.* New York: McGraw-Hill.

Blalock, Hubert M., Jr. 1964. *Causal Inference in Nonexperimental Research.* Chapel Hill: University of North Carolina Press.

Blalock, Hubert M., Jr. 1969. *Theory Construction: From Verbal to Mathematical Formulations.* Englewood Cliffs, NJ: Prentice-Hall.

Blalock, Hubert M., Jr. 1982. *Conceptualization and Measurement in the Social Sciences.* Beverly Hills: Sage.

Blalock, Hubert M., Jr. (ed.). 1971. *Causal Models in the Social Sciences.* Chicago: Aldine-Atherton.

Blaug, Mark. 1978. *Economic Theory in Retrospect.* Cambridge: Cambridge University Press.

Blaug, Mark. 1980. *The Methodology of Economics, Or How Economists Explain.* Cambridge: Cambridge University Press.

Bloch, Marc. 1941/1953. *The Historian's Craft.* New York: Vintage Books.

Bohm, David. 1957. *Causality and Chance in Modern Physics.* London: Routledge.

Bohman, James. 1991. *New Philosophy of Social Science: Problems of Indeterminacy.* Cambridge, MA: MIT Press.

Bok, Derek. 1982. *Beyond the Ivory Tower: Social Responsibilities of the Modern University.* Cambridge: Harvard University Press.

Boring, Edwin G. 1923. "Intelligence as the Tests Test It." *The New Republic* (June 6) 35–37.

Bouma, Gary D. and G. B. J. Atkinson. 1995. *A Handbook of Social Science Research: A Comprehensive and Practical Guide for Students.* Oxford: Oxford University Press.

Bowen, John R. and Roger Petersen (eds.). 1999. *Critical Comparisons in Politics and Culture.* Cambridge: Cambridge University Press.

Bowker, Geoffrey C. and Susan Leigh Star. 1999. *Sorting Things Out: Classification and Its Consequences.* Cambridge, MA: MIT Press.

Boyd, Richard. 1984. "The Current Status of Scientific Realism." In Jarrett Leplin (ed), *Scientific Realism.* Berkeley: University of California Press.

Boyd, Richard, Philip Gasper, and J. D. Trout (eds.). 1991. *The Philosophy of Science.* Cambridge, MA: MIT Press.

Brady, Henry E. 1995. "Doing Good and Doing Better. Symposium on *Designing Social Inquiry, Part 2.*" *Political Methodologist* 6:2 (Spring).

Braithwaite, Richard B. 1955. *Scientific Explanation: A Study of the Function of Theory, Probability and Law in Science.* Cambridge: Cambridge University Press.

Braumoeller, Bear F. 1999. "Small-N Logic and Large-N Research." Paper presented at the annual meetings of the American Political Science Association, Atlanta, GA (September).

Brodbeck, May (ed.). 1968. *Readings in the Philosophy of the Social Sciences.* New York: Macmillan.

Brody, B. A. (ed.). 1970. *Readings in the Philosophy of Science.* Englewood Cliffs, NJ: Prentice Hall.

Brown, Robert. 1984. *The Nature of Social Laws: Machiavelli to Mill.* Cambridge: Cambridge University Press.

Brown, Steven R. and Richard W. Taylor. 1972. "Perspective in Concept Formation," *Social Science Quarterly* 52, 852–60.

Bulmer, Martin and Robert G. Burgess. 1986. "Do Concepts, Variables and Indicators Interrelate?" In Robert G. Burgess (ed.), *Key Variables in Social Investigation* (London: Routledge).

Bunge, Mario. 1959. *Causality.* Cambridge, MA: Harvard University Press.

Bunge, Mario. 1983. *Treatise on Basic Philosophy, Vol. 5. Epistemology and Methodology I: Exploring the World.* Dordrecht: D. Reidel.

Burawoy, Michael. 1989. "Two Methods in Search of Science." *Theory and Society* 18 (1989) 759–805.

Burger, Thomas. 1976. *Max Weber's Theory of Concept Formation: History, Laws, and Ideal Types.* Durham: Duke University.

Burgess, R. and D. Bushell. 1969. *Behavioral Sociology.* New York: Columbia University Press.

Campbell, Angus, Philip E. Converse, Warren P. Miller, and Donald E. Stokes. 1960. *The American Voter.* New York: Wiley.

Campbell, Donald T. 1975. "'Degrees of Freedom' and the Case Study." *Comparative Political Studies* 8 (July).

Campbell, Donald T. 1988. *Methodology and Epistemology for Social Science,* ed. E. Samuel Overman. Chicago: University of Chicago Press.

Campbell, Donald T. and Julian Stanley. 1966. *Experimental and Quasi-Experimental Designs for Research.* Chicago: Rand McNally.

Campbell, Norman Robert. 1919/1957. *Physics: The Elements.* Reprinted as *Foundations of Science.* New York: Dover.

Caporaso, James A. 1995. "Research Design, Falsification, and the Qualitative-Quantitative Divide." *American Political Science Review* 89:2 (June) 457–60.

Carlsnaess, Walter. 1981. *The Concept of Ideology and Political Analysis.* London: Greenwood Press.

Carnap, Rudolf. 1962. *Logic and Language.* Dordrecht: D. Reidel.

Carnap, Rudolf. 1967. *The Logical Structure of the World: Pseudoproblems in Philosophy,* trans. Rolf A. George. Berkeley: University of California Press.

Carr, Edward Hallett. 1939/1964. *The Twenty Years' Crisis, 1919–1939: An Introduction to the Study of International Relations.* New York: Harper.

Carr, Edward Hallett. 1961. *What Is History?* New York: Vintage Books.

Carroll, Lewis. 1939. *Alice's Adventures in Wonderland and Through the Looking Glass.* London: William Collins Sons.

Caton, Charles E. (ed.). 1963. *Philosophy and Ordinary Language.* Urbana: University of Illinois Press.

Cavell, Stanley. 1969. *Must We Mean What We Say?* Cambridge (reprint): Cambridge University Press.

Cavell, Stanley. 1979. *The Claim of Reason: Wittgenstein, Skepticism, Morality, and Tragedy.* Oxford: Oxford University Press.

Chafetz, Janet Saltzman. 1978. *A Primer on the Construction and Testing of Theories in Sociology.* Itasca, IL: Peacock.

Chapin, F. Stuart. 1939. "Definition of Definitions of Concepts." *Social Forces* 18:2 (December).

Chappell, V. C. (ed.). 1964. *Ordinary Language.* Englewood Cliffs, NJ: Prentice Hall.

Charlesworth, J. C. 1962. *The Limits of Behavioralism in Political Science.* Philadelphia: American Academy of Political and Social Science.

Clarke, Barry. 1979. "Eccentrically Contested Concepts," *British Journal of Political Science* 9:1 (January).

Cohen, Bernard P. 1989. *Developing Sociological Knowledge,* 2d ed. Chicago: Nelson-Hall.

Cohen, Morris R. and Ernest Nagel. 1934. *An Introduction to Logic and Scientific Method.* New York: Harcourt.

Cohen, Ronald (ed.). 1986. *Justice: Views from the Social Sciences.* New York: Plenum. [MU]

Coleman, James S. 1990. *Foundations of Social Theory.* Cambridge, MA: Harvard University Press.

Collier, David. 1993. "The Comparative Method." In Ada W. Finifter (ed.), *Political Science: The State of the Discipline II* (Washington, DC: American Political Science Association).

Collier, David. 1995a. "Trajectory of a Concept: 'Corporatism' in the Study of Latin American Politics." In Peter Smith (ed.), *Latin America in Comparative Perspective* (Boulder: Westview) 135–62.

Collier, David. 1995b. "Translating Quantitative Methods for Qualitative Researchers: The Case of Selection Bias." *American Political Science Review* 89:2 (June) 461–6.

Collier, David. 1998. "Putting Concepts to Work: Toward a Framework for Analyzing Conceptual Innovation in Comparative Research." Paper presented at the annual meetings of the American Political Science Association, Boston, MA (September).

Collier, David. 1999. "Data, Field Work and Extracting New Ideas at Close Range." *APSA-CP: Newsletter of the APSA Organized Section in Comparative Politics* 10:1 (Winter).

Collier, David and Robert Adcock. 1999. "Democracy and Dichotomies: A Pragmatic Approach to Choices about Concepts." *Annual Review of Political Science* 2.

Collier, David and Henry Brady. 1998. "Studies of Major Concepts in Political Analysis: An Illustrative Inventory." Unpublished manuscript, Department of Political Science, University of California at Berkeley, Berkeley CA.

Collier, David and Steven Levitsky. 1997. "Democracy with Adjectives: Conceptual Innovation in Comparative Research." *World Politics* 49 (April) 430–51.

Collier, David and James E. Mahon, Jr. 1993. "Conceptual 'Stretching' Revisited: Adapting Categories in Comparative Analysis." *American Political Science Review* 87:4 (December).

Collier, David and James Mahoney. 1996. "Insights and Pitfalls: Selection Bias in Qualitative Research." *World Politics* 49 (October) 56–91.

Collier, David and Richard E. Messick. 1975. Prerequisites Versus Diffusion: Testing Alternative Explanations of Social Security Adoption." *American Political Science Review* 69:4 (December) 1299–1315.

Collier, Ruth Berins and David Collier. 1991. *Shaping the Political Arena: Critical Junctures, the Labor Movement, and Regime Dynamics in Latin America.* Princeton: Princeton University Press.

Collingwood, R. G. 1940. *An Essay on Metaphysics.* Oxford: Oxford University Press.

Collins, Randall. 1985. *Three Sociological Traditions.* New York: Oxford University Press.

Comte, Auguste. 1975. *Auguste Comte and Positivism: The Essential Writings,* ed. Gertrud Lenzer. Chicago: University of Chicago Press.

Connolly, William E. 1974/1983. *The Terms of Political Discourse,* 2d ed. Princeton: Princeton University Press.

Converse, Philip E. 1964. "The Nature of Belief Systems in Mass Publics." In David E. Apter (ed.), *Ideology and Discontent* (London: Free Press) 206–61.

Converse, Philip E. 1982. "Response to Lecture by Professor Cronbach." In W. H. Kruskal (ed.), *The Social Sciences: Their Nature and Uses* (Chicago: University of Chicago Press).

Converse, Philip E. 1986. "Generalization and the Social Psychology of 'Other Worlds.'" In Donald W. Fiske and Richard A. Shweder (eds.), *Metatheory in Social Science: Pluralisms and Subjectivities* (Chicago: University of Chicago Press).

Cook, Thomas and Donald Campbell. 1979. *Quasi-Experimentation: Design and Analysis Issues for Field Settings.* Boston: Houghton Mifflin.

Coons, John E. and Patrick M. Brennan. 1999. *By Nature Equal: The Anatomy of a Western Insight.* Princeton: Princeton University Press.

Coppedge, Michael. 1999. "Thickening Thin Concepts and Theories: Combining Large N and Small in Comparative Politics." *Comparative Politics* 31:4 (July) 465–76.

Cox, Gary W. 1999. "The Empirical Content of Rational Choice Theory: A Reply to Green and Shapiro." *Journal of Theoretical Politics* 11:2 (April) 147–70.

Cox, Richard H. 1969. "The Original Concept of Ideology." In Richard H. Cox (ed.), *Ideology, Politics, and Political Theory* (Belmont, CA: Wadsworth) 9–27.

Cunningham, Adrian. 1973. "Reflections on Projections: The Range of Ideology." In Robert Benewick, R. N. Berki, and Bhikgu Parekh (eds.), *Knowledge and Belief in Politics: The Problem of Ideology* (London: Allen & Unwin) 36–56.

Dahl, Robert A. 1957/1969. "The Concept of Power." Reprinted in Roderick Bel, David V. Edwards, and R. Harrison Wagner (eds.), *Political Power: A Reader in Theory and Research* (New York: Free Press).

Dahl, Robert A. 1961/1969. "The Behavioral Approach in Political Science: Epitaph to a Successful Protest." In Heinz Eulau (ed.), *Behavioralism in Political Science* (Chicago: Aldine, Atherton).

Dahl, Robert A. 1968. "Power." In David L. Sills (ed.), *International Encyclopedia of the Social Sciences,* Vol. XII (New York: Macmillan) 405–15.

Dahl, Robert A. 1971. *Polyarchy: Participation and Opposition.* New Haven, Yale University Press.

D'Andrade, Roy G. 1995. *The Development of Cognitive Anthropology.* Cambridge: Cambridge University Press.

David, Paul A. 1993. "Path-Dependence and Predictability in Dynamic Systems with Local Network Externalities: A Paradigm for Historical Economics." In Dominique Foray and Christopher Freeman (eds.), *Technology and the Wealth of Nations: The Dynamics of Constructed Advantage* (London: Pinter) 208–31.

Davidson, Donald. 1993. "Causal Relations." In Ernest Sosa and Michael Tooley (eds.), *Causation* (Oxford: Oxford University Press).

Davis, David Brion. 1988. *The Problem of Slavery in Western Culture*. Oxford: Oxford University Press.

Davis, James A. 1985. *The Logic of Causal Order*. Thousand Oaks: Sage.

Day, Timothy and Harold Kincaid. 1994. "Putting Inference to the Best Explanation in its Place." *Synthese* 98, 271–95.

Debnam, Geoffrey. 1984. *The Analysis of Power: Core Elements and Structure*. New York: St. Martin's.

DeFelice, E. Gene. 1986. "Causal Inference and Comparative Methods." *Comparative Political Studies* 19:3 (October) 415–37.

Delbanco, Andrew. 1999. "The Decline and Fall of Literature." *New York Review of Books* XL VI:17 (November 4) 32–8.

de Marchi, Neil (ed.). 1988. *The Popperian Legacy in Economics*. Cambridge: Cambridge University Press.

Dewey, John. 1938. *Logic: The Theory of Inquiry*. New York: Holt.

Dion, Douglas. 1998. "Evidence and Inference in the Comparative Case Study." *Comparative Politics* (January) 127–45.

DiRenzo, Gordon J. 1966a. "Conceptual Definition in the Behavioral Sciences." In Gordon J. DiRenzo (ed.), *Concepts, Theory, and Explanation in the Behavioral Sciences* (New York: Random House) 6–18.

DiRenzo, Gordon J. (ed.). 1966b. *Concepts, Theory, and Explanation in the Behavioral Sciences*. New York: Random House.

Dittberner, Job L. 1979. *The End of Ideology and American Social Thought: 1930–1960*. Ann Arbor: UMI Research.

Dower, John. 1999. *Embracing Defeat*. New York: Norton.

Drass, Kriss and Charles C. Ragin. 1992. *QCA: Qualitative Comparative Analysis*. Evanston, IL: Institute for Policy Research, Northwestern University.

Dray, William H. 1952. *Laws and Explanations in History*. Oxford: Oxford University Press.

Dray, William H. (ed.). 1966. *Philosophical Analysis and History*. New York: Harper.

Dreze, Jean and Amartya Sen. 1989. *Hunger and Public Action*. Oxford: Clarendon.

Dreze, Jean, Amartya Sen, and Arhar Hussain (eds.). 1995. *The Political Economy of Hunger: Selected Essays*. Oxford: Clarendon.

Dugger, William. 1979/1984. "Methodological Differences between Institutional and Neoclassical Economics." In Daniel M. Hausman (ed.), *The Philosophy of Economics: An Anthology* (Cambridge: Cambridge University Press).

Dumont, Richard G. and William J. Wilson. 1967. "Aspects of Concept Formation, Explication, and Theory Construction in Sociology," *American Sociological Review* 32:6 (December) 985–95.

Dupre, John. 1984. "Probabilistic Causality Emancipated." In Peter A. French, Theodore E. Uehling, Jr., and Howard K. Wettstein (eds.), *Midwest Studies in Philosophy Volume IX: Causation and Causal Theories* (Minneapolis: University of Minnesota Press).

Durbin, Paul T. 1988. *Dictionary of Concepts in Philosophy of Science.* New York: Greenwood Press.

Durkheim, Emile. 1895/1964. *The Rules of Sociological Method.* New York: Free Press.

Durkheim, Emile. 1897/1951. *Suicide: A Study in Sociology.* New York: Free Press.

Durkheim, Emile. 1947. *The Elementary Forms of the Religious Life: A Study in Religious Sociology,* trans. Joseph Ward Swain. Glencoe, IL: Free Press.

Duverger, Maurice. 1963. *Political Parties: Their Organization and Activity in the Modern State.* New York: Wiley.

Dworkin, Ronald M. 1977. *Taking Rights Seriously.* Cambridge, MA: Harvard University Press.

Eagleton, Terry. 1991. *Ideology: An Introduction.* London: Verso.

Earman, John (ed.). 1992. *Inference, Explanation, and Other Frustrations: Essays in the Philosophy of Science.* Berkeley: University of California Press.

Easton, David. 1953. *The Political System.* New York: Knopf.

Easton, David. 1965/1979. *A Systems Analysis of Political Life.* Chicago: University of Chicago Press.

Eckstein, Harry. 1975. "Case Studies and Theory in Political Science." In Fred I. Greenstein and Nelson W. Polsby (eds.), *Handbook of Political Science, Vol. 7. Political Science: Scope and Theory* (Reading, MA: Addison-Wesley).

Eckstein, Harry. 1992. *Regarding Politics: Essays on Political Theory, Stability, and Change.* Berkeley: University of California Press.

Eggan, F. 1954. "Social Anthropology and the Method of Controlled Comparison." *American Anthropologist* 56 (October) 743–63.

Eidlin, Fred. 1983. "Area Studies and/or Social Science: Contextually-Limited Generalizations versus General Laws." In Fred Eidlin (ed.), *Constitutional Democracy: Essays in Comparative Politics* (Boulder: Westview).

Einhorn, Hillel J. and Robin M. Hogarth. 1986. "Judging Probable Cause." *Psychological Bulletin* 99:3, 3–19.

Einstein, Albert. 1940/1953. "The Fundaments of Theoretical Physics." In Herbert Feigl and May Brodbeck (eds.), *Readings in the Philosophy of Science* (New York: Appleton) 253–62.

Eldridge, J. E. T. 1983. *C. Wright Mills.* Chichester: Ellis Horwood.

Ellis, John. 1999. *Literature Lost: Social Agendas and the Corruption of the Humanities.* New Haven: Yale University Press.

Elster, Jon. 1982. "Belief, Bias, and Ideology." In Martin Hollis and Steven Lukes (eds.), *Rationality and Relativism* (Oxford: Basil Blackwell) 123–48.

Elster, Jon. 1989a. *Nuts and Bolts for the Social Sciences.* Cambridge: Cambridge University Press.

Elster, Jon. 1989b. *Solomonic Judgments.* Cambridge: Cambridge University Press.

Elster, Jon (ed.). 1986. *Rational Choice.* New York: New York University Press.

Ember, Melvin. 1991. "The Logic of Comparative Research." *Behavior Science Research* 25, 143–54.

Ember, Melvin and Keith F. Otterbein. 1991. "Sampling in Cross-Cultural Research." *Behavior Science Research* 25, 217–34.

Emigh, Rebecca. 1997. "The Power of Negative Thinking: The Use of Negative Case Methodology in the Development of Sociological Theory." *Theory and Society* 26, 649–84.

Eulau, Heinz (ed.). 1969. *Behavioralism in Political Science.* Chicago: Aldine, Atherton.

Faeges, Russell S. 1999. "Theory-Driven Concept Definition: The Challenge of Perverse Classifications." Paper presented at the annual meetings of the American Political Science Association, Atlanta, GA (September).

Fay, Brian. 1976. *Social Theory and Political Practice.* London: Allen & Unwin.

Fay, Brian. 1983/1994. "General Laws and Explaining Human Behavior." In Michael Martin and Lee C. McIntyre (eds.), *Readings in the Philosophy of Social Science* (Cambridge, MA: MIT Press).

Feagin, Joe R., Anthony M. Orum, and Gideon Sjoberg. 1991. *A Case for the Case Study.* Chapel Hill: University of North Carolina Press.

Fearon, James. 1991. "Counter Factuals and Hypothesis Testing in Political Science." *World Politics* 43 (January) 169–95.

Fearon, James D. and David D. Laitin. 2000. "Ordinary Language and External Validity: Specifying Concepts in the Study of Ethnicity." Paper presented at the annual meetings of the American Political Science Association, Washington, D.C. (August-September).

Fenno, Richard F., Jr. 1978. *Home Style: House Members in Their Districts.* Boston: Little, Brown.

Feyerabend, Paul. 1975. *Against Method.* London: New Left Books.

Field, Harry. 1972. "Tarski's Theory of Truth." *Journal of Philosophy* 69, 347–75.

Fine, Gary Alan and Kent Sandstrom. 1993. "Ideology in Action: A Pragmatic Approach to a Contested Concept." *Sociological Theory* 11:1 (March) 21–38.

Finley, M. I. 1963. "Generalizations in Ancient History." In Louis Gottschalk (ed.), *Generalization in the Writing of History* (Chicago: University of Chicago Press).

Firebaugh, Glenn. 1999. "Empirics of World Income Inequality." *American Journal of Sociology* 104:3 (November) 1597–1630.

Fischer, David Hackett. 1970. *Historians' Fallacies: Toward a Logic of Historical Thought.* New York: Harper.

Fischer, David Hackett. 1989. *Albion's Seed: Four British Folkways in America.* New York: Oxford University Press.

Fishburn, Peter C. 1985. *Interval Orders and Interval Graphs: A Study of Partially Ordered Sets.* New York: Wiley.

Fiske, Donald W. 1986. "Specificity of Method and Knowledge in Social Science." In Donald W. Fiske and Richard A. Shweder (eds.), *Metatheory in Social Science: Pluralisms and Subjectivities* (Chicago: University of Chicago Press).

Fiske, Donald W. and Richard A. Shweder (eds.). 1986. *Metatheory in Social Science: Pluralisms and Subjectivities.* Chicago: University of Chicago Press.

Fodor, Jerry A. 1998. *Concepts: Where Cognitive Science Went Wrong.* Oxford: Oxford University Press.

Fodor, Jerry A. and Jerrold J. Katz (eds.). 1964. *The Structure of Language: Readings in the Philosophy of Language.* Englewood Cliffs, NJ: Prentice Hall.

Freeden, Michael. 1994. "Political Concepts and Ideological Morphology." *The Journal of Political Philosophy* 2:1, 140–64.

Freeden, Michael. 1996. *Ideologies and Political Theory: A Conceptual Approach.* Oxford: Oxford University Press.

Freedman, David, Robert Pisani, Roger Purves, and Ani Adhikari. 1991. *Statistics,* 2d ed. New York: Norton.

French, Peter A., Theodore E. Uehling, Jr., and Howard K. Wettstein (eds.). 1984. *Midwest Studies in Philosophy Volume IX: Causation and Causal Theories.* Minneapolis: University of Minnesota Press.

Frendreis, John P. 1983. "Explanation of Variation and Detection of Covariation: The Purpose and Logic of Comparative Analysis." *Comparative Political Studies* 16:2 (July) 255–72.

Friedman, Jeffrey (ed.). 1996. *The Rational Choice Controversy: Economic Models of Politics Reconsidered.* New Haven: Yale University Press.

Friedman, Kenneth S. 1972. "Empirical Simplicity as Testability." *British Journal for the Philosophy of Science* 23, 25–33.

Friedman, Michael. 1992. "Philosophy and the Exact Sciences: Logical Positivism as a Case Study." In John Earman (ed), *Inference, Explanation, and Other Frustrations: Essays in the Philosophy of Science.* Berkeley: University of California Press.

Friedman, Milton. 1953. "The Methodology of Positive Economics." In *Essays in Positive Economics* (Chicago: University of Chicago Press).

Friedman, Milton. 1953/1984. "The Methodology of Positive Economics." In Daniel M. Hausman (ed.), *The Philosophy of Economics: An Anthology* (Cambridge: Cambridge University Press).

Frohlich, Norma and Joe A. Oppenheimer. 1992. *Choosing Justice.* Berkeley: University of California Press.

Fukuyama, Francis. 1992. *The End of History and the Last Man.* New York: Avon.

Gadamer, Hans-Georg. 1975. *Truth and Method,* trans. Garrett Barden and John Cumming. New York: Seabury Press.

Gallie, W. B. 1956/1962. "Essentially Contested Concepts," reprinted in Max Black (ed.), *The Importance of Language* (Englewood Cliffs, NJ: Prentice Hall).

Gardiner, Patrick. 1952/1961. *The Nature of Historical Explanation.* Oxford: Oxford University Press.

Gardner, Riley W. and Roberet A. Schoen. 1962. "Differentiation and Abstraction in Concept Formation," *Psychological Monographs: General and Applied* 76:41.

Garfinkel, Alan. 1981. *Forms of Explanation: Rethinking the Questions of Social Theory.* New Haven: Yale University Press.

Garfinkel, Harold. 1967. *Studies in Ethnomethodology.* Englewood Cliffs, NJ: Prentice Hall.

Gasking, D. 1955. "Causation and Recipes." *Mind* 64, 479–87.

Gay, Peter. 1984–98. *The Bourgeois Experience: Victoria to Freud,* 5 vols. New York: Oxford University Press and Norton.

Geddes, Barbara. 1990. "How the Cases You Choose Affect the Answers You Get: Selection Bias in Comparative Politics." In James A. Stimson (ed.), *Political Analysis,* vol. 2 (Ann Arbor: University of Michigan Press).

Geddes, Barbara. 1996. *Politician's Dilemma: Building State Capacity in Latin America*. Berkeley: University of California Press.

Geertz, Clifford. 1964/1973. "Ideology as a Cultural System." In *The Interpretation of Cultures* (New York: Basic Books).

Geertz, Clifford. 1973. *The Interpretation of Cultures*. New York: Basic Books.

Geertz, Clifford. 1983. *Local Knowledge: Further Essays in Interpretive Anthropology*. New York: Basic Books.

Gellner, Ernest. 1973. *Cause and Meaning in the Social Sciences*. London: Routledge.

Gellner, Ernest. 1985. *Relativism and the Social Sciences*. Cambridge: Cambridge University Press.

George, Alexander. 1979. "Case Studies and Theory Development: The Method of Structured, Focused Comparison." In Paul Gordon Lauren (ed.), *Diplomacy: New Approaches in History, Theory, and Policy* (New York: Free Press).

George, Alexander L. and Andrew Bennett. In press. *Case Studies and Theory Development*. Cambridge, MA: MIT Press.

George, Alexander L. and Timothy J. McKeown. 1985. "Case Studies and Theories of Organizational Decision Making." *Advances in Information Processing in Organizations*, Vol. 2 (Santa Barbara: JAI Press).

Gerring, John. 1997. "Ideology: A Definitional Analysis." *Political Research Quarterly* 50:4 (December) 957–94.

Gerring, John. 1998. *Party Ideologies in America, 1828–1996*. Cambridge: Cambridge University Press.

Gerring, John. 1999. "What Makes a Concept Good?: An Integrated Framework for Understanding Concept Formation in the Social Sciences." *Polity* 31:3 (Spring).

Gerring, John. 2000a. "Corruption: A Large-N Framework." Unpublished manuscript, Boston University, Department of Political Science, Boston, MA.

Gerring, John. 2000b. "Culture Concepts in Social Science Research: Recurring Problems in Concept Formation and Research Design." Unpublished manuscript, Boston University, Department of Political Science, Boston, MA.

Gillies, Donald. 1993. *Philosophy of Science in the Twentieth Century: Four Central Themes*. Oxford: Blackwell.

Glaser, Barney G. and Anselm L. Strauss. 1967. *The Discovery of Grounded Theory: Strategies for Qualitative Research*. New York: Aldine de Gruyter.

Glymour, Clark. 1980. *Theory and Evidence*. Princeton: Princeton University Press.

Glymour, Clark. 1993. "A Review of Recent Work on the Foundations of Causal Inference." In Vaughn R. McKim and Stephen P. Turner (eds.), *Causality in Crisis?: Statistical Methods and the Search for Causal Knowledge in the Social Science* (Notre Dame, IN: University of Notre Dame Press).

Glymour, Clark, Richard Scheines, Peter Spirtes, and K. Kelly. 1987. *Discovering Causal Structures*. New York: Academic Press.

Goffman, Erving. 1974. *Frame Analysis*. Cambridge: Harvard University Press.

Goldie, Mark. 1989. "Ideology." In Terence Ball et al. (eds.), *Political Innovation and Conceptual Change* (Cambridge: Cambridge University) 266–91.

Goldstone, Jack A. 1997. "Methodological Issues in Comparative Macro-sociology." *Comparative Social Research* 16, 121–32.

Goldstone, Jack A. 1998. "Initial Conditions, General Laws, Path Dependence, and Explanation in Historical Sociology." *American Journal of Sociology* 104:3 (November) 829–45.

Goldthorpe, John H. 1997. "Current Issues in Comparative Macrosociology: A Response to the Commentaries." *Comparative Social Research* 16, 121–32.

Goodman, Nelson. 1965. *Fact, Fiction, Forecast,* 2d ed. Indianapolis: Bobbs-Merrill.

Gottschalk, Louis (ed.). 1963. *Generalization in the Writing of History.* Chicago: University of Chicago Press.

Gourevitch, Peter Alexis. 1978. "The International System and Regime Formation: A Critical Review of Anderson and Wallerstein." *Comparative Politics* 10, 419–38.

Graham, George J., Jr. 1971. *Methodological Foundations for Political Analysis.* Waltham, MA: Xerox College Publishing.

Gray, John N. 1977. "On the Contestability of Social and Political Concepts," *Political Theory* 5:3 (August).

Green, Donald P. and Ian Shapiro. 1994. *Pathologies of Rational Choice Theory: A Critique of Applications in Political Science.* New Haven: Yale University Press.

Griffin, Larry J. 1992. "Temporality, Events, and Explanation in Historical Sociology: An Introduction." *Sociological Methods and Research* 20:4 (May) 403–27.

Griffin, Larry J. 1993. "Narrative, Event-Structure, and Causal Interpretation in Historical Sociology." *American Journal of Sociology* 98, 1094–1133.

Gruenbaum, Adolf. 1976. "Can a Theory Answer More Questions than One of Its Rivals?" *British Journal for the Philosophy of Science* 27, 1–23.

Gujarati, Damodar N. 1995. *Basic Econometrics,* 3d ed. New York: McGraw-Hill.

Gutting, Gary (ed.). 1980. *Paradigms and Revolutions: Appraisals and Applications of Thomas Kuhn's Philosophy of Science.* Notre Dame, IN: University of Notre Dame Press.

Haan, Norma, Robert Bellah, Paul Rabinow, and William M. Sullivan (eds.). 1983. *Social Science as Moral Inquiry.* New York: Columbia University Press.

Habermas, Jurgen. 1972. *Knowledge and Human Interests,* trans. Jeremy J. Shapiro. Boston: Beacon Press.

Hagood, Margaret Jarman. 1941. *Statistics for Sociologists.* New York: Reynal and Hitchcock.

Hahn, Frank and Martin Hollis (eds.). 1979. *Philosophy and Economic Theory.* Oxford: Oxford University Press.

Hall, Peter and Rosemary C. R. Taylor. 1996. "Political Science and the Three New Institutionalisms." *Political Studies,* 936–57.

Hall, Stuart, Bob Lumley, and Gregor McLennan. 1977. "Politics and Ideology: Gramsci." In *On Ideology* (London: Center for Contemporary Cultural Studies/Hutchinson) 45–76.

Halle, Louis J. 1972. *The Ideological Imagination.* Chicago: Quadrangle Books.

Hamilton, Lawrence C. 1992. *Regression with Graphics: A Second Course in Applied Statistics*. Pacific Grove, CA: Brooks/Cole.

Hamilton, Malcolm B. 1987. "The Elements of the Concept of Ideology." *Political Studies* 35.

Hamilton, Richard F. 1996. *The Social Misconstruction of Reality: Validity and Verification in the Scholarly Community*. New Haven: Yale University Press.

Hammel, E. A. 1980. "The Comparative Method in Anthropological Perspective." *Comparative Studies in Society and History* 22:2, 145–55.

Hanson, Norwood Russell. 1961. "Is There a Logic of Discovery?" In H. Feigle and G. Maxwell (eds.), *Current Issues in the Philosophy of Science* (New York: Holt), 20–35.

Hanson, Stephen E. 1997. *Time and Revolution: Marxism and the Design of Soviet Institutions*. Chapel Hill: University of North Carolina Press.

Harman, Gilbert. 1965. "The Inference to the Best Explanation." *Philosophical Review* xxiv, 88–95.

Harre, R. 1972. *The Philosophies of Science*. London: Oxford University Press.

Harre, R. and E. H. Madden. 1975. *Causal Powers: A Theory of Natural Necessity*. Oxford: Basil Blackwell.

Harris, Marvin. 1978. *Cannibals and Kings: The Origins of Cultures*. New York: Vintage Books.

Harris, Marvin. 1985. *Good to Eat: Riddles of Food and Culture*. New York: Simon & Schuster.

Hart, H. L. A. and A. M. Honoré. 1959. *Causality in the Law*. Oxford: Oxford University Press.

Hart, H. L. A. and A. M. Honoré. 1966. "Causal Judgment in History and in the Law." In William H. Dray (ed.), *Philosophical Analysis and History* (New York: Harper).

Hartz, Louis. 1955. *The Liberal Tradition in America*. New York: Harcourt.

Hausman, Daniel M. 1992. *The Inexact and Separate Science of Economics*. Cambridge: Cambridge University Press.

Hawthorn, Geoffrey. 1991. *Plausible Worlds: Possibility and Understanding in History and the Human Sciences*. Cambridge: Cambridge University Press.

Hayek, Friedrich A. von. 1955–56. "Degrees of Explanation." *British Journal for the Philosophy of Science* 6.

Hayek, Friedrich A. von. 1956. "The Dilemma of Specialization." In L. D. White (ed.), *The State of the Social Sciences* (Chicago: University of Chicago Press).

Heckscher, Gunnar. 1957. *The Study of Comparative Government and Politics*. London: Allen & Unwin.

Hedstrom, Peter and Richard Swedberg (eds.). 1998. *Social Mechanisms: An Analytical Approach to Social Theory*. New York: Cambridge University Press.

Heidenheimer, Arnold J. 1986. "Politics, Policy and *Policey* as Concepts in English and Continental Languages: An Attempt to Explain Divergences." *Review of Politics* 48:1, 3–31.

Heise, David. 1988. "Computer Analysis of Cultural Structures." *Social Science Computer Review* 6, 183–96.

Heise, David. 1989. "Modeling Event Structures." *Journal of Mathematical Sociology* 14, 139–69.

Held, Virginia. 1973. "The Terms of Political Discourse: A Comment on Oppenheim," *Political Theory* 1:1 (February).

Hempel, Carl G. 1952. "Fundamentals of Concept Formation in Empirical Science." *Foundations of the Unity of Science* 2:7.

Hempel, Carl G. 1963. "Typological Methods in the Social Sciences." In Maurice Natanson (ed.), *Philosophy of the Social Sciences: A Reader* (New York: Random House).

Hempel, Carl G. 1965. *Aspects of Scientific Explanation: And Other Essays in the Philosophy of Science.* New York: Free Press.

Hempel, Carl G. 1966. *Philosophy of Natural Science.* Englewood Cliffs, NJ: Prentice Hall.

Hempel, Carl G. 1991. "Empiricist Criteria of Cognitive Significance: Problems and Changes." In Richard Boyd, Philip Gasper, and J. D. Trout (eds.), *The Philosophy of Science* (Cambridge, MA: MIT Press).

Hesse, Mary. 1974. *The Structure of Scientific Inference.* London: Macmillan.

Hexter, J. H. 1979. *On Historians: Reappraisals of Some of the Masters of Modern History.* Cambridge, MA: Harvard University Press.

Hicks, Alexander. 1999. *Social Democracy and Welfare Capitalism: A Century of Income Security Politics.* Ithaca: Cornell University Press.

Hicks, Alexander, Toya Misra, and Tang Hah Ng. 1995. "The Programmatic Emergence of the Social Security State." *American Sociological Review* 60 (June) 329–49.

Hirsch, E. D. 1967. *Validity in Interpretation.* New Haven: Yale University Press.

Hirschman, Albert O. 1970a. *Exit, Voice, Loyalty: Responses to Decline in Firms, Organizations, and States.* Cambridge, MA: Harvard University Press.

Hirschman, Albert O. 1970b. "The Search for Paradigms as a Hindrance to Understanding." *World Politics* 22:3 (March) 329–43.

Hirst, Paul. 1979. *On Law and Ideology.* London: Macmillan.

Holland, Paul W. 1986. "Statistics and Causal Inference." *Journal of the American Statistical Association* 81, 945–60.

Hollis, Martin. 1994. *The Philosophy of Social Science: An Introduction.* Cambridge: Cambridge University Press.

Hollis, Martin and Steven Lukes (eds.). 1982. *Rationality and Relativism.* Oxford: Basil Blackwell.

Holt, R. T. and J. E. Turner. 1970. "The Methodology of Comparative Research." In R. T. Holt and J. E. Turner (eds.), *The Methodology of Comparative Research* (New York: Free Press).

Homans, George C. 1951. *The Human Group.* Cambridge, MA: Harvard University Press.

Homans, George C. 1961. *Social Behavior: Its Elementary Forms.* New York: Harcourt.

Homans, George C. 1967. *The Nature of Social Science.* New York: Harcourt.

Hook, Sidney. 1946. "Illustrations." In Social Science Research Council, Committee on Historiography, *Theory and Practice in Historical Study: A Report of the Committee on Historiography* (New York: Social Science Research Council).

Horwich, Paul. 1982. *Probability and Evidence.* Cambridge: Cambridge University Press.

Hoy, David Couzens. 1982. *The Critical Circle: Literature, History, and Philosophical Hermeneutics.* Berkeley: University of California Press.

Huaco, George A. 1971. "On Ideology," *Acta Sociologica* 14:4, 245–55.

Hume, David. 1888. *Treatise of Human Nature.* Oxford: Oxford University Press.

Hume, David. 1960. "The Idea of Necessary Connexion [from *An Enquiry Concerning Human Understanding*, Sect. 7]. In Edward H. Madden (ed.), *The Structure of Scientific Thought: An Introduction to Philosophy of Science* (London: Routledge).

Hume, David. 1985. *Essays: Moral, Political, and Literary,* ed. Eugene F. Miller. Indianapolis: Liberty Classics.

Hunter, Floyd. 1963. *Community Power Stucture: A Study of Decision Makers.* New York: Anchor.

IDEA. 1997. *Voter Turnout from 1945 to 1997: A Global Report on Political Participation.* Stockholm: International Institute for Democracy and Electoral Assistance.

Immergut, Ellen M. 1996. "The Normative Roots of the New Institutionalism: Historical Institutionalism and Comparative Policy Studies." In Arthur Benz and Wolfgang Seibel (eds.), *Beitrage zur Theorieentwicklung in der Politik- und Verwaltungswissenschaft* (Baden-Baden: Nomos Verlag).

Irwin, Galen. 1974. "Compulsory Voting Legislation: Impact on Voter Turnout in the Netherlands." *Comparative Political Studies* 7 (October) 292–315.

Jackman, Robert W. 1985. "Cross-National Statistical Research and the Study of Comparative Politics." *American Journal of Political Science* 29:1 (February) 161–82.

Jacoby, Russell. 1987. *The Last Intellectuals: American Culture in the Age of Academe.* New York: Farrar, Straus & Giroux.

Janoski, Thomas and Alexander Hicks (eds.). 1993. *Methodological Advances in Comparative Political Economy.* Cambridge: Cambridge University Press.

Jarausch, Konrad H. and Kenneth A. Hardy. 1991. *Quantitative Methods for Historians: A Guide to Research, Data, and Statistics.* Chapel Hill: University of North Carolina Press.

Jeffrey, Richard. 1983. *The Logic of Decision.* Chicago: University of Chicago Press.

Jevons, W. Stanley. 1877/1958. *The Principles of Science.* New York: Dover.

Johnson, Paul E. 1999. "Simulation Modeling in Political Science." *American Behavioral Scientist* 42:10 (August) 1509–30.

Jones, Charles O. 1974. "Doing Before Knowing: Concept Development in Political Research." *American Journal of Political Science* 18, 215–28.

Kafker, Frank A. and James M. Laux (eds.). 1983. *The French Revolution: Conflicting Interpretations.* Malabar, FL: Robert E. Krieger.

Kalleberg, Arthur L. 1969. "Concept Formation in Normative and Empirical Studies: Toward Reconciliation in Political Theory," *American Political Science Review* LXIII:1 (March).

Kamarck, Andrew. 1983. *Economics and the Real World.* Oxford: Basil Blackwell.

Kantorowicz, Ernst H. 1957. *The King's Two Bodies: A Study in Medieval Political Theology.* Princeton: Princeton University Press.

Kaplan, Abraham. 1964. *The Conduct of Inquiry: Methodology for Behavioral Science.* San Francisco: Chandler.

Karl, Barry D. 1982. "The Citizen and the Scholar: Ships That Crash in the Night." In W. H. Kruskal (ed.), *The Social Sciences: Their Nature and Uses* (Chicago: University of Chicago Press).

Karl, Terry Lynn. 1997. *The Paradox of Plenty: Oil Booms and Petro-States.* Berkeley: University of California Press.

Katz, Jerrold. 1966. *The Philosophy of Language.* New York: Harper.

Katznelson, Ira. 1997. "Structure and Configuration in Comparative Politics." In Mark Irving Lichbach and Alan S. Zuckerman (eds.), *Comparative Politics: Rationality, Culture, and Structure* (New York: Cambridge University Press).

Keith, Bruce E., David B. Magleby, Candice J. Nelson, Elizabeth Orr, Mark C. Westlye, and Raymond E. Wolfinger. 1992. *The Myth of the Independent Voter.* Berkeley: University of California Press.

Kennedy, Peter. 1998. *A Guide to Econometrics.* Cambridge, MA: MIT Press.

Keohane, Nannerl O. 1976. "Philosophy, Theory, Ideology: An Attempt at Clarification." *Political Theory* 4:1 (February) 80–100.

Kernan, Alvin (ed.). 1997. *What's Happened to the Humanities?* Princeton: Princeton University Press.

Kincaid, Harold. 1990/1994. "Defending Laws in the Social Sciences." In Michael Martin and Lee C. McIntyre (eds.), *Readings in the Philosophy of Social Science* (Cambridge, MA: MIT Press).

Kinder, Donald R. and Thomas R. Palfrey (eds.). 1993. *The Experimental Foundations of Political Science.* Ann Arbor: University of Michigan Press.

King, Gary. 1989. *Unifying Political Methodology: The Likelihood Theory of Statistical Inference.* New York: Cambridge University Press.

King, Gary. 1995. "Replication, Replication." *PS: Political Science and Politics* XXVIII:3 (September) 443–99.

King, Gary, Robert O. Keohane, and Sidney Verba. 1994. *Designing Social Inquiry: Scientific Inference in Qualitative Research.* Princeton: Princeton University Press.

King, Gary, Robert O. Keohane, and Sidney Verba. 1995. "The Importance of Research Design in Political Science." *American Political Science Review* 89:2 (June) 475–81.

Kirkham, Richard L. 1992. *Theories of Truth: A Critical Introduction.* Cambridge, MA: MIT Press.

Kiser, Edgar. 1996. "The Revival of Narrative in Historical Sociology: What Rational Choice Can Contribute." *Politics and Society* 24, 249–71.

Kiser, Edgar and Michael Hechter. 1991. "The Role of General Theory in Comparative-Historical Sociology." *American Journal of Sociology* 97, 1–30.

Komarovsky, Mirra. 1940. *The Unemployed Man and His Family: The Effect of Unemployment upon the Status of the Man in Fifty-nine Families.* New York: Dryden Press.

Kornblith, Hilary (ed.). 1985. *Naturalizing Epistemology.* Cambridge, MA: MIT Press.

Korzeniewicz, Roberto P. and Timothy P. Moran. 1997. "World-Economic Trends in the Distribution of Income, 1965–1992." *American Journal of Sociology* 102, 1000–39.

Kosselleck, Reinhart. 1989. "Linguistic Change and the History of Events." *Journal of Modern History* 61 (December) 649–66.

Krasner, Stephen D. 1978. *Defending the National Interest: Raw Materials Investments and U.S. Foreign Policy.* Princeton: Princeton University Press.

Krieger, Susan. 1991. *Social Science and the Self: Personal Essays on an Art Form.* New Brunswick: Rutgers University Press.

Krimerman, Leonard I. (ed.) 1969. *The Nature and Scope of Social Science.* New York: Appleton, Century, Crofts.

Kroeber, A. L. and Clyde Kluckhohn. 1952/1963. *Culture: A Critical Review of Concepts and Definitions.* New York: Vintage/Random House.

Kruskal, W. H. (ed.). 1982. *The Social Sciences: Their Nature and Uses.* Chicago: University of Chicago Press.

Kuhn, Thomas S. 1962/1970. *The Structure of Scientific Revolutions.* Chicago: University of Chicago Press.

Kuhn, Thomas S. 1977. *The Essential Tension.* Chicago: University of Chicago Press.

Laclau, Ernesto. 1977. *Politics and Ideology in Marxist Theory: Capitalism, Fascism, Populism.* London: New Left Books.

Laitin, David D. 1995. "The Qualitative-Quantitative Disputation: Gary King, Robert O. Keohane, and Sidney Verba's *Designing Social Inquiry: Scientific Inference in Qualitative Research.*" *American Political Science Review* 89:2 (June) 454.

Lakatos, Imre. 1978. *The Methodology of Scientific Research Programmes.* Cambridge: Cambridge University Press.

Lakatos, Imre and A. Musgrave (eds.). 1970. *Criticism and the Growth of Knowledge.* Cambridge: Cambridge University Press.

Lakoff, George. 1987. *Women, Fire, and Dangerous Things: What Categories Reveal about the Mind.* Chicago: University of Chicago Press.

Lakoff, George and Herbert F. York. 1989. *A Shield in Space: Technology, Politics, and the Strategic Defense Initiative.* Berkeley: University of California Press.

Lamberts, Koen and David Shanks (eds.). 1997. *Knowledge, Concepts, and Categories.* Cambridge, MA: MIT Press.

Landau, Martin. 1972. "Comment: On Objectivity." *American Political Science Review* 66:3 (September).

Landes, David S. and Charles Tilly (eds.). 1971. *History as Social Science.* Englewood Cliffs, NJ: Prentice Hall.

Lane, Robert. 1962. *Political Ideology: Why the American Common Man Believes What He Does.* New York: Free Press.

Larrain, Jorge. 1979. *The Concept of Ideology.* London: Hutchinson.

Larrain, Jorge. 1983. *Marxism and Ideology.* London: Macmillan.

Lasswell, Harold and Abraham Kaplan. 1950. *Power and Society: A Framework for Political Inquiry.* New Haven: Yale University Press.

Latour, Bruno and Steve Woolgar. 1979. *Laboratory Life: The Social Construction of Scientific Facts.* Beverly Hills: Sage.

Laudan, Larry. 1977. *Progress and Its Problems: Toward a Theory of Scientific Growth.* Berkeley: University of California Press.

Laudan, Larry. 1983. *Science and Values.* Berkeley: University of California Press.

Laudan, Larry. 1996. *Beyond Positivism and Relativism: Theory, Method, and Evidence.* Boulder: Westview.

Lave, Charles and James March. 1975. *An Introduction to Models in the Social Sciences.* New York: Harper.

Lazarsfeld, Paul F. 1966. "Concept Formation and Measurement in the Behavioral Sciences: Some Historical Observations." In Gordon J. DiRenzo (ed.), *Concepts, Theory, and Explanation in the Behavioral Sciences* (New York: Random House) 144–204.

Lazarsfeld, Paul F. and Allen H. Barton. 1951. "Qualitative Measurement in the Social Sciences: Classification, Typologies, and Indices." In Daniel Lerner and Harold D. Lasswell (eds.), *The Policy Sciences* (Stanford: Stanford University Press).

Lazarsfeld, Paul F. and Morris Rosenberg. 1955. *The Language of Social Research.* Glencoe, IL: Free Press.

Leontief, Wassily. 1982/1983. "Foreword." In Alfred S. Eichner (ed.), *Why Economics Is Not Yet a Science* (Armonk: M. E. Sharpe).

Leplin, Jarrett (ed.). 1984. *Scientific Realism.* Berkeley: University of California Press.

Lerner, Daniel (ed.). 1959. *The Human Meaning of the Social Sciences.* New York: Meridian.

Lerner, Daniel and Harold D. Lasswell (eds). 1951. *The Policy Sciences.* Stanford: Stanford University Press.

Lerner, Daniel and Harold D. Lasswell (eds). 1951. *The Policy Sciences.* Stanford: Stanford University Press.

Levey, Geoffrey Brahm. 1996. "Theory Choice and the Comparison of Rival Theoretical Perspectives in Political Sociology." *Philosophy of the Social Sciences* 26:1 (March) 26–60.

Levi, Margaret. 1999. "Producing an Analytic Narrative." In John R. Bowen and Roger Petersen (eds.), *Critical Comparisons in Politics and Culture* (Cambridge: Cambridge University Press).

Levinson, Paul (ed.). 1988. *In Pursuit of Truth: Essays on the Philosophy of Karl Popper on the Occasion of His Eighteenth Birthday*. Atlantic Highlands, NJ: Humanities Press.

Lévi-Strauss, Claude. 1969. *The Elementary Structures of Kinship*. Boston: Beacon Press.

Lewis, David K. 1973. *Counterfactuals*. Oxford: Basil Blackwell.

Lewis, David K. 1973/1993. "Causation." In Ernest Sosa and Michael Tooley (eds.), *Causation* (Oxford: Oxford University Press).

Lichtheim, George. 1967. "The Concept of Ideology." In *The Concept of Ideology and Other Essays* (New York: Random House) 3–46.

Lieberson, Stanley. 1985. *Making it Count: The Improvement of Social Research and Theory*. Berkeley: University of California Press.

Lieberson, Stanley. 1991. "Small N's and Big Conclusions: An Examination of the Reasoning in Comparative Studies Based on a Small Number of Cases." *Social Forces* 70:2 (December) 307–20. Reprinted in Charles S. Ragin and Howard S. Becker (eds.), *What Is a Case? Exploring the Foundations of Social Inquiry* (Cambridge: Cambridge University Press, 1992).

Lieberson, Stanley. 1994. "More on the Uneasy Case for Using Mill-Type Methods in Small-N Comparative Studies." *Social Forces* 72:4 (June) 1225–37.

Liebow, Elliot. 1967. *Tally's Corner: A Study of Negro Streetcorner Men*. Boston: Little, Brown.

Lijphart, Arend. 1971. "Comparative Politics and the Comparative Method." *American Political Science Review* 65:3 (September).

Lijphart, Arend. 1975a. "The Comparable Cases Strategy in Comparative Research." *Comparative Political Studies* 8, 158–77.

Lijphart, Arend. 1975b. *The Politics of Accommodation: Pluralism and Democracy in the Netherlands*. Berkeley: University of California Press.

Lindblom, Charles E. 1997. "Political Science in the 1940s and 1950s." In Thomas Bender, Carl E. Schorske, Stephen R. Graubard, and William J. Barber (eds.), *American Academic Culture in Transformation: Fifty Years, Four Disciplines* (Princeton: Princeton University Press).

Lindblom, Charles E. and David K. Cohen. 1979. *Usable Knowledge: Social Science and Social Problem Solving*. New Haven: Yale University Press.

Linsky, Leonard. 1969. "Reference and Referents." In Thomas M. Olshewsky (ed.), *Problems in the Philosophy of Language* (New York: Holt).

Lipset, Seymour Martin and Richard Hofstadter (eds.). 1968. *Sociology and History: Methods*. New York: Basic Books.

Little, Daniel. 1991. *Varieties of Social Explanation: An Introduction to the Philosophy of Social Science*. Boulder: Westview Press.

Little, Daniel. 1998. *Microfoundations, Method, and Causation*. New Brunswick: Transaction.

Loewenstein, Karl. 1953. "The Role of Ideologies in Political Change." *International Social Science Bulletin* 5:1, 51–74.

Luebbert, Gregory M. 1991. *Liberalism, Fascism, or Social Democracy: Social Classes and the Political Origins of Regimes in Interwar Europe*. Berkeley: University of California Press.

Lukes, Steven. 1973. *Individualism*. New York: Harper.

Lynd, Robert Staughton. 1939/1964. *Knowledge for What?: The Place of Social Science in American Culture*. New York: Grove Press.

Lynd, Robert Staughton and Helen Merrell Lynd. 1929/1956. *Middletown: A Study in American Culture*. New York: Harcourt.

Mach, Ernest. 1902/1953. "The Economy of Science." In Philip P. Wiener (ed.), *Readings in Philosophy of Science* (New York: Scribner's) 446–52.

MacIntyre, Alasdair. 1971. *Against the Self-Images of the Age: Essays on Ideology and Philosophy*. London: Duckworth.

MacIver, R. M. 1942/1964. *Social Causation*. New York: Harper.

Mackie, John L. 1965/1993. "Causes and Conditions." In Ernest Sosa and Michael Tooley (eds.), *Causation* (Oxford: Oxford University Press).

Mackie, John L. 1974. *The Cement of the Universe: A Study of Causation*. Oxford: Clarendon.

Mahon, James E., Jr. 1998. "Political Science and Ordinary Language: Why Don't We Have Conferences on 'The Transition to Polyarchy?'" Paper presented to the International Social Science Council Committee on Conceptual and Terminological Analysis, 14th World Congress of Sociology, Montreal (July).

Mahoney, James. 1999a. "Nominal, Ordinal, and Narrative Appraisal in Macro-Causal Analysis." *American Journal of Sociology* 104:4 (January) 1154–96.

Mahoney, James. 1999b. "The Uses of Path Dependence in Historical Sociology." Paper presented at the annual meetings of the American Political Science Association, Atlanta, GA (September).

Mahoney, James. 2000. "Strategies of Causal Inference in Small-N Analysis." *Sociological Methods and Research* 28:4 (May) 387–424.

Mahoney, James and Michael Ellsberg. 1999. "Goldhagen's *Hitler's Willing Executioners:* A Clarification and Methodological Critique." *Journal of Historical Sociology* 12:4 (December).

Malinowski, Bronislaw. 1922/1984. *Argonauts of the Western Pacific*. Prospect Heights, IL: Waveland.

Manning, David John (ed.). 1980. *The Form of Ideology*. London: Allen & Unwin.

Manning, David John and T. J. Robinson. 1985. *The Place of Ideology in Political Life*. London: Croom Helm.

Mansbridge, Jane. 1983. *Beyond Adversarial Democracy*. Chicago: University of Chicago Press.

Mapel, David. 1989. *Social Justice Reconsidered: The Problem of Appropriate Precision in a Theory of Justice*. Urbana: University of Illinois Press.

March, James G. and Johan P. Olsen. 1984. "The New Institutionalism: Organizational Factors in Political Life." *American Political Science Review* 78:3 (September).

March, James G. and Johan P. Olsen. 1989. *Rediscovering Institutions: The Organizational Basis of Politics*. New York: Free Press.

Marini, Margaret and Burton Singer. 1988. "Causality in the Social Sciences." In Clifford Clogg (ed.), *Sociological Methodology* 18, 347–409.

Marks, Lawrence E. 1974. "The Nature of Scale Types." In *Sensory Processes: The New Psychophysics* (New York: Academic Press) 245–49.

Martin, Michael and Lee C. McIntyre (eds.). 1994. *Readings in the Philosophy of Social Science.* Cambridge, MA: MIT Press.

Mayer, Thomas. 1993. *Truth versus Precision in Economics.* London: Edward Elgar.

Mayhew, David R. 1986. *Placing Parties in American Politics: Organization, Electoral Settings, and Government Activity in the Twentieth Century.* Princeton: Princeton University Press.

Mazlish, Bruce. 1998. *The Uncertain Sciences.* New Haven: Yale University Press.

McCall, George J. and George H. Weber (eds.). 1984. *Social Science and Public Policy: The Roles of Academic Disciplines in Policy Analysis.* New York: Associated Faculty Press.

McCloskey, Donald. 1990. *If You're So Smart.* Chicago: University of Chicago Press.

McCloskey, Donald. 1992. "The Art of Forecasting, from Ancient to Modern Times." *Cato Journal* 12:1 (Spring/Summer) 23–43.

McClosky, Herbert. 1964. "Consensus and Ideology in American Politics." *American Political Science Review* 58 (June) 361–82.

McIntyre, Lee C. 1996. *Laws and Explanation in the Social Sciences: Defending a Science of Human Behavior.* Boulder: Westview.

McKeown, Timothy. 1999. "Case Studies and the Statistical World View." *International Organization* 53:1 (Winter) 161–90.

McKim, Vaughn R. 1997. "Introduction." In Vaughn R. McKim and Stephen P. Turner (eds.), *Causality in Crisis?: Statistical Methods and the Search for Causal Knowledge in the Social Science* (Notre Dame, IN: Notre Dame Press).

McKim, Vaughn R. and Stephen P. Turner (eds.). 1997. *Causality in Crisis?: Statistical Methods and the Search for Causal Knowledge in the Social Science.* Notre Dame, IN: Notre Dame Press.

McKinney, John C. 1966. *Constructive Typology and Social Theory.* New York: Appleton.

McLellan, David. 1986. *Ideology.* Minneapolis: University of Minnesota.

McMullin, Ernan. 1984. "Two Ideals of Explanation in Natural Science." In Peter A. French, Theodore E. Uehling, Jr., and Howard K. Wettstein (eds.), *Midwest Studies in Philosophy Volume IX: Causation and Causal Theories* (Minneapolis: University of Minnesota Press).

Meckstroth, Theodore. 1975. "'Most Different Systems' and 'Most Similar Systems': A Study in the Logic of Comparative Inquiry," *Comparative Political Studies* 8:2 (July) 133–77.

Meehan, Eugene J. 1971. *The Foundations of Political Analysis: Empirical and Normative.* Homewood, IL: Dorsey Press.

Merton, Robert K. 1949/1968. *Social Theory and Social Structure.* New York: Free Press.

Mill, John Stuart. 1843/1872. *System of Logic,* 8th ed. London: Longmans, Green.

Miller, David. 1976. *Social Justice.* Oxford: Clarendon.

Miller, John William. 1980. *The Definition of a Thing, with Some Notes on Language.* New York: Norton.

Miller, Richard W. 1983/1991. "Fact and Method in the Social Sciences." In In Richard Boyd, Philip Gasper, and J. D. Trout (eds.), *The Philosophy of Science* (Cambridge, MA: MIT Press).

Miller, Richard W. 1987. *Fact and Method: Explanation, Confirmation and Reality in the Natural and the Social Sciences.* Princeton: Princeton University Press.

Mills, C. Wright. 1959. *The Sociological Imagination.* New York: Oxford University Press.

Mink, Louis. 1987. "History and Fiction as Modes of Comprehension." In Brian Fay, Eugene Golob, and Richard Van (eds.), *Historical Understanding* (Ithaca: Cornell University Press).

Miron, Jeffrey A. 1994. "Empirical Methodology in Macroeconomics: Explaining the Success of Friedman and Schwartz's 'A Monetary History of the United States, 1867–1960.'" *Journal of Monetary Economics* 34, 17–25.

Mitchell, G. Duncan (ed.). 1979. *A New Dictionary of the Social Sciences.* New York: Aldine.

Mitchell, Joel. 1990. *An Introduction to the Logic of Psychological Measurement.* Hillsdale, NJ: Lawrence Erlbaum.

Moore, Barrington, Jr. 1958. *Political Power and Social Theory.* Cambridge, MA: Harvard University Press.

Moore, Barrington, Jr. 1978. *Injustice: The Social Bases of Obedience and Revolt.* White Plains, NY: M. E. Sharpe.

Morgan, Edmund S. 1975. *American Slavery/American Freedom: The Ordeal of Colonial Virginia.* New York: Norton.

Morgan, Mary S. 1997. "Searching for Causal Relations in Economic Statistics." In Vaughn R. McKim and Stephen P. Turner (eds.), *Causality in Crisis?: Statistical Methods and the Search for Causal Knowledge in the Social Science* (Notre Dame, IN: University of Notre Dame Press).

Morgenthau, Hans J. 1946. *Scientific Man versus Power Politics.* Chicago: University of Chicago Press.

Morgenthau, Hans J. 1955. "Reflections on the State of Political Science." *Review of Politics* 17, 431–60.

Morriss, Peter. 1987. *Power: A Philosophical Analysis.* New York: St. Martin's.

Most, Benjamin A. and Harvey Starr. 1982. "Case Selection, Conceptualization and Basic Logic in the Study of War." *American Journal of Political Science* 26, 834–56.

Mueller, Dennis C. (ed.). 1997. *Perspectives on Public Choice: A Handbook.* Cambridge: Cambridge University Press.

Mullins, Willard A. 1974. "Sartori's Concept of Ideology: A Dissent and an Alternative." In Allen R. Wilcox, ed., *Public Opinion and Political Attitudes.* New York: John Wiley & Sons.

Munck, Gerardo L. 1998. "Canons of Research Design in Qualitative Analysis." *Studies in Comparative International Development* 33:3, 18–45.

Munck, Gerardo L. and Jay Verkuilen. 2000. "Measuring Democracy: Evaluating Alternative Indices." Paper presented at the annual meetings of the American Political Science Association, Washington, DC (August–September).

Murphey, Murray G. 1994. *Philosophical Foundations of Historical Knowledge.* Albany: SUNY Press.

Murphy, Gregory L. and Douglas L. Medin. 1985. "The Role of Theories in Conceptual Coherence." *Psychological Review* 92:3 (July) 289–315.

Murray, Charles A. 1984. *Losing Ground: American Social Policy, 1950–1980.* New York: Basic Books.

Myrdal, Gunnar. 1944. *An American Dilemma: The Negro Problem and Modern Democracy.* New York: Harper.

Myrdal, Gunnar. 1970. *The Challenge of World Poverty: A World Anti-Poverty Program in Outline.* New York: Pantheon.

Nagel, Ernest. 1961. *The Structure of Science: Problems in the Logic of Scientific Explanation.* New York: Harcourt.

Naroll, Raoul. 1965. "Galton's Problem: The Logic of Cross-Cultural Analysis." *Social Research* 32.

Natanson, Maurice (ed.). 1963. *Philosophy of the Social Sciences: A Reader.* New York: Random House.

Nettl, J. P. 1967. *Political Mobilization: A Sociological Analysis of Methods and Concepts.* New York: Basic Books.

Neuman, W. Lawrence. 1997. *Social Research Methods: Qualitative and Quantitative Approaches,* 2d ed. Boston: Allyn & Bacon.

Nichols, Elizabeth. 1986. "Skocpol and Revolution: Comparative Analysis vs. Historical Conjuncture." *Comparative Historical Research* 9, 163–86.

Norris, Christopher. 1997. *Against Relativism: Philosophy of Science, Deconstruction, and Critical Theory.* Oxford: Basil Blackwell.

Nowak, Stefan. 1960. "Some Problems of Causal Interpretation of Statistical Relationships." *Philosophy of Science* 27 (January) 23–38.

Nozick, Robert. 1974. *Anarchy, State, and Utopia.* New York: Basic Books.

Ogden, C. K. and I. A. Richards. 1923/1989. *The Meaning of Meaning.* San Diego: Harcourt.

Olshewsky, Thomas M. (ed.). 1969. *Problems in the Philosophy of Language.* New York: Holt.

Oppenheim, Felix E. 1961. *Dimensions of Freedom: An Analysis.* New York: St. Martin's.

Oppenheim, Felix E. 1975. "The Language of Political Science: Problems of Clarification." In Fred Greenstein and Nelson Polsby (eds.), *Handbook of Political Science, Vol, 1: Political Science Scope and Theory* (Reading, MA: Addison-Wesley).

Oppenheim, Felix E. 1981. *Political Concepts: A Reconstruction.* Chicago: University of Chicago Press.

Ordeshook, Peter C. 1986. *Game Theory and Political Theory: An Introduction.* Cambridge: Cambridge University Press.

Ordeshook, Peter C. 1990. "The Emerging Discipline of Political Economy." In James E. Alt and Kenneth A. Shepsle (eds.), *Perspectives on Positive Political Economy* (Cambridge: Cambridge University Press).

Page, Benjamin I. and Calvin C. Jones. 1979. "Reciprocal Effects of Policy Preferences, Party Loyalties and the Vote." *American Political Science Review* 73:4 (December) 1071–89.

Palmer, Anthony. 1988. *Concept and Object: The Unity of the Proposition in Logic and Psychology.* London: Routledge.

Pap, Arthur. 1969. "Theory of Definition." In Thomas M. Olshewsky (ed.), *Problems in the Philosophy of Language* (New York: Holt).

Parsons, Talcott. 1951. *The Social System.* Glencoe, IL: Free Press.

Partridge, P. H. 1961. "Politics, Philosophy, Ideology." *Political Studies* 9:3, 217–35.

Passmore, John. 1961/1967. "Arguments to Meaninglessness: Excluded Opposites and Paradigm Cases." Reprinted in Richard Rorty (ed.), *The Linguistic Turn: Recent Essays in Philosophical Method* (Chicago: University of Chicago Press).

Patterson, Orlando. 1982. *Slavery and Social Death: A Comparative Study.* Cambridge, MA: Harvard University Press.

Pawlowski, Tadeusz. 1980. *Concept Formation in the Humanities and the Social Sciences.* Boston: D. Reidel.

Pearce, David W. (ed.). 1992. *The MIT Dictionary of Modern Economics.* Cambridge, MA: MIT Press.

Pearl, Judea. 2000. *Causality: Models, Reasoning, and Inference.* Cambridge, MA: Harvard University Press.

Petersen, Roger. 1999. "Mechanisms and Structures in Comparisons." In John R. Bowen and Roger Petersen (eds.), *Critical Comparisons in Politics and Culture* (Cambridge: Cambridge University Press).

Piaget, Jean. 1968/1970. *Structuralism.* New York: Harper.

Pierson, Paul. 2000. "Increasing Returns, Path Dependence, and the Study of Politics." *American Political Science Review* 94:2 (June).

Piore, Michael J. 1979. "Qualitative Research Techniques in Economics." *Administrative Science Quarterly* 24 (December).

Pitkin, Hanna Fenichel. 1967. *Representation.* Berkeley: University of California Press.

Pitkin, Hanna Fenichel. 1972. *Wittgenstein and Justice: On the Significance of Ludwig Wittgenstein for Social and Political Thought.* Berkeley: University of California Press.

Plamenatz, John. 1970. *Ideology.* New York: Praeger.

Pocock, J. G. A. 1975. *The Machiavellian Moment: Florentine Political Thought and the Atlantic Republican Tradition.* Princeton: Princeton University Press.

Polkinghorne, Donald. 1983. *Methodology for the Human Sciences: Systems of Inquiry.* New York: SUNY Press.

Popper, Karl. 1934/1968. *The Logic of Scientific Discovery.* New York: Harper.

Popper, Karl. 1936/1957. *The Poverty of Historicism.* New York: Harper & Row.

Popper, Karl. 1945. *The Open Society and Its Enemies.* London: Routledge.

Popper, Karl. 1969. *Conjecture and Refutations.* London: Routledge.

Popper, Karl. 1972. *Objective Knowledge.* Oxford: Oxford University Press.

Popper, Karl. 1976. *Unended Quest: An Intellectual Autobiography.* LaSalle, IL: Open Court.

Porter, T. M. 1986. *The Rise of Statistical Thinking 1820–1900.* Princeton: Princeton University Press.

Przeworski, Adam and Henry Teune. 1970. *The Logic of Comparative Social Inquiry.* New York: Wiley.

Putnam, Hilary. 1975. "The Meaning of 'Meaning.'" In Putnam, *Mind, Language and Reality, Philosophical Papers, Volume 2* (Cambridge: Cambridge University Press) 215–71.

Putnam, Hilary. 1978. *Meaning and the Moral Sciences.* London: Routledge.

Putnam, Hilary. 1984. "What Is Realism?" In Jarrett Leplin (ed.), *Scientific Realism* (Berkeley: University of California Press).

Putnam, Hilary. 1987. *The Many Faces of Realism.* LaSalle, IL.: Open Court.

Quadagno, Jill and Stan J. Knapp. 1992. "Have Historical Sociologists Forsaken Theory?: Thoughts on the History/Theory Relationship." *Sociological Methods and Research* 20, 481–507.

Quine, Willard van Orman. 1953. "Two Dogmas of Empiricism." In *From a Logical Point of View* (Cambridge, MA: Harvard University Press).

Quine, Willard van Orman. 1960. *Word and Object.* Cambridge, MA: MIT Press.

Quine, Willard van Orman. 1966. "Simple Theories of a Complex World." In *the Ways of Paradox and Other Essays* (New York: Random House).

Quine, Willard van Orman. 1977. "Natural Kinds." In S. P. Schwartz (ed.), *Naming, Necessity, and Natural Kinds* (Ithaca: Cornell University Press) 155–75.

Rabinow, Paul and William M. Sullivan (eds). 1979. *Interpretive Social Science: A Reader.* Berkeley: University of California Press.

Rachlin, H. 1970. *Introduction to Modern Behaviorism.* San Francisco: Freeman.

Radcliffe-Brown, A. R. 1958. *Method in Social Anthropology.* Chicago: University of Chicago Press.

Ragin, Charles C. 1987. *The Comparative Method: Moving Beyond Qualititative and Quantitative Strategies.* Berkeley: University of California Press.

Ragin, Charles C. 2000. *Fuzzy-Set Social Science.* Chicago: University of Chicago Press.

Ragin, Charles C. and Howard S. Becker (eds.). 1992. *What Is a Case? Exploring the Foundations of Social Inquiry.* Cambridge: Cambridge University Press.

Ragin, Charles C. and David Zaret. 1983. "Theory and Method in Comparative Research: Two Strategies." *Social Forces* 61, 731–54.

Rawls, John. 1971. *A Theory of Justice.* Cambridge, MA: Harvard University Press.

Redman, Deborah A. 1991. *Economics and the Philosophy of Science.* New York: Oxford University Press.

Reinharz, Shulamit. 1992. *Feminist Methods in Social Research.* New York: Oxford University Press.

Rejai, Mostafa. 1991. *Political Ideologies: A Comparative Approach.* Armonk, New York: M.E. Sharpe.

Rescher, Nicholas. 1977. *Methodological Pragmatism.* New York: New York University Press.

Reynolds, Paul Davidson. 1971. *A Primer in Theory Construction.* Indianapolis: Bobbs-Merrill.

Riggs, Fred W. 1975. "The Definition of Concepts." In Giovanni Sartori, Fred W. Riggs, and Henry Teune (eds.), *Tower of Babel: On the Definition and Analysis of Concepts in the Social Sciences* (International Studies, occasional paper no. 6) 39–76.

Riker, William H. 1986. *The Art of Political Manipulation.* New Haven: Yale University Press.

Ritsert, Jurgen. 1990. *Models and Concepts of Ideology.* Amsterdam: Rodopi.

Roberts, Clayton. 1996. *The Logic of Historical Explanation.* University Park: Pennsylvania State University Press.

Roberts, Fred S. 1976. *Discrete Mathematical Models, with Applications to Social, Biological, and Environmental Problems.* Englewood Cliffs, NJ: Prentice Hall.

Robinson, Richard. 1954. *Definition.* Oxford: Clarendon.

Rogowski, Ronald. 1995. "The Role of Theory and Anomaly in Social-Scientific Inference." *American Political Science Review* 89:2 (June) 467–70.

Rorty, Amelia (ed.). 1966. *Pragmatic Philosophy: An Anthology.* Garden City, NY: Doubleday Anchor.

Rosch, Eleanor, Carolyn Mervis, Wayne Gray, David Johnson, and Penny Boyes-Braem. 1976. "Basic Objects in Natural Categories," *Cognitive Psychology* 8, 382–439.

Rosenau, Pauline Marie. 1992. *Post-Modernism and the Social Sciences: Insights, Inroads, and Intrusions.* Princeton: Princeton University Press.

Rosenberg, Alexander. 1988. *Philosophy of Social Science.* Boulder: Westview.

Rosenberg, Alexander. 1992. *Economics – Mathematical Politics or Science of Diminishing Returns?* Chicago: University of Chicago Press.

Rosenberg, Morris. 1968. *The Logic of Survey Analysis.* New York: Basic Books.

Rosenkrantz, Roger. 1977. *Inference, Method and Decision.* Dordrecht: D. Reidel.

Ross, Marc Howard. 1988. "Studying Politics Cross-Culturally: Key Concepts and Issues." *Behavior Science Research* 22, 105–29.

Rostow, W. W. 1960. *The Stages of Economic Growth: A Non-Communist Manifesto.* Cambridge: Cambridge University Press.

Roth, David. 1987. *Meanings and Methods: A Case for Methodological Pluralism in the Social Sciences.* Ithaca: Cornell University Press.

Roth, Paul A. 1994. "Narrative Explanations: The Case of History." In Michael Martin and Lee C. McIntyre (eds.), *Readings in the Philosophy of Social Science* (Cambridge, MA: MIT Press).

Roucek, Joseph Slabey. 1944. "A History of the Concept of Ideology." *Journal of the History of Ideas* 5, 479–88.

Rude, George. 1980/1995. *Ideology and Popular Protest.* Chapel Hill: University of North Carolina Press.

Rueschemeyer, Dietrich. 1991. "Different Methods – Contradictory Results? Research on Development and Democracy." *International Journal of Comparative Sociology* 32:1–2 (January–April) 9–38.

Rueschemeyer, Dietrich and John D. Stephens. 1997. "Comparing Historical Sequences–A Powerful Tool for Causal Analysis." *Comparative Social Research* 16, 55–72.

Rueschemeyer, Dietrich, Evelyne Huber Stephens, and John D. Stephens. 1992. *Capitalist Development and Democracy*. Chicago: University of Chicago Press.

Rule, James B. 1997. *Theory and Progress in Social Science*. Cambridge: Cambridge University Press.

Russell, Bertrand. 1913. "On the Notion of Cause." *Proceedings of the Aristotelian Society* 13, 1–26.

Russell, Bertrand. 1917/1968. *Mysticism and Logic*. Garden City, NY: Doubleday Anchor.

Russell, Bertrand. 1969. "On Denoting." In Thomas M. Olshewsky (ed.), *Problems in the Philosophy of Language* (New York: Holt).

Ryle, Gilbert. 1949. *The Concept of Mind*. New York: Barnes & Noble.

Ryle, Gilbert. 1953/1964. "Ordinary Language." In V.C. Chappell (ed), *Ordinary Language*. Englewood Cliffs, New Jersey: Prentice-Hall.

Ryle, Gilbert. 1964. *Dilemmas*. Cambridge: Cambridge University Press.

Salmon, Wesley C. 1967. *The Foundations of Scientific Inference*. Pittsburgh: University of Pittsburgh Press.

Salmon, Wesley C. 1984. *Scientific Explanation and the Causal Structure of the World*. Princeton: Princeton University Press.

Samuelson, Paul A. 1959. "What Economists Know." In Daniel Lerner (ed.), *The Human Meaning of the Social Sciences* (New York: Meridian).

Sartori, Giovanni. 1969. "Politics, Ideology, and Belief Systems." *American Political Science Review* 63:2 (June).

Sartori, Giovanni. 1970. "Concept Misformation in Comparative Politics." *American Political Science Review* 64:4 (December) 1033–46.

Sartori, Giovanni. 1975. "The Tower of Babble." In Giovanni Sartori, Fred W. Riggs, and Henry Teune (eds.), *Tower of Babel: On the Definition and Analysis of Concepts in the Social Sciences* (International Studies, occasional paper no. 6) 7–38.

Sartori, Giovanni. 1976. *Parties and Party Systems*. Cambridge: Cambridge University Press.

Sartori, Giovanni. 1984a. "Guidelines for Concept Analysis." In *Social Science Concepts: A Systematic Analysis* (Beverly Hills: Sage) 15–48.

Sartori, Giovanni. 1991. "Comparing and Miscomparing." *Journal of Theoretical Politics* 3:3, 243–257.

Sartori, Giovanni (ed.). 1984b. *Social Science Concepts: A Systematic Analysis*. Beverly Hills: Sage.

Sartori, Giovanni, Fred W. Riggs, and Henry Teune (eds.). 1975. *Tower of Babel: On the Definition and Analysis of Concepts in the Social Sciences*. International Studies, occasional paper no. 6.

Savolainen, Jukka. 1994. "The Rationality of Drawing Big Conclusions Based on Small Samples: In Defense of Mill's Methods." *Social Forces* 72, 1217–24.

Sayer, R. Andrew. 1992. *Method in Social Science: A Realist Approach*, 2d ed. London: Routledge.

Schaffer, Frederic C. 1998. *Democracy in Translation: Understanding Politics in an Unfamiliar Culture*. Ithaca: Cornell University Press.

Schmitter, Philippe C. 1974. "Still the Century of Corporatism?" In Frederick B. Pike and Thomas Stritch (eds), *The New Corporatism*. Notre Dame: University of Notre Dame Press.

Scott, James C. 1998. *Seeing Like a State: How Certain Schemes to Improve the Human Condition Have Failed*. New Haven: Yale University Press.

Scriven, Michael. 1962. "Explanations, Predictions, and Laws." In Herbert Feigl and Grover Maxwell (eds.), *Minnesota Studies in the Philosophy of Science. Vol. 3: Scientific Explanation, Space, and Time* (Minneapolis: University of Minnesota).

Scriven, Michael. 1966/1993. "Defects of the Necessary Condition Analysis of Causation." In Ernest Sosa and Michael Tooley (eds.), *Causation* (Oxford: Oxford University Press).

Searle, John R. 1969. *Speech Acts: An Essay in the Philosophy of Language*. Cambridge: Cambridge University Press.

Secord, Paul F. 1986. "Explanations in the Social Sciences and in Life Situations." In Donald W. Fiske and Richard A. Shweder (eds.), *Metatheory in Social Science: Pluralisms and Subjectivities* (Chicago: University of Chicago Press).

Seliger, Martin. 1976. *Ideology and Politics*. London: Allen & Unwin.

Seliger, Martin. 1977. *The Marxist Conception of Ideology: A Critical Essay*. Cambridge: Cambridge University Press.

Sewell, William H., Jr. 1992. "Introduction: Narratives and Social Identities." *Social Science History* 16, 479–88.

Sewell, William H., Jr. 1996. "Three Temporalities: Toward an Eventful Sociology." In Terrence J. McDonald (ed.), *The Historic Turn in the Human Sciences* (Ann Arbor: University of Michigan Press) 245–80.

Shively, W. Phillips. 1990. *The Craft of Political Research*. Englewood Cliffs, NJ: Prentice Hall.

Sil, Rudra. 2000. "The Division of Labor in Social Science Research: Unified Methodology or 'Organic Solidarity'?" *Polity* (Summer).

Sills, David L. (ed.). 1968. *International Encyclopedia of the Social Science*. New York: Macmillan.

Simon, Herbert Alexander. 1982. "Are Social Problems that Social Science Can Solve?" In W. H. Kruskal (ed.), *The Social Sciences: Their Nature and Uses* (Chicago: University of Chicago Press).

Simowitz, Roslyn and Barry L. Price. 1990. "The Expected Utility Theory of Conflict: Measuring Theoretical Progress." *American Political Science Review* 84:2 (June) 439–60.

Skinner, B. F. 1953. *Science and Human Behavior*. New York: Macmillan.

Skocpol, Theda. 1979. *States and Social Revolutions: A Comparative Analysis of France, Russia, and China*. Cambridge: Cambridge University Press.

Skocpol, Theda. 1986. "Analyzing Causal Configurations in History: A Rejoinder to Nichols." *Comparative Social Research* 9, 187–94.

Skocpol, Theda (ed.). 1984. *Vision and Method in Historical Sociology*. Cambridge: Cambridge University Press.

Skocpol, Theda and Margaret Somers. 1980. "The Uses of Comparative History in Macrosocial Inquiry." *Comparative Studies in Society and History* 22:2 (April).

Skyrms, Brian. 1966. *Choice and Chance*. Belmont, CA: Dickenson.

Skyrms, Brian. 1980. *Causal Necessity: A Pragmatic Investigation of the Necessity of Laws*. New Haven: Yale University Press.

Small, Albion. 1910. *The Meaning of Social Science*. Chicago: University of Chicago Press.

Smelser, Neil J. 1973. "The Methodology of Comparative Analysis." In D. P. Warwick and S. Osherson (eds.), *Comparative Research Methods* (Englewood Cliffs, NJ: Prentice-Hall) 42–86.

Smelser, Neil J. 1976. *Comparative Methods in the Social Sciences*. Englewood Cliffs, NJ: Prentice-Hall.

Smelser, Neil J. and Dean Gernstein (eds.). 1986. *Behavioral and Social Science: Fifty Years of Discovery*. Washington: National Academy Press.

Smith, Roger. 1997. *The Norton History of the Human Sciences*. New York: Norton.

Smith, T. V. and Leonard D. White (eds.). 1929. *Chicago: An Experiment in Social Science Research*. Chicago: University of Chicago Press.

Sobel, Michael E. 1995. "Causal Inference in the Social and Behavioral Sciences." In Gerhard Arminger, Clifford C. Clogg, and Michael E. Sobel (eds.), *Handbook of Statistical Modeling for the Social and Behavioral Sciences* (New York: Plenum).

Sober, Elliot. 1975. *Simplicity*. Oxford: Oxford University Press.

Sober, Elliot. 1988. *Reconstructing the Past: Parsimony, Evolution and Inference*. Cambridge, MA: MIT Press.

Soltan, Karol Edward. 1982. "Empirical Studies of Distributive Justice." *Ethics* 92, 673–91.

Soltan, Karol Edward. 1987. *The Causal Theory of Justice*. Berkeley: University of California Press.

Somers, Margaret R. 1992. "Narrativity, Narrative Identity, and Social Action: Rethinking English Working-Class Formation." *Social Science History* 16, 591–630.

Sosa, Ernest and Michael Tooley (eds.). 1993. *Causation*. Oxford: Oxford University Press.

Steinbruner, John D. 1974. *The Cybernetic Theory of Decision: New Dimensions of Political Analysis*. Princeton: Princeton University Press.

Steinmo, Sven, Kathleen Thelen, and Frank Longstreth (eds.). 1992. *Structuring Politics: Historical Institutionalism in Comparative Analysis*. Cambridge: Cambridge University Press.

Sternberg, Robert J. and Douglas K. Detterman (eds.). 1986. *What Is Intelligence? Contemporary Viewpoints of its Nature and Definition*. Norwood, NJ: Ablex.

Stevens, S. S. 1946. "On the Theory of Scales of Measurement." *Science* 103, 677–80.

Stinchcombe, Arthur L. 1968. *Constructing Social Theories*. New York: Harcourt.

Stinchcombe, Arthur L. 1978. *Theoretical Methods in Social History*. New York: Academic Press.

Stinchcombe, Arthur L. 1992. "The Conditions of Fruitfulness of Theorizing about Mechanisms in Social Science." *Philosophy of the Social Sciences* 21, 367–88.

Stone, Lawrence. 1979. "The Revival of Narrative: Reflections on a New Old History." *Past and Present* 85, 3–24.

Strauss, Leo. 1953/1963. "Natural Right and the Distinction Between Facts and Values." In Maurice Natanson (ed.), *Philosophy of the Social Sciences: A Reader* (New York: Random House).

Strawson, P. F. 1969. "On Referring." In Thomas M. Olshewsky (ed.), *Problems in the Philosophy of Language* (New York: Holt).

Stryker, Robin. 1996. "Beyond History versus Theory: Strategic Narrative and Sociological Explanation." *Sociological Methods and Research* 24, 304–52.

Suppes, Patrick C. 1970. *A Probabilistic Theory of Causality.* Amsterdam: North-Holland.

Swanson, Guy. 1971. "Frameworks for Comparative Research: Structural Anthropology and the Theory of Action." In Ivan Vallier (ed.), *Comparative Methods in Sociology: Essays on Trends and Applications* (Berkeley: University of California Press) 141–202.

Sykes, Adam and Iain Sproat. 1967. *The Wit of Westminster.* London: Leslie Frewin.

Tarrow, Sidney. 1995. "Bridging the Quantitative-Qualitative Divide in Political Science." *American Political Science Review* 89:2 (June) 471–74.

Tarski, Alfred. 1944. "The Semantic Conception of Truth." *Philosophy and Phenomenological Research* 4, 341–76.

Taylor, Charles. 1962. *The Explanation of Behavior.* New York: Routledge.

Taylor, Charles. 1967/1994. "Neutrality in Political Science." In Michael Martin and Lee C. McIntyre (eds.), *Readings in the Philosophy of Social Science* (Cambridge, MA: MIT Press). In Peter Laslett and W. G. Runciman (eds.), *Philosophy, Politics and Society,* 3d. ser. (New York: Barnes & Noble).

Taylor, Charles. 1970. "The Explanation of Purposive Behavior." In Robert Borger and Frank Cioffi (eds.), *Explanation in the Behavioral Sciences* (Cambridge: Cambridge University Press).

Taylor, Charles. 1985. "Interpretation and the Sciences of Man." In *Philosophy and the Human Sciences: Philosophical Papers, Vol. II.* Cambridge: Cambridge University Press.

Taylor, John R. 1995. *Linguistic Categorization: Prototypes in Linguistic Theory.* Oxford: Clarendon.

Tetlock, Philip E. and Aaron Belkin (eds.). 1996. *Counterfactual Thought Experiments in World Politics.* Princeton: Princeton University Press.

Therborn, Goran. 1980. *The Ideology of Power and the Power of Ideology.* London: Verso.

Thomas, David. 1979. *Naturalism and Social Science: A Post-empiricist Philosophy of Social Science.* Cambridge: Cambridge University Press.

Thompson, Edward P. 1963. *The Making of the English Working Class.* New York: Vintage Books.

Thompson, Edward P. 1978. *The Poverty of Theory and Other Essays.* New York: Monthly Review Press.

Thompson, John B. 1984. *Studies in the Theory of Ideology.* Berkeley: University of California Press.

Thompson, Michael, Richard Ellis, and Aaron Wildavsky. 1990. *Cultural Theory.* Boulder: Westview.

Toulmin, Stephen. 1970. "Reasons and Causes." In Robert Borger and Frank Cioffi (eds.), *Explanation in the Behavioral Sciences* (Cambridge: Cambridge University Press).

Toulmin, Stephen. 1972. *Human Understanding, Vol. 1.* Princeton: Princeton University Press.

Trigg, Roger. 1985. *Understanding Social Science: A Philosophical Introduction to the Social Sciences.* Oxford: Basil Blackwell.

Turner, Stephen P. 1997. "'Net Effects': A Short History." In Vaughn R. McKim and Stephen P. Turner (eds.), *Causality in Crisis?: Statistical Methods and the Search for Causal Knowledge in the Social Science* (Notre Dame, IN: Notre Dame Press).

Tversky, Amos and Itamar Gati. 1978. "Studies of Similarity." In Eleanor and B. B. Lloyd (eds.), *Cognition and Cateogrization* (Hillsdale, NJ: Lawrence Erlbaum).

Vallier, I. (ed). 1971. *Comparative Methods in Sociology: Essays on Trends and Applications.* Berkeley: University of California Press.

Van Deth, Jan W. (ed.). 1998. *Comparative Politics: The Problem of Equivalence.* New York: Routledge.

Van Evera, Stephen. 1997. *Guide to Methods for Students of Political Science.* Ithaca: Cornell University Press.

van Fraassen, Bas C. 1980. *The Scientific Image.* Oxford: Clarendon.

Verba, Sidney, Kay Lehman Schlozman, and Henry Brady. 1995. *Voice and Equality: Civic Voluntarism in American Life.* Cambridge: Harvard University Press.

Verba, Sidney, Norman H. Nie, and Jae-on Kim. 1978. *Participation and Political Equality.* Cambridge: Cambridge University Press.

Vico, Giambattista. 1744/1984. *The New Science of Giambattista Vico,* trans. T. G. Bergin and M. H. Fisch. Ithaca: Cornell University Press.

Vijver, Fons van and Kwok Leung. 1997. *Methods and Data Analysis for Cross-Cultural Research.* Thousand Oaks: Sage.

Vogt, W. Paul. 1993. *Dictionary of Statistics and Methodology.* Newbury Park: Sage.

von Wright, Georg Henrik. 1971. *Explanation and Understanding.* Ithaca: Cornell University Press.

Wagner, David G. and Joseph Berger. 1985. "Do Sociological Theories Grow?" *American Journal of Sociology* 90:4, 697–728.

Wallerstein, Immanuel Maurice et al. 1996. *Open the Social Sciences: Report of the Gulbenkian Commission on the Restructuring of the Social Sciences.* Stanford: Stanford University Press.

Walzer, Michael. 1983. *Spheres of Justice: A Defense of Pluralism and Equality.* New York: Basic Books.

Watkins, J. W. N. 1994. "Historical Explanation in the Social Sciences." In Michael Martin and Lee C. McIntyre (eds.), *Readings in the Philosophy of Social Science* (Cambridge, MA: MIT Press).

Weber, Max. 1905/1949. *The Methodology of the Social Sciences*. New York: Free Press.

Weiner, Myron. 1967. *Party Building in a New Nation: The Indian National Congress*. Chicago: University of Chicago Press.

Westen, Peter. 1990. *Speaking of Equality*. Princeton: Princeton University Press.

Whitbeck, C. 1977. "Causation in Medicine: The Disease Entity Model." *Philosophy of Science* 44, 619–37.

White, Leonard. 1956. *The State of the Social Sciences*. Chicago: University of Chicago Press.

White, Leonard (ed.). 1930. *The New Social Science*. Chicago: University of Chicago Press.

Whorf, B. L. 1956. *Language, Thought and Reality*. Cambridge, MA: MIT Press.

Whyte, William Foote. 1943/1955. *Street Corner Society: The Social Structure of an Italian Slum*. Chicago: University of Chicago Press.

Wildavsky, Aaron. 1995. *But Is it True?: A Citizen's Guide to Environmental Health and Safety Issues*. Cambridge, MA: Harvard University Press.

Wilensky, Harold L. 1997. "Social Science and the Public Agenda: Reflections of Knowledge to Policy in the United States and Abroad." *Journal of Health Politics, Policy and Law* 22:5 (October) 1241–65.

Williams, Howard. 1988. *Concepts of Ideology*. Sussex: Wheatsheaf Books.

Williams, Raymond. 1983. *Keywords: A Vocabulary of Culture and Society*. New York: Oxford University Press.

Williamson, John B., David A. Karp, and John R. Daphin et al. 1977. *The Research Craft: An Introduction to Social Science Methods*. Boston: Little, Brown.

Wilson, Edward O. 1998. *Consilience: The Unity of Knowledge*. New York: Knopf.

Winch, Peter. 1958. *The Idea of a Social Science, and its Relation to Philosophy*. London: Routledge.

Winks, Robin W. (ed.). 1969. *The Historian As Detective: Essays on Evidence*. New York: Harper.

Wirth, Louis (ed.). 1940. *Eleven Twenty-six: A Decade of Social Science Research*. Chicago: University of Chicago Press.

Wittgenstein, Ludwig. 1921/1988. *Tractatus logico-philosophicus*, trans. D. F. Pears and B. F. McGuinness. London: Routledge.

Wittgenstein, Ludwig. 1953. *Philosophical Investigations*. New York: Macmillan.

Wolfinger, Raymond E. and Steven J. Rosenstone. 1980. *Who Votes?* New Haven: Yale University Press.

Wolin, Sheldon S. 1969. "Political Theory as a Vocation." *American Political Science Review* 63 (December) 1062–82.

Woodward, C. Vann. 1951. *The Origins of the New South: 1877–1913*. Baton Rouge: Louisiana State University Press.

Woolgar, Steve. 1988. *Science: The Very Idea*. Chichester: Ellis Horwood.

Wright, Arthur F. 1963. "On the Uses of Generalization in the Study of Chinese History." In Louis Gottschalk (ed.), *Generalization in the Writing of History* (Chicago: University of Chicago Press).

Young, J. Z. 1978. *Programs of the Brain*. Oxford: Oxford University Press.

Zald, Mayer. 1990. "Sociology as a Discipline: Quasi-Science and Quasi-Humanities." *The American Sociologist* 22:3–4, 165–87.

Zannoni, Paolo. 1978. "The Concept of Elite." *European Journal of Political Research* 6 (March) 1–30.

Zelditch, M., Jr. 1971. "Intelligible Comparisons." In I. Vallier (ed.), *Comparative Methods in Sociology: Essays on Trends and Applications* (Berkeley: University of California Press) 267–307.

Zeller, Richard A. and Edward G. Carmines. 1980. *Measurement in the Social Sciences: The Link Between Theory and Data*. Cambridge: Cambridge University Press.

Zerubavel, Eviatar. 1996. "Lumping and Splitting: Notes on Social Classification." *Sociological Forum* 11:3, 421–33.

Ziff, Paul. 1960. *Semantic Analysis*. Ithaca: Cornell University Press.

Index

accuracy, 10, 20, 24, 40t, 54, 90, 91t, 99–101 (defined), 119, 174, 192, 217, 232; and causation, 149, 192. *See also* proposition, truth, validity

adequacy, *See* criteria

Adorno, Theodore , 110

analysis: causal, 96, 122, 128n2, 129, 137, 145, 155, 170, 172, 183, 189, 198, 199, 253; comparative, 199, 214; counterfactual, 183, 221–22 (defined), 229; cross-case, 162, 216, 227; definitional, 83; descriptive, 124, 155, 156, 175; diachronic, 161t, 163, 180, 189, 201, 211, 222, 224, 225, 229; longitudinal, 187; methods of, 7n14, 82, 170, 205, 214, 215, 223, 233; most different/most similar, 212–14 (defined), 221, 229; ordinary language, 36, 68, 69, 75; small-N/large-N, 168, 169, 171, 175, 211, 226, 227; statistical, 1, 90n5, 103, 169, 180, 205, 206, 209, 220, 242; styles, 55; synchronic, 161t, 163, 180, 189, 201, 211, 222, 224, 229; tools of, 8, unit of, 160 (defined), 161t, 174, 178, 190, 206, 216, 217; within-case, 162–63, 191, 218, 227. *See also* QCA

analytic/empirical utility, *See* concepts; propositions; research design

anomie, 58

anthropology, xiii, xiv, 1, 89, 106, 107, 251, 254

Arendt, Hannah, 100

Aristotle, 9, 83, 131, 131n6, 246n6

Arrow, Kenneth, xiv

autocorrelation, 164t, 180, 242

Bacon, Francis, 6n11, 75, 232

Bartels, Larry, 13,

Barthes, Roland, 75

behavioralism, vxii, ix, 2, 3, 8, 9, 25, 74, 76, 108, 197

Benedict, Ruth, 122

Bentham, Jeremy, 58

Bloch, Marc, 99, 100, 244

boundedness, *See* research design

breadth, *See* proposition formation

Carr, E. H., 116

cases, 159–160 (defined); diachronic, 222; independence, 159, 163, 164t, 170, 178–81, 189, 203, 224; least-likely, 220; most-likely, 220; relevance, 149, 172–173, 249–52, (*see also* boundedness); representative, 167, 181–83, 189, 192, 193, 205, 218, 225–28 *passim*, 241; selection, 21, 30, 145, 183, 189, 201, 205, 207, 212, 219, 241; small-N/large-N, 166, 172, 178, 192, 206, 209, 225; synchronic, 222

293

P 75 FECUNDITY
P. 118 DESIDERATA

DE STENCIL